July 1914

July 1914

The Outbreak of the First World War:
Selected Documents

Edited by Imanuel Geiss

CHARLES SCRIBNER'S SONS · NEW YORK

To Bernadotte E. Schmitt

Acknowledgment
and Note on the Translation

The Introduction, the chapter on the 'Origins of the First World War' (except for pp. 48–53) and the Conclusion have been written by the author, in English, especially for this edition. The introductory chapters to each section have been translated by Henry Meyric Hughes, who has also translated the following documents: 4, 7, 13, 15, 28, 32, 41, 43, 59, 61, 63–6, 76–8, 86, 87, 118, 123 (last para.), 124, 138, 146, 155 and 176. The author himself is responsible for the translations of documents 1 and 5 and for the quotations in the introductory chapter; he has also amended occasionally faulty or clumsy translations, mainly of German and Austrian documents.

In all other cases translations have been taken from the following publications, for which acknowledgment is due to the respective publishers:

GERMAN DOCUMENTS (*D.D.*) from *Outbreak of the World War: German Documents collected by Karl Kautsky* (Carnegie Endowment for International Peace, 1924).

AUSTRIAN DOCUMENTS (*Ö.D.*) from the Austrian Red Book (George Allen & Unwin 1920, 3 vols), except for document 3 from L. Albertini, *Origins of the First World War*, II, pp. 129f.

FRENCH DOCUMENTS (*D.F.*) from the French Yellow Book in *Collected Diplomatic Documents relating to the Outbreak of the European War* (HMSO, 1915).

RUSSIAN DOCUMENTS (*Int. Bez.* 1) from Schilling, *How the War Began in 1914* (George Allen & Unwin, 1925), except for documents 102 and 136 from the Russian Orange Book in *Collected Diplomatic Documents* (HMSO *op. cit.*, 1915).

All the BRITISH DOCUMENTS (*B.D.*) are taken from G. P. Gooch and Harold Temperley (ed.), *British Documents on the Origins of the War 1898–1914*: vol. XI 'The Outbreak of War', edited by J. W. Headlam Morley (HMSO, 1926).

Other sources from which the documents in this edition are taken are listed, along with the abbreviations used, in the Bibliography (pp. 383–4). In addition, the following occur:
  A.A. – Politisches Archiv des Auswärtigen Amts
  D.Z.A. (R.A.d.1) – Deutsches Zentralarchiv, Potsdam (Reichsamt des Innern)
The abbreviations of journals referred to in the text will be found on p. 389.

The author's special thanks for help in the preparation of this volume are due to John Röhl of the University of Sussex and to Hartmut Pogge-v. Strandmann of Balliol College, Oxford, for their vigorous and helpful criticism of the first chapter and the conclusion. He also wishes to thank Geoffrey Barraclough of St John's College, Cambridge, for encouraging the publication of the English edition.

Contents

Introduction

The outbreak of the First World War has become—one generation after the outbreak of the Second—a controversial subject in Germany. For the first time there is a genuine debate on principles among German historians: the united front against the common enemy, both abroad and at home, no longer exists. The new debate was provoked by Fritz Fischer's book on Germany's role in the First World War,[1] which strongly criticised hitherto orthodox views.

For decades a remarkable cooperation between professional historians and the State had succeeded in building up and maintaining the taboo of German innocence, or relative innocence, in the First World War. Article 231 of the Versailles Treaty, by declaring Germany responsible for the outbreak of the war, established the legal basis for claiming reparations from defeated Germany without, however, the moralising implications read into it by the Germans:[2] this Article was the main object of German interest in the so-called 'war guilt question', a term which was often replaced by the polemical form 'war guilt lie'

---

[1] Fritz Fischer, *Griff nach der Weltmacht: Die Kriegszielpolitik des kaiserlichen Deutschland 1914–1918* (Düsseldorf, 1961; 3rd ed. 1964). An English, somewhat abridged, version recently appeared under the title, *Bid for Power* (London and New York, 1967).

[2] Alma Luckau, *The German Delegation at the Paris Conference* (New York, 1941), pp. 81ff; Hajo Holborn, 'Diplomats and Diplomacy in the Early Weimar Republic' in *The Diplomats 1919–1939*, ed. Gordon Craig (Princeton, 1953), pp. 141ff. For a recent German account see Fritz Dickmann, 'Die Kriegsschuldfrage auf der Friedenskonferenz von Paris 1919', in *H.Z.*, 197/1 (August 1963), pp. 1–101.

(*Kriegsschuldlüge*). During the war, emphasising German innocence had been a matter of course, but the main work in establishing the national taboo was done in the period of the Weimar Republic. The chief agency for manipulating public opinion at home and abroad was the 'War Guilt Section' (*Kriegsschuldreferat*) in the German Auswärtiges Amt. It directed and financed the German propaganda campaign by various methods.[1] German historians never questioned the righteousness of the German cause and defended uncritically the official line, without taking the trouble to produce anything comparable to the great works of professional historians in the 'enemy countries'.[2] Instead they allowed either foreigners or amateurs to do the spade-work when creating the 'scholarly' basis of the orthodox apologia.[3] Even after 1945 no fundamental revision took place in Germany. After some confusion and wavering, reflected in Friedrich Meinecke's and Gerhard Ritter's first publications after the Second World War,[4] a slightly modified version of the traditional line was adopted. In the era of German democratic Europeanism it even received the sanction of a formal agreement between leading German and French historians in 1951–2.[5] Now more than ever German historians, and public opinion in general, clung to Lloyd George's politically in-spired dictum of 1920, that 'all nations tumbled into war', that all participants had an equal share in the responsibility for its outbreak. When going into detail, however, one can detect a general tendency to blame above all Russia and Austria,[6] which boils down to saying that all the Powers were equally guilty, but that some were more guilty than others.

[1] For a first provisional sketch see I. Geiss, 'The Outbreak of the First World War and German War Aims', in *J.C.H.*, vol. I, no. 3 (July 1966), pp. 75–7.

[2] Above all, Pierre Renouvin, *Les Origines Immédiates de la Guerre* (Paris, 1925); Bernadotte E. Schmitt, *The Coming of the War*, 2 vols (New York and London 1930); Luigi Albertini, *Le Origini della Guerra del 1914*, 3 vols (Milano, 1942–3) (English edition, *The Origins of the War of 1914*, London, New York, Toronto 1952–7, second impression 1966).

[3] The most influential were: Harry E. Barnes, *The Genesis of the World War: An introduction to the problem of War Guilt* (New York, 1927); Sydney B. Fay, *The Origins of the World War*, 2 vols (New York, 1928); Hermann Lutz, *Lord Grey und der Weltkrieg:* (English version, *Lord Grey and the World War*, London, 1928); Alfred v. Wegerer, *Der Ausbruch des Weltkrieges 1914*, 2 vols (Hamburg, 1939). Recently, Friedrich Haselmayer, *Diplomatische Geschichte des Zweiten Reichs von 1871–1918*, 6 vols (München 1955–64), vol. 6, pp. 5, 351–506.

[4] Gerhard Ritter, *Europa und die deutsche Frage* (Munich, 1948); republished in 1962 as *Das deutsche Problem* (2nd impression, Munich, 1966); Friederich Meinecke, *Die deutsche Katastrophe* (Wiesbaden, 1947), English edition, *The German Catastrophe* (Cambridge, Mass., 1950).

[5] The agreement was published in *W.A.G.*, vol. XII (1952), 2, pp. 139–148; the joint declara-tion was the result of discussions between German and French historians in 1951. It figures also as an item in G. Ritter's bibliography, which suggests the prominent part he played in them. See G. Ritter, *Lebendige Vergangenheit* (Munich, 1958), p. 323, no. 121.

[6] As the most prominent of recent examples see G. Ritter, *Staatskunst und Kriegshandwerk. Das Problem des 'Militarismus' in Deutschland*, 3 vols (Munich, 1954–64), vol. II, pp. 282, 320.

On the other hand, Gerhard Ritter did deal more critically with the role of the Germany Army in July 1914.[1] But, hedged about by so many traditional excuses, his contribution only slightly modified the traditional creed. This is borne out by his, frequently, unjustified polemics against Luigi Albertini,[2] whose massive contribution he otherwise ignored, as did most German historians.[3] By the late 1950s, the whole problem seemed to be definitely settled for German historians; as Walther Hubatsch put it in a university textbook, 'the history of the years 1914–18 is studied almost more thoroughly than any other era. The historian moves everywhere on firm ground.'[4] This magisterial pronouncement of quasi-official weight is the more remarkable as the German documents on the First World War had at that time not been tapped by serious research, and German historians always insisted that final judgments would be impossible without knowledge of the archives. It is not surprising that, only a few years after Hubatsch's proclamation, this complacency[5] was rudely shattered by Fritz Fischer.[6] In one of his two introductory chapters Fischer did nothing more than introduce Albertini's results into Germany for the first time, when he showed that German policy was the main cause of the First World War. Yet a good deal of the immediate and violent attacks against him was concentrated on the crisis of July 1914. With promptitude otherwise rare in German historiography, the first attacks were published a few months after the book's appearance in November 1961. 'Liberals' like Golo Mann, Ludwig Dehio, Michael Freund and Hans Herzfeld[7] took as great a part in the campaign against Fischer as

---

[1] *Ibid.*, pp. 282–343.

[2] *Ibid.*, p. 381, n. 11; p. 382, n. 17, 22; p. 383, n. 25, 28; p. 384, n. 32.

[3] Only Hans Herzfeld, *Die Moderne Welt 1789 bis 1945* (3rd edn, Braunschweig, 1961), part II, p. 1, and Karl Dietrich Erdmann, 'Die Zeit der Weltkriege' in Bruno Gebhardt, *Handbuch der deutschen Geschichte*, vol. IV (8th edition, 2nd impression, Stuttgart, 1961), pp. 18, 22, mention or even quote Albertini, without, however, doing justice to him, let alone accepting his conclusions.

[4] Walter Hubatsch, 'Der Weltkrieg 1914–1918' in *Handbuch der deutschen Geschichte*, ed. Leo Just, vol. IV, section 2 (Konstanz, 1955), p. 2.

[5] Hubatsch, however, stuck to his guns. Eight years later he repeated his dictum with only verbal modifications when he maintained that a 'historian can write about the war from a reasonably firm and definite basis'; W. Hubatsch, *Germany and the Central Powers in the World War 1914–1918* (Lawrence, Kansas, 1963), p. 15.

[6] See note 1 (p. 9); two years before Fischer had published a preview of his results, 'Deutsche Kriegsziele: Revolutionierung und Separatfrieden im Osten 1914–1918' in *H.Z.*, 188/2, pp. 249–310. This article was recently republished in *Deutsche Kriegsziele 1914–1918*, ed. Ernst W. Graf Lynar (Ullstein 616, Berlin 1964), pp. 18–83.

[7] Ludwig Dehio, 'Deutschlands Griff nach der Weltmacht? Zu Fritz Fischers Buch über den Ersten Weltkrieg' in *Der Monat*, no. 161 (February 1962), pp. 65–9; Golo Mann, 'Der Griff nach der Weltmacht' in *Neue Zürcher Zeitung* (28 April 1962) (Ullstein 616, pp. 183–93); H. Herzfeld, review article in *G.W.U.*, 13/4 (April, 1962), pp. 246–54; H. Herzfeld, 'Die deutsche Kriegspolitik im Ersten Weltkrieg' in *Vh.G.Z.*, 11/3 (July 1963), pp. 224–45.

Conservatives like Gerhard Ritter[1], or right-wing extremists such as Erwin Hölzle and Giselher Wirsing.[2] Even politicians joined the fray, in particular the 'liberal' Christian Democrat Eugen Gerstenmaier, President of the German Bundestag,[3] while the Auswärtiges Amt intervened indirectly in spring 1964 by withdrawing funds for Fischer's lecture tour through the U.S.A. originally arranged by the Goethe-Institut, the German Cultural Institute.

The year 1964, the fiftieth anniversary of the outbreak of the First World War, brought an interesting development in the debate. While on the one hand the shrill polemics of Michael Freund and Giselher Wirsing and the more muffled interventions of Gerstenmaier and the Auswärtiges Amt added fuel to the raging debate, more rational elements made their appearance. Freund's charge that Fischer had relapsed into the attitudes of the 1920s and that he had made Bethmann Hollweg the Hitler of Imperial Germany, and Wirsing's jibe at Fischer's 'national masochism', were bound only to discredit the attackers themselves. Whereas Ritter and Freund pretended to accept a certain revision of the traditional line (without, however, dispensing with most of the traditional arguments), a new group emerged, represented by Karl-Dietrich Erdmann, the President of the German Historical Association, and Egmont Zechlin, Fischer's closest colleague at Hamburg University.

Erdmann, in his first contribution to the controversy, admitted that Bethmann Hollweg had seen and accepted the danger of Britain's joining a continental conflict, resulting from his 'leap into the dark'. Yet, by emphasising Bethmann Hollweg's subjective honesty and relative pacifism he suggested that Fischer was wrong in his essential points. His main new evidence was the diary of Kurt Riezler, the Chancellor's young aide and intimate adviser.[4] Unfortunately, Erdmann confused the issue by claiming

---

[1] G. Ritter, 'Griff nach der Weltmacht?' in *Löbecker Nachrichten* (20 May 1962); 'Eine neue Kriegsschuldthese? In Fritz Fischers Buch *Griff nach der Weltmacht*' in *H.Z.*, 194/4 (June 1962), pp. 646-68 (Ullstein 616, pp. 121-44); *Der Erste Weltkrieg. Studien zum deutschen Geschichtsbild* (Bonn, 1964); *Schriftenreihe der Bundeszentrale für Politische Bildung; Staatskunst und Kriegshandwerk*, vol. III, p. 8 and in many footnotes; 'Zur Fischer-Kontroverse', *H.Z.*, 200/3 (June 1965), pp. 783-7; 'Die politische Rolle Bethmann Hollwegs während des Ersten Weltkrieges' in *Congrès International des Sciences Historiques* (Vienna, 29 August-5 September 1965), vol. IV, pp. 271-8.

[2] Erwin Hölzle, 'Griff nach der Weltmacht?' in *Das Historisch-Politische Buch*, X, 3 (March 1962), pp. 65-9; Giselher Wirsing, '... auch am ersten Weltkrieg schuld?' in *Christ und Welt* (8 May 1964); *Der Bauchredner, ibid.* (10 July 1964).

[3] Eugen Gerstenmaier, 'Die Last des Vorwurfs. Zweimal deutsche Kriegsschuld?' in *Christ und Welt* (2 September 1964); almost identical in *Bulletin der Bundesregierung* (4 September 1964); re-published in E. Gerstenmaier, *Neuer Nationalismus?* (Stuttgart, 1965), pp. 82-85.

[4] K.-D. Erdmann, 'Zur Beurteilung Bethmann Hollwegs' in *G.W.U.*, 15/9 (September 1964), pp. 525-40.

that, when the Chancellor rejected Riezler's idea of German world domination, he also rejected Germany's claim to the status of a world power. When Rudolf Augstein, the editor of *Der Spiegel*, pointed out the inconsistency in Erdmann's argument,[1] the Professor peremptorily maintained that Riezler could not have thought of German world domination when he actually spoke of it.[2] This was doubly unfortunate, as Erdmann advanced no proof for his dogmatic statement, and completely ignored Riezler's pre-war writing in which he clearly spoke of the tendency of all nations to embrace world domination as the supreme aim.[3] At the same time, in his polemical rejoinder to Augstein, Erdmann defined Germany's policy as one of obtaining 'a share in world domination', so that, as he triumphantly concluded, Germany would merely have become 'a World Power beside other World Powers'. Erdmann's line of attack is the more surprising as his formula admirably sums up the essence of Fischer's thesis which Erdmann had tried to demolish.

In the same issue of the *Historische Zeitschrift* in which Fischer answered his critics for the first time and gave additional material on German pre-war policy in the Balkans,[4] Egmont Zechlin tried to refute Fischer by developing a complicated line of argument. Like Erdmann, he admitted that Bethmann Hollweg had taken the conscious risk of world war in July 1914, but said that he had wanted to fight only a limited, national, war in the style of the cabinet wars of the eighteenth century. Unfortunately, Grey had misunderstood Bethmann Hollweg and forced upon Germany a war *à outrance*, which had, in its turn, compelled the Chancellor to draw up his memorandum of September 1914 in self-defence and in order to bring down Britain. As proof, Zechlin advanced the theory that Bethmann Hollweg was shaken by the collapse of international law, when, for instance, dividends to German shareholders from Entente countries were withheld in August 1914.[5] Unwittingly, however, Erdmann and Zechlin cracked the former united front against heretical views. It is interesting to see that in subsequent contributions to the debate, Zechlin has moved closer still to Fischer's position, without, however, admitting it and without giving sufficient credit to Fischer for his own new insights. On the basis of a document first discovered and quoted during the Inter-

---

[1] Rudolf Augstein, 'Bethmann—einen Kopf kürzer?' in *Die Zeit* (25 September 1964).

[2] K.-D. Erdmann, 'Bethmann Hollweg, Augstein und die Historiker-Zunft', *Die Zeit* (2 October 1964).

[3] See below, pp. 33f.

[4] F. Fischer, 'Weltpolitik, Weltmachtstreben und deutsche Kriegsziele' in *H.Z.*, 199/2 (October 1964), pp. 265–346.

[5] Egmont Zechlin, *Deutschland zwischen Kabinettskrieg und Wirtschaftskrieg. Politik und Kriegführung in den ersten Monaten des Weltkrieges 1914*, pp. 347–458, especially p. 365.

national Historical Congress in Vienna 1965 by this author, Zechlin now goes so far as to admit that there was a strong element of preventive war thinking on the German side but, again, he finds many 'explanations' which amount to as many excuses.[1]

It was to be expected that Fritz Fischer would be walking straight into a hornet's nest when he dared to destroy the national taboo of successive German political régimes since 1914; that his new view on July 1914 would be indignantly challenged; that German historians would not easily admit a rational discussion on the subject. In order to provide a broader basis to Fischer's rapid sketch on July 1914 it was decided to publish a compilation of the most important documents on the outbreak of the First World War. As the documentary material was so massive, the problem so complicated, and as the documents were spread over so many varied and often no longer readily available editions, the German public had remained dependent for decades on whatever their professional historians thought fit to tell them, which was not very much and mostly misleading. Also the non-specialist historian must have found it hard to form an independent judgment based on solid knowledge of the facts and the documentary evidence. But even the present writer's two-volume documentary collection which organised Austrian, German, Russian, French and British documents strictly chronologically and gave short introductions to the 16 chapters,[2] turned out to be too detailed for the non-specialist. While Fischer's critics used the fiftieth anniversary of the outbreak of the First World War for more polemics,[3] a further effort was made by the other side to provide a firm basis for future discussion on this delicate question.

The lively interest of the German public in the Fischer controversy was increased by the fiftieth anniversary, by the violent polemics against Fischer, and by the German Historical Congress in Berlin in October 1964 where, in front of an audience of 2,000 consisting mainly of senior history students and graduates, a fair confrontation of the conflicting views took

---

[1] E. Zechlin, 'Bethmann Hollweg, Kriegsrisiko und SPD 1914' in *Der Monat*, 208 (January 1966), pp. 17–32; 'Motive und Taktik der Reichsleitung 1914. Ein Nachtrag' in *Der Monat*, 209 (February 1966), pp. 91–5.

[2] I. Geiss, *Julikrise und Kriegsausbruch 1914*. 2 vols (Hannover, 1963–4).

[3] G. Ritter, *Der Erste Weltkrieg* (see above, p. 12, n.1); G. Wirsing (see above, p. 12, n.2); G. Mann in *Suddeutsche Zeitung* (2 August 1964); H. Herzfeld in *Die Welt* (2 August 1964). The only attempt at a positive synthesis by one of Fischer's critics is so short and full of elementary mistakes, and so biased, that it is useless; see W. Hubatsch, 'Ursachen und Anlass des Weltkrieges 1914' in *1914–1939–1944. Schicksalsjahre deutscher Geschichte*, ed. Klaus-Jürgen Müller (Boppard, 1964); see also Hubatsch's even less substantial article, 'So kam es zum Ersten Weltkrieg' in *Deutsche Korrespondenz* (4 July 1964). Undaunted, Hubatsch recently repeated his mediocre performance in *Deutschland im Weltkrieg, 1914–1918* (Frankfurt/M., Berlin, 1966), pp. 23–33.

place. All this suggested the idea of compressing the documentary evidence still further, to form a single readable volume. For this purpose, the German edition of this volume was prepared. Obviously not all details could be dealt with. Instead, it was my aim to concentrate the narrative and the documentation on the central points.

The present volume does not seek to impose a certain view on the reader. The combination of an interpretative account with the key documents ready for critical inspection provides the suspicious reader with the means of checking the views expressed. If he is not satisfied he may turn to the original two-volume documentation. If he still does not trust my conclusions, he may turn either to the original documents themselves or to Albertini's great work (a second edition of which has appeared recently, and which could usefully be read in conjunction with the present volume). In any case, this succinct compilation of documents should be a help for the further study of a very complicated subject.

Some critics of both the large and the abridged documentation have made the point that they simply provide a documentary reconstruction of *German* policy in the crisis of July 1914, or, less charitably, that they were only arranged to prove a thesis, formulated beforehand, that Germany bears the major share for causing the War. Both views, however, are false. After making a careful selection of those documents which charted the main course of events and illustrated the state of mind and the reasons for the decisions of the statesmen and diplomats concerned, it so happened that most of them came either from the German side or reflected German actions and thoughts. True, this does reflect the preponderant part played by Germany in the crisis, but this cannot be blamed on the historian. It would be a distortion to create an artificial balance in the documentation when none existed. Similarly, in the present volume, by compressing the documentary material even more and concentrating on the really essential points, the German part is thrown into an even sharper relief than in the larger work. Again, this cannot be helped: it is a reflection of the events, not of personal bias.

For the compilation and re-editing of the documents I have followed the same principles as in the original large, two-volume selection. All documents are arranged in strict chronological order, day by day, hour by hour. In the case of telegrams, the hour of their despatch usually determines their place, unless they are known to have been drafted at an earlier date. Written despatches, memoranda and so forth are placed at the end of the telegrams. When passages from literature fill in a documentary gap, they are used as documents; this is particularly the case with Conrad's memoirs. Since Russian documents contain no hours of despatch or arrival, the chronological arrangement has had to be modified in such a way that for each day documents appear in the following order: Austrian, German, Russian, French, British. Most documents are unabridged; in a few cases some unimportant passages have been omitted and replaced by dots. In the German documents the Kaiser's remarks are printed in small type; words appearing in italics were underlined by the Kaiser in the original. The introductions to each chapter are sometimes fairly long, in particular that to Chapter I, as documentary sources for the first few days are very scant. The introductory remarks have been written so that they can stand by themselves, without needing constant reference to the documents in the relevant chapter. At the same time, of course, the critical reader is invited to use both parts together. Footnotes to the documents are reduced to a minimum. They dispense with criticisms of older literature, in order to avoid a running battle with authors who are mostly either unknown or irrelevant to English-speaking readers. The figures in bold type refer to the document numbers.

The original intention in publishing this volume was to make a constructive contribution to the present debate in Germany on the outbreak of the First World War, by presenting the facts as objectively as possible. But quite apart from the controversy, which in itself is only of passing interest, the subject is clearly of sufficient importance to warrant a detailed study by successive generations of students of modern history. In helping to clarify an important issue which has for too long been clouded by national passions and political considerations, it is hoped that this volume will present the relevant material in a convenient form for both present and future students.

It should be added that the present volume is not just a translation of the German original. Although the documentary material is the same, the Introduction, first chapter and Conclusion have been re-written, in the light both of new material and of new points raised in the debate. At the same time the presentation of the texts has been adapted to the English-speaking reading public, which either does not know the more detailed original selection of documents or cannot readily refer to it. For this reason texts have been expanded and regrouped. Similarly, some of the introductory remarks to individual chapters have been modified in the light of new material or criticism. In many ways the English version represents an enlarged and improved second edition of the German original.

Oxford, November 1966   Imanuel Geiss

Origins of the First World War

The events of July and early August 1914 cannot be properly understood without a knowledge of the historical background provided by the preceding decades of Imperialism. On the other hand, that background alone is not sufficient to explain the outbreak of the First World War. Two general historical factors proved to be decisive and both were fused by a third to produce the explosion known as the First World War. Imperialism, with Wilhelmine *Weltpolitik* as its specifically German version, provided the general framework and the basic tensions; the principle of national self-determination constituted, with its revolutionary potential, a permanent but latent threat to the old dynastic Empires and built up tensions in south-east Europe. The determination of the German Empire—then the most powerful conservative force in the world after Czarist Russia— to uphold the conservative and monarchic principles by any means against the rising flood of democracy, plus its *Weltpolitik*, made war inevitable.

Although the forces of national and revolutionary democracy were most active in south-east Europe just before the war, their roots go back to the French Revolution of 1789. Before 1914 the principle of national self-determination directly threatened the Ottoman Empire and caused the First Balkan War against Turkey, as a kind of war of national liberation. After the new Balkan nations had practically pushed Turkey out of Europe, the next target was inevitably Austria-Hungary, which, however, was closely allied to Germany. Although the German Empire was a nation-state, it in fact included compact national minorities on its borders consti-tuting about ten per cent of its population: Frenchmen in Alsace and Lorraine; Walloons in Eupen-Malmédy; Danes in Schleswig; Poles in West Prussia, Posen and Upper Silesia. They led the more or less marginal existence of second-class citizens; they resented the arbitrary separation from their compatriots and their enforced inclusion in the German Reich. Thus, at least indirectly, even the German Empire was implicated in the rise of national self-determination.

The third factor which made the First World War inevitable in the form and at the time it did occur, was the German Empire itself. It was important for two main reasons: its ambition to attain the status of 'a World Power beside other World Powers' (Erdmann), but without seeking an agreement with at least one of the world powers already firmly established; and secondly, its self-proclaimed role as the great bulwark against revolution and democracy. It is significant that both factors, even if in a rather confused way, had played a dominant role in the revolution of 1848–9. While we will probably never know whether a victory of liberal and democratic forces in Germany at that time would really have meant large-scale expansion of a newly founded Empire,[1] it is certain that Bismarck started his career by fighting both liberalism and democracy on the one hand, and expansion to at least a Greater German Empire, in-cluding Austria (with or without the non-German provinces) on the other. His Lesser German Empire founded in 1871 was a modest affair com-pared with the daydreams of many a liberal Greater-German patriot. But it established Prussian predominance and was accomplished only by three wars in rapid succession. The victories of the Prussian armies—in 1870 over Bonapartist France, about to liberalise herself, and after Sedan over post-Bonapartist, democratic France who resisted German demands for annexations[2]—in themselves introduced a new, disquieting element into the European scene. It was partly Bismarck's cunning diplomacy and Moltke's strategy of *blitzkrieg* (to use a fitting expression of a later period) that made it possible for Bismarck to unite the Germans in the face of misgivings in Europe.

[1] As even G. Ritter argues, although he thus refutes his own thesis that more positive alternatives to what actually happened were possible in modern German history; see G. Ritter, *Europa und die deutsche Frage*, pp. 72–6.

[2] Recent research shows how Bismarck himself, from the first days of the Franco-Prussian War, manipulated the press and let it make propaganda for German demands, so that he could later claim that he had only been reluctantly forced by the pressure of German public opinion into the annexation of Alsace-Lorraine. See Walter Lipgens, 'Bismarck, die öffentliche Meinung und die Annexion von Elsass und Lothringen 1870' in *H.Z.*, 199/1 (August 1964), pp. 31–112.

The immediate effect of the re-establishment of the Reich was to change profoundly the balance of power in Europe. Since the late Middle Ages Europe had been accustomed to weakness in its centre, in one form or another. Either there existed a confused political vacuum, created by the old Reich in its perennial agony, or two great German powers largely neutralised each other by their rivalries. The unification of a majority of Germans in the 'Lesser' German Reich under the leadership of Prussia helped to make the new Germany 'into the greatest concentration of power on the mainland in Europe'.[1] Unification, rapid industrialisation, military power and bureaucratic efficiency were sufficient to raise even Bismarck's 'Lesser' Germany almost automatically into a position of 'latent hegemony' (Theodor Schieder) over the Continent. Since then, the future of Europe and the Reich depended on the wisdom of Germany's political leaders, whether or not they successfully resisted the temptation to convert this latent hegemony into an open one.

Just as Frederick II of Prussia lay low after his conquest of Silesia, so did Bismarck after his successful coups. He wanted to accustom Europe to the new balance of power and to the emergence of Germany as the potential leading power in the centre of Europe. Bismarck's 'peaceful' policy after 1871 thus finds a very simple explanation. On the other hand, his new caution, after nearly a decade of gambling, recklessness and limited wars, probably also appealed to his conservative instincts. He had been successful beyond reasonable expectations, he did not want to run the risk of losing everything by aiming at even higher prizes. Bismarck's watchword that Germany was 'satiated' had two aims: to reassure Europe about the danger of German hegemony, and to restrain elements in Germany which were not satisfied with his achievements.[2] In the short run, Bismarck seemed to have succeeded again, at least as long as he was Chancellor. After 1871 he figures as the statesman of moderation and peace. Yet, in the long run, he and his work became the victim of those elements with which he had cooperated and which he afterwards tried to moderate or channel. And after his fall we see him allying himself with those very elements which dreamt of expansionist schemes.[3]

The real roots of Bismarck's triumph and of Germany's emergence as the leading power on the Continent in 1871 had been Prussia's industrial

[1] Charles A. Fisher, 'The Changing Dimensions of Europe' in *J.C.H.*, vol I, no. 3 (July 1966), p. 6; see also F. H. Hinsley, *Power and the Pursuit of Peace* (Cambridge, 1963), p. 301.

[2] See Hans Herzfeld, *Moderne Welt*, I, p. 219; the most recent and succinct discussion of Bismarck's policy after 1871 is by Martin Winckler, *Bismarcks Bündnispolitik und das europäische Gleichgewricht* (Stuttgart, 1964), especially pp. 43–6.

[3] See below, pp. 20–1.

preponderance over her more agrarian Austrian and French rivals.[1] Soon after the foundation of the Second Reich heavy industry was developed beyond the immediate needs of an expanding economy. From the early 1890s onwards industrialists, in particular Krupp, pressed for fuller use to be made of the inflated capacity for steel production. The demands were translated into political agitation by the Navy League, which was one of the first modern pressure groups in Germany and inspired and largely financed by Krupp.[2]

Similarly, the German economy expanded overseas and entered into conscious rivalry with British industry and finance, even though this was mitigated by short-term cooperation on such schemes as the Baghdad Railway. Soon after 1871 the pressure of foreign trade and increasing participation in world markets created the demand for a German share in world domination, or *Weltpolitik* as it was called. At least that was the explanation given, not by a Marxist but by Kurt Riezler, writing under a pseudonym shortly before the outbreak of the First World War.[3] Bismarck, mainly for domestic reasons, had tried to give these expansionist elements a limited outlet by inaugurating German colonial policy in the early 1880s.[4] Anti-British and an anti-Russian economic policy (in order to satisfy agrarian interests) made Germany drift into a hopeless dilemma.[5]

In spite of his sound insights into the dangers of open German hegemony, even Bismarck was unable to hold down for good the new demands for greater German power. After his fall, which was widely welcomed over practically the whole of Germany,[6] Caprivi's cautious policy of consolidation stood on the shoulders of Bismarck's 'peaceful' policy of the post-1871 period. Caprivi cared little for colonial and less for naval ambitions, but concentrated his efforts rather on strengthening Germany's position on the Continent, especially *vis-à-vis* Russia—to the chagrin of many German Conservatives and patriots. In particular, the Zanzibar-Heligoland deal of 1890 provoked the anger of the new forces in Germany, and Bismarck, now in enforced retirement, viciously denounced the very policy of restraint that he himself had pursued for almost two decades. Out of this agitation against the 'soft' Caprivi arose the Pan-German

[1] See Helmut Böhme, *Deutschlands Weg zur Grossmacht. Studien zum Verhältnis von Wirtschaft und Staat während der Reichsgrundungszeit 1848–1881* (Köln, 1966).

[2] See John C. G. Röhl, *Germany Without Bismarck* (London, 1967) Chap. 7.

[3] See below, p. 34.

[4] See Hartmut Pogge-v. Strandmann (Ph.D. diss., Oxford, 1967), Chapter I.

[5] E. Kehr, *Der Primat der Innenpolitik* (Berlin 1965), pp. 149–175.

[6] See J. C. G. Röhl, 'The Disintegration of the Kartell and the Politics of Bismarck's Fall from Power, 1887–90' in *H.J.*, vol. IX (1966), no. 1, pp. 60–89.

League.[1] For the period of Caprivi's Chancellorship, and again mainly for domestic reasons, Bismarck now openly allied himself with the incipient Pan-German movement. Yet the old Bismarck apparently did not realise in his anger that he was supporting a cause which, in the long run, would endanger his own work. Consequently, especially after his death in 1898, Bismarck became the patron of a new wave of German chauvinism, embracing all champions of German *Weltpolitik*.

GERMAN WELTPOLITIK

The new feeling was articulated for the first time in a powerful and persuasive way by Max Weber. In his famous Inaugural Lecture at Freiburg University in 1895, he pleaded for a new policy of striving for world power:

> We must understand that the unification of Germany was a youthful folly, which the nation committed in its declining days and which would have been better dispensed with because of its expense, if it should be the conclusion and not the starting point for a German *Weltmachpolitik*.[2]

Max Weber's eloquent plea was immediately taken up by Friedrich Naumann and by a vociferous group of Liberal imperialists,[3] in constant rivalry with the more conservative Pan-Germans in whose ranks Max Weber had played a role as one of the founder members. Between them they provided the climate of public opinion and the ideology for the actual change of German foreign policy.

The emergence of the Pan-German and Liberal Imperialists was one of the results of the new movement in German public opinion that clamoured for Germany to play a bigger role in the world. It is not surprising that the young Kaiser Wilhelm II, flamboyant and constantly torn between cutting a figure as a great Prince of Peace (*Friedenskaiser*) and a great Warlord (*Oberster Kriegsherr*), should have been amongst the first to voice the new sentiment, even if only in the strictest privacy. As early as summer 1892 he revealed to his intimate friend and adviser Count Eulenburg the 'fundamental principle' of his policy: 'a sort of Napoleonic supremacy . . . in the peaceful sense'. In the Kaiser's versatile mind 'Napoleonic supremacy', albeit 'in the peaceful sense', seemed perfectly compatible with his extraordinary illusion that the Poles were craving to be 'liberated from the Russian yoke' by the Germans: 'In the

---

[1] See Alfred Kruck, *Geschichte des Alldeutschen Verbands 1890–1939* (Wiesbaden, 1954).
[2] Wolfgang J. Mommsen, *Max Weber und die deutsche Politik 1890–1920* (Tübingen, 1959), p. 78.   [3] *Ibid.*, pp. 139ff.

event of a war with Russia the whole of Poland would revolt and come over to my side with the express intention of being annexed by me'.[1]

Perhaps even more significant is a private memorandum composed in 1896 by Georg Alexander von Müller, later Chief of the Imperial Naval Cabinet, under the title *Zukunftspolitik*.[2] Müller proceeded from the assumption that world history was at present characterised by a violent economic struggle, especially in Europe. While *Mitteleuropa* was becoming too narrow, the 'free expansion of the nations living there was limited by the existing distribution of the inhabitable parts of the globe, in particular by England's world domination'. Out of the tensions 'war can and, as many maintain, must arise'. According to Müller there was common agreement in Germany (*nach einer bei uns landläufigen Ansicht*) that the aim of such a war must be 'the destruction of English world domination in order to acquire the necessary colonies for the mid-European states in need of expansion'. Apart from Germany, Austria-Hungary and Italy were rated as such states 'in need of expansion', while Müller also considered the candidacy of Scandinavia and Switzerland. But, 'In the necessity and justification of expansion . . . Germany excels by far.'[3]

However, Müller, who had some liberal inclinations (liberal, that is, by German standards) did not entirely agree with that common view, since Germany would gain little from the destruction of the British Empire. Instead he preferred an alliance with Britain against Russia. As Britain, for reasons of racial comity (*Rassengemeinschaft*), would be Germany's 'natural ally', such an alliance would also give the 'economic struggle an ideological trait, the preservation of the Germanic race against Slavs and Romans'.[4] While the final result might be a clash between the two powerful 'Germanic empires' he preferred permanent cooperation between them in the interest 'of the future struggle for the hegemony of the Germanic race'. Müller clearly saw the two alternatives for Germany: 'Either to commit all the power of the nation, recklessly, not even shirking a great war, or else to limit ourselves to a Continental Power.'[5] He was against both a feeble compromise and the attempt to forge ahead against Britain.

[1] J. C. G. Röhl, 'A Document of 1892 on Germany, Prussia and Poland' in *H.J.*, vol. VII (1964), no. 1, pp. 143–9; the quotation on p. 144; the following on p. 147.

[2] *Der Kaiser: Aus den Tagebüchern des Chefs des Marinekabinetts Admiral Georg Alexander von Müller*, ed. Walter Görlitz (Göttingen, Berlin, Frankfurt, 1965), pp. 36–41.

[3] *Ibid.*, p. 37.

[4] *Ibid.*, p. 38 ('dem wirtschaftlichen Kampf einen ideellen Zug verleihen würde, das Hochhalten der germanischen Rasse im Gegensatz zu Slawen und Romanen').

[5] *Ibid.*, p. 40 ('Mit der ganzen Kraft der Nation einsetzen, rücksichtslos, auch den grossen Krieg nicht scheuend, oder aber die Beschränkung auf die Kontinentalmacht'); on the same page also the previous quotation.

The most interesting aspects of Müller's analysis and recommendations are his testimony of how general the German desire in 1896 must have been for expansion of the Reich (*landläufige Ansicht*); the realisation that the desired breakthrough to the status of World Power would be possible only by war was, it seems, equally widespread; and the emergence of a crude racism, even in one of 'liberal' repute. The implication of the new *Weltpolitik*—the Great War—was thus clearly seen in Wilhelmine Germany, even before it was launched. Although it would be of interest to assemble all the evidence showing that Germany's political élite understood this implication—before and after the crucial decision to plunge into the breakneck adventure of *Weltpolitik*—one more example must here suffice. Again, we quote not an extremist but a well-known moderate, the liberal-conservative historian and publicist Hans Delbrück, who, as one of the few German 'critic[s] of the Wilhelmine era',[1] was certainly not prone to extravagant pronouncements. As early as 26 November 1899 he proclaimed in his *Preussische Jahrbücher*:

> We want to be a World Power and pursue colonial policy in the grand manner. That is certain. Here there can be no step backward. The entire future of our people among the great nations depends on it. We can pursue this policy with England or without England. With England means in peace; against England means—through war.[2]

Like Müller, Delbrück would have preferred the former solution, but the Government's *Weltpolitik* was conducted not only without Britain, but even against Britain. Müller and Delbrück differed from the mainstream of political thought, as represented by the Kaiser, the Court and the Navy, in their caution *vis-à-vis* Britain. But all were agreed on the need for a powerful German fleet as the most important instrument of *Weltpolitik*. Even before 1897 the Navy pressed for a more powerful Battle Fleet. After the Kaiser had revealed to his intimate friend Eulenburg his Napoleonic dream in 1892, Eulenburg persistently pushed Bülow's candidacy as Foreign Secretary and Chancellor, while Bülow was only too willing to translate his Kaiser's ideas into action. Both were convinced that only a spectacular success in foreign policy could restore and enhance the popularity of the monarchy and establish the Kaiser's personal rule.[3] Out of all those dreams, sentiments, ambitions, crosscurrents and pressures emerged German *Weltpolitik*. It was apparently advocated for the first time at Government level in July 1897 by the

[1] A. Thimme, *Hans Delbrück als Kritiker der Wilhelminischen Epoche* (Düsseldorf, 1955).
[2] Quoted after J. Steinberg, 'The Copenhagen Complex' in *J.C.H.*, vol. I, no. 3, p. 27.
[3] J. C. G. Röhl, op. cit., and 'A Document of 1892 on Germany, Prussia, and Poland', *Historical Journal*, VII, 1 (1964), p. 144.

national-liberal Prussian Minister of Finance, Johannes von Miquel, as an indispensable part of his new policy of 'Collection' (*Sammlungspolitik*)—of rallying the well-to-do classes around the throne against Social Democracy.[1] At the same time, the new emphasis on foreign policy was to help overcome serious differences between the industrial and agrarian wings of Germany's wealthier classes and to create a united front of the whole nation against the world. Thus German *Weltpolitik* was partly created by a domestic policy, which aimed at diverting the attention of the masses from social and political problems at home by a dynamic expansion abroad. In this the essentially demagogic slogan of *Weltpolitik* proved only too successful. Through its 'national' appeal it soon acquired a momentum of its own, and finally domesticated the Catholic Centre Party, the left-wing Liberals, and even the SPD. It gave rise to a distinct political tradition that prevented even the most sensible and strong-willed German statesman from avoiding the collision course on which Germany was set. If there is anything tragic about Bethmann Hollweg, as is nowadays often claimed, it lay in the situation he inherited and was unable to affect, even if this had been his genuine desire. By 1914 the Reich had become victim of its own most valued slogan.

Bülow's arrival at the Auswärtiges Amt, the launching of Tirpitz's crash programme of naval armament, and Germany's seizure of Kiaochov in 1897, all point to the effective inauguration of German *Weltpolitik*.[2] The German Navy, built not only 'for our commerce, our security, our future', but also 'especially for the person of our dear Kaiser',[3] was understood by Britain as a challenge to her naval supremacy. Both Tirpitz's concept of the *Risikoflotte*, designed to frighten Britain at least into neutrality,[4] and the Battle of Jutland in 1916[5] prove that British fears were not unfounded. As late as February 1914 Jagow, the Secretary

---

[1] Kehr, *Der Primat der Innenpolitik*, pp. 150–75.

[2] There is, unfortunately, not yet a satisfactory comprehensive study of German *Weltpolitik*. The nearest to it is George W. F. Hallgarten, *Imperialismus vor 1914. Die soziologischen Grundlagen der Aussenpolitik europäischer Grossmächte vor dem Ersten Weltkrieg*, 2 vols (2nd edition, Munich, 1963); all other studies are more or less rapid sketches. Although it deals only with one aspect of *Weltpolitik*, J. Steinberg's article on the Copenhagen complex (above p. 23, n. 2) gives many important insights, as does the article by C. A. Fisher (see above, p. 19, n. 1).

[3] J. C. G. Röhl, *Germany Without Bismark*, Chap. 7. The quotation is taken from a letter of Bülow to Eulenburg (1898).

[4] For the most recent treatment of this important aspect see J. Steinberg, *Yesterday's Deterrent. Tirpitz and the Birth of the German Battle Fleet* (London, 1965). See also Eckart Kehr, *Schlachtflottenbau und Parteipolitik. Historische Studien*, vol. 197 (Berlin, 1930), especially pp. 21, 27, 125–48, 208–21.

[5] There is much force in the argument that, given equal visibility and tactical advantages, the result of the Battle of Jutland might have been different, judging from the short spells when these conditions actually existed. See Corelli Barnett, *The Sword Bearers: Studies in Supreme Command in the First World War* (London, 1963), 'Jellicoe,' pp. 165–71.

of State at the Auswärtiges Amt, wrote to Lichnowsky, the German Ambassador in London, on the question of British neutrality in a future conflict:

> We have not built our fleet in vain, and in my opinion, people in England will seriously ask themselves whether it will be just that simple and without danger to play the role of France's guardian angel against us.[1]

German *Weltpolitik* pursued the tactics of claiming equality with the established World Powers and demanded 'compensations' for any territorial or other changes of the status quo anywhere on the globe. The character of Germany's new course was thus one of irritating vagueness, but it was clearly based on the consciousness of growing power. German uncertainty about the present status of Germany in the world and her future role only increased confusion at home and suspicion abroad. Whereas Max Weber in 1895 still demanded a new *Weltmachtpolitik*, the Kaiser proclaimed that Germany had already become a 'world empire' (*Weltreich*) as early as 18 January 1896. Nobody doubted or disputed Germany's status as a great continental Power. But it was increasingly hard to define her position in world politics.

THE EFFECT OF WELTPOLITIK ON THE BALANCE OF POWER

Germany's *Weltpolitik* had far-reaching effects. A less obvious one was the change in the character of the Triple Alliance. The Dual Alliance between Germany and Austria had originally been concluded in 1879 as a purely defensive treaty. The inclusion of Italy in 1882 did not alter that basic fact, although complications were introduced on account of Austro-Italian rivalry. The new *Weltpolitik*, however, gradually transformed the Triple Alliance into the basis for German ambitions as a fledgling world power. When Italy tried to do the same on a limited scale with her Libyan war against Turkey in 1911 (a power open to German influence), and when Austria tried to use the Triple Alliance to support her own policy in the Balkans, the Triple Alliance lost much of its defensive character and its superficially imposing unity and power.[2]

Even more startling was the effect on the other Powers. In 1871 there was no system of alliance in existence; in 1885, when the 'scramble for Africa' began, there existed only one alliance—the Triple Alliance; by

[1] *G.P.*, XXXVII, no. 14692. It is interesting that Jagow should realise that France needed Britain as a 'guardian angel' against Germany. The German Battle Fleet was meant to discourage Britain from exercising this role.
[2] This is stressed by Fritz Fellner, *Der Dreibund. Europäische-Diplomatie vor dem Ersten Weltkrieg* (München, 1960).

1907, however, the Triple Entente had emerged. Among the first symptoms of the new development had been the Franco-Russian Alliance of 1892–4, which put an end to the isolation of France, created by Bismarck's diplomacy after 1871. It also ended for good the cooperation between the great conservative Powers of the East, Russia, Germany and Austria. Partly as a reaction to Germany's *Weltpolitik*, her naval armament and her refusal to enter into a loose arrangement with Britain, and partly as a counter-move to the completion of the Trans-Siberian Railway in 1902,[1] Britain's foreign policy after the Boer War was designed to end her erstwhile 'splendid isolation'.[2] The alliance with Japan in 1902 was followed in 1904 by the Entente Cordiale with France. Although it was primarily an arrangement over colonial questions, political cooperation between the two Western Powers soon followed. In 1907, after the Russo-Japanese War of 1904–5, Britain and Russia concluded an even looser arrangement. The so-called 'Triple Entente' was, therefore no solid alliance. There was no formal treaty of alliance between all three partners; there was only the Treaty between Russia and France. There were no formal and binding agreements for military cooperation between Britain and the other partners. The tensions between Britain and Russia over Persia were a constant source of friction between the two countries, even in early July 1914.[3] Neither the Triple Alliance nor the Triple Entente were the monolithic power blocks they seemed to be.[4] But most contemporaries and participants in the diplomatic negotiations at the time felt strongly about the differences between the two groups. At least Jagow, on 1 August 1914, attributed the deeper reasons for the outbreak of war to 'this d—d system of alliances', as he remarked in a conversation with Sir Edward Goschen, the British Ambassador in Berlin.[5]

Contrary to traditional German belief, the Triple Entente was not conceived as an offensive alliance. None of the three Powers pursued expansionist aims, over which they would or could have gone to war: British

---

[1] C. A. Fisher (see above, p. 19, n. 1).

[2] For the most recent and detailed study see George W. Monger, *The End of Isolation: British Foreign Policy 1900–1907* (London, Edinburgh, 1963).

[3] A point in particular stressed by Oswald Hauser, *Deutschland und der englisch-russische Gegensatz 1900–1914* (Göttingen, Berlin, Frankfurt, 1958). For a general treatment of the age of Imperialism before 1914 see William L. Langer, *European Alliances and Alignments 1871–1890* (New York, 1931; 2nd impression 1951); *The Diplomacy of Imperialism 1890–1902*, 2 vols (New York, 1935); L. Albertini: *Origins*, vol. I; A. S. Jerussalimski, *Die Aussenpolitik und die Diplomatie des deutschen Imperialismus Ende des 19 Jahrhunderts* (Berlin, 1954). An excellent survey of the literature on the period is provided by Hans Herzfeld, *Moderne Welt*, II, pp. 12f., 22ff., 33f., 45f., 53f., 62ff., 79ff., 88f., and 96f.; Herzfeld's own account is, of course, also important. For the earlier periods see E. Kehr, *Schlachtflottenbau*.

[4] See above, p. 25, n. 2.

[5] *B.D.*, XI, no. 510.

'envy of the German economy' (*Handelsneid*), French 'Revanchism' and Russian 'Pan-Slavism' were, and still are, grossly exaggerated in Germany. Alsace-Lorraine was of course in the minds of many Frenchmen, but France would never have gone to war in order to reconquer the two provinces, if only because public opinion was on the whole pacific, as the German Ambassador in Paris stressed in detailed reports from France.[1] On the other hand, the French, in their *nouvel esprit*, were no longer prepared to swallow such a humiliation as having to sack Delcassé merely to avert threats from Germany, as happened during the first Moroccan crisis of 1905–6.[2]

Russian 'Pan-Slavism' amounted to a vague feeling of solidarity among all Slavs, and active, chauvinistic Pan-Slavs in Russia were limited to small circles as, again, the Kaiser and the Chancellor could have learned from their top expert on the question, the German Ambassador in St Petersburg.[3] Czarist Russia, it is true, had her traditional ambitions for Constantinople. Yet there she encountered not only German interests, but also traditional British and French suspicions, which by themselves would have been enough to neutralise any Russian aggression against Turkey. The Russians, furthermore, faced a serious dilemma: 'a struggle for Constantinople was not possible without a general European war', as was pointed out in the famous secret Conference of 21 February– 6 March 1914 in St Petersburg,[4] but in a general war military action against Constantinople would be impossible, as all forces would be needed on other fronts. Nor would an isolated coup against Constantinople succeed because it was bound to provoke a general war which the Russians knew they were too weak to wage on their own; neither France nor Britain would come to their help in a provoked war, let alone one provoked by the seizure of Constantinople. This dilemma proved to be insoluble, and in fact during the crisis of July 1914 Constantinople figured only in the back of the minds of a few statesmen: Sazonov apparently wanted to prevent

[1] See Schoen's reports of 10 November 1912 and 15 November 1913 in *G.P.*, XXXIV, no. 12522, and XXXIX, no. 15657.

[2] On Delcassé see Christopher Andrew, *The Foreign Policy of Théophile Delcassé to 1905* (Ph.D. diss., Cambridge, 1965), and the same author's article 'German World Policy and the Reshaping of the Dual Alliance' in *J.C.H.*, I, no. 3, pp. 137–51.

[3] Pourtalès' reports of 2 March, 26 April and 30 June 1913, and of the German consul in Moscow of 10 and 18 April and 3 May 1913 in *Politisches Archiv des Auswärtigen Amts. Russland 85 geh.* vol. 1; *Russland 61*, vol. 121; they had not been published in the *Grosse Politik*, as one would have expected.

[4] For a recent discussion of the importance of the Straits see E. Zechlin, 'Die türkischen Meerengen—ein Brennpunkt der Weltgeschichte' in *G.W.U.*, 17/1 (January 1966), pp. 1–31, especially pp. 12–17; see also I. V. Bestuzhev, 'Russian foreign policy February–June 1914' in *J.C.H.*, I, no. 3, pp. 93–112, especially p. 107.

the Germans from taking over in Constantinople once Serbia was crushed by Austria, while the Austrians and Germans apparently feared Russia's expansion through the alliance with the south Slavs, whose success would isolate the Central Powers from Turkey. Constantinople was not a direct cause of war in 1914.

The two most highly industrialised countries of Europe—Britain and Germany—were each other's best trading partners, and in Britain there was a strong pro-German current, from the monarchy down to a rather sentimental feeling of 'kith and kin' on the part of the Left, who were most outspoken in their opposition to entering the war on the side of Czarist Russia. Britain was also opposed to any offensive war against Germany provoked by Russia or France and would effectively have vetoed it. [1]

There were, however, circles in Britain who were disturbed and even frightened by the menace of the German Fleet, of Germany's vague, ill-defined demands, her pretensions and the ostentatious display of her military and naval power. This group became strong in the Navy, the Army and the Foreign Office. The most detailed articulation of their misgivings is to be found in Sir Eyre Crowe's famous memorandum of 1 January 1907. [2] His memorandum is, it seems, more denounced as anti-German than actually read (at least in Germany), perhaps on account of its length. [3] In the light of subsequent events and of our present knowledge, it proves to have been the most intelligent and precise analysis of German *Weltpolitik* for a very long time to come. Far from being crudely anti-German, it was a balanced judgment of German intentions and sought to find a rational explanation for the apparently irrational and bewildering manifestations of German *Weltpolitik*. Crowe set it in historical perspective, in the same sort of way as many German historians, then and later,

[1] The British attitude was most effectively analysed as early as 1929 by Hermann Kantorowicz, *Der Geist der englischen Politik und das Gespenst der Einkreisung Deutschlands* (Berlin, 1929), pp. 351–4, a book which has been undeservedly forgotten.

[2] The text in *B.D.*, III, appendix A, pp. 397–420. A short but fair appraisal of its main points is in G. W. Monger, *The End of Isolation*, pp. 313–15.

[3] The last example is G. Wirsing's attack on Fischer (see above, p. 12, n. 2). When challenged by Rudolf Augstein in *Der Spiegel* that his was a typical 'Nazi legend', Wirsing retorted that this was not so, as the Nazis 'were too little educated in history to ever have heard of such a figure in the background, such as Crowe. We do not know that there exists any Nazi literature on Crowe.' (G. Wirsing, *Der Bauehredner*.) In fact, the Nazis had used the argument in abundance, and one of them was Wirsing himself who accused Crowe of having interpreted the principle of the balance of power as 'Germaniam esse delendam!' G. Wirsing, *Das Zeitalter des Ikaros* (Jena, 1944), p. 97. Also G. Wirsing, *Der Masslose Kontinent. Roosevelts Kampf um die Weltherrschaft* (Jena, 1942) p. 17. Similarly distorted interpretations by Heinz Günter Sasse, *England—Deutschlands Widerpart* (Berlin, 1941) p. 162, and Wilhelm Schüssler, *Deutschland zwischen Russland und England* (Leipzig, 1940) pp. 182–92.

have traced the rise of little Brandenburg into the mighty German Empire, via Prussia. A close look at Crowe's memorandum is, therefore, highly relevant in the present context, if only because it was long considered in Germany as a major factor contributing to war.

Crowe saw the rational core of German *Weltpolitik* in the drive for equality of Germany overseas:

> Germany had won her place as one of the leading, if not, in fact, the foremost Power on the European continent. But over and beyond the European Great Powers there seemed to stand the 'World Powers'. It was at once clear that Germany must become a 'World Power'. (p. 404)

The result was the inauguration of German colonial policy. Crowe's way of summing up political sentiment in Germany is worth quoting. In answering the question why Germans thought they must have colonies, a powerful fleet and coaling stations, he answers for the German mind:

> A healthy and powerful State like Germany, with its 60 million inhabitants, must expand, it cannot stand still, it must have territories to which its overflowing population can emigrate without giving up its nationality . . . When it is objected that the world is now actually parcelled out among independent States, and that territory for colonization cannot be had except by taking it from the rightful possessor, the reply again is: 'We cannot enter into such considerations. Necessity has no law. The world belongs to the strong. A vigorous nation cannot allow its growth to be hampered by blind adherence to the status quo. . . !'

After quoting some of the most revealing remarks of the Kaiser ('The trident must be in our hand', 'No question of world politics may be settled without the consent of the German Emperor', etc.), Crowe reached a provisional conclusion, which is more moderate than extreme:

> The significance of these individual utterances may easily be exaggerated. Taken together, their cumulative effect is to confirm the impression that Germany distinctly aims at playing on the world's political stage a much larger and much more dominant part than she finds allotted to herself under the present distribution of material power. (p. 405)

Crowe warned that it was not a matter of moralising, as examples of history showed. Again he revealed how well he knew the German mind:

> No modern German would plead guilty to a mere lust of conquest for the sake of conquest. But the vague and undefined schemes of Teutonic expansion (*die Ausbreitung des deutschen Volkstums*) are but the expression of the deeply rooted feeling that Germany has established for herself . . . the right to assert the primacy of German national ideas. And as it is an axiom of her political faith that right, in order that it may prevail, must be

backed by force, the transition is easy to the belief that the 'good German sword', which plays so large a part in patriotic speeches, is there to solve any difficulties that may be in the way of establishing the reign of those ideas in a Germanized world.   (p. 406)

Turning to the analysis of German *Weltpolitik* proper, Crowe made it clear that he was no anti-German, for he did not question 'that the mere existence and healthy activity of a powerful Germany is an undoubted blessing to the world' (p. 406).

In spite of all English 'sympathy and appreciation of what is best in the German mind', created by 'intellectual and moral kinship', Crowe attached one condition to his welcoming an increase of Germany's influence and power in the world:

> There must be respect for the individualities of other nations, equally valuable coadjutors, in their way, in the work of human progress, equally entitled to full elbow-room in which to contribute, in freedom, to the evolution of a higher civilization.   (p. 406)

On the following page Crowe put the same argument in a different form:

> So long, then, as Germany competes for an intellectual and moral leadership of the world in reliance of her own national advantages and energies England can not but admire, applaud, and join in the race. If, on the other hand, Germany believes that greater relative preponderance of material power, wider extent of territory, inviolable frontiers, and supremacy at sea are necessary and preliminary possessions without which any aspirations to such leadership must end in failure, then England must expect that Germany will surely seek to diminish the power of any rivals, to enhance her own by extending her dominion, to hinder the co-operation of other States, and ultimately to break up and supplant the British Empire. (p. 407)

Crowe noted that, of course, German statesmen denied any such intentions. He pointed out that, even if such assurances were sincere, they might be 'incapable of fulfilment'. Furthermore, 'ambitious designs against one's neighbours are not as a rule openly proclaimed'. Crowe cautiously introduced the idea of what is now called 'continuity' in German policy, by suggesting 'that a further development [of German policy] on the same general lines would not constitute a break with former traditions, and must be considered at least as possible.' And he asked:

> Whether it would be right, or even prudent, for England to incur any sacrifice or see other, friendly, nations sacrificed merely in order to assist Germany in building up step by step the fabric of a universal preponderance, in the blind confidence that in the exercise of such preponderance

Germany will confer unmixed benefits on the world at large, and promote the welfare and happiness of all other peoples without doing injury to any one. (p. 407)

Crowe had his doubts. Again he stressed 'that a recognition of the dangers of the situation need not and does not imply any hostility to Germany'; he was ready to mete out to Germany the same as he expected for England: 'not to be wantonly hampered by factitious opposition', when pursuing schemes which are not harmful to third nations.

After a lengthy and detailed survey of the many frictions between Germany and Britain, which Crowe blamed on Germany's *Weltpolitik*, he returned to the question of what German intentions could be. He saw two possible explanations:

Either Germany is definitely aiming at a general political hegemony and maritime ascendancy, threatening the independence of her neighbours and ultimately the existence of England; or Germany, free from any such clear-cut ambition, and thinking for the present merely of using her legitimate position and influence as one of the leading Powers in the council of nations, is seeking to promote her foreign commerce, spread the benefits of German culture, extend the scope of her national energies, and create fresh German interests all over the world wherever and whenever a peaceful opportunity offers, leaving it to an uncertain future to decide whether the occurrence of great changes in the world may not some day assign to Germany a larger share of direct political action over regions not now a part of her dominions, without that violation of the established rights of other countries which would be involved in any such action under existing political conditions.

(p. 417)

And he added: 'In either case Germany would clearly be wise to build as powerful a navy as she can afford.' One might add today: the overall result would have been the same—the Great War.[1] To meet either possibility Crowe recommended falling back on the traditional policy of the balance of power. This would not mean that Germany need be reduced to the rank of a weak power, for:

So long as Germany's action does not overstep the line of legitimate protection of existing rights she can always count upon the sympathy and good-will, and even the moral support, of England. Further, it would be neither just nor politic to ignore the claims to a healthy expansion which a vigorous and growing country like Germany has a natural right to assert in the field of legitimate endeavour. . . . It cannot be good policy for England to thwart such a process of development where it does not directly conflict either with British interests or with those of other nations to which England

[1] See above, p. 22.

is bound by solemn treaty obligations. If Germany, within the limits imposed by these two conditions, finds the means peacefully and honourably
to increase her trade and shipping, to gain coaling stations or other har-
bours, to acquire landing rights for cables, or to secure concessions for the
employment of German capital or industries, she should never find
England in her way. Nor is it for British Governments to oppose Germany's building as large a fleet as she may consider necessary or desirable
for the defence of her national interests. . . .   (p. 417)

Crowe summed up his policy, which could be called one of 'containment',[1]
in a remarkable passage:

It would be of real advantage if the determination not to bar Germany's
legitimate and peaceful expansion, nor her schemes of naval development,
were made as patent and pronounced as authoritively as possible, provided care was taken at the same time to make it quite clear that this
benevolent attitude will give way to determined opposition at the first
sign of British or allied interest being adversely affected. This alone would
probably do more to bring about lastingly satisfactory relations with
Germany than any other course.   (p. 418)

But he warned of one road which would be disastrous:

That is the road paved with graceful British concessions—concessions
made without any conviction either of their justice or of their being set off
by equivalent counter-services. The vain hopes that in this manner
Germany can be 'conciliated' and made more friendly must be definitely
given up.   (p. 419)

Crowe's memorandum can be regarded as the key document of British
policy before 1914, which amounted to accepting the expansion of German influence and power in the world, as long as it was peaceful; provided that is, that it did not violate vital British interests either directly
or indirectly, nor tried to upset the then existing balance of power in
Europe and in the world. Crowe was against a policy of concessions,
merely to 'conciliate' (we would now say 'appease') Germany on her road
to more power. British policy of containing Germany could only lead to
collision if Germany were to bear out the worst suspicions and fears of
Crowe and his group.

No one who knows the course of German history since Bismarck, or
the attitude of pre-1914 Germany (as reflected both in the writings of the
time and in the minds of the present older generation), can doubt that

[1] This expression is not an anachronism, as one might think. Berchtold, the Austrian Foreign
Minister, used the German equivalent *Eindämmung* on 1 August 1914 when describing British
policy *vis-à-vis* Germany. *D.A.*, III, 96.

Crowe's assessment, on the whole, was to the point, was just and fair. Even if Crowe had not read Max Weber's Inaugural Lecture of 1895 and had not known Müller's ideas on Germany's *Zukunftspolitik*, even if one were to dismiss the Pan-Germans as representing the 'lunatic fringe' in German society (which they certainly were not), he could not have known the revealing German counterpart of his own analysis of the situation and of the German mind, since it was published only some years later.

Kurt Riezler is not a figure whose historical relevance can easily be ignored or belittled: he came from a respectable, well-educated family, was the young but influential adviser of Chancellor Bethmann Hollweg and had written two important books, couched in the traditional (and often unreadable) jargon of German philosophical idealism.[1] His second book, published under a pseudonym, appeared just before the outbreak of the First World War and reflects the position of the most liberal and peaceful wing of German patriotism. Nevertheless, in it Riezler gave expression to the widespread Social Darwinism of the time and he seems certainly to have been influenced by Max Weber, the greatest intellect of German Liberal Imperialists. It is not surprising that for the same reason Riezler, in spite of his criticism of the Pan-Germans over details of policy, betrayed many affinities with them over basic questions of German *Weltanschauung*.[2] In many respects Riezler confirmed Crowe's analysis of the German mind before 1914, as did Müller's, almost 20 years earlier.[3]

For Riezler there was no question of a rational principle which would allow or make desirable the peaceful coexistence of nations, small and large. He not only fell back on a Hobbesian philosophy of war of all against all, but even proclaimed the theory that the eternal struggle—not for survival, but for obtaining world-domination—was the supreme aim of all nations. If this was true of all nations, then it applied to the Germans:

[1] Kurt Riezler, *Die Erforderlichkeit des Unmöglichen, Prolegomena zu einer Theorie der Politik und zu anderen Theorien* (Munich, 1912).

J. J. Ruedorffer (=K. Riezler), *Grundzüge der Weltpolitik* (Stuttgart and Berlin, 1914). A critical analysis of his basic political ideas by I. Geiss, 'Zur Beurteilung der deutschen Reichspolitik im ersten Weltkrieg' in H. Pogge–v. Strandmann and I. Geiss, *Die Erforderlichkeit des Unmöglichen: Deutschland am Vorabend des ersten Weltkrieges. Hamburger Studien zur neueren Geschichte*, ed. Fritz Fischer, vol. 2 (Frankfurt, 1965), pp. 55–64, 78–80. See also Andreas Hillgruber, 'Riezlers Theorie des kalkulierten Risikos und Bethmann Hollwegs politische Konzeption in der Julikrise 1914' in *H.Z.*, 202/2 (April 1966), pp. 333–51.

[2] This explains why there were so many basic points which Liberal Imperialists, like Riezler and Bethmann Hollweg, Max Weber and Friedrich Naumann, had in common with the Pan-Germans over war aims, even if they disagreed substantially over extent, priorities and methods.

[3] See above, pp. 22f.

Ideally, every nation wants to grow, to expand, to rule and to subject [others] without end, wants to coalesce and to incorporate ever more [nations], wants to become an even more powerful unit, until the Universe has under its own rule, become one organic unit.[1]

In his next book, Riezler went as far as to use the precise term for this circumlocution—'world domination'—as the supreme prize in the political struggle.[2] It is logical that for Riezler enmity was the underlying principle governing the relations between nations, a principle which could only be temporarily modified by tactics and expediency.[3] In his more popular book, he pleaded for the supremacy of German *Kultur* in the world by endorsing the Kaiser's view that the world should one day be healed by German ideas and methods.[4] Like Max Weber, Riezler saw in Germany's economic expansion the impulse towards German *Weltpolitik*; he also saw in the foundation of the Reich by Bismarck in 1871 the basis for further political expansion:

> The young German Empire pushed out into the world. Its population grows annually by 8–900,000 people, and for these new masses food must be found, or, what amounts to the same, work. . . . The economic interest had to be followed by the political. The enormous potential and achievement of the rising nation pushed the young Empire into its *Weltpolitik* . . . Germany's unification was, on the one hand, a culmination of the national development, a fulfilment of national aspirations. On the other hand, it was the beginning of a new development, the germ for new, more far-reaching aspirations. Just as in the strivings of the individual, so in the aspirations of the nations there is neither culmination nor end. Parallel to the increasing interest in *Weltpolitik*, German nationalism orientated itself towards *Weltpolitik*. The demands of the German nation for power and prestige, not only in Europe, but throughout the world, have increased rapidly.[5]

But Riezler feared that Germany's territorial basis in Europe for pursuing her *Weltpolitik* was too narrow. He wanted to free the Reich from Bismarck's *cauchemar des coalitions* by making Germany so powerful that, in the interest of her *Weltpolitik*, she would have the chance of victory in 'any possible constellation', thus deterring any possible combination of adversaries or rivals throughout the world. And Riezler concluded his analysis of German *Weltpolitik*, which he took for granted:

[1] K. Riezler, *Die Erforderlichkeit des Unmöglichen*, p. 203.
[2] J. J. Ruedorffer, *Grundzüge*, pp. 23, 32.
[3] K. Riezler, *Die Erforderlichkeit des Unmöglichen*, pp. 227ff.
[4] J. J. Ruedorffer, *Grundzüge*, p. 22: 'dass die Welt am deutschen Wesen genesen werde'; compare Crowe's doubts, above, p. 31.
[5] *Ibid.*, pp. 115ff.

Hemmed in by unfavourable frontiers it [the German nation] needs to display great power, so long as it is obstructed in many ways from freely pursuing its *Weltpolitik*. For the sake of freedom in its world policy it must be guarded against any eventuality. It cannot allow those spheres of activity to be blocked which are still open for its world policy. The attempt to contain this policy might be temporarily successful, but in the long run it will fail because of the nation's effective power and its tremendous *élan vital* [*Lebensdrang*].[1]

Riezler's philosophy amounted to a thinly disguised claim to German world domination to be attained in successive stages. His views, which were still the more 'moderate', 'soft' version of the prevalent German *Weltanschauung* of the time, were bound to produce war, once translated into practical policy. For on the one hand, it was unlikely that the other Powers would passively allow Germany to advance towards world domination; on the other hand, Riezler apparently saw even a policy of containment as hostile obstruction, which would be brushed aside by Germany's 'effective power and her tremendous *élan vital*'.

THE GROWING CRISIS

German *Weltpolitik*, the containment policy of the Entente and Germany's refusal to be contained made war inevitable. The elements of containment became apparent from the time of the Entente Cordiale of 1904. Germany's first political reaction of significance was the move against France over Morocco in 1905–6. It would have been a success but for German insistence on a fully-fledged international conference to underscore the German diplomatic triumph, after Delcassé's fall under German pressure. The Bosnian crisis of 1908–9 brought another temporary victory for Germany, when Serbia was dropped by Russia under the veiled threat of German mobilisation against Russia. But Russian humiliation was such that a repetition of the same manoeuvre was unlikely to be successful—as Prince Bülow, then German Chancellor, claims to have warned his sovereign while taking his farewell after his dismissal in 1909.[2]

The second crisis over Morocco in 1911 was in many ways a repetition of the first, but this time without the initial German success. The despatch of the German gunboat *Panther* to Agadir produced anxieties in Britain,

[1] *Ibid.*, pp. 115f.
[2] Fürst von Bülow, *Denkwürdigkeiten*, 3 vols (Berlin, 1931–2), vol. 2, pp. 513ff.; English edition, *Memoirs 1903–1909* (London, 1931), p. 502.

and British warnings, expressed by Lloyd George in his famous Guildhall speech, were prompter and clearer this time than ever before or after. When Italy and Austria refused to support Germany on her course of collision, Germany backed down with the help of a face-saving compromise, which gave her some additional territory in the Cameroons. The net effect of German endeavours was to weld together the Triple Entente, and to raise a new spirit of national defiance in France. Sir Edward Grey, the British Foreign Secretary, and Paul Cambon, the French Ambassador in London, exchanged their famous letters in which they promised to coordinate the foreign policy of their countries in future periods of crisis, while arrangements for naval and military cooperation between Britain and France were made in the event of a German attack against France. The possibility of Germany's trying to breach Belgian neutrality was seriously considered and cooperation with the Belgian General Staff sought for that contingency.

The effect of the German diplomatic defeat in the second Moroccan crisis was even more dramatic in Germany: German propaganda, from now on, loudly proclaimed that the Reich was 'encircled' by the Entente Powers, by a coalition of envious and mischievous Powers, who were only waiting for their chance to overwhelm the Central Powers. Probably the first, at any rate the best-known, expression of the new 'encirclement' complex had come a few years before from Field-Marshal Count Schlieffen, the prolific ex-Chief of the Prussian General Staff. In his famous article 'Der Krieg in der Gegenwart', written as early as January 1909 we find most of the relevant clichés gathered together: Britain envious of Germany's economic and industrial progress, France thirsting for revenge, Russia full of Slav resentment against the Teuton, treacherous Italy lined up against Austria. They all had built up powerful fortresses around unprotected Germany and Austria-Hungary.

> An endeavour is afoot to bring all these Powers together for a concentrated attack on the Central Powers. At the given moment, the drawbridges are to be let down, the doors are to be opened and the million-strong armies let loose, ravaging and destroying, across the Vosges, the Meuse, the Niemen, the Bug and even the Isonzo and the Tyrolean Alps. The danger seems gigantic. [1]

These were not just the wild rantings of a frustrated retired general, who had never had the chance of conducting a great battle in actual warfare, but views shared by many of the Wilhelmine Establishment. Schlieffen's

---

[1] Graf Alfred von Schlieffen, *Gesammelte Werke*, 2 vols (Berlin, 1913), vol. 1, pp. 20ff. The English version after G. Ritter, *The Schlieffen Plan: Critique of a Myth* (London, 1958), p. 100.

successor, General Moltke, to whom Schlieffen had sent the manuscript of his article before publication, warmly praised it. The Minister of War, General Einem, had nothing against publication and merely suggested that Schlieffen should discuss his article before publication with the Auswärtiges Amt (which he did not do). The Kaiser read the article aloud to his commanding generals on 2 January 1909 and commented with a succinct 'Bravo'.[1]

The naval equivalent of Schlieffen's hair-raising nightmare has recently been well described by Jonathan Steinberg as the 'Copenhagen Complex', the almost obsessive fear of many Germans that the British Fleet might attack the German Fleet any day without warning, in order to cripple the unwelcome commercial and naval rival. Those fears arose even before *Weltpolitik*, at a time when there was virtually no German fleet in existence.[2] The German fear of 'encirclement', as outlined above, was mistaken—and there are reasons to doubt whether the German leaders themselves believed in the 'fairy tale of encirclement' (H. Kantorowicz). In any case, at least some of them seem to have realised that the Entente Powers, with their sometimes conflicting aims (Persia, Constantinople), had no aggressive intentions. In the comparatively quiet pre-*Weltpolitik* and pre-Entente days, in early December 1894, Holstein had countered the argument that a successful war might help to establish the Kaiser's personal rule by pointing out to Eulenburg that there was 'little prospect just now of a defensive war, for no one wants to do us any harm'.[3] The exact wording recurs just over one decade later: one of the most capable and level-headed German diplomats, Count Metternich, wrote to his Government in 1905 during the first crisis over Morocco: 'If we eliminate the problem of Morocco, our position in the world will be completely unchallenged, for no one wants to do us any harm.'[4] In 1910 Kiderlen-Wächter, rated as one of the most brilliant German Foreign Secretaries, went even further: 'If we do not provoke the war, others will hardly do so.'[5]

Schlieffen concluded his alarmist article of 1909 on a more sober note, admitting that war might be delayed or indeed, might not break out at all, as the 'enemies' were still hesitating.[6] The Pan-Germans seem to have

---

[1] *Generalfeldmarschall Graf Alfred von Schlieffen: Briefe*, edited and introduced by Eberhard Kessel (Göttingen, 1958), pp. 308ff.

[2] J. Steinberg, *J.C.H.*, 3/1, p. 42.

[3] *Philipp Eulenburg, The Kaiser's Friend*, 2 vols., ed. Johannes Haller (London, n.d.). See also J. Haller, *Aus dem Leben des Fürsten Philipp zu Eulenburg-Hertefeld* (Berlin, 1924), pp. 170–3.

[4] *G.P.*, XX, 2, no. 6681.

[5] *Kiderlen-Wächter. Der Staatsmann und Mensch. Briefwechsel und Nachlass*, ed. Ernst Jäckh, 2 vols (Stuttgart, Berlin, Leipzig, 1924), vol. II, pp. 234ff.

[6] Schlieffen, *Briefe*, pp. 21ff. See above, p. 36, n. 1.

shared the sentiment, even after the second crisis over Morocco. In November 1913 one of their leaders, the retired General Gebsattel, wrote in a memorandum for the Kaiser and the Chancellor that the Entente Powers were unlikely to take the initiative in starting a war (which Gebsattel fervently hoped for in order to improve the domestic situation in the Reich), since they would not dare to attack Germany.[1] In the early days of July 1914 there was no talk in Berlin of an immediate danger of attack from the other Powers. On the contrary, their present peaceful intentions were given by the Government as arguments for the policy of localisation (see documents 4, 18, 25, 28, 30, 33).

Those Germans who sincerely believed in the threat constituted by 'encirclement'—and this was the overwhelming majority—clearly misunderstood the intentions of the Entente. But German public opinion by now understood well enough that to become a world power within a short time, and in opposition to the established Powers, could not be achieved without conflict. The answer, however, was not drastically to revise or forgo *Weltpolitik*, pursued now for half a generation; rather the widespread German desire to achieve the breakthrough must be intensified. In the years before 1914 public opinion was characterised by a strange mixture of pride in Germany's growing power and gloom about the future, of the obsessive will to push ahead with *Weltpolitik* and of Germany's *Weltpolitische Angst*.[2]

THE GERMAN CONCEPT OF A PREVENTIVE WAR

The only major modification of German foreign policy was that introduced by Bethmann Hollweg. While armaments were increased in both the military and naval sectors, German efforts were concentrated on the Continent itself. At the same time, Berlin sought to improve relations with London, hoping to bring about, by means of peripheral agreements not involving concessions on German naval armaments—such as the Baghdad Railway and the future of Portuguese colonies—an understanding with Britain that would keep the latter neutral in a continental war. Such a war was thought to be inevitable and imminent by many circles within Germany. Leading German geographers, especially Friedrich Ratzel, had taught that growing populations needed growing territories, that industrialised countries needed *Ergänzungsräume*, i.e. colonial or quasi-colonial territories of lower population density. Eminent

---

[1] H. Pogge-v. Strandmann, 'Staatsstreichpläne, Alldeutsche und Bethmann Hollweg' in H. Pogge and I. Geiss, *Hamburger Studien*, no. 2, pp. 17f.

[2] J. Steinberg, *J.C.H.*, 3/1, p. 41.

German historians had helped to implant the idea that Germany in a changing world had either to stagnate and be relegated to the status of a minor power, or to promote herself to the status of a firmly established world power.[1] They saw Germany as a fortress besieged by enemies, and as they felt the ring around Germany drawing closer and closer the idea of a sudden desperate charge out of the fortress became respectable.

The logical consequence was the concept of preventive war. Objectively German fears were unfounded. But the more Russia recovered her former military strength after her defeat at the hands of Japan and the Revolution of 1904–5, the more urgently the idea of preventive war was formulated in Germany. The agitation of the Pan-Germans more or less openly accused the Imperial Government of cowardice for not taking the plunge. General Bernhardi's widely-read book, which appeared in several impressions before 1914, spoke openly of the next war.[2] It is true that the group around Richard Kühlmann, Secretary of State in the Auswärtiges Amt in 1917–18, did plead meekly for a *Weltpolitik* without war.[3] But Chancellor Bethmann Hollweg, although after 1945 credited with having subscribed to such a programme, apparently could not and did not dare to come out in the open with what was, by German standards, a near-pacifist line: he was afraid of a new outburst of Pan-German agitation which might have endangered his position.[4] Ruedorffer's (Riezler's) book, which, until recently, also belonged to those books that are more often quoted than read, was equally far from advocating a peaceful German policy, as he was accused of before 1945 and praised for since then in Germany. He only warned of Pan-German impatience and pleaded for a more temperate pursuit of *Weltpolitik*.

Traditional German historians have always angrily denied the existence of the concept of preventive war in Germany before 1914.[5] There is, however, sufficient evidence to support the view that it not only existed, but also exercised a strong influence on German policy. It is natural that

[1] For the geographers, see C. A. Fisher (see p. 19, n. 1), p. 12; for the historians, see Ludwig Dehio, *Deutschland und die Weltpolitik* (München, 1955).

[2] Friedrich v. Bernhardi, *Deutschland und der nächste Krieg* (6th edition, Stuttgart, Berlin, 1913). G. Ritter tries to create the impression that Bernhardi was no more than an isolated representative of what could be called the lunatic fringe in Germany—certainly an underestimation of Bernhardi's standing in German society before 1914; see G. Ritter in his polemics against F. Fischer in *H.Z.*, 194/3, p. 657, and *Staatskunst und Kriegshandwerk*, III, pp. 141ff.

[3] Hans Plehn, *Deutsche Weltpolitik und kein Krieg* (Berlin, 1913).

[4] Maximilian von Hagen, 'Deutsche Weltpolitik und kein Krieg' in *H.Z.*, 179/2 (April 1955), pp. 297–307, especially p. 297. For a violent denunciation of the Chancellor's timidity, see H. Herzfeld, *Die deutsche Rüstungspolitik vor dem Weltkriege* (Bonn, Leipzig, 1923), pp. 147–52.

[5] A. v. Wegerer, *Ausbruch*, vol. I, p. 355; G. Ritter, *Staatskunst*, vol. II, pp. 140f., 146f., 310ff. W. Kloster, *Der deutsche Generalstab und der Praventivkriegsgedanke* (Stuttgart, 1932).

preventive war should have found its keenest champions amongst the military, whereas the Government, following the post-1871 tradition of Bismarck, was reluctant. It is also significant that the concept of preventive war very soon included an attack through neutral Belgium. At the beginning of German *Weltpolitik*, in 1897, there existed a plan—initiated by the Kaiser and seriously discussed by the Navy—to seize Antwerp by sea in a sudden commando raid, without any declaration of war, and to hold it until troops were marched through Belgium. For Antwerp was thought to be important for mounting an invasion of Britain. The idea was quietly dropped, not on moral grounds or because international law would have been violated, but for technical reasons.[1] In the event, the seizure of Liège in the first days of the First World War took the place of a coup against Antwerp.

During the Russo-Japanese War at least part of the German General Staff were for seizing the chance of a preventive war against Russia, weakened by war and revolution. Even if Count Schlieffen, Chief of the General Staff, had not been a member of the war party,[2] at least junior officers in the General Staff were vaguely for war, and Groener after 1919 proudly confessed that even after 1919 he supported the concept of preventive war.[3] General Einem, Prussian Minister of War, boasts in his memoirs that he had supported Chancellor Bülow in his struggle against Delcassé, 'hoping fervently then that the matter would be decided by the sword. Militarily, the situation then was more favourable for us than at any other moment.'[4] Schlieffen's successor, Count Moltke, was of even softer metal than Schlieffen. But as 1914 approached he became more and more outspoken about the need for a war. Just before the peaceful settlement of the second Moroccan crisis he deplored that the chance had been lost to seek a showdown with Britain:

> If we again slink out of this affair with our tail between our legs, if we cannot pull ourselves together to present demands which we are prepared to enforce by the sword, then I despair of the future of the German Reich. Then I shall resign. But first I shall ask that we abolish the Army and put ourselves under the protectorate of Japan.[5]

[1] J. Steinberg, 'A German Plan for the Invasion of Holland and Belgium, 1897' in *H.J.*, vol. VI (1963), no. 1, pp. 107–19.
[2] As G. Ritter maintains in *Der Schlieffenplan. Kritik eines Mythos* (München, 1958), pp. 114ff.; *Staatskunst*, II, p. 240.
[3] Wilhelm Groener, *Lebenserinnerungen: Jugend, Generalstab und Weltkrieg*, ed. by Friedrich Frhr. Hiller v. Gaertringen (Göttingen, 1957), pp. 83f.
[4] *V. Einem: Erinnerungen eines Soldaten; 1853–1933* (Leipzig, 1933), p. 111.
[5] Helmuth v. Moltke, *Erinnerungen, Briefe, Dokumente 1877–1916* (Stuttgart, 1922), p. 362.

In the summer of 1911 Kiderlen-Wächter, Secretary of State in the Auswärtiges Amt, pursued a policy which his formal superior, Chancellor Bethmann Hollweg, was not sure aimed at war or not. He could only find out by making Kiderlen-Wächter drink heavily one night. The Secretary, according to Riezler's diary, did not aim at war under all circumstances (and in fact did avoid war on that occasion), but even the comparatively mild Bethmann Hollweg was then convinced that a war was necessary for the German nation.[1] Apart from the Social-Democrats and the left-wing Liberals, the parliamentary spokesmen of the German nation apparently were of the same opinion. For, in the great Reichstag debate after the settlement of the crisis, the Conservative and National Liberal parties were furious at the Chancellor because he had disappointed a nation which had been ready for war. It was on this occasion, on 9 November 1911, that August Bebel, the veteran leader of the SPD, gave his impressive warning of a general war and its revolutionising effects. But his warning was laughed at and went unheeded. One heckler in Parliament is recorded to have interrupted him with the words: 'After every war things are better!'[2] Only a few months later, on 2 February 1912, Spahn, the leader of the Catholic Centre Party, construed in the Reichstag the precise situation which was to lead to war in August 1914: Austria would attack Serbia, Russia would support Serbia. Spahn interpreted Russian assistance as aggression against Germany, so that the *casus foederis* would arise for Germany as well.

After the second Moroccan crisis the disposition towards war in Germany only increased. The pre-war diaries of Admiral Müller give the impression that leading circles in Germany were obsessed with the inevitability of a great war, without admitting that they themselves, by their own *Weltpolitik*, created the essential conditions for it. During the crisis the Kaiser had told Müller in an argument on whether the German Navy was prepared for war or not:

> Its unpreparedness has always been objected to me in a moment of crisis. Now, in any case, is the moment for action. The people demand it. If the Chancellor and Kiderlen and Wermuth[3] do not want to comply, they will be sacked. The Chancellor should inform himself better of the mood of the people.[4]

Admiral Müller himself was convinced that war with Britain could not be avoided in the long run. One of his reasons for preferring to see the

---

[1] K. D. Erdmann, *Zur Beurteilung Bethmann Hollwegs*, p. 534.

[2] For this and on Spahn see G. W. F. Hallgarten, *Imperialismus*, II, pp. 266ff., 363f.

[3] Secretary of State for Finance (1909–12), afterwards Lord Mayor of Berlin.

[4] *Der Kaiser* (see above p. 22, n. 2), p. 90 (4 September 1911).

showdown postponed for the time being was that the Kiel Canal, which would have allowed the free passage of German capital ships from the Baltic to the North Sea, was still under construction.[1] The Canal was finished in June 1914.

During the First Balkan War the Kaiser suddenly recognised Serbian aspirations and was for holding back Austria against Serbia.[2] But on 8 December 1912, the Kaiser, Müller, Tirpitz and the Chiefs of the General and the Naval Staffs held a kind of war council. Prince Lichnowsky, the new German Ambassador in London, had reported a warning of Haldane's that, if Germany were to attack France, Britain would have to come to the aid of France. The Kaiser welcomed this declaration, because it clarified the situation, and went on to outline the shape of things to come:

> Austria had to act vigorously against the foreign Slavs (Serbs), because she would otherwise lose her power over the Serbs in the Austro-Hungarian Monarchy. If Russia were to support the Serbs [Sazonov's declaration: Russia would immediately invade Galicia, if Austria were to invade Serbia], war would be inevitable for us . . .. The Fleet, of course, would have to face the war against Britain.[3]

The Kaiser's analysis, it should be noted, is the same as that made by Spahn only ten months before. Moltke's reaction to his Sovereign's expectorations is typical: 'In my opinion war is inevitable, and the sooner the better.' But he advised that 'the popularity of a war against Russia as outlined by the Kaiser, should be better prepared' in the press. The Kaiser agreed and gave instructions accordingly. Admiral Müller himself passed on the imperial injunction to the Chancellor, who had not even attended that important policy-making meeting: 'to enlighten the people through the press of the great national interests, which would be at stake also for Germany, if a war were to break out over the Austro–Serbian conflict.' The reason is simple:

> The people must not be in the position of asking themselves only at the outbreak of a great European war, what are the interests that Germany would be fighting for. The people ought rather to be accustomed to the idea of such a war beforehand.[4]

One week later the Chancellor too had apparently 'accustomed' himself 'to the idea of such a war', as the Kaiser told Admiral Müller. He ex-

[1] *Ibid.*, p. 92 (6 September 1911).
[2] *Ibid.*, pp. 121f. (19 October 1912).
[3] *Ibid.*, pp. 124f.
[4] F. Fischer, *Griff nach der Weltmacht*, p. 42; I. Geiss, *Julikrise*, vol. I, p. 45. This is another of those documents not to be found in the *Grosse Politik*—for obvious reasons.

pressed his surprise because Bethmann Hollweg had said one year earlier that he could never advise a war.[1]

Again two weeks later the Kaiser related his conversation with the Belgian King Albert to Moltke and Bethmann Hollweg. When Wilhelm II and Albert had met in Munich on 19 December 1912, Albert had expressed anxieties over a possible threat to Belgian neutrality, but the Kaiser assured him that 'his desire was only to have the right flank safeguarded in the case of war'. By now the Chancellor must have learned of the German intention to march through Belgium at the beginning of the war. For Moltke replied to the Kaiser's account:

> He had to consider the situation. Our plan of deployment against France is based, as is well known [*bekanntlich*], on our advance through Belgium. Nothing could be changed in regard to the deployment.[2]

The following year gave ample opportunity to 'accustom the people to the idea of such a war'. The centenary of the war of 1813 and the twenty-fifth anniversary of the Kaiser's reign, occasioned military and academic ceremonies all over Germany during 1913, and was perhaps the emotional climax of Wilhelmine Germany before 1914. But in early 1913 the German Government did not yet want to risk a great war. On 10 February, both Moltke and Bethmann Hollweg warned their respective Austrian counterparts in separate letters of the danger of making war with Serbia at the present moment over the Albanian question. Moltke expressed his conviction 'that a European war is bound to come sooner or later, in which the issue will be one of a struggle between Germandom and Slavdom', and he proclaimed: 'To prepare themselves for that contingency is the duty of all states which are the champions of Germanic ideas and culture [*Geisteskultur*].' But he warned Conrad, the Austrian Chief of Staff, that the great war 'necessitates the readiness of the people to make sacrifices, and popular enthusiasm', and therefore he was against provoking war with Serbia, especially after Serbia had gone back on her Albanian demands. Now, Moltke wrote, it would be difficult for Germany to 'find an effective slogan' for a great war.[3] At the same time, he told the Austrian military attaché in Berlin: 'When starting a world war one has to think very carefully.'[4]

In his letter to Berchtold, the Austrian Minister of Foreign Affairs, the

---

[1] *Der Kaiser* (see above, p. 22, n. 2), p. 126 (14 December 1912).

[2] I. Geiss, *Julikrise*, vol. II, p. 575, n. 3; another of those key documents, for which no place could be found in *Grosse Politik*.

[3] *G.P.*, XXXIV, no. 12824; Feldmarschall Conrad, *Aus meiner Dienstzeit 1906–1918*, 5 vols (Vienna, Leipzig, Munich, 1922), vol. III, pp. 144ff.

[4] G. Ritter, *Staatskunst*, II, p. 311 ('Der Beginn eines Weltkrieges sei wohl zu überlegen'.)

Chancellor raised two other points which became relevant in the crisis of July 1914: Russian intervention in the case of Austria attacking Serbia, and British neutrality:

> After analysing the situation objectively, one has to conclude that, considering her traditional relations with the Balkan States, it will be nearly impossible for Russia passively to watch military action by Austria against Serbia without a tremendous loss of face. The exponents of a pacific orientation, whom we can see no doubt in Messrs. Kokovzov and Sazonov, would be simply swept away by the indignation of public opinion, if they were to try to resist it. The consequences of Russian intervention, however, are obvious. They would result in a warlike conflict of the Triple Alliance —probably without enthusiastic support by Italy—against the Triple Entente, and Germany would have to bear the full brunt of the French and British attack.

Bethmann Hollweg hoped instead for a 're-orientation of British policy', in other words for a drifting apart or even disintegration of the Triple Entente, which would automatically improve prospects for the Triple Alliance:

> The British attitude [in the Balkan Crisis] is only one of several symptoms which suggest that the Entente has passed its climax and that we may look forward to a re-orientation of British policy if we succeed in emerging from this crisis without conflicts. These are, of course, developments which are just beginning and which will take some time to bear fruit. But to precipitate a violent solution—even if some interests of the Austrian-Hungarian Monarchy were to demand one—at the very moment when we seem to have the chance, if only a remote one, to have the conflict under conditions much more favourable for us, would be, in my opinion, a mistake of incalculable consequences.[1]

Only 17 months later the 'much more favourable conditions' for the showdown seemed to have arrived: the treaties over the Baghdad Railway and over the future of the Portuguese colonies as a further step towards the creation of a German *Mittelafrika*, and the visit of a British naval squadron to Kiel in June 1914, seemed to inaugurate a new phase of Anglo-German cooperation and to offer the chance of eventual British neutrality in a continental war. If neutrality were not to be had, at least the Kiel Canal had been completed by now.

Meanwhile, the diplomatic crisis over the Second Balkan War provoked new outbursts of warlike sentiment behind the scenes in Germany. During the spectacular ceremony at Leipzig, when the great monument in memory of the Battle of Leipzig in 1813 was unveiled, the Kaiser told

[1] *G.P.*, XXXIV, no. 12818.

the Austrian Chief of Staff, Baron Conrad, that he supported Austria against the Serbs:

> I am with you there. The others [i.e. the other powers] are not prepared, they will not do anything against it. Within a few days you must be in Belgrade. I was always a partisan of peace; but this has its limits. I have read much about war and know what it means. But finally a situation arises in which a Great Power can no longer just look on, but must draw the sword.[1]

About the same time, the Kaiser commented on Berchtold's appreciation of German support for an Austrian *démarche* in Belgrade and the hope expressed that the Serbs would give in forthwith, so that extreme measures would be unnecessary, with the words: 'This would be very regrettable! Now or never! For once things down there have to be put right and calm restored!'[2] The Kaiser's patience was apparently wearing thin, and he voiced some sentiments which were to reappear in July 1914—even the magic formula of 'Now or never!'[3] While the Government did not dare openly to embrace the course of '*Weltpolitik* and no war', in late 1913 they came under pressure from the Pan-Germans, this time mainly for reasons of domestic policy. The elections of 1912 had made the SPD the strongest party in the Reichstag; the policy of *Weltpolitik* for diverting the attention of the masses from the Socialists had apparently failed. (In fact it had only failed superficially because the SPD in the process had become largely nationalist in their turn, as not only the war in 1914 was to show.) This is why some circles now returned to the old idea of a coup against Reichstag and Constitution.[4] After legislation for a massive expansion of the army had been passed by the Reichstag in summer 1913, the Pan-Germans stepped up their campaign against the Chancellor.

In October 1913 their leaders sent an important memorandum to the Crown Prince, whose Pan-German sympathies were notorious; he passed it on to the Kaiser in mid-November, at the peak of the crisis over the Zabern incident.[5] The memorandum suggested the abolition of the constitution, the suppression of freedom of the press and discriminatory legislation aimed at the Jews; and it accused the Government of wanting to preserve peace at any price. Even an unsuccessful war would be

[1] Conrad, *Aus meiner Dienstzeit*, vol. III, p. 470.
[2] *G.P.*, XXXVI, no. 14176.
[3] See below, Document no. 2.
[4] I follow here Hartmut Pogge-v. Strandmann, 'Staatsstreichpläne, Alldeutsche und Bethmann Hollweg' in H. Pogge-v. Strandmann and I. Geiss, *Hamburger Studien*, no. 2, pp. 11–45.
[5] For a modern account of the Zabern crisis see Hans Ulrich Wehler, 'Der Fall Zabern. Rückblick auf eine Verfassungskrise des wilhelminischen Kaiserreichs' in *Die Welt als Geschichte*, vol. 23 (1963).

preferable to a 'long and cowardly peace'. Since the other Powers would
hardly attack Germany, the Reich had to take the initiative. While Bethmann Hollweg, in a long letter to the Kaiser, rejected all the concrete
proposals of the Pan-Germans, he revealed that he did not differ basically
from them on some points, but differed rather on tactics and emphasis.
He merely maintained that what counted was to be successful: a coup
against the Reichstag would fail, because it would start a civil war which
in its turn would lead to war with foreign Powers. The Chancellor also
rejected the charge of wanting to preserve peace at any price. He could
envisage only two cases in which he would advocate war, if the 'honour
and dignity of Germany were to be affected by another nation' which had
not happened so far, according to Bethmann Hollweg, and if he could
'envisage vital aims for the nation' which 'could not be accomplished
without war'. As examples he quoted Bismarck's wars: 'In order to
accomplish such tasks and aims Bismarck wanted, and made, the wars
of 1864, 1866 and 1870.'[1]

One such 'vital aim' for Germany was to achieve the status of a World
Power on an equal footing with the others. It was Riezler who formulated
this in 1914, a few weeks before the outbreak of war. Although the geographical basis was apparently too narrow for such a course, he insisted
that:

> *Weltpolitik* must nevertheless be pursued . . . German policy must escape
> the *circulus vitiosus*. It cannot opt for a purely continental policy. The task
> which arises out of the situation is the essential problem of the foreign
> policy of the German Reich. Everything that happens can be interpreted
> as an attempt at its solution.[2]

And what was the supreme task of German policy? To make the Reich
stronger than any combination of possible enemies.[3] Such a *Lebensaufgabe*,
to quote Bethmann Hollweg, was, of course, impossible without war; of
this others besides Riezler were well aware. Again, the final logic points
to preventive action, before the potential enemies were strong enough to
prevent German expansion, which would sweep away the barriers of
containment.

The tensions with Russia over the mission of the German General
Liman von Sanders to Turkey had hardly abated when Moltke was
pressing more urgently than ever before for an early war. He was especially
worried about the military recovery of Russia. On 12 May 1914 he spoke
to Conrad at Carlsbad about the possibility of war. According to Conrad
he said that 'any delay meant a lessening of our chances; we could not

[1] Hartmut Pogge-v. Strandmann, *ibid*; see above, p. 45, n. 4.
[2] J. J. Ruedorffer, *Grundzüge der Weltpolitik*, p. 106.   [3] *Ibid.*

compete with Russia in masses'.[1] The same obsession with Russian armaments was revealed a few days later by a conversation between Jagow and Moltke, on either 20 May or 3 June 1914 when both travelled in Moltke's car from Potsdam to Berlin.[2] Moltke feared that Russia would have built up maximum armaments in two to three years and thought no other way was left but to 'wage a preventive war in order to beat the enemy while we still have some chance of winning'. Moltke, therefore, advised Jagow 'to orientate our policy at the early provocation of a war'. Jagow refused, pointing to the steady improvement of Germany's economic situation, but after the war he admitted that he himself 'never condemned in principle and *a limine* the idea of the preventive war'. In his view even Bismarck's wars had been preventive. It is perhaps as a consequence of this conversation between Moltke and Jagow that Beth-mann Hollweg spoke with the Bavarian Minister in Berlin, Count Lerchenfeld, early in June 1914, about 'the preventive war demanded by many generals'. When Lerchenfeld objected that the right moment had passed already, the Chancellor agreed, but added:

> There are circles in the Reich who expect of a war an improvement in the domestic situation in Germany—in a Conservative direction. He, the Chancellor, however, thought that on the contrary a World War with its incalculable consequences would strengthen tremendously the power of Social Democracy, because they preached peace, and would topple many a throne.[3]

In spite of his correct insight into the consequences of a world war Bethmann Hollweg was either too weak or too inconsistent to translate his theoretically sound judgment into practical politics. Apparently he was the prisoner of the tradition of *Weltpolitik*, now nearly two decades old, of some of his own ideas and of his surroundings: he himself was no longer in principle against a war, and he was ready to fight one to accomplish the great, vitally important aims of the nation.[4] Riezler had pointed to one such vital aim—the need to broaden the basis for pursuing the *Weltpolitik*. Moltke pressed for an early preventive war, and Jagow was not against it in principle. The Pan-Germans and most political parties accused him of cowardice, while the Kaiser oscillated.

The Kaiser's person was an additional reason for Jagow's hesitation to

---

[1] Conrad, *Aus meiner Dienstzeit*, vol. III, p. 597.

[2] *Politisches Archiv des Auswärtigen Amts. Nachlass Jagow*, vol. VIII. Meanwhile, Jagow's account of that conversation, which was written down after the war, has been published by E. Zechlin; see above p. 14, n. 1.

[3] *Bayerische Dokumente zum Kriegsausbruch und zum Versailler Schuldspruch*, ed. Pius Dirr, (3rd impression, Munich, 1925), no. 1; see also F. Fischer, *Griff nach der Weltmacht*, pp. 59f.

[4] See above, pp. 42f., 46.

risk a preventive war, because he thought Wilhelm II would not have the strength to see a great war right through.[1] A similar view had been expressed by Tschirschky, the German Ambassador in Vienna, a few months earlier. When, on 16 March 1914, Conrad suggested an early war against Russia, Tschirschky objected: 'Two important people are against it, your Archduke Franz Ferdinand and my Kaiser.' Tschirschky added that only under compulsion of a *fait accompli* would they resolve to go to war.[2]

On 28 June 1914, one of the two obstacles to war had been removed—Archduke Franz Ferdinand. His murder provided Berlin with the chance to 'find an effective slogan' in Germany for a great war, for which the German nation had been psychologically and materially prepared since at least December 1912. The showdown came at a time when the German 'chance . . . to have the conflict under conditions much more favourable' than in February 1913 seemed to be brighter than ever before.

AUSTRIA-HUNGARY AND SERBIA: THE ASSASSINATION
OF ARCHDUKE FRANZ FERDINAND

The spark which set off the First World War sprang from the apparently only secondary field of tension between Serbia and Austria-Hungary.[3] In reality there lay concealed beneath this the secular conflict between the dynastic, supra-national, conservative idea of state and the modern national revolutionary and national democratic principle of self-government, which in its many different forms has determined the course of world history from the French Revolution down to the present day—a conflict which opens up perspectives of a universal historical nature far beyond and above the mere consideration of the question of 'war guilt'.

The Danube Monarchy had had to contend with the problem of the emergent nations, in one form or another, throughout the nineteenth century. As the successor to the Holy Roman Empire of the German nation on southern European soil, the Hapsburg Monarchy had never been able to come to terms with a modern world of heterogeneous nationalities all agitating for emancipation. As far back as 1859, in circumstances strikingly similar to those which led to the First World War in 1914, she had been defeated by a national revolutionary movement

---

[1] See above, p. 47, n. 2.   [2] Conrad, *Aus meiner Dienstzeit*, vol. III, p. 670.
[3] There is a brief survey of the most important literature on the south Slav problem in I. Geiss, *Julikrise und Kriegsaubruch 1914*, I, 47, n. 103. See also Z. A. B. Zeman, 'The Break-up of the Hapsburg Empire, 1914–18', *A Study in National and Social Revolution*, London, New York and Toronto, 1961, pp. 1–35. See also A. J. P. Taylor, *The Hapsburg Monarchy, 1809–1918* (London, 1948; Penguin, 1964).

allied with a European Great Power—the then emergent Italy, which could count upon active support from France under Napoleon III. Then, to be sure, Austria had only lost the greater part of her Italian possessions, but the loss left behind an incurable resentment against the liberal, national revolutionary Italy of the Risorgimento. At least as important as this was the Austrian quest for a substitute for Venetia and Lombardy. Almost two decades later the Danube Monarchy found itself in occupation of Bosnia-Herzegovina, which only intensified the underlying problem. With the occupation and annexation respectively of these two south Slav provinces (in 1878 and 1908), the Danube Monarchy incorporated the political explosive which was to cause its destruction in 1918. Yet it was the south Slav nationalists, above all, who were struck by the example of Piedmont and the need to win the support of a Great Power in the struggle against Austria. The same combination as in 1859—a national revolutionary movement inside Austria and its support by an already existing national state, receiving help in turn from a Great Power—led in 1914–18 to the collapse of the Danube Monarchy.

Since the almost total elimination of the Italian element after the war of 1859, the Danube Monarchy found itself confronted with the nationalist movements of the Slavs, mainly south Slavs and Czechs. After the defeat in 1866 in the internal war for German hegemony, the Hapsburgs could only prevent the secession of the Magyars by allowing them to share power with the Germans who had, in effect, had a monopoly of power up till then. For the Hungarians, and more especially the powerful and self-assertive Magyar aristocracy, it was in the interest of survival to keep down the south Slavs. The reorganisation of the Imperial State into the Dual Monarchy by means of the Compromise of 1867 (which had to be endorsed and modified every ten years in laborious negotiations), gave the Magyar aristocracy a kind of veto over Vienna. Even the threat of withdrawal from the Imperial Alliance would have been enough to block any kind of federal or democratic reform which could have undermined the dualism of Austrians and Magyars or even granted to the Slav nationalities complete equality of rights.

For decades Austria-Hungary had been content with a system of 'muddling through' which had led to a state of complete political paralysis. As a result of her anachronistic construction and concomitant stagnation, she had from the turn of the century drifted helplessly into the maelstrom of the Slav nationalist movement. After the overthrow of the Obrenović dynasty in 1903 the Serbs constituted the most dynamic element in the Balkans and, as such, the greatest threat to the Monarchy: for the immediate aims of unification of the Serbs with Montenegro, parts of

Macedonia and ultimately the south Slav provinces of the Danube
Monarchy, Bosnia and Herzegovina would inevitably result in the
addition of Dalmatia, Croatia and Slovenia to an enlarged south Slav
national state. The realisation of the national right of self-determination
for south Slavs (whether of the Greater Serbian, Centralist or south Slav
Federalist variety) thus constituted a threat to the Dual Monarchy if she
failed to remodel herself in time into a federalist and democratic structure.
The leading Austro-Hungarian statesmen were fully aware of the basic
problem; thus Conrad von Hötzendorf wrote to the Heir Apparent,
Archduke Franz Ferdinand on 14 December 1912:

> The unification of the south Slav race is one of the powerful national
> movements which can neither be ignored nor kept down. The question can
> only be, whether that unification will take place within the boundaries of
> the Monarchy—that is at the expense of Serbia's independence—or under
> Serbia's leadership at the expense of the Monarchy. The cost to the
> Monarchy would be the loss of its south Slav provinces and thus of almost
> its entire coast-line. The loss of territory and prestige would relegate the
> Monarchy to the status of a small power.[1]

With his realistic analysis Conrad unwittingly anticipated the end of the
Danube Monarchy, for it proved incapable of creating the necessary basis
for a constructive solution; and the development of Serbia from 1903
onwards had already progressed too far for it still to be possible to compel
a unification of the south Slavs with the increasingly self-assertive Serbs
within the framework of the Danube Monarchy. The ruling class of
Austria-Hungary, notoriously unable to adapt their conservative, dynastic
régime to the exigencies of modern times, abandoned themselves to a
chivalrous mood of decline: if their traditional positions of power could
no longer be assured by political means, there was a wish at least to 'go
down with honour'. For the ruling class, still adhering to their feudal
modes of thought, this was only conceivable in a war, which it was hoped
—against all reason—would somehow succeed in prolonging an existence
which had long since become questionable.

The most influential exponent of this fatalistic conception of war was
Conrad. He hoped to save the Danube Monarchy by a preventive war,
at one moment against Italy, which although officially a member of the
Triple Alliance sympathised with the south Slavs, and at the next against
national democratic and national revolutionary Serbia herself.

Austria-Hungary had already on two occasions demonstrated her
hostility to the expansion of Serbia and had even partially mobilised her

[1] Conrad, *Dienstzeit*, II, 380. See also Robert Kann, *The Multinational Empire* (New York,
1950).

army in the annexation crisis of 1908–09 and the Balkan Wars of 1912–13. The tense atmosphere was shattered by the shots at Sarajevo on 28 June 1914. Several factors combined to make the outrage possible.

Franz Ferdinand, the Heir Apparent, had the reputation of wanting to reconstruct the Dual Monarchy into a Trialism, with the south Slav nationalities as the third pillar, thereby saving the situation and taking the wind out of the sails of south Slav nationalism. In the light of this the choice of the Heir Apparent as the victim of the assassination was certainly no coincidence, the less so since Franz Ferdinand made his entry into Sarajevo at the close of the manoeuvres in Bosnia on 28 June, the anniversary of the Battle of Kasovo in 1389.

The second factor was the south Slav movement emanating from Serbia. Earlier German and Austrian interpretations which take the guilt or complicity of the Serbian Government as their point of departure[1] do not withstand examination. Still less tenable, if only because the murder was the most extreme and violent expression of south Slav nationalism, is the monstrous theory of collective guilt which attempts to pin the responsibility for the outrage of Sarajevo on to the Serbian people as a whole. Rather it would seem necessary to show careful discrimination: the outrage of Sarajevo was by no means the work of the Serbian Government; in any case, the latter did not have enough knowledge of the plans to take preventive measures in time.[2] On the contrary, Sarajevo was planned and organised by the extreme wing of Serbian nationalism, the secret society 'Death or Unification', better known under the name of the 'Black Hand'. This consisted of an association of nationalist officers, officials and intellectuals. In the summer of 1914 the 'Black Hand' was locked in a struggle with the Serbian Government, which may have led to the fall of the head of the society, Colonel Dimitriević-Apix, Chief of the military Secret Service.

In this tense situation the outrage resembled an attempt to plunge the more prudent Government of the Old Radicals, under Nikola Pašić, headlong into the alternative of either submitting to the Austrians, with the subsequent risk of an armed revolution such as was frequently feared in

[1] Thus also G. Ritter, *Staatskunst*, II, pp. 291f.: 'In the general excitement scarcely a single person asked for documentary proof of the complicity of Serbian Government circles such as the Austrian Government strove in vain to procure; everyone was instinctively convinced, and we indeed know today that this instinct did not come amiss'.

[2] Here I am making use of the extensive research work of Vladimir Dedijer, *The Road to Sarajevo* (New York and London, 1966), pp. 385–95. For an extract of his findings, see Vladimir Dedijer, 'Sarajevo: Fifty Years After', *Foreign Affairs*, July 1964, pp. 569ff. His treatment is by far superior to the old-fashioned and pro-Austrian study by Joachim Remak, *Sarajevo* (London, 1959.)

the July crisis,[1] or postponing its more cautious programme for the liberation of the south Slav provinces and taking on a war with Austria-Hungary instead.

Recent research has shown that Pašić had certainly heard rumours of arms smuggling over the frontier into Bosnia and that he consequently demanded an enquiry. Dimitriević-Apix however, whilst conceding in a long written report to Pašić that the pistols emanated from army stores, claimed that they were only employed for the protection of his secret service agents in Bosnia.[2] Despite this deliberate deception by Apix, Pašić did not allow matters to rest there and issued an order to the frontier authorities to prevent arms' smuggling and the illicit entry of young men.[3] In view of this, Apix attempted to call off the whole undertaking. Like the *Norodna Odbrana*,[4] whose agent heard of the planned attempt, Apix tried at the last moment to put a stop to the outrage through his contact man with the group of conspirators in Sarajevo. The conspirators however, with Gavrilo Princip at their head, refused to abandon their plan for assassinating the Archduke.

At this point a third factor comes into play: the perpetrators all came from Bosnia itself and were thus Austro-Hungarian subjects. They were much less blind and willing tools of the 'Black Hand' than has up till now generally been accepted in Germany and Austria. Princip and his circle of friends belonged to the national revolutionary movement among young intellectuals, students and school-children, commonly known as 'Young Bosnia'. In contrast to the more exclusively Pan-Serbian ideas of the 'Black Hand', they stood for a south Slav, federal solution on the basis of equality for all south Slav groups. The idea of an attempt on the life of Franz Ferdinand in Sarajevo originated in 'Young Bosnian' circles, and merely happened to fit in with similar, but as yet uncrystallised ideas of the 'Black Hand' which finally took over the practical preparations for the attempt (such as procuring the weapons and equipment, training the accomplices, and helping them over the frontier). At the decisive point in the crisis, when Apix tried hard to prevent the outrage, it was Princip's firm determination to carry out the attempt at all costs that prevailed. In the last analysis, the murder at Sarajevo was thus primarily

---

[1] See **56, 67, 100** below; also *D.F.*, XI, 20; *D.D.*, 328; *Int. Bez.*, I, 5, appendix 7.

[2] Cf. Vladimir Dedijer, *The Road to Sarajevo*, p. 388.

[3] Pašić sent a loosely phrased warning against Franz Ferdinand's entry into Sarajevo through the Serbian Minister in Vienna, to Finance Minister Biliński, the Minister with responsibilities for Bosnia-Herzegovina, but this was not heeded in Vienna.

[4] An initially quasi-official partisan organisation for propaganda in Belgrade, founded during the Annexation Crisis. After the crisis was over, it lost its semi-official and militant character and confined itself to nationalist propagandist activity.

the deed of Princip himself and can only indirectly be charged to the 'Black Hand', and virtually not at all to the Serbian Government (let alone the Serbian people).

In a deeper sense the ultimate responsibility falls on the ruling class in Austria-Hungary, less because it sent Franz Ferdinand into an 'alley of bomb throwers'[1] than on account of its inability to satisfy the legitimate struggle of their various nationalities for freedom, equality and social justice (a motive which is generally overlooked in the wholesale condemnation in Germany and Austria of the conspirators of Sarajevo). By their rigid adherence to outdated political and social conceptions the traditional powers left no room for the political agitations of the young south Slav intelligentsia who, in their desperation, were finally driven to the crime of political murder. No historical account seeking to do justice to the complicated events of July and August 1914 can any longer afford to ignore this important aspect, neglected for so long in Germany and Austria. It becomes clear that the Austrian and German Governments were in fact mistaken in their assumptions about the background to the outrage.

Sarajevo was the dramatic culmination of the conflict between the Danube Monarchy and the south Slav national movement which had been smouldering for so long. Everything now depended on how Austria-Hungary would react. The manner of her reaction could give rise to a confrontation with Russia, and create the constellation which would make world war inevitable, a constellation so accurately predicted by Spahn in February 1912, by Bethmann Hollweg in February 1912 and by the Kaiser in October 1913.[2]

---

[1] Thus Prince Lichnowsky, the German Ambassador in London, to Bethmann Hollweg on 16 July 1914; *D.D.* 62.

[2] See above, pp. 41, 44f.

1 The Reaction to Sarajevo
28 June – 4 July

The shots in Sarajevo brought all the gathering tensions in the world, on the Continent and in the Balkans in particular, into sudden eruption. While these tensions cannot be ignored, their significance should not be exaggerated. The course of diplomatic and political events, which culminated in the outbreak of the First World War a mere six weeks later, was no automatic and irreversible process. Rather, it was inaugurated and subsequently sustained, and even hastened, by a conscious decision on the part of leading figures in Europe.

This does not mean, as is so frequently asserted, that the assassination at Sarajevo was synonymous with the outbreak of world war. Nor was a war against Serbia Austria-Hungary's only conceivable and possible reaction (as was until recently the view of traditional German historians).[1] The assassination naturally caused a profound shock to Europe, and in general sympathies were overwhelmingly on the side of the Danube Monarchy and the House of Hapsburg. Yet, despite their appreciation of the severe loss to Austria-Hungary, the Cabinets of the Powers did not think in terms either of a local war against Serbia or of world war. Thus Sir Arthur Nicolson, Under-Secretary of State in the British Foreign Office, wrote on 30 June a confidential letter to Sir George Buchanan, British Ambassador in St Petersburg: 'The tragedy which has just taken place in Sarajevo will not, I trust, lead to further complications.'[2] A week

[1] See, e.g., Karl-Dietrich Erdmann, *Die Zeit de Weltkriege*, p. 16: 'Austria had to act. It was not enough to fight the Pan-Serbian movement on Austrian territory.' [2] *B.D.* 19.

later Nicolson showed a similar reserve in his confidential letter of 6 July to Sir Maurice Bunsen, British Ambassador in Vienna.[1] The French President, Poincaré, sent his condolences in a spirit of sincere sympathy. However, when Count Szécsen, the Austro-Hungarian Ambassador at Paris, had dutifully thanked him on 4 July, Poincaré combined a reiteration of his condolences with an indirect warning against anti-Serbian excesses on the territory of the Danube Monarchy.[2] In contrast the French press (as Szécsen was quick to report on 1 July) immediately suspected that the Vienna Government would use the assassination as a pretext for severe reprisals against Serbia.[3]

Russia's reaction was not substantially different. On the one hand the assassination caused acute embarrassment and on the other Russia intimated that she would agree to the Danube Monarchy seeking satisfaction provided this did not touch on either the sovereignty and integrity of Serbia or the prestige of Russia as Serbia's protector.[4]

Scarcely anyone disputed the right of Austria-Hungary to impose moderate demands on Serbia, but the Great Powers, or at least Russia and France, did not give Vienna a free hand against Serbia. The reaction of French public opinion amounted to an indirect appeal to Vienna not to bear out the suspicion already aired, that she would exploit the pretext against Serbia. The Russian attitude clearly indicated to the Austro-Hungarian leaders the path between peaceful pursuance of Austria's legitimate objectives and a warning against an armed settlement of differences. Now it was up to the Danube Monarchy to tread the narrow path which led to the maintenance of peace.

The mood in Austria-Hungary after the assassination was by no means such that war against Serbia should have seemed inevitable: no one could have guessed from the reaction in the Danube Monarchy that the incident would lead to a war against Serbia. Franz Ferdinand, on account of his cold and distant manner, was anything but popular with his future subjects, and official circles wavered between suspicion of his plans for reform and blind hatred. Neither the Viennese people nor the authorities within whose jurisdiction it lay to order a temporary closure of the *Prater* were particularly affected by the murder, for there was no interruption of the lively activity in Vienna's pleasure park, even on the day of the murder or on 29 June.[5] But Emperor Franz Joseph bore his nephew a grudge on account of his marriage 'below his station' to a Bohemian

[1] *B.D.* 33. [2] *Ö.D.* 10047. [3] Szécsen to Berchtold, 1 July; *Ö.D.* 9970.
[4] *Int. Bez.*, I, 4, 128; *B.D.* 76.
[5] See *Schicksalsjahre Osterreichs 1908–1918, Das politische Tagebuch Joseph Redlichs*, 2 vols, ed. Fritz Fellner (Graz/Cologne, 1953), p. 235: 'In the town no mood of mourning; in the *Prater* and with us here in Grienzing music everywhere on both days!' (Entry of 29 June).

countess, and right up to the end the Imperial court had systematically humiliated the unwanted spouse of the Heir Apparent by innumerable petty jibes and slights. In view of the aged Emperor's simple conceptions of God and the world, it is entirely plausible that his first comment on the murder of Franz Ferdinand, recounted by one of his closest confidants, should have been: 'Horrible! The Almighty is not mocked! . . . Order, which, alas, I had not the strength to maintain, has been restored by a Higher Will.'[1] This remark is perhaps the most apt illustration of the bigoted reaction of the Danube Monarchy to the assassination of its unloved Heir Apparent.

The leading men in the Government scarcely reacted differently from their Imperial master. In Hungary the Magyar aristocracy breathed a deep sigh of relief, and the murder in no way disturbed the splendid wedding celebrations in the families of two magnates.[2] A wedding in Budapest and the *Prater* in Vienna—these were no symptoms of a sincere mourning. Nor was the Government in Vienna plunged into grief at the Archduke's sudden death—rather the contrary. From a recently discovered report by Tschirschky on 2 July, we learn something of the atmosphere immediately after the assassination. Tschirschky reported that one significant outcome of the loss of Franz Ferdinand was that it had been decided by the leading Austrian statesmen in their first, strictly confidential discussion, to take care 'not in any circumstances to allow the formation of another "subsidiary government" such as had arisen under Franz Ferdinand'.[3]

Despite the embarrassing discrepancy between official horror and the 'third class funeral'[4] on the one hand, and public indifference and internal relief over the disappearance of the Heir Apparent on the other, the assassination aroused in many Austrians a desire to force a showdown with troublesome Serbia. Pressure for war against Serbia stemmed mainly from the greater part of the middle-class German-speaking press. Within

[1] Albert von Margutti, *Vom alten Kaiser. Persönliche Erinnerungen an Franz Joseph* (Leipzig/ Vienna, 1921), English edition, p. 148. Likewise also Tisza: 'The Almighty has willed it thus and we owe everything to the Almighty.' Quoted from Hermann Wendel, *Die Habsburger und die Südslawenfrage. Das Werk des Untersuchungsausschusses*, 1st Series, vol. 10 (Berlin, 1930), p. 646.

[2] Max Müller, the British Consul-General in Budapest, to Grey, 14 July (*B.D.* 70) gives further information on this subject.

[3] AA, *Österreich, 103*, vol. 7; see I. Geiss, *Julikrise und Kriegsausbruch 1914*, I, no. 10.

[4] The term may stem from Karl Kraus; at any rate it is to be found in his *Die letzten Tage der Menschheit* (Munich, 1964) ('Sonderreihe dtv', vols. 23 and 24), Part I, p. 28. More recently, the term has been taken over by Ladislaus Singer, *Eine Welt bricht zusammen. Die letzen Tage vor dem Weltkrieg* (Graz/Vienna/Cologne, 1961), pp. 47f., in the chapter 'Begräbnis dritter Klasse'.

the administration there was also support for this among leading officials in the Foreign Ministry and Count Hoyos, Forgách and Macchio in particular. On the military side they were joined by Baron Conrad von Hötzendorf, the Chief of the General Staff, Krobatin the Minister of War, and General Potiorek the Governor of Bosnia-Herzegovina. Conrad saw in the Sarajevo murder an occasion for the preventive war against Serbia which he had long been advocating[1] and for which there was now a psychological advantage. To be sure, Conrad at first concealed his true opinion by merely demanding mobilisation (1), but in the existing state of affairs this would have been virtually certain to provoke war. Thus the Chief of the General Staff clearly emerged as the pace-maker in his initial discussion with Berchtold on 29 June.

Count Berchtold, the Austro-Hungarian Foreign Minister, found himself in a difficult position. Although not in the least belligerent by temperament,[2] he saw the dangers for the Danube Monarchy that would necessarily result from the emergence of south Slav nations outside Austria-Hungary, and from the structural inability of the Danube Monarchy to grant full autonomy and political rights to its many differing nationalities. On the other hand, Berchtold was exposed to the pressure of German-Austrian public opinion which had neither forgotten nor forgiven his alleged weakness towards Serbia in the great Balkan crises. There were also the demands of his subordinates, Hoyos, Forgách and Macchio, and of his military antagonist, Conrad. However, he knew that Emperor Franz Joseph and (for quite different reasons) Count Tisza, the Hungarian Prime Minister, were opposed to war against Serbia. Finally, Berchtold was not yet clear as to the German attitude, especially as Berlin had restrained rather than spurred on her ally in the Balkan crises. In the first days of general confusion, therefore, Berchtold tried, as best he could, to manoeuvre between the two fronts.

On 29 June Berchtold attempted at first to curb Conrad, who was thirsting for action. To Conrad's displeasure he had planned a different approach in anticipation of the proposal for immediate mobilisation: 'We send Serbia a demand to dissolve certain societies, relieve the Minister of Police of his post, etc.' Above all he advocated first awaiting the outcome of the enquiry in Sarajevo (1). Conrad was not pleased with Berchtold's timidity. However, in a discussion with the hesitant Tisza, who advised against any use of force, Berchtold changed his tack and spoke instead of

---

[1] For a summary of Conrad's ideas on a preventive war see Gerhard Ritter, *Staatskunst*, II, pp. 282–97.

[2] See Hugo Hantsch, *Leopold Graf Berchtold Grandseigneur und Staatsmann*, 2 vols (Cologne/Graz/Vienna, 1963).

'the intention of using the abomination of Sarajevo as the pretext for a settlement of accounts with Serbia'. Disturbed by Berchtold's belligerence, Tisza thereupon made eloquent representations to the Emperor.[1]

In a second conversation with Conrad on 1 July, Berchtold again placated the Chief of the General Staff by pointing out that Tisza and Count Stürgkh (the Austrian Prime Minister), no less than the Emperor himself, were pleading 'for the need to keep a cool head'. Berchtold particularly played on Tisza's fears that Russia would intervene in a war against Serbia, while Germany would refuse to come to Austria's assistance. Thus, even the bellicose Conrad could not deny the force of this argument, for he was quite explicit in making the decision for a war against Serbia contingent upon Germany protecting the rear against Russia in the event of an advance against Serbia.[2] This meant that Germany's attitude was crucial to the final decision in Vienna.

In taking a preliminary sounding of the German position immediately after Sarajevo Berchtold had already struck a remarkably vigorous note in the presence of Tschirschky. It is evidently with Berchtold in mind that the latter informed Berlin on 30 June that 'I frequently hear expressed here, even among serious people, the wish that at last a final and fundamental reckoning should be made with the Serbs' (2). However, whilst Tschirschky, in ignorance of the intentions of his Imperial Master and of the Government in Berlin, was still trying to placate the Ballhausplatz, his compatriot Victor Naumann (political confidant of Count Hertling, the Bavarian Prime Minister, and of Baron von Stumm of the German Auswärtiges Amt), was calling an altogether different tune (3).

Since Conrad recommended that Austria should first obtain Germany's support before taking any action on her own account and Berchtold inclined to the same view, it only remained to learn the *official* German views on the matter. The quickest and safest way was to make enquiries directly in Berlin. Accordingly Count Hoyos, the *Chef de Cabinet* in the Austro-Hungarian Foreign Ministry was despatched to Berlin on 4 July to ascertain the policy of the German Reich. He took with him two documents which he was to deliver to Count Szögyény, the Austro-Hungarian Ambassador, who in turn was to pass them on to Kaiser Wilhelm II and his Government. The most important basis for diplomatic action was a detailed memorandum which had already been drawn up before the assassination in Sarajevo. It called upon Germany to use diplomatic means to strengthen the position of the Danube Monarchy and in particular to win back the by now unreliable Roumania to the

---

[1] Tisza to Franz Joseph, 1 July; *Ö.D.* 9978.
[2] L. Albertini, *Origins*, II, p. 125 (Conrad, *Dienstzeit*, IV, p. 34).

Triple Alliance. At the same time it was envisaged that Bulgaria should be drawn into the Triple Alliance, so that the isolation of Serbia could be achieved. After the assassination the memorandum, which was in no way bellicose, was strengthened by the addition of a forceful closing paragraph and further supplemented with a letter in the same vein from Franz Joseph to Wilhelm II.[1]

On 5 July, when Hoyos was already in Berlin, Conrad once more proved in an audience with Franz Joseph that the purpose of the Hoyos Mission was not to confront the Berlin Government with the final and firm resolve of her Austrian ally, but rather to pose an open question. There followed a revealing dialogue between the Emperor and his Chief of Staff in conjunction with Conrad's observation to the effect that war with Serbia was inevitable. At its close Conrad expressly declared: 'We must have the answer (from Berlin I.G.) but have it soon, as the great decision depends upon it.' Conrad summarised his impressions of the conversation with the words that the Emperor 'does not feel certain of Germany and consequently hesitates to decide'.[2] Although Conrad was doubtless the more insistent partner, we may assume that this also applied in principle to himself. Conrad, too, was not anxious to stand 'alone' if Germany refused to endorse his belligerent *élan*. In any case— as he told Berchtold in as many words on 29 June—he was fully prepared to make 'the great decision' (which had not yet, then, been taken) contingent upon Germany's answer to the question he himself had put in Berlin. Thus, even the most vehement advocate of a preventive war against Serbia, who is alleged to have been 'undoubtedly the focal point of all martial energy in those critical weeks',[3] by no means wanted war at all costs, but was prepared to make the final decision dependent upon the vote of the more powerful ally.

In reality, Austria-Hungary could not even begin a war against Serbia without German protection of the rear. Everything, therefore, hinged upon the official German attitude. After Sarajevo, Berlin was in as much of a quandary as Vienna as to the course it should follow, until a clear line eventually prevailed. Three factors were decisive for the formulation of Reich policy: the Kaiser, the General Staff and the Imperial Government.

Theoretically there were two ways in which Imperial policy might have responded to the assassination: either Germany could have restrained her ally from aggressive actions against Serbia and assisted the other Powers

[1] *Ö.D.* 9984; both documents also in *D.D.* 13 and 14; Franz Joseph's hand-written letter in *Julikrise und Kriegsausbruch 1914*, no. 9; likewise a résumé of Bethmann Hollweg's memorandum under no. 22.
[2] Conrad, *Dienstzeit*, IV, pp. 36f.
[3] Thus G. Ritter, *Staatskunst*, II, p. 282.

in their search for a peaceful solution, or she could have tolerated, protected, demanded and even furthered such aggressive acts as the Danube
Monarchy might have planned. The Auswärtiges Amt, or at least one
section of it, initially inclined to the former alternative and the General
Staff to the latter (4, 5).

In past years the military had already discussed amongst themselves
the possibility of a preventive war—evidently with such candour that
only three weeks before the outrage of Sarajevo Bethmann Hollweg, in a
private conversation with Count Lerchenfeld, the Bavarian Minister in
Berlin, felt obliged to dissociate himself from such ideas. A few weeks later,
Lerchenfeld could report that Moltke, months ago, had thought the
present moment the best for war, as Russia and France were militarily
unprepared but had envisaged a war for 1917. And in early January 1918,
the ex-Chancellor Bethmann Hollweg, when privately asked, obliquely
admitted that the war was a German preventive war, started under the
pressure of the generals.[1] But even Bethmann Hollweg was convinced
of the inevitability of the great conflict, although he did not realise that
it was basically the German Reich and its ambitious plans for world power
which had made the great war in the long run inevitable. Under the influence of Socialist Darwinist beliefs, with which he moreover came into
direct contact through the pseudo-philosophical speculations of Kurt
Riezler,[2] his closest adviser, the Chancellor developed a fatalism towards
the preservation of world peace which stifled any inclination for a policy
to avoid world war.[3]

Immediately after Sarajevo the General Staff again pressed their view.
Given the structure of the Wilhelminian Reich, it was plain that their
opinions would not pass unnoticed. From the scant documents available
we can conclude that in this situation the General Staff emphatically
interposed in favour of war, on the assumption that Russia was still
militarily but ill-prepared (4, 5). In any case, the harsh course tallied
with the traditional sentiment of the Prussian military, who were spoilt by
the memory of three successful and relatively easy campaigns half a
century earlier.

We are scarcely better informed on the attitude of the political leaders.
As in the case of the General Staff, whose Chief, Moltke, had just gone on
a cure to Carlsbad on 28 June, the Reich gave the appearance of being
leaderless at the onset of the crisis. Thus, shortly after Sarajevo, the

[1] *D.D.*, Annex IV, nos. 27 (31 July, 1914) and 35 (5 August).
[2] Wolfgang Steglich, *Die Friedenspolitik der Mittelmächte 1917/18*, vol. 1(Wiesbaden, 1964)
p. 418, n. 3.
[3] For Bethmann Hollweg's paralysing war fatalism, see now, too, K.-D. Erdmann, *Zur
Beurteilung Bethmann Hollwegs*, pp. 527f., 536.

Chancellor had withdrawn to his Hohenfinow estate; he returned thence, however, for secret conferences with the Kaiser on 1, 3 and 5 July.[1] Secretary of State Jagow was on his honeymoon at the time, so that Under-Secretary of State Zimmermann was deputising for him at the Auswärtiges Amt. For the first few days, so far as we can tell, Zimmermann pursued Bethmann Hollweg's original line of opposing a preventive war. Initially he even departed from the basic assumption that the Serbian Government was largely free from complicity in the murder plot. He displayed no belligerence and exercised a pacifying influence on all quarters, towards Austrians and Russians, French and Serbs alike.[2] The Auswärtiges Amt, in harmony with Tschirschky's parallel endeavours in Vienna (2), expressed the hope that a war between Austria and Serbia could be avoided, as it predicted that Russian mobilisation and what it specifically named as 'world war' would be the inevitable consequence (4).

Three points ought to be borne in mind when analysing the sober assessment which the Auswärtiges Amt made of the political situation in the first days of July:

I. There was no mention of any threat to Germany or the Triple Alliance from the Triple Entente. The 'informant' (possibly Zimmermann) cited by the Saxon Minister even underlined the fundamentally peaceful character of Russian, French and British policies. This disposes of the traditional German thesis of a 'surprise attack' against Germany.

II. At that time the Auswärtiges Amt clear-sightedly held world war to be inevitable from the moment that local war broke out between Austria-Hungary and Serbia. The Saxon minister explicitly wrote: 'If if does not, then, come to a war between Serbia and Austria, my informant believes the peace will be preserved' (4).

III. The arguments on which the Auswärtiges Amt based its optimism (on the condition that there was no war against Serbia) are almost identical with those which only shortly afterwards were used to sustain the fiction of localisation, namely the apparent passivity of Russia, France and England.

The beginning of July, then, was characterised in Berlin by a divergence between the views of the political and the military leaders. However, one can hardly speak of a struggle between the two factions over the final line to be adopted, as the brief space of time before the final decision precluded any open confrontation of divergent opinions. Moreover, the onset of the holiday season and the archaic structure of the Reich, lacking as it did any constitutional provision for the formal deliberation of major

[1] See p. 12.
[2] B.D. 22; Ö.D. 10039; Bayr. Dok. no. 4.

problems, combined to rule out the possibility of any such debate. In fact, the entire constitution of the Prusso-German Reich determined that the onus of deciding the issue lay with the Kaiser himself. In the past Wilhelm II had repeatedly oscillated between a realistic evaluation of Serbia's national aspirations and an unreserved support of the allied Danube Monarchy consistent with his sense of a dynastic-aristocratic solidarity in the face of the national revolutionary and democratic south Slav movement.[1]

The Kaiser's Leipzig proposals of October 1913 had already contained all the elements of the German policy of localisation in July 1914— encouragement, even incitement, of the Austrians to a rapid attack on Serbia, the promise that Germany would protect Austria's rear, and the speculation that the other powers would remain inactive. Now, after the Sarajevo assassination the Kaiser apparently felt that the time had come for Austria to put her hand to the sword and act. The assassination also appears to have dealt a severe blow to Wilhelm II's self-esteem as a monarch. Given his easily excitable temperament, the extent of his fury against the Serbs can well be imagined, for they appeared to have robbed him of his political friend, Franz Ferdinand (whose personal friendship he had only recently won), and ruined his beloved regatta at Kiel. Hence the reported spontaneous reaction of the Kaiser. When Wilhelm II received Tschirschky's preliminary report after the assassination he covered the document with uncontrolled marginal notes, which—this time—made world history. His drastically formulated wish to dispose of the Serbs 'soon' and his 'Now or never' (2) supplied the decisive catchwords for subsequent German policy in the July crisis. At the same time it was the authority of the Kaiser which settled the differences between the political and military leadership. No matter how often the Chancellor and the Auswärtiges Amt may have mocked at the Kaiser's outbursts and circumvented or even contravened his instructions if they considered them to be mistaken, this time the marginal notes had the effect of an Imperial command.

Whatever differences of opinion there may have been within the Auswärtiges Amt itself as to the course to be adopted, when Tschirschky's report was returned to the Wilhelmstrasse on 4 July, the Auswärtiges Amt swung round wholly and unreservedly to the harsh course ordered by the Kaiser in his marginalia. After that date there is no further trace of moderation towards Austria or of a realistic understanding that a local war against Serbia would immediately provoke world war. After the Kaiser had come down on the side of the General Staff, the political leaders

[1] See pp. 42, 44f.

fell in with the Monarch's commands, in accordance with time-honoured German tradition, and, contrary to their earlier and better judgment, assumed responsibility for the diplomatic implementation of the new line.

The effect of this victory for the harsher line in Berlin was immediately noticeable in Vienna. There, by some means which will probably remain a mystery, Tschirschky must have instantly learned of the Kaiser's outburst of anger at his hesitation. This was a sufficient cue for him, from that moment onwards, to champion the (for him at any rate more fitting) harsh line. Otherwise it could not be explained how, on that same 4 July, he was able indirectly to inform the Ballhausplatz through Ganz, the Viennese correspondent of the *Frankfurter Zeitung*, that 'Germany would support the Monarchy through thick and thin in whatever it might decide regarding Serbia', and: 'The sooner Austria-Hungary went into action the better. Yesterday would have been better than today, and today would be better than tomorrow.' And he closed with the assertion: 'It would not be possible for one Great Power to speak more candidly to another.'[1] In point of fact the interchange of views between Germany and Austria-Hungary now relapsed into the conciliating, concealing language of official diplomacy; never again were Germans to speak to the Austrians with such candour.

On 4 July in Berlin all confusion and divergences over the course of Imperial policy in the July crisis which was now unfolding were henceforth put aside. The Kaiser had decided on war against Serbia even before he knew whether that was what the Austrians really desired. In his bellicose 'Now or never' mood, Wilhelm II calmly looked forward to subsequent events.

1 Conversation between Berchtold and Conrad, 29 June 1914

Conrad IV, pp. 33f.

On 29 June in the evening, before a Ministerial Council scheduled at 8 o'clock, I saw Berchtold. I had greeted him with the words: 'We meet under circumstances which are quite different from what they used to be.'

Count Berchtold told me that Kaiser Wilhelm would come to the funeral, which would offer an opportunity to discuss the situation. I answered that this was certainly desirable, but that Sarajevo had been a

[1] L. Albertini, *Origins*, II, p. 150 (Minute by Forgách of the conversation with Ganz on 4 July; *Ö.D.* 10038).

blow against the Monarchy, which ought to be followed by immediate measures. In my opinion it would consist of mobilisation against Serbia. This seemed to me inevitable, however little it suited the Monarchy at present. The Minister answered that the outward occasion was lacking and that public opinion must first be prepared.

Count Berchtold: 'Do you not think that a revolution might break out?'

I: 'Where?'

Count B.: 'In Bohemia.'

I: 'Do not let anyone persuade you of such a thing.'

Count B.: 'I thought of a different form of procedure. We send Serbia a demand to dissolve certain societies, relieve the Minister of Police of his post, etc.'

I: 'The Serbs will quietly dismiss the Minister of Police; it will have no effect whatsoever; nothing will have effect but the use of force. The Moslems and the Croats are against the Serbs. Vis-à-vis Russia we ought to stress the anti-monarchic element of the murder, and King Carol could hardly be actively hostile to us under such circumstances.'

Even Count Berchtold agreed that the moment had come to solve the Serbian question and that he would discuss the matter with His Majesty. Above all, however, one should wait for the result of the investigation.

2   Tschirschky to Bethmann Hollweg

Report 212   Vienna, 30 June 1914
D.D. 7   R. 2 July, afternoon

Count Berchtold told me today that *everything* pointed to the fact that the threads of the conspiracy to which the Archduke fell a sacrifice, *ran together at Belgrade.* The affair was so well thought out that very young men were intentionally selected for the perpetration of the crime, against whom *only a mild punishment could be* *decreed.* The Minister spoke very bitterly about the Serbian plots.

I hope not.

Now or never.

Who authorised him to act that way?

That is very stupid!

I frequently hear expressed here, even among serious people, the wish that at *last a final and fundamental reckoning should be had with the Serbs.* The Serbs should first be presented with a number of demands, and in

It is none of his business, as it is solely the affair of Austria, what she plans to do in this case. Later, if plans go wrong, it will be said that Germany did not want it! Let Tschirschky be good enough to drop this nonsense! The Serbs must be disposed of, *and* that right *soon*!

Goes without saying; nothing but truisms.

case they should not accept these, energetic measures should be taken.[1] *I take opportunity of every such occasion to advise quietly but very impressively and seriously against too hasty steps.*[2] First of all, they must make sure what they want to do, for so far I have heard only indefinite expressions of opinion. Then the chances of every kind of action should be carefully weighed, and it should be kept in mind that Austria-Hungary does not stand alone in the world, that it is her duty to think not only of her allies, but to take into consideration the entire European situation, and especially to bear in mind the attitude of Italy and Roumania on all questions that concern Serbia.[3]

3 Hoyos' Conversation with Victor Naumann

Strictly secret
Ö.D. 9966   Vienna, 1 July 1914

The German publicist Victor Naumann came to see me today and expressed his indignation at the terrible murder of Sarajevo. Thereafter, Dr Naumann discussed the general political situation, dwelling on the great uneasiness felt in Berlin over Russian armaments and the test mobilisation, recently fixed for the autumn, of considerable Russian forces.[4] He himself had observed that not only in army and navy circles but also in the Foreign Ministry the idea of a preventive war against Russia was regarded with less disfavour than a year ago.[5] A settlement had been arrived at with England over Africa and the Portuguese colonies, and the visit of the English fleet to Kiel had been arranged to document the improvement in relations. For this reason there was believed to be the certainty that England would not intervene in a European war. The Foreign Ministry had been much impressed by the verbal account of the German consul until lately in Moscow who has now been appointed as *vortragender Rat* at the Foreign Ministry and has brought a great deal of

---

[1] See 1.
[2] See, in contrast, Tschirschky's subsequent attitude from 4 July in 11 and 17.
[3] See also p. 61.
[4] See, e.g., Bethmann Hollweg to Lichnowsky, 24.6.1914 (*D.D.* 3); see also 30.
[5] See 4 and 5.

information about Russian armaments. Herr von Stumm has spoken very seriously with Dr Naumann of this danger and has described the war 'which Germany could have when she wants' as not impossible. I thanked Dr Naumann for this interesting survey and let fall the remark that this state of affairs would be not unpleasing to us if we should ever find ourselves under the necessity of taking action against Serbia. Dr Naumann eagerly seized on this remark and said that this was exactly what he had been going to suggest to me. In his opinion, after the Sarajevo murder, it was a question of life and death for the Monarchy not to leave this crime unpunished but to annihilate Serbia. For Germany such a course of action would be the touchstone whether Russia meant war or not. Berlin no longer counted on Roumania as an ally, but thought that the Roumanians would at first stay neutral. Opinion had come round to agreement to the accession of Bulgaria and Turkey to the Triplice and the Bulgarians would receive a subsidy. It was hoped that Greece could be forced to be neutral. France would probably be obliged by financial embarrassments to urge Russia not to go to war, but if a European war should come after all, the Triplice was now strong enough.[1] Dr Naumann thinks that if at the present moment, when Kaiser Wilhelm is horrified at the Sarajevo murder, he is spoken to in the right way, he will give us all assurances and this time go to the length of war, because he perceives the dangers for the monarchical principle. The Foreign Ministry will do nothing to oppose this state of mind because they regard this as the favourable moment for bringing about the great decision. Public opinion, says Naumann, would never have supported a war for Jakova but now he would guarantee that it would stand by the Austrian ally to a man and regard war as a liberating action. Austria-Hungary will be finished as a Monarchy and as a Great Power if she does not take advantage of this moment.[2] I answered that I, too, regarded a solution of the Serbian question as urgently necessary and that it was of great value to us to reckon with the certainty that Germany will cover our rear. Dr Naumann offered on his part, without mentioning me by name, to bring up the matter informally with Herr von Stumm and let me know his answer. Naumann has tried to influence all the German press to be anti-Serbian and thinks that public opinion in Germany will force the Auswärtiges Amt to support us.

[1] See 30.
[2] See also 11, 18, 30, 31 and 33. Victor Naumann has also given in his memoirs (Victor Naumann, *Dokumente und Argumente*, Berlin, 1928, p. 7) a considerably shorter account of the discussion, which is, on the whole, complementary to that of Hoyos.

4 Lichtenau[1] to Vitzthum[2]   Berlin, 2 July 1914
Report 1045
Confidential
Bach no. 2

I have the honour of informing you that I have taken the opportunity of making inquiries at the Auswärtiges Amt with regard to the European situation and the way in which it has been affected by the death of the Archduke, Heir to the Throne. Here, as indeed everywhere, there is a general feeling of horror at the crime, but it is held that this would hardly give cause for any kind of harmful consequences to Europe. It is extremely regrettable for the internal situation in Austria-Hungary that, with the Archduke, a powerful force should have disappeared from the scene and that there is no one else at present capable of taking control of affairs, since even Count Berchtold does not show any great inclination or determination to pursue the course which has been set. On the military side the Chief of the General Staff, Conrad von Hötzendorf, whom the Archduke initially removed but was subsequently obliged to recall, will resume full command and, it is believed, provide a perfectly satisfactory leadership. This will ensure that there is no discontinuity in relations with Europe and in the last analysis it might perhaps even result in a clarification and easing of relations, as the Archduke was always regarded as an unknown quantity. His attitude to the Triple Alliance was likewise problematic as he was an outspoken enemy of Italy and his sympathies with Germany were only occasioned by his friendship for His Majesty the Kaiser, whereas previously he had generally been taken for a Russophile. His efforts had been directed towards the establishment of a Greater Austria and centralisation of the Government; however, this would no longer have been practicable nowadays as Hungary would no longer allow herself to be robbed of her independence. Had he ruled, therefore, he might also have been the cause of severe crises in the Dual Monarchy. The main difficulty for the policy of the German Reich was caused by the alliance with Austria-Hungary; however it would be too late to withdraw from this now and we can only strive to prevent being placed in too difficult a position by our Imperial ally. The death of the Archduke with his restless and unstable plans may bring about an improvement in this respect.

Austria-Hungary is planning to take vigorous action against Serbia on account of the murder. The German Government has advised the Serbian

---

[1] Saxon Minister in Berlin.
[2] Saxon Minister of State for Foreign Affairs.

Government to afford the maximum cooperation in this matter in which it finds all Europe against Serbia, and the Russian Ambassador to Berlin has also been approached and has given assurances that he will urge his Government to influence Serbia accordingly.[1] The Auswärtiges Amt believes that a war between Austria-Hungary and Serbia will consequently be avoided. Should it break out nonetheless, Bulgaria would immediately declare war on Greece—the dispute between Greece and Turkey fortunately having been settled—Russia would mobilise and world war could no longer be prevented.[2] There is renewed pressure from the military for allowing things to drift towards war while Russia is still unprepared,[3] but I do not think that His Majesty the Kaiser will allow himself to be induced to do this.

The Auswärtiges Amt believes, as before mentioned, that it will not come to a war between Austria and Serbia. As far as our relations with our neighbours are concerned, neither Russia nor France has any desire to start a war. France is too preoccupied with her internal affairs and her financial troubles. Russia, it is true, has been rattling the sabre, but the reason for this is apparently only to ensure that she receives the 500 million promised by France for next year, as she, too, is suffering from a lack of money. Our relations with England have improved, even though we should not indulge in the illusion that we are popular on the other side of the Channel. But England does not desire a war either, as the times are past when she could allow nations to slaughter each other on the continent; she would be drawn in herself and moreover her trade would be destroyed; besides our Fleet is still a factor with which England would now have to reckon.[4] Her colonies would also give her a great deal of trouble. If it does not come to a war between Serbia and Austria, then my informant believes that peace will be preserved. . . .

[1] See also p. 61.

[2] This was, in effect, precisely what happened after the declaration of war on Serbia on 28 July; see also 33.

[3] See 3 and 5. Also Lerchenfeld's report of 6 June 1914 on his conversation with the German Chancellor, who on this occasion 'brought up the subject of the preventive war demanded by many of the generals'. The Chancellor and Lerchenfeld, however, considered that the right moment for this had already been missed. 'But the Kaiser had never conducted nor ever would conduct a preventive war. Certain circles in the Reich, however, expected that war would provide a cure to Germany's internal problems—and that in a conservative sense' (*Bayr. Dok.* 1).

[4] See p. 23.

5   Leuckart[1] to Carlowitz[2]

Despatch 73/3472   Berlin, 3 July 1914
Bach no. 3

I have to report to your Excellency that in competent circles here the political situation is regarded as very serious—also for us. The memorial service for Archduke Franz Ferdinand gave me the chance to talk things over with Major-General Count Waldersee, Quartermaster-General in the Grand General Staff. What he said seemed to be the view of the Chief of the Army General Staff. He gave it as his opinion that we might become involved in a war from one day to another. Everything, he thinks, depends on what attitude Russia takes in the Austro-Serbian business. In any case the course of events is being closely watched by Supreme Headquarters. I had the impression that they would regard it with favour there if war were to come about now. Conditions and prospects would never become better for us.[3] But on the other hand H.M. the Kaiser is said to have pronounced in favour of maintaining peace.[4]

The Royal Minister has learned the same—as far as I know from the Auswärtiges Amt[5]. . . .

[1] Saxon Military Plenipotentiary in Berlin.
[2] Saxon Minister of War.
[3] See 4.
[4] See, in contrast, 2, the Kaiser's marginalia.
[5] See 4.

2 The Plot Thickens
5 – 7 July

At approximately midday on 5 July Szögyény handed to the Kaiser in the Neues Palais in Potsdam the two documents which Hoyos had brought with him from Vienna. How the Austro-Hungarian Ambassador explained his mission has not been recounted, but we may conclude from his own report (6) (the only source on his discussion with Wilhelm II) that, not unlike Hoyos in his conversation with Zimmermann in Berlin at the same time,[1] he gave a somewhat bellicose interpretation to his *démarche*.

The Kaiser, thus abruptly confronted with reality, initially avoided committing himself: he would have to 'bear in mind the possibility of grave complications in Europe' and preferred therefore 'not to give a definite answer until he had consulted the Chancellor'. After lunch however, when Szögyény once again urged him for a reply, Wilhelm II had changed his mind. He now promised that Germany would give her unreserved support to Austria-Hungary, even if Russia should intervene. The so-called blank cheque had thus been made out. But Wilhelm II did not leave it at that: he even went so far as to fill it in for the (still undecided)

[1] For information about the discussions which Hoyos had in Berlin, we had, until recently, to rely upon vague allusions in the small number of extant documents, since Hoyos' official record was evidently lost and in his book (*Der deutsch–englische Gegensatz und sein Einfluss auf die Balkanpolitik Österreich-Ungarns*, Berlin, 1922) Hoyos gave no indications which are of any further assistance. A new source confirms the prevalent confusion. See H. Hantsch, *Berchtold*, II, p. 572.

Austrians. There were echoes of Leipzig, October 1913,[1] when he stated that in his opinion 'this action must not be delayed' (6).

Shortly after Szögyény's departure, the Kaiser summoned those of his highest military and political advisers who were available at a moment's notice. The Chancellor arrived from Hohenfinow and Zimmermann (who had been hastily informed by Bethmann Hollweg), from Berlin; those of the military to attend included Falkenhayn, Prussian Minister of War, Aide-de-camp General Plessen, General Lyncker, Chief of the Military Cabinet, and Captain Zenker as representative of the Navy.

The Kaiser repeated in outline to his Chancellor the formulation of the blank cheque which he had just given to their Austrian ally through the intermediary of Szögyény; at the same time, he outlined the concept of localisation. Bethmann Hollweg ratified the Imperial pledge and thus also gave it constitutional legality.[2] The Kaiser read the Austrian documents to his advisers by apparently rattling them off with unceremonious speed —at least Falkenhayn found some difficulty in forming an opinion because of 'the hurriedness of the proceedings' (7). The dominant mood among the military and political leaders of the Reich after the Kaiser's disclosures on 5 July is perhaps best illustrated by Plessen's entry of the same date in his diary: 'The opinion prevailed among us that the sooner the Austrians make their move against Serbia the better, and that the Russians—though friends of Serbia—will not join in after all.'[3]

This optimism was based on the assumption that Russia would not intercede on behalf of Serbia, 'which had stained itself by an assassination', as Wilhelm II remarked to Zenker. In the opinion of the Kaiser France, too, would 'scarcely let it come to a war as it lacked the heavy artillery for the field armies'. Although a war against France and Russia in the event of an Austrian attack on Serbia was now suddenly no longer considered to be 'probable', nevertheless it was the Kaiser's opinion that 'the possibility of such a war must be borne in mind from the military point of view'.[4] Falkenhayn, the Minister of War, was asked by the Kaiser 'whether the army was ready for all eventualities' and the General replied in the affirmative. When he enquired 'whether any kind of preparations should be made' the Kaiser stalled—no, matters had not yet gone that far.[5] Accordingly, he did not trouble the Chief of Naval Staff, who was on holiday, and there was no change in the plan for the High Seas Fleet to undertake its journey to Norway.

---

[1] See above, pp. 44f.
[2] See Theobald von Bethmann Hollweg, *Betrachtungen zum Weltkriege*, 2 vols (Berlin, 1919–1922), vol. I, pp. 134ff.
[3] L. Albertini, *Origins*, II, p. 142 (Bach., 14).   [4] *D.D.* XXI.   [5] *Ibid.*, XII.

It is significant that Austria's *démarche* at Potsdam does not seem to have been uniformly interpreted in Germany. For instance Plessen, who probably reflected the Kaiser's own state of mind, deduced from the two documents delivered to Wilhelm II that 'the Austrians want to prepare for war against Serbia and to be certain beforehand of German support'. This interpretation was still in advance of events (although Plessen may not have known this with such certainty), for the decision in Vienna only took place on 7 July, after Hoyos' return from Berlin. In contrast, Falkenhayn (quite justifiably) recorded in his letter to Moltke on the same day that 'these documents did not succeed in convincing me that the Vienna Government had taken any firm resolution' (7). Like Bethmann Hollweg, Falkenhayn even doubted 'that the Austrian Government is really in earnest with its undeniably more resolute language' (7). Thus the Chancellor and the War Minister had come closer to the truth than all those who took it for granted that the Austro-Hungarian Government was already firmly resolved on war.

Bethmann Hollweg, however, in his ensuing conversation with Szögyény and Hoyos on 6 July in the Wilhelmstrasse did nothing to sow doubt in the minds of his allies as to the wisdom of a war against Serbia. On the contrary the Chancellor, just like his Imperial master, saw an immediate Austrian intervention in Serbia as the 'best solution' to the Monarchy's difficulties in the Balkans (8). This joint discussion, in which Zimmermann also took part on the German side, only served to give constitutional legality to the Imperial pledge. Only Bethmann Hollweg's reply to Szögyény endorsing the Imperial dictate gave it political and constitutional effect.

On the morning of 6 July Wilhelm II resumed his consultations with the military in a number of individual audiences. He informed Admiral von Capelle, acting Secretary of State for the Imperial Navy, of the events leading up to the present state of affairs and added (as Capelle recalled in October 1919) that 'he did not believe there would be further military developments'. The Kaiser went on to repeat the arguments he had given to Zenker on 5 July: 'The Czar would not in this case place himself on the side of the regicides. Besides that, Russia and France were not prepared for war.'[1] The Kaiser also made similar comments in the presence of General von Bertrab[2], the senior-ranking Quartermaster-General on the Grand General Staff, and he for his part immediately informed Moltke by letter.[3]

The Kaiser now boarded his special train for Kiel, from where he would begin his customary journey to Scandinavia. In Kiel he still found the

[1] *Ibid.*, XIXf.   [2] *Ibid.*   [3] Bach., 14.

time to inform Krupp, the cannon king, of the resolutions which had just been taken, whereupon Krupp sent a confidential enquiry to his Board of Directors, asking 'whether anything should be done to supplement the firm's stocks in case of mobilisation'. Nothing needed to be done, however, for the concern, like the army, was permanently prepared for war.[1]

From the improvised deliberations in Potsdam between the Kaiser and his political and military advisers immediately after the audience with Szögyény, there grew up during the war itself the legend of the so-called 'Potsdam Privy Council', about which the most absurd rumours have from time to time been circulated. Historical research has indeed established that no such 'Privy Council' ever took place, and the legend has been dismissed.[2] But most legends have a grain of historical truth and this one is no exception. On 5 and 6 July 1914 several discussions did in fact take place in Potsdam, even if not in the regular form of a 'Privy Council'. Indeed, it was then that the crucial decision was taken which alone made the July crisis possible—at least so far as Germany was concerned.

Equally the legend cannot simply be discounted as a malevolent invention of 'hostile' foreign propaganda. Evidently it was merely an attempt to bring official policy into line with the events of 5 and 6 July. Nevertheless the fiction of a 'Privy Council' imputed to the German constitution of 1914 a modern rationality of structure which was contradicted by the facts themselves. Foreign observers probably naively assumed that such an important decision would first have been discussed and prepared for by a proper constitutional conference. They would certainly never have thought that one of the most momentous decisions of world history could have been made by the semi-private utterance of one man over his lunch, and was only belatedly endorsed, without any discussion, at a private meeting between three individuals. Meetings of the Council of Ministers took place even in the old monarchies of Austria-Hungary and Russia during the July crisis, and the work of the historian is enormously facilitated by the more or less exhaustive protocols, whereas for an account of the central discussions of 5 and 6 July, the historian is reduced to Szögyény's reports, two contemporary letters, an entry in a diary and a number of extremely vague disclosures subsequently made by a few of the participants.

By piecing together the sparse and fragmentary documentary evidence of the consultations of 5 and 6 July, it is possible to glean the basic elements of German policy, even at this early stage in the July crisis: in

---

[1] See *Untersuchungsausschuss*, vol. II, supplement, p. 87: 'Zur Vorgeschichte des Weltkrieges'.
[2] Finally in L. Albertini, *Origins*, II, pp. 178ff.; an exhaustive analysis also in B. Schmitt, *Coming of the War*, I, pp. 329–41.

reply to a vague enquiry, Berlin not only unreservedly allowed her ally a free hand against Serbia, but went on to encourage her to strike with the greatest possible speed and energy. The Germans certainly envisaged the possibility that the Russians might intervene—a last dim reflection of the realistic assessment of the Auswärtiges Amt on 2 July (4)—but they speculated on the Czarists' dynastic solidarity and on the inadequate preparedness of Russia and France for war. If Russia were in fact to come to the defence of Serbia, Berlin would be prepared to cover Austria. The German Government thus consciously took upon itself the risk of a conflict with Russia and of the continental war which would ensue.[1] All these resolutions were taken in such secrecy that no official minutes are to be found among the German documents—an extraordinary omission in view of the otherwise pedantic exactness of Prusso-German bureaucracy.

The Chancellor, after his conversation with Szögyény and Hoyos in Berlin on 6 July, immediately informed the German Ambassador in Vienna about the Hoyos Mission. The two final sentences of the telegram go to the root of the matter: the German Kaiser could not commit himself further at this stage, yet 'the Emperor Franz Joseph may, however, rest assured that His Majesty will faithfully stand by Austria-Hungary, as is required by the obligations of his alliance and of ancient friendship.'[2] As an understandable precaution, all reference to the German pressure for an early war, such as Szögyény had reported, is lacking (8). But since Tschirschky immediately and expressly confirmed the agreement between Szögyény's reports and the Chancellor's telegram (10), it is possible that Tschirschky may have received an additional communication of this kind from Berlin, which would have left no trace in the archives. Tschirschky apparently knew of the German pressure for an immediate war against Serbia—even at the risk of a conflict with Russia. At any rate, in the following weeks he acted as if he had been fully initiated into the secrets of the Wilhelmstrasse.

Szögyény's communication of the Germans' unconditional promise to cover Austria's rear and of the German pressure for an immediate war against Serbia (6, 8) made a profound impression on Vienna, especially on Berchtold. Only when he had the pledge of the German Kaiser and his Chancellor in his pocket did Berchtold overcome his initial hesitation and himself decide in favour of vigorous action against Serbia. Gerhard Ritter gives an excellent summary of the effect of the German attitude on the

---

[1] See now the particularly revealing passages from Riezler's diary, quoted by K.-D. Erdmann (GWU, 9, 1964, p. 536), which make it abundantly clear that the Chancellor consciously accepted even the risk of world war.   [2] *D.D.* 15.

Austro-Hungarian Foreign Minister: 'Berchtold, previously so timid and unsure of himself, now that he was certain of German support (he had even been advised by Berlin to make a rapid assault!) suddenly emerged as the strong man regarding a final settlement of accounts with the hated neighbour as indispensable, and all diplomatic attempts to reach an understanding and political agreement with Serbia as virtually useless.'[1] The devastating effect was even greater in Vienna. Once the cautious and timid Berchtold had been won over to the idea of war, a line of august statesmen followed in rapid succession: Emperor Franz Joseph and the Austrian Prime Minister, Stürgkh (each initially as irresolute as the other), and finally even Tisza, who had originally been opposed to war.

Berchtold's change of heart can be followed step by step from irresolute temporising to preparedness for war. As early as 6 July he informed Tisza of the German pledge in a brief paraphrase of the telegram from Berlin, but he omitted to give any indication as to his own intentions.[2] In a conversation with Conrad later the same day, and in answer to pressure from the latter—'We must before anything know for certain whether Germany will take her stand at our side'—Berchtold referred to the provisional character of the Imperial reply from Berlin, which only the Chancellor's vote could make binding. Berchtold spoke out for a later dateline in the event of war but suggested a trial mobilisation, an idea which Conrad rejected out of hand.[3] Szögyény's second telegram, reporting his discussion with the Chancellor, arrived in Vienna at 8.00 in the evening (8). Apparently under its influence, but also under that of the verbal report of Hoyos, who had returned from Berlin shortly afterwards, Berchtold finally swung over to the harsh line against Serbia from 7 July onwards.

7 July saw the great clash between Berchtold and Tisza in the combined Council of Ministers. Now certain of support from Germany, the Foreign Minister outlined a scheme for a preventive war against Serbia to forestall both the threat of a victory for the national revolutionary south Slav movement (which would, in the long run, have rendered the existence of the Dual Monarchy illusory) and Russia's attempts to unite the Slav Balkan states under Russian leadership. Berchtold also pointed to the danger of a conflict with Russia, which he regarded as in any case inevitable. Tisza, in contrast, warned against a war 'sans crier gare', such as Hoyos had evidently advocated in Berlin, since Austria-Hungary (and not Russia, *nota bene*) would thus be provoking world war from a dis-

[1] G. Ritter, *Staatskunst*, II, p. 294.
[2] Ö.D., 10091.
[3] L. Albertini, *Origins*, II, p. 164 (Conrad, *Dienstzeit*, IV, pp. 39f.).

advantageous moral position. Instead he spoke in favour of placing severe but *acceptable* conditions before Serbia and only proceeding to mobilisation and subsequently war if these were rejected. However the Council of Ministers tended towards Berchtold's viewpoint, which, in its turn, was a compromise between the demand for an immediate war represented by Hoyos and Berlin, and the more resolute cautiousness of Tisza: war against Serbia, to be sure, but diplomatically introduced by an ultimatum which would be formulated in terms deliberately intended to be *unacceptable*. In the second part of the consultations Conrad and Admiral von Kailer, as representative of the Austro-Hungarian Fleet, were present. On this occasion the main question was mobilisation and the probable course of a European war in which the attitude of Roumania played an important role (9).

The scene for the coming drama had been set. The plot was outlined by Vienna, worked out in Potsdam and Berlin and finally approved by Vienna as a result of the German pressure for immediate war against Serbia.

6 Szögyény to Berchtold

Telegram 237   Berlin, 5 July 1914
Strictly confidential   D. 7.35 p.m.
Ö.D. 10058   R. 10.00 p.m.

When I had informed Kaiser Wilhelm that I had an autograph letter from His Imp. and Roy. Apostolic Majesty, which Count Hoyos had just brought and which I was to give to him, I received an invitation to lunch with Their Majesties at noon in the Neues Palais. I gave the autograph letter[1] and the enclosed memoir into the hands of His Majesty. In my presence the Kaiser read both with the greatest attention. The first thing he assured me was, that he had expected some serious step on our part towards Serbia, but that at the same time he must confess that the detailed statement of His Majesty made him regard a serious European complication possible and that he could give no definite answer before having taken council with the Imperial chancellor.

After lunch, when I again called attention to the seriousness of the situation, the Kaiser authorised me to inform our gracious Majesty that we might in this case, as in all others, rely upon Germany's full support.

[1] See pp. 58f.

He must, as he said before, first hear what the Imperial Chancellor has to say, but he did not doubt in the least that Herr von Bethmann Hollweg would agree with him. Especially as far as our action against Serbia was concerned. But it was his (Kaiser Wilhelm's) opinion that this action must not be delayed. Russia's attitude will no doubt be hostile, but to this he had been for years prepared, and should a war between Austria-Hungary and Russia be unavoidable, we might be convinced that Germany, our old faithful ally, would stand at our side. Russia at the present time was in no way prepared for war, and would think twice before it appealed to arms. But it will certainly set other powers on to the Triple Alliance and add fuel to the fire in the Balkans. He understands perfectly well that His Apostolic Majesty in his well-known love of peace would be reluctant to march into Serbia; but if we had really recognised the necessity of warlike action against Serbia, he (Kaiser Wilhelm) would regret if we did not make use of the present moment, which is all in our favour.[1] As to Roumania he would take care that King Carol and his councillors would observe a correct attitude. He cannot sympathise with the idea of concluding an alliance with Bulgaria; he never trusted King Ferdinand and does not trust him now, nor his former or present councillors. Still he would make no objections to a treaty between the monarchy and Bulgaria, but this treaty must contain nothing to offend Roumania and it must—as the memoir proposes, be communicated to Roumania. Kaiser Wilhelm intends leaving to-morrow morning for Kiel, whence he starts for his northern tour; but before leaving, His Majesty will discourse with the Imperial Chancellor on the subject in question. For this purpose he has sent for him to Hohenfinow, and will see him in the Neues Palais this evening. I shall certainly have an opportunity of seeing the Imperial Chancellor in the course of to-morrow.[2]

7 Falkenhayn to Moltke

To be delivered by hand.
Strictly confidential
D.D., p. XII

Berlin, 5 July 1914

This afternoon H.M. the Kaiser and King sent for me at the Neues Palais to inform me that Austria-Hungary seemed resolved no longer to tolerate the hatching of intrigues against Austria on the Balkan Peninsula and

[1] See 2 and 4.   [2] See 8.

therefore, if necessary, to march into Serbia as a beginning; if the Russians refused to tolerate this, Austria would not be disposed to give way.

H.M. felt justified in drawing this inference from the words of the Austrian Ambassador, when the latter this afternoon delivered a memorandum from the Government in Vienna and a hand-written communication from Emperor Franz Joseph.[1]

I was not present during this conversation, so am unable to permit myself to form any opinion in this matter. On the other hand, H.M. read aloud both the autograph letter and the memorandum. Insofar as the hurriedness of the proceedings gave one a chance to arrive at any opinion, these documents did not succeed in convincing me that the Vienna Government had taken any firm resolution. Both paint a very gloomy picture of the general situation of the Dual Monarchy as a result of Pan-Slav agitations. Both consider it necessary that something should be done about this with the greatest urgency. But neither speaks of the need for war, rather both expound 'energetic' political action such as the conclusion of a treaty with Bulgaria, for which they would like to be certain of the support of the German Reich.

This support should be granted with some indication that it would, in the first place, be a matter for Austria-Hungary to take the requisite steps which are in her own interest.

The Chancellor, who was also in Potsdam, appears to have as little faith as I do that the Austrian Government is really in earnest, even though its language is undeniably more resolute than in the past.[2] At any rate, not only has he raised no objections about the Scandinavian journey taking place, but he has even recommended it. Certainly in no circumstances will the coming weeks bring any decision. It will be a long time before the treaty with Bulgaria is concluded. Your Excellency's stay at the Spa will therefore scarcely need to be curtailed. Nonetheless, although I have not been authorised to do so, I considered it advisable to inform you of the gravity of the situation so that anything untoward which could, after all, occur at any time, should not find you wholly unprepared.

[1] See 6.
[2] See 15 and 33.

8 Szögyény to Berchtold

Telegram 239   Berlin, 6 July 1914
Strictly confidential   D. 5.10 p.m.
Ö.D. 10076   R. 8.00 p.m.

In addition to my telegram 237 of yesterday.[1] Have just had a long discourse with the Imperial Chancellor and the Under-Secretary of State,
Count Hoyos being present. Herr von Bethmann Hollweg began by saying
that Kaiser Wilhelm had instructed him to express his thanks for the
autograph letter, which he would answer personally in a few days.[2] He
(the Imperial Chancellor) was also authorised by his Imperial master to
give a precise account of the position of the German Government towards
the imperial letter and the memoir, which he did in these words: German
Government perceives all the dangers arising for Austria-Hungary and
for the Triple Alliance as well, from Russia's plan of a Balkan league; it
perceives also that in this situation we should be desirous to induce
Bulgaria to join the Triple Alliance formally, but it must insist that this
should be done in a way—as indeed is intended—not to violate our
obligations towards Roumania. German Minister in Sofia was authorised
to negotiate in this sense with the Bulgarian government, when his Austro-
Hungarian colleague will call upon him to do so. At the same time he (the
Imperial Chancellor) intends instructing the German Minister in
Bucharest to speak openly with the King of Roumania, to inform him of
the negotiations carried on in Sofia and to call his attention to the fact that
he ought to stop the Roumanian agitation against us. Herr von Bethmann
Hollweg will also cause the King to be told, that he (Chancellor) has in
the past always advised us to remain friends with Serbia, but that after
the late events he perceives that this is as good as impossible; Roumania
should also take this into account. With regard to our relations towards
Serbia the German Government is of opinion that we must judge what is
to be done to clear the course; whatever way we decide, we may always
be certain that we will find Germany at our side, a faithful ally and friend
of our monarchy.

In the further course of conversation I ascertained that the Imperial
Chancellor like his Imperial master considers immediate action on our part
as the best solution of our difficulties in the Balkans. From an international
point of view he considers the present moment as more favourable than
some later time; he agrees with us that we need inform neither Italy nor
Roumania beforehand of an intended action against Serbia. On the other

[1] See 6.   [2] See p. 95.

hand Italy should even now be informed of the intention to allow Bulgaria to join the Triple Alliance.

Both the Imperial Chancellor and the Under-Secretary of State were of opinion that it would be best to negotiate a treaty with Bulgaria only at present and to leave it to the future whether Turkey and eventually Greece would bind themselves to Bulgaria. Chancellor remarked that in view of the great interests which Germany has in Turkey, this country's accession would be most desirable.

With regard to the step to be undertaken in Bucharest by the representative of Germany, Herr von Bethmann Hollweg thinks it might be useful, when King Carol's answer has reached Berlin, that Count Czernin should shortly afterwards speak with the king on the same subject.

At the conclusion of our discourse, the Chancellor asked how matters were going on in Albania and warned earnestly against plans which might endanger our relations towards Italy or the duration of the Triple Alliance.

Herr von Tschirschky will be informed of our discourse in strict privacy.[1]

9 Protocol of the Council of Ministers for Common Affairs, with Berchtold in the chair

Ö.D. 10118   7 July 1914

Present: The Imp. and Roy. President of the Council of Ministers Count Stürgkh, the Roy. Hungarian Premier Count Tisza, the Imp. and Roy. Joint Minister for Finances Ritter von Biliński, the Imp. and Roy. Minister of War F.Z.M. Ritter von Krobatin, the Imp. and Roy. Chief of the General Staff G. d. I. Baron von Conrad, the Deputy Chief of the Naval Staff, Rear-Admiral von Kailer,

Keeper of the Protocol: Secretary of legation Count Hoyos,

Subject of Council: Bosnian concerns. The diplomatic action against Serbia.

The *President*[2] opens the sitting remarking that the Council of Ministers had been called together to advise on the measures to be taken for meeting the evils which in Bosnia and Herzegovina have resulted from the catastrophe of Sarajevo. According to his view there would be a number of internal measures which the critical state of Bosnia has made desirable; but before deciding in their favour there should be clearness whether the

[1] See p. 74.   [2] Berchtold.

moment has not come when a show of force might put an end to Serbia's intrigues once and for all. A decisive stroke of this kind cannot be dealt without previous diplomatic preparation, and for this reason the German Government was informed and consulted. The discussions with Germany brought about a most satisfactory result, since Kaiser Wilhelm as well as Herr von Bethmann Hollweg solemnly promised the support and aid of Germany in the eventuality of a warlike complication with Serbia.[1] We must still take into account Italy and Roumania, he agreed with the Berlin cabinet that it would be better to act first and wait for eventual claims to compensation afterwards.

He is by no means convinced that an expedition to Serbia must necessarily involve us in a war with Russia. Russia's present policy, which is farsighted, is aiming at a league of the Balkan states including Roumania, which it would at a suitable moment play out against our monarchy. It is his belief that we must take into account that in the face of this policy our situation must become more precarious as time goes on, all the more because if we do not act, our own South Slavs and Roumanians will interpret our attitude as weakness, and would be all the more disposed to lend a willing ear to the persuasions of our neighbours across the frontier.

The logical result of what has been said, would be to get in advance of our foes and by coming to terms with Serbia, to stop the development of the process at present going on, a result which we may not be able to attain later on.

The *Royal Hungarian Premier* agrees with us that during the last days the situation has changed on account of the facts which judicial examination has brought forth and also on account of the attitude of the Serbian press, and fully admits that the possibility of a warlike action against Serbia seems nearer than he believed just after the crime of Sarajevo. But he would never consent to a surprise attack upon Serbia without a previous diplomatic action, such as he is afraid is being intended and he is sorry to hear, has been discussed by Count Hoyos in Berlin. We should, he believes, in this case play a sorry figure in the eyes of all Europe, and should draw upon ourselves the enmity of all the Balkan states with the exception of Bulgaria, which is too weak just now to be of any effective help.

It is absolutely necessary that we address demands to Serbia and if these are rejected we must make out an ultimatum. Our exactions may be hard, but not such that they cannot be complied with. If Serbia accepted them, we should have a splendid diplomatic success and our *prestige* in the Balkans would gain immensely. If our demands are refused, he would also

[1] See **6** and **8**.

vote for a warlike action, but he must call attention to the fact that by a war we could reduce the size of Serbia, but we could not completely annihilate it. Russia would fight to the death before allowing this and he, as Hungarian Premier, could never consent to the Monarchy's annexing any part of Serbia.

It is not for Germany to decide whether we ought to go to war with Serbia just now or not. Personally he holds the belief that it is not absolutely necessary to begin a war at the present moment. We must remember that agitation against us in Roumania is exceedingly busy just now and that in view of the excited feelings of the population we should almost certainly have to look forward to a Roumanian attack and we should doubtless have to protect Transylvania by a strong force to intimidate the Roumanians. Now that Germany has happily opened the way to Bulgaria's joining the Triple Alliance, a promising perspective for successful diplomatic action in the Balkans opens out, since by the accession of Bulgaria and Turkey to the Triple Alliance we may outbalance Roumania and Serbia and perhaps induce Roumania to return to the Triple Alliance. With regard to European countries it must be considered that the forces of France when compared to those of Germany are diminishing on account of the continual reduction of the French birth-rate, so that Germany will be in a position to muster more troops against Russia.

All these circumstances must be considered, when a resolution involving such exceedingly heavy responsibility was to be taken, and he must again declare, that notwithstanding the crisis in Bosnia, where a great deal might be done by a reform of the administration, he could not make up his mind in favour of the war, but still thought that a marked diplomatic success, which would cause a deep humiliation of Serbia, would decidedly improve our situation and give a chance of initiating an advantageous policy in the Balkans.

The *Presiding Minister* (Berchtold) took up this argument and remarked that diplomatic successes against Serbia had increased the Monarchy's *prestige* for the time being, but had in the end also increased the tension in the relations with Serbia. Neither our success in the crisis of the annexion, nor that of creating the Albanian state, nor yet Serbia having had to give way after the ultimatum of the autumn of last year changed any of our circumstances. A radical solution of the question raised by the propaganda for a Greater Serbia, which is systematically set to work in Belgrade and whose corrupting effects we feel from Agram to Zara,[1] can only be brought about by the exertion of main force.

With regard to the danger of a hostile attitude in Roumania,

[1] Now Zagreb and Zadar respectively.

mentioned by the Hungarian premier, the presiding minister was of opinion that it is less to be feared at the present time than in the future, when the partnership of interests between Roumania and Serbia will have developed. King Carol, it is true, has expressed doubts whether under present circumstances he would be able to do his whole duty as an ally by giving active help when it was wanted. But we cannot assume that he would consent to a warlike operation against the monarchy, or that he would be unable to oppose public feeling in such an eventuality. Besides it must be remembered that Roumania stands in fear of Bulgaria and would not be free to act freely, even under present circumstances.

As to the Hungarian Premier's remark with regard to the proportion of forces between France and Germany, he thought it right to call attention to the fact that the reduction of the growth of the population in France was more than balanced by the increasing number of inhabitants in Russia, so that the assertion that Germany would in time have more troops at its disposition against France cannot be taken into account.

The *Imp. and Roy. Premier* (Stürgkh) remarked that the present Council of Ministers had been called for the purpose of discussing the measures to be taken in Bosnia and Herzegovina, to ensure the success of the judicial examinations on the assassination and to counteract the Pan-Serbian movement that is taking place in Bosnia. These questions must go to the rear if the greater question arises, whether we might not solve the Bosnian difficulty by exercising force against Serbia.

Two reasons make this question very pressing just now; in the first place the Governor in Bosnia and Herzegovina declares that it is his belief that no successful measures could be applied in the interior of these provinces unless we deal Serbia a forcible stroke first. His opinion is founded on his own perceptions and on his thorough knowledge of the country. These perceptions on General Potiorek's part make it imperative to ask whether we are at all able to stop the subversive activity which originates in Serbia, and whether we are able to keep the two provinces in question if we do not promptly deal a blow to Serbia.

During the last few days the whole situation has changed. It now shows a psychological character and is decidedly more than ever pointing to a solution at the point of the sword. He cannot help agreeing with the Hungarian premier that it is for us and not for the German Government to decide whether a war is necessary or not; still he must say that our decision should be influenced strongly by the fact that where we look to for the most faithful support of our policy in the Triple Alliance, we are promised unreserved loyalty and are advised to act without delay. Count Tisza should consider this circumstance and remember that by a weak and hesitating policy we might risk not being so certain of German support at some future time. This is surely of the highest importance, next to the interest we have in restoring order in Bosnia, and should be carefully considered.

It is but a question of detail how we are to begin and if the Hungarian government thinks that a surprise attack, *sans crier gare* as Count Tisza expresses it, is not feasible, we will have to find some other way; but what he thinks is absolutely necessary is to act without delay and to spare our national economy a protracted period of suspense. But all this is mere detail considered side by side with the question of principle, whether it is absolutely necessary to have a war or not. Here the *prestige* and the existence of the Monarchy must decide, whose south Slav provinces he holds to be lost if nothing is done to prevent it.

We should therefore decide in principle today that action must and shall follow. He shares the presiding Minister's belief that a mere diplomatic success would not improve the situation. If a foregoing diplomatic action is therefore resorted to for international reasons, it should be taken with the firm resolve that this action can only end in war. . . .

The *Imp. and Roy. War Minister* (Krobatin) is of opinion that a diplomatic success would be of no use at all. A success of this kind would be interpreted as weakness. From a military point of view he must remark that it would be better to go to war immediately, rather than at some later period, because the balance of power must in course of time change to our disadvantage. As to the modality of the beginning of war, he must call attention to the fact that the two big wars of latter years, the war between Russia and Japan, as also the Balkan war began without a foregoing declaration of war. It was his belief that we should at first only carry through the mobilisation as it is prepared against Serbia, and postpone the general mobilisation to such a time when it becomes clear that Russia is acting.

We have already lost two opportunities for solving the Serbian question and have postponed the decision each time. If we do this again and allow this provocation to pass unavenged, this will be taken for a proof of weakness in all south Slav provinces and would be an encouragement to agitation against us.

From a military point of view it is desirable that the mobilisation should be carried through immediately and as secretly as possible, and that an ultimatum should be addressed to Serbia when the mobilisation is complete. This would also be in our favour with regard to the Russian forces, because just now the Russian army corps at the frontier are incomplete on account of the leave given for harvesting.

After this a discussion began on the aims of a war against Serbia, during which the Royal Hungarian Premier's view, that Serbia might be reduced as to size but not annihilated out of consideration for Russia, was adopted by all. The *Imp. and Roy. Premier* (Stürgkh) said that he should advise that the Karageorgevich dynasty be removed, and the crown given to a European prince. The reduced kingdom should also be placed in a dependent position towards the Monarchy, at least from a military point of view.

The *Royal Hungarian Premier* (Tisza) still holds the belief that a successful Balkan policy could be created by the addition of Bulgaria to the Triple Alliance, and calls attention to the terrible calamity of a European war under present circumstances. It should not be overlooked that all kinds of eventualities are possible in the near future—Russia might be absorbed by Asian complications, Bulgaria, when it regains its strength might want to revenge itself upon Serbia, etc. which would all improve our position towards the problem of Greater Serbia, to what it is at present.

The *presiding Minister* (Berchtold) replied to these arguments that certainly one might imagine many possibilities in the future, which would place us in a favourable situation. But he feared that there was no time to wait for such developments. The fact must be taken into account that our enemies are preparing for a decisive conflict with the Monarchy and that Roumania is lending a helping hand to the diplomacy of Russia and France. One must not assume that our policy with Bulgaria will be a full equivalent for the loss of Roumania. It is his belief that Roumania cannot be won back as long as Serbian agitation continues, because agitation for Greater Roumania follows the Serbian and will not meet with opposition until Roumania feels isolated by the annihilation of Serbia and sees that its only chance of being supported is to join the Triple Alliance. We must moreover not forget the fact that with regard to Bulgaria's accession to the Triple Alliance the very first step has not been made. All we know is that the present Bulgarian government a few months ago expressed this wish and was then about to conclude an alliance with Turkey. This has not been accomplished; on the contrary, Turkey has since allowed Russia and France to gain influence with it. The attitude of the Radoslawoff cabinet is certainly such, that we cannot doubt that Bulgaria is still disposed to lend a willing ear to any positive propositions we might make in the sense referred to. Still we cannot make these assumptions a safe cornerstone of our Balkan politics even so, because the present Bulgarian government has no sound basis; public opinion, which is always influenced by Russia to a certain degree, might object to joining the Triple Alliance and Radoslawoff's cabinet might be turned out. We must also remember that

Germany accepted the accession of Bulgaria to the Triple Alliance at the condition only that the agreement should not be directed against Roumania. This condition is rather difficult to comply with and might at some future time be the cause of misunderstandings.

A lengthy debate on the question of the war followed. The result of the discussion may be summarised as follows:

1 That all present wish for a speedy decision of the controversy with Serbia, whether it be decided in a warlike or a peaceful manner;

2 that the Council of Ministers is prepared to adopt the view of the Royal Hungarian Premier according to which the mobilisation is not to take place until after concrete demands have been addressed to Serbia and after being refused, an ultimatum has been sent.

All present except the Royal Hungarian Premier hold the belief that a purely diplomatic success, even if it ended with a glaring humiliation of Serbia, would be worthless and that therefore such stringent demands must be addressed to Serbia, that will make a refusal almost certain, so that the road to a radical solution by means of a military action should be opened.

Count Tisza remarked that he was anxious to meet the others halfway and was prepared to concede that the demands addressed to Serbia should be hard indeed, but not such as to make our intention of raising unacceptable terms clear to everybody. Otherwise we should not have a lawful basis for our declaration of war. The text of the note must be composed with utmost care and he should very much beg to be allowed to see it before it is sent. He must also clearly state that if his point of view was disregarded, he would draw the unavoidable consequences.

After this the sitting was suspended to be reopened in the afternoon.

When the Council of Ministers met again, the Chief of the General Staff and the Deputy Chief of the Naval Staff were also present.

The *War Minister* (Krobatin) at the request of the presiding Minister spoke first to ask the Chief of the General Staff three questions as follows:

1 Whether it is possible to mobilise against Serbia only at first and against Russia not until necessity arises.

2 Whether it is possible to retain a large body of troops in Transylvania to intimidate Roumania.

3 Where the conflict with Russia could be taken up.

The *Chief of the General Staff* answered these questions privately and begged that the answers should not appear in the protocol.

A lengthy debate followed these explanations, touching upon the proportion of forces and the probable course of a European war, which being of a private character are not suitable to be taken into the protocol.

Before the debate was closed the *Hungarian Premier* (Tisza) again explained his point of view on the question of the war and appealed again to all present to consider carefully what they were about to decide.

The points which were to be contained in the note to Serbia were then discussed.

With regard to these points the Council of Ministers did not take a resolution; but they were formed, so as to give a clear idea of what might be asked of Serbia.

At this point the Chief of the General Staff and the Deputy Chief of the Naval Staff left the Council, which discussed the internal situation of Bosnia and the necessary measures to be taken . . . .

All present agree that some of General Krobatin's propositions should be accepted, whilst others went too far. That it was not possible to decide definitely over measures relating to administration, before the great question whether there was to be war with Serbia or not, was decided.

The *presiding Minister* (Berchtold) declares that though there were yet differences of opinion between the members of the Council and Count Tisza, still an agreement had been arrived at, since the propositions of the Hungarian Premier would in all probability lead to a war with Serbia, the necessity of which he and all the other members of the Council had understood and admitted.

Count Berchtold then told the Council that he intended going to Ischl on the 8th of the month to report to His Imp. and Roy. Apostolic Majesty. The Royal Hungarian Premier begged that the Minister would present to His Majesty a memorandum in which he (Tisza) would record his view of the situation.[1]

After a communication to the press had been agreed upon, the presiding Minister closed the sitting.

10   Tschirschky to Jagow

Telegram 83
Confidential
D.D. 18

Vienna, 7 July 1914
D. 3.25 p.m.
R. 6.55 p.m.

I was asked to be present today at a conference between Count Berchtold and the two Premiers, at which Count Hoyos read the reports of Count Szögyény in which the latter advised them of the preliminary reply of His

[1] *Ö.D.* 10146.

Majesty after the reading of the personal letter from the Emperor and of the memorandum, as well as about the succeeding conference had by him with Your Excellency.[1] Furthermore, Count Hoyos read us a memorandum that he had drawn up concerning a talk on the same matter with the Under-Secretary of State.[2]

In regard to the latter memorandum, I may remark that Count Berchtold as well as Count Tisza, the latter most especially, wants it to be most plainly understood that everything that Count Hoyos said during this conference with the Under-Secretary of State is to be regarded only as his own personal opinion. (This limitation refers particularly to the fact that Count Hoyos stated that a complete partition of Serbia was under consideration here.)[3]

Count Berchtold requested me, in the names of both Premiers as well as in his own, to express to His Majesty our Most Gracious Master as well as to Your Excellency, their most sincere gratitude for the attitude, so clearly in accord with the compact of alliance and with the dictates of friendship, which you have assumed.

The reports of Count Szögyény[1] correspond exactly to the tenor of the most graciously addressed telegram from Your Excellency on the sixth of the month, no. 113.[4]

In connection with this preliminary conference, a Ministerial Council is to take place, which today is to concern itself exclusively with those measures of an internal political nature which are to be taken in Bosnia and Herzegovina.[5]

---

[1] See 6 and 8.
[2] Not among the documents.
[3] See also 26.
[4] *D.D.* 15; see p. 74.
[5] See 9.

3   Lull Before the Storm
8 – 18 July

The basic decision to declare war against Serbia was made in Vienna and
Berlin between 5 and 7 July, but it was obvious that the necessary preparations would require a certain amount of time. The first task, therefore,
was to conceal the measures being taken in Vienna by general preparations
for the summer vacation, and Vienna and Berlin worked with rare accord
to set up this smoke-screen. By sheer luck, Moltke happened to have just
left to take the waters in Carlsbad on 28 June and both Tirpitz, Secretary
of State for the Navy, and the Chief of Naval Staff had already set out
on their summer holiday. Kaiser Wilhelm II was for cancelling his
Scandinavian journey in view of possible complications but the Chancellor
dissuaded him from such a dramatic step in order to avoid attracting
unnecessary attention; it might have created alarm and suspicion abroad
if he had brusquely dropped this almost traditional visit. Moltke had no
need to interrupt his cure, and his second-in-command, General von
Waldersee, likewise went on leave on 8 July, on the recommendation of
Jagow, Secretary of State for Foreign Affairs, who had returned to Berlin
the same day;[1] but Waldersee remained 'ready to jump' as 'we are all
prepared here at the General Staff; in the meantime there is nothing for us
to do.'[2] On 23 July, the date of delivery of the ultimatum, Waldersee
returned to Berlin in ample time to go into action. Shortly after him
Falkenhayn joined the solemn procession of holiday-making monarchs,
generals and admirals, only to arrive back at Berlin, punctually on 25 July

[1] *D.D.* p. XX.   [2] *D.D.* 74.

(which was incidentally the date of Moltke's premature return from Carlsbad).

The Chancellor ostensibly spent most of the July crisis at nearby Hohenfinow, but made several secret journeys to Berlin and Potsdam, the better to retain a firm hand on affairs.[1] Vice Chancellor and Secretary of State for the Interior, Clemens von Delbrück, was allowed to resume his holiday after a fleeting return visit to Berlin for private reasons on 9 July; it was then that Bethmann Hollweg, Jagow and Zimmermann took the opportunity of letting him into the state secret. He was recalled to Berlin on 23 July and left his holiday-place furtively, using his wife's illness as an excuse for his sudden departure.[2]

Those who were directly involved, however, had to remain at their posts: Jagow, Secretary of State at the Auswärtiges Amt, was not asked to extend his brief honeymoon-week, and none of the key figures in the Auswärtiges Amt or in the Ballhausplatz were on leave in July 1914. Similarly the German and Austrian Ambassadors remained in the major European capitals, while a number of the Entente Ambassadors who were on leave had to hasten back to their posts when the crisis broke out into the open after the delivery of the ultimatum.[3] It is for this reason that for the greater part of July 1914 on the side of the Entente it was the great hour of the chargés d'affaires, who like Rumbold and Bronewski in Berlin, and Kudaschev in Vienna, did not acquit themselves badly, to judge from their reports.

As for the Austrians, Emperor Franz Joseph indulged in his customary summer visit to Bad Ischl and Berchtold sent away Conrad and Krobatin, the Minister of War, for a holiday until 22 July. As early as 8 July Berchtold had remarked to Conrad: 'It would be a good thing if you and the Minister of War would go on leave for a while, so as to keep up an appearance that nothing is going on.'[4] When Tschirschky informed Berlin of the demonstrative departure on leave of absence of both generals, together with Berchtold's explanation that 'this is being done on purpose, in order to prevent any disquiet', the Kaiser in his pleasure yacht *Hohenzollern* scribbled 'Childish!' in the margin of the telegram (16), little knowing that his Chancellor in Berlin was pursuing identical tactics with regard to his own Scandinavian journey and the annual holiday of leading officers and statesmen. Thus on 18 July Schoen, the Bavarian Chargé d'Affaires, was able to report to Munich on the policy of the German

[1] See also 15.
[2] *Untersuchungsausschuss* pp. 79f.; Clemens von Delbrück, *Die wirtschaftliche Mobilmachung in Deutschland* (Munich 1924), p. 96.
[3] See p. 92.
[4] Conrad, *Dienstzeit*, IV, p. 61 (Albertini, *Origins*, II, p. 171).

Reich: 'The administration will, immediately upon the presentation of the Austrian note at Belgrade, initiate diplomatic action with the Powers in the interest of the localisation of the war. It will *claim* that the Austrian action has been just as much of a surprise to it as to the other Powers, pointing out the fact that the Kaiser is on his northern journey and that the Chief of the Grand General Staff and the Prussian Minister of War are away on leave of absence' (33).

In other ways, too, Vienna and Berlin were at pains to 'keep up the appearance that nothing is going on'. The Austrian papers it is true carried on a heated dispute with the Serbian press, but in general the Ballhausplatz did its best to prevent any leakage of information as to its intentions. In Germany the Chancellor carefully restrained the press from anti-French polemics so as to avoid scaring the French and to facilitate localisation (25). When the Crown Prince, who was notorious for his Pan-German sympathies, looked like sundering the fine threads of the German policy of localisation by his provocative demonstrations in the days immediately before the delivery of the ultimatum to Serbia, the Chancellor, in despair, turned to his imperial father in an attempt to restore him to reason. His explanation for this is revealing: the noisy demonstrations of the Crown Prince might be interpreted abroad 'as wilful war-baiting, whereas it is our task, according to Your Majesty's admonitions, to localise the conflict. The accomplishment of this task is in itself so difficult, that even minor incidents may determine its fate.'[1] It was evidently clear to Bethmann Hollweg that he had to perform a balancing act without the net, and he had no wish to be disturbed in his breakneck activity by any ill-timed clamouring for war.

In those first days, the maintenance of a peaceful exterior towards Serbia was extended even to court formalities. On 11 July Wilhelm II sent to enquire of the Auswärtiges Amt whether the customary birthday telegram which was due just then, should in fact be sent to Peter I, the Serbian King. After all, it was to be expected that Germany, or at any rate Austria-Hungary, would shortly find herself at war with Serbia. The enquiry speaks for the human delicacy of the Kaiser, the answer for the cold-bloodedness of the Auswärtiges Amt: 'As Vienna has so far inaugurated no action of any sort against Belgrade, the omission of the customary telegram would be too noticeable and might be the cause of premature uneasiness.'[2] The customary telegram, with good wishes from the Kaiser to the King, was accordingly despatched to Belgrade.

The European Powers were in fact deluded, to a certain extent, by the

[1] *D.D.* 84.
[2] Exchange of telegrams of 11 July in *D.D.* 30a, 32a.

deceptive calm in Vienna. As they could do nothing but wait and see how Vienna would react in response to Sarajevo, it only remained for them to hope that the Danube Monarchy would not act in a way that was over-dramatic or even a threat to peace. The Russian and British Ambassadors to Berlin both went on holiday, the Russian Ambassador to Vienna actually departing for Russia on 21 July, trusting in the assurances of the Ballhaus-platz that Austria would make no demands on Serbia which might lead to international complications.[1]

Behind this smokescreen of official holidaymaking, however, Vienna and Berlin were making their arrangements for the imminent conflict. The Vienna Government drew up the ultimatum to Serbia whilst the German Government, even before its delivery, attempted to prepare the position on localisation which it intended to adopt immediately on publica-tion of the ultimatum. At the same time the Berlin administration, allegedly with concern for the maintenance of peace, continued to urge the Austro-Hungarian Government to act with greater celerity.

Soon after the Council of Ministers on 7 July (9), the Austrian Foreign Ministry set about composing the ultimatum to Belgrade. Its main features were already worked out on 10 July: a dead-line of 48 hours for a reply, participation of the Austrian Government in the surveillance of Pan-Serbian intrigues, 'perhaps also . . . the dissolution of the associations and the dismissal of some compromised officers'. In accordance with the general principles guiding the Council of Ministers, the ultimatum was to be made unacceptable (16).

Wiesner, the Legal Adviser in the Austrian Foreign Ministry, whom Berchtold had sent to Sarajevo on 11 July to supply information on the current investigations, provided further suggestions on 19 July. Although his provisional report of 13 July, which arrived by telegraph, poured water into the wine of all those who believed in the complicity of the Serbian Government, he was able, nonetheless, to confirm that some Serbian civil servants had taken part in the planning and organisation of the plot (19) and his suggestions were finally turned to good account in the formulation of the ultimatum (37).

On 19 July the text of the document was by now sufficiently well established to receive ratification at a sitting of the Council of Ministers (35). On this occasion, the Council also reached a firm agreement on the date for its delivery in Belgrade. Originally Berchtold had envisaged 18 or 24 July, out of consideration for the French state visit to St Petersburg arranged for 20–23 July, in order if possible to prevent a coordination of French and Russian policies. The Minister preferred the later date, how-

[1] *D.F.*, X, 554; *Bayr. Dok.* 19.

ever, in view of the harvest (17). On 14 July Berchtold suggested 25 July to Tschirschky (22), but shortly afterwards advanced the date to 23 July, the day of Poincaré's departure from St Petersburg 'with the hope of hastening the occurrence as much as possible' (27). On 19 July this date was confirmed and the time of delivery fixed for five o'clock in the afternoon (35).

Work on the ultimatum was paralleled in the first week after the great Council of Ministers (9) by the struggle for final unity among the leading figures of the Danube Monarchy. Even though Berchtold had been won over by 7 July to the idea of a war against Serbia,[1] it was only on 9 July that Franz Joseph announced 'that he was quite of our opinion that it was necessary now to come to some determination, in order to put an end to the intolerable conditions in connection with Serbia' (16). But according to a new source, he did not altogether exclude the possibility of a peaceful settlement. He did, however, seek to bring about an understanding between Berchtold and Tisza through Berchtold and Burián, the permanent representative for Hungary in Vienna with the rank of Minister (13). In view of Tisza's deep respect for Franz Joseph, it is to be assumed that the latter's admonitions contributed towards Tisza's final conversion to Berchtold's line on 14 July (21).[2]

The first military preparations were now already begun. As early as 7 July Conrad had discussed mobilisation in general terms at the Council of Ministers (9). Initially, approximately 16 days were envisaged for the deployment of troops against Serbia (12). But by mid-July the Austrian batteries facing Belgrade on the Danube were already in possession of accurate maps of the Serbian capital to assist them in marking their targets (32). On 19 July Krobatin, the Minister of War, informed the Council of Ministers of the secret measures for mobilisation which had been carried out in the meantime (35).

The official line which Schoen communicated to Munich ahead of time on 18 July (33) was that Berlin had no knowledge of the contents of the ultimatum to Serbia, or even of the belligerent intentions of her ally. The elder generation of German historians not only uncritically accepted this official line but for almost half a century presented it as the historical truth,[3] despite the fact that documents which have been made known since 1919 unequivocally prove the contrary.

[1] See pp. 74f.
[2] See *Journal of Contemporary History*, no. 3.
[3] Recently in G. Ritter, *Staatskunst*, II, p. 312; a more flexible interpretation of the same view can still be found in W. Hubatsch, *Ursachen und Anlass des Weltkrieges, 1914*. According to Hubatsch the German Government was 'only insufficiently and reluctantly informed' by Vienna (p. 28) and 'the wording' of the Austrian note of 23 July was only known in Berlin on

After the Hoyos Mission the German Government was constantly informed through the normal diplomatic channels of the most important
moves of its Austro-Hungarian ally throughout the entire July crisis;
in the following weeks Tschirschky in Vienna and Szögyény in Berlin
paid almost daily visits to the Austrian and German Foreign Ministries
respectively and saw to the necessary information and coordination. The
running commentaries provided by Tschirschky and his deputy, Stolberg,
were supplemented by reports from both Count Kageneck, the German
Military Attaché in Vienna, and the German Consul General in Budapest.

Tschirschky was able to inform the Wilhelmstrasse of the outcome of the
Council of Ministers as early as 8 July, both before and after he had held
lengthy consultations with Berchtold (10, 12). On 10 July Tschirschky
telegraphed news of the 48-hour time limit, one of the basic conditions
of the ultimatum, and also of Berchtold's intention of making the ultimatum unacceptable in any circumstances (16). On 11 July Tschirschky
communicated in a 'strictly confidential' personal letter to Jagow what
was later to become the principle clause of the ultimatum, namely the
publication of a Royal army order, to be dictated to the Serbian King,
in which he was to dissociate himself from all Pan-Serbian activities (17).
On 18 July Schoen was able to inform Munich on all these points (33)
and Koester, the Chargé d'Affaires for Baden-Baden, did likewise for his
Government in Karlsruhe two days later.[1] Although it was alleged in the
official version for consumption at home and abroad that the German
Government was still in ignorance of 'the exact contents of the note' a
closer examination reveals that the indications given by Koester accord
with the principle clause and points 1–7 (out of a total of ten) of the ultimatum. The Wilhelmstrasse and at least two regional governments were
not only informed of the general tenor of the note—that it was deliberately
unacceptable—but also of its basic content.

Had it wanted to, the German Government would thus have had time
enough to lodge a protest or at least raise objections to too forceful a
measure on the part of her ally.[2] But nothing of the kind happened, even

---

the previous evening (p. 30). A final illustration from G. Ritter, *Der Erste Weltkrieg. Studien
zum deutschen Geschichtsbild. Schriftenreihe der Bundeszentrale für politische Bildung*, no. 64
(Bonn, 1964), p. 22: 'This intention [of "making inevitable" this war against Serbia] naturally
had to be kept a strict secret from the rest of the world—even from Germany from whom the
wording of the ultimatum was withheld (despite all inquiries) almost up to the last moment,
because it was feared that she might raise objections'.

[1] Bach, no. 5.

[2] See also G. Ritter, 'Eine neue Kriegsschuldthese?' in *Historische Zeitschrift*, vol. 194, no. 3,
pp. 646–68, p. 659, n. 18, also republished in *Deutsche Kriegsziele 1914–1918*, edited by Ernst
W. Graf Lynar (Berlin, 1964), p. 134, n. 18. Here Ritter upholds the traditional view, maintaining that there was no time for the Germans to raise objections in Vienna between the evening

on 14 July when the Wilhelmstrasse learned that the Ballhausplatz intended after the ultimatum to break off relations with Serbia, mobilise and possibly shell Belgrade.[1] The German Government's past attitude, however, made such a protest most unlikely as it had only recently given Austria the explicit assurance that it desired the quickest and most drastic action possible.[2]

After the Hoyos Mission Szögyény took the opportunity, on 8 July, of seeing a number of people, including Zimmermann, in the Auswärtiges Amt. The Germans repeated their commitment in principle and added 'that our decisions are awaited here with impatience, as it is thought to be the right moment ... to take vigorous action against Serbia'. Jagow confirmed this the following day and assured Szögyény 'in a most emphatic manner that he also was of the opinion that the proposed action against Serbia should be taken in hand without delay'.[3] That day the Auswärtiges Amt despatched to the *Hohenzollern* a letter addressed to Franz Joseph, which Wilhelm II merely had to sign. This contained a ceremonious repetition of the assurance given to Szögyény 'that you will find me and my Empire standing faithfully at your side in this dark hour, in full accord with our old and tried friendship and with the obligations of our alliance'.[4] On 12 July Szögyény gave an impressive résumé of the considerations which lay behind the German pressure for the 'action' against Serbia (18).

At the same time Tschirschky in Vienna urged a quickening of tempo for the 'action proposed against Serbia'.[5] As early as 11 July he was exhorting Berchtold to greater haste—though not for the first time, as he had already written to Jagow in his private letter of the same date: 'I took the opportunity *again* today to discuss the proceedings against Serbia with Count Berchtold, principally to impress upon the Minister *once more*, emphatically, that quick action was called for' (17). Two days later he renewed the pressure, for on that day he had 'once more taken the opportunity of emphasising to the Minister the need for a quick decision'.[6] Thus Kaiser Wilhelm II would certainly not have been alone in heaving a sigh of relief when on 14 July Tschirschky was finally able to announce a broad agreement between Berchtold and Tisza and a further advance in the concrete preparations against Serbia (21, 22).

---

of 22 July and the delivery of the Note in Belgrade. This may have been true for that limited period, but it leaves out of account the fact that *before* 22 July the Auswärtiges Amt was already in possession of ample information.
[1] Ö.D. 10236, 10259; also 7 and 32. [2] See pp. 70ff.
[3] Ö.D. 10127, 10154. [4] D.D. 26.
[5] Ö.D. 10154 (A.R.B., I, no. 13).
[6] I. Geiss, *Julikrise und Kriegsausbruch 1914*, I, no. 82, n. 2.

The Auswärtiges Amt was unhappy at any postponement of the Austrian action. On 14 July Berchtold had explained to Tschirschky the desirability of a postponement until 25 July. But on the following day he evidently saw the need for instructing Szögyény (23) specifically to draw attention to his affirmation 'that they could feel absolutely assured in Berlin that there was not a thought of hesitation or uncertainty in existence here' (22). Jagow complied with what he had no power to alter, but he was apparently unable altogether to suppress his displeasure at the delay (24).

The Wilhelmstrasse thus welcomed any indication of Austrian resolve and immediately gave its support. When on 14 July Szögyény at Berchtold's behest put out a feeler to the German Government to ascertain whether it was prepared to take charge of Austro-Hungarian interests in Belgrade after relations with Serbia and Montenegro had been broken off, Jagow quickly assented. He even went on to add 'that Germany would also have to recall her representatives in the event of an armed conflict between the Monarchy and the other two countries'.[1]

The Germans had suspected from the very beginning that their allies were not sufficiently earnest in their desire to go through with the 'action proposed against Serbia'. On 5 July Falkenhayn and the Chancellor had already cast doubts upon the strength of Austrian intentions (7). Whether or not at the time this had been a correct assessment of Vienna's firmness of purpose after the Hoyos Mission, there soon developed a widespread doubt in the Wilhelmstrasse as to whether Austria was even capable of summoning up the requisite energy for a war. On 8 July Zimmermann declared to Schoen, who in turn informed Munich on 9 July, that he would 'consider the present moment as very favourable to Austria for undertaking what he called a "punitive expedition" against her southern neighbour, and definitely believes this would succeed in localising the war. He doubts however that Vienna will decide to do this' (15). On 17 July the Saxon Minister in Berlin announced after a discussion with Zimmermann that 'the Government in Vienna seems only with some difficulty to be summoning up the requisite energy for a *démarche*' (28), although, as Schoen put it on 18 July, Germany had given Austria a '"blanket authority" even though it was at the risk of a war with Russia' (33).

On 17 July Stolberg, as Tschirschky's deputy, was able to report from Vienna that the delivery of the ultimatum had now definitely been fixed for 23 July but Berchtold still only half suggested the 'hope' (rather than the certainty) 'that Serbia would not agree to the Austro-Hungarian

[1] *Ö.D.* 10259.

demands' (27). At this Stolberg appears to have let fly in a somewhat un-diplomatic manner—at all events, he enquired sharply 'what would happen, then, should the matter come to nothing in this fashion'. And in a private letter he launched forth in no uncertain terms on the bad impression that would be created by a failure to take action (31).

Jagow and Zimmermann expressed their views even more forcibly to Schoen on 18 July: 'Here they are absolutely willing that Austria should take advantage of the favourable opportunity even at the risk of further complications. But whether they will actually rise to the occasion in Vienna still seems doubtful to Herr von Jagow as it does to Herr Zimmermann. The Under-Secretary of State made the statement that Austria-Hungary, thanks to her indecision and desultoriness, has really become the Sick Man of Europe.' And at another point in the same report: 'In Vienna they do not seem to have expected such an unconditional support of the Danube Monarchy by Germany, and Herr Zimmermann has the impression that it is almost embarrassing to the always timid and undecided authorities at Vienna not to be admonished by Germany to caution and self-restraint' (33).

The German fears, however revealing they may appear in retrospect, were all too justified, as the 'always timid and undecided authorities at Vienna' did indeed only 'rise to the occasion' with a decision for 'action' against Serbia as a result of the German pledge and pressure from Berlin. But even now the Austrians wanted to take their time over proceedings, for they adopted a relatively circumspect *modus procedendi*, which obviously jangled the nerves of the German statesmen. Vienna's plan was to break off relations with Serbia and issue the order for mobilisation on expiry of the 48-hour time limit and on receipt of the unsatisfactory reply which was expected from Serbia. But, as has been mentioned above, a period of 16 days had been envisaged for Austrian mobilisation (12). It was only intended to declare war on Serbia and effectually open hostilities once mobilisation and the deployment of troops against Serbia had been completed (42). Thus the local war against Serbia would only have started around 12 August, which would still have given time for diplomatic intervention by the European Powers. However, it was just such a mediation between Vienna and Belgrade that the German Government sought to prevent. It learned of the planned duration of Austrian mobilisation as early as the evening of 8 July or the morning of 9 July, but only on 24 July did it receive news of the timetable which was envisaged: breaking off of relations, mobilisation, completion of the deployment of troops, declaration of war. And it immediately reacted in its own fashion (71).

repeatedly been asserted that it was merely for the sake of
localisation that the Germans were so insistent in their
or precipitate action from Austria. The sooner the Austrians
t is argued, the more willing the other Powers would have been
to acquiesce, while the impression of the Sarajevo murder remained fresh
in their memory.[1] The Germans in July may have thought in terms of a
blitzkrieg (to borrow the word used by the victorious armies in September
1939), but nothing to this effect was set down in German or Austrian
documents. Rather, the argument first crops up after the War in attempts
to justify Germany's role in 1914.[2] Closer analysis of the document reveals that it was purely speculative, or at best naive, to suppose that the
Entente Powers would have allowed themselves to be influenced by sentiments (such as disgust), rather than by political interests. Indeed their
political interests would have looked no different in the event of a surprise
attack on Serbia immediately after the assassination or after the consultations in Potsdam and Berlin than they did after three weeks of a deceptive
calm and a further week of agitation over the ultimatum to Belgrade.

Moreover, only once in the documents does there appear to be any
motivation for the German pressure on Vienna for haste and even here
there was no talk of preserving world peace, but only of the fear that the
Austrians might, by their delay, give the Serbian Government time and
occasion 'to make an offer of satisfaction on its own account, perhaps
acting under Russo-French pressure' (33). In other words, the Austrians
might, by dallying too long over the time-consuming preliminaries, let
slip their chance for the war against Serbia which Germany desired. The
greatest fear of the German Government was not, then, that the Austrians
might proceed too ruthlessly against Serbia, but the exact opposite, that
they might not prove ruthless enough for a war and might show weakness
in the event and content themselves with less than a complete subjection
of Serbia by force.

Simultaneously with pressing Vienna for speed and consistency, the

[1] More recently in Michael Freund, 'Bethmann Hollweg, der Hitler des Jahres 1914? Zu
einer Spätfrucht des Jahres 1914 in der Geschichtsschreibung' in *FAZ*, 28/29 March 1964,
reprinted in *Deutsche Kriegsziele 1914–1918*, p. 177.

[2] Only recently has K.-D. Erdmann brought to light a single passage in Riezler's diary which
indicates the contemporary nature of the argument without, however, rendering the behaviour
of the German Administration in July 1914 any more intelligible from an objective viewpoint.
See K.-D. Erdmann, *GWU* 9, 1964, p. 536. See also once more G. Ritter, *Eine neue Kriegsschuldthese?* Here it is stated that the motive for the haste in Berlin was 'not the burning zeal for war
of some militarists or other but the quite justified fear of belated and half-hearted action by the
Austrians who left their opponents time for diplomatic and military counter measures and thus
spoilt the political and moral impact of the assassination and equally the practical success of
any undertaking against Serbia.' (*Deutsche Kriegsziele*, p. 135).

Auswärtiges Amt also began to make careful preparations for a localisation of the conflict. As early as 7 July it drafted instructions to Prince Lichnowsky, the German Ambassador in London. In these instructions (which were only despatched on 12 July) the Auswärtiges Amt formulated the German policy of localisation with absolute clarity: 'We should desire under all circumstances a localisation of the conflict. For this purpose it is necessary that public opinion throughout Europe should make it possible for the various Governments to look on while Austria and Serbia decide their difference, without taking sides. . . . Kindly try to influence the local press according to this suggestion as far as is feasible, being careful, however, to avoid everything that might give the appearance that we are inciting the Austrians to war.'[1] The last part of this diplomatic mission was particularly delicate for, as has been shown, the main substance of German policy during the July crisis consisted, specifically, in 'inciting' the Austrians to war against Serbia. Similar instructions were sent to both Bucharest and Sofia, so as to ensure the accession of Roumania and Bulgaria to the Triple Alliance,[2] and also to Rome, that the Italian press might be prejudiced against Serbia and the way thereby paved for a favourable attitude from the Italian Government towards Germany and Austria-Hungary.[3]

As the date for delivery of the ultimatum drew nearer, the Germans increased their efforts to achieve localisation. Their aims and motives, even their plan of action, had all been worked out in general and in particular by 18 July at the latest and formulated in impressive turns of phrase: Berlin welcomed vigorous measures on the part of her ally 'since it is held that this would enhance the prestige of Austria-Hungary abroad, especially within the Balkan States, and resolute action would be a suitable means of retarding, for some time at least, the inner decomposition of the Monarchy' (28). The German Government was anxious to 'lay stress upon the fact that it is a matter of interest for all the monarchical Governments that "the Belgrade nest of anarchists" be once and for all rooted out' (33).

Finally, 'Austria, which has forfeited more and more prestige as the result of her lack of vigour, hardly counts any longer as a really Great Power. . . . Nor have we at the present time forced Austria to take her decision. But we neither could nor should attempt to stay her hand. If we should do that, Austria would have the right to reproach us (and we ourselves) with having deprived her of her last chance of political rehabilitation. And then the process of her wasting away and her internal decay would be still further accelerated. . . . If we cannot attain localisation

[1] *D.D.* 36.   [2] *D.D.* 16; *D.D.* 17.   [3] *D.D.* 33; *D.D.* 44.

(of the conflict) and Russia attacks Austria, a *casus foederis* will then arise; we could not throw Austria over then. . . . I desire no preventive war, but if war should come, we cannot hide behind the fence' (30). After Sarajevo war was plainly the order of the day for the German Government and the Reich did not in fact 'hide behind the fence' but fought it out—right on to the bitter end.

At the same time, the first administrative preparations for the Great War began to gather momentum in a number of Berlin offices. In his discussion with Bethmann Hollweg on 9 July Delbrück, the Secretary of State for the Interior, had already drawn the correct conclusion from the Chancellor's exposition of the foreign situation: 'That is war.' Although Delbrück was allegedly acting on his own initiative, he used his 'leisure time in the following days once more to think out in detail the individual problems in connection with mobilisation which would come within my province, and cautiously to discuss some of these with the permanent Heads of Department.' He again arrived at 'the conclusion that we were "ready for the fight".'[1] Delbrück could now resume his holiday as 'all drafts of bills relating to mobilisation' had long since 'lain ready' and 'all other measures in connection with this had also been prepared down to the smallest detail'. It only remained for the final signal to be given for despatches to 'fly to all corners of the German Fatherland'.[2] On 19 July, in a letter drafted on 17 July and completed on 18 July, the Ministry of the Interior urged the War Ministry to join forces in making a fresh scrutiny of all ordinances and decrees against the eventuality of mobilisation.[3]

While the political designs of Berlin and Vienna were taking their final shape and preparations were being made for action, the Entente Powers were left to make their own conjectures. On the whole their Ambassadors in Vienna were willing to accept the assurances of the Ballhausplatz that Austria's designs were innocuous.[4] It was not until 16 July that Bunsen, the British Ambassador, was able to pass on, from a private source, indications of the Austrian Government's true intentions.[5] Grey, the British Foreign Minister, was more disturbed than Benckendorff, the optimistic Russian Ambassador in London. Lichnowsky, who had been in Berlin as recently as 5 July, and had been able to some extent to brief himself on events there, sought out Grey immediately on his return to London on 6 July. Without authority from his Government

---

[1] C. v. Delbrück, *Mobilmachung*, pp. 96f.   [2] *Ibid.*, p. 107.
[3] *D.Z.A.*, Potsdam, R.A.d. J., no. 1244.
[4] Thus Bunsen to Grey with characteristic marginalia by the Foreign Office on 9 July; *B.D.* 40.   [5] *B.D.* 50, 56.

(indeed in contradiction of its intentions), but spurred on by his concern for the maintenance of peace, Lichnowsky had given the first hint of Austrian aims. Grey had at once interposed anxiously that the Austrians 'surely did not think of appropriating any territory?'[1] In a further conversation on 9 July Grey took care to make it clear that any Austrian measures against Serbia would have to be kept within bounds if they were to meet with approval in London (14). A week later he repeated and clarified his premonitory warning by intimating that 'everything would depend on the kind of intervention that might ensue; in no case ought a diminution of Serbian territory be considered.'[2] On the other hand, like Paul Cambon, the French Ambassador in London, he spontaneously declared himself in favour of exercising restraint on St Petersburg, should the need arise.[3] This for the time being exhausted the resources of French diplomacy.

Austria and Germany deliberately left Italy in the dark, for fear that Rome would prematurely 'betray' and thus sabotage the action envisaged. In spite of this, however, the Italian Government gained some idea of Austria's intentions and on 16 July sent a discreet warning to the Russian Foreign Ministry through Carlotti, its Ambassador at St Petersburg, couched in the question: 'How would Russia react to an Austrian move if the latter decided to act against Serbia?' On 18 July an enraged Sazonov summoned Count Szápáry, the Austro-Hungarian Ambassador, to the Foreign Ministry and affirmed Russia's determination 'in no circumstances to agree to any blow to Serbia's independence'. Szápáry, who had perhaps not even yet received precise instructions, denied any such intention, with the result that the Russian Foreign Minister calmed down again: 'Il a été doux comme un agneau', Sazonov noted after the conversation (34).

The Great Powers, then, were still by no means seriously disquieted. Thus on 15 July Poincaré, the French President, and Viviani, his Prime Minister and Foreign Minister, set out on their pre-arranged journey to St Petersburg with the intention of making state visits to the Scandinavian countries on their return.

---

[1] Grey to Rumbold, 6 July; *B.D.* 32. Lichnowsky's substantially identical version in *D.D.* 20.
[2] Lichnowsky to Jagow, 15, 7; *D.D.* 52.
[3] Grey to Bertie, 8 July; *B.D.* 38.

11 Berchtold to Tisza

Private letter
Ö.D. 10145   Vienna, 8 July 1914

Tschirschky has just left me, who told me that he had received a telegram from Berlin, by which his Imperial master instructs him to declare emphatically that in Berlin an action of the Monarchy against Serbia is fully expected and that Germany would not understand why we should neglect this opportunity of dealing a blow.[1] My remark that in taking a decisive resolution we should consider it of the greatest importance to know how far we could rely upon Germany's influence being used in Roumania, and what result we might hope for, was answered by the ambassador to the effect that Berlin thinks it is altogether out of question that Roumania would in this case act against the monarchy. Kaiser Wilhelm has already addressed a letter on the subject to King Carol and we might be very sure that it left nothing to be desired in plainness of speech! The ambassador's further remarks showed me that Germany would consider further negotiating with Serbia a confession of weakness on our part, and this would damage our position in the Triple Alliance and might influence Germany's future policy.[2] Tschirschky's remarks impressed me so much that I thought they might in some degree influence your ultimate decisions, and for this reason I am informing you without delay and begging you, if you are of the same mind, to telegram to me (in cypher) while I am at Ischl, where I stay all tomorrow and shall be glad to be your interpreter with His Majesty.

12 Tschirschky to Jagow

Telegram 84   Vienna, 8 July 1914
Confidential   D. 8.10 p.m.
D.D. 19   R. 10.40 p.m.

After the conclusion of the official Ministerial Council yesterday,[3] a conference concerning the attitude to be adopted toward Serbia was held in connection with it, at which a general idea of the reply received from

---

[1] No telegram of this description can be traced. With regard to Tschirschky's visit at 3.30 p.m. on 8 July, Berchtold noted in his diary: 'Most emphatic that Berlin expects action against Serbia.' See Hugo Hantsch, *Berchtold*, II. p. 570.
[2] See also **9, 18, 28, 30, 31** and **33**.   [3] See **9**.

His Majesty our Most Gracious Master was given to the Ministers who had not been present at the preliminary conference[1] which I had attended.

Two currents of opinion made themselves evident in relation to the proceedings against Serbia. One, that represented by Count Berchtold and the Ministry of Foreign Affairs, would make direct use, as the occasion of any action, of the Serbian policy in general and of the state of affairs created by the intrigues against the Monarchy which came to a culmination in the recent assassination; whereas the other, represented by Count Tisza, holds it to be advisable first to put concrete demands up to Serbia. I have the impression that Count Berchtold regards Count Tisza as an element of encumbrance. The latter wishes to set down his point of view in a memorandum which Count Berchtold will not receive before this evening shortly before he starts on his journey to Ischl. Count Berchtold stated that he would advise his Emperor, in case the latter should adopt this point of view, at least to make demands of such a nature that the possibility of their acceptance would be precluded.[2]

Count Berchtold also said quite *confidentially* that according to Baron Conrad von Hötzendorf, mobilisation could not be completed until after sixteen days. The Chief of the General Staff, so Count Berchtold tells me, has called attention to the decisive significance of Roumania's attitude in connection with the arrangement and progress of military operations.

The Minister further remarked that after thorough consideration he had come to the conclusion that it would be wiser not to enter upon the prospective alliance with Bulgaria at once, particularly as in such an event Roumania might be disturbed. On the contrary, he was going to advise Sofia most urgently to maintain an attitude of peace and quiet.

13 Macchio[3] to Tisza

Unnumbered telegram[4]
Budapest

Vienna, 9 July 1914
D. 5.53 p.m.

Count Berchtold requested me to communicate the following to Your Excellency:

[1] See 6.   [2] See 16, 17, 31 and 33.
[3] Head of Department (Under-Secretary of State) in the Imp. and Royal Foreign Ministry.
[4] Handwritten copy of the telegram. This document, found amongst the Burián private papers, was placed at my disposal by the kindness of Dr Peter Hánák, of the Hungarian Academy of Sciences, whom I should like to take this opportunity of thanking. Dr Hánák first quoted it in a paper he gave at a symposium on Sarajevo and its immediate consequences, held in the Belvedere, Vienna, June 1964.

'His Imp. & Roy. Apostolic Majesty has decided with regard to my report[1] that the attempt should be made to settle the small contradictions which are still apparent in my interpretation and that of C[oun]t Tisza.

His Majesty agrees with my opinion that a peaceful solution of the crisis would be worthless without positive guarantees that the Pan-Serbian movement will in fact be suppressed on the initiative of Belgrade.

His Majesty also shares my view that diplomatic exchanges should not precede an ultimatum. However, His Majesty, like C[oun]t Tisza, does not preclude the possibility of a peaceful settlement with Serbia if the aforementioned conditions are hereby fulfilled.'

News from Uskub today announces Serbian troop movements in the direction of Lovnica.

14   Lichnowsky to Bethmann Hollweg

Confidential   London, 9 July 1914
D.D. 30   R. 11 July, morning

Sir E. Grey asked me to call on him today and first of all communicated to me the memorandum which he made concerning our conference which took place shortly before my visit to Berlin and Kiel.[2] He said that he could add nothing today to the words he had uttered at that time, and could only repeat to me that secret agreements between Great Britain on the one hand and France and Russia on the other, which would entail obligations on Great Britain in case of a European war, did not exist. England wished to preserve an absolutely free hand, in order to be able to act according to her own judgment in the event of continental complications. The Government had to a certain extent obligated itself to Parliament not to commit itself to any secret liabilities. In no case would the British Government be found on the side of the aggressors in the event of continental complications.

But as he did not wish to put me on the wrong track—'as I did not want to mislead you'—he at once added that his relations to the Powers referred to had none the less lost nothing of their earlier intimacy. So that even if there existed no agreements which imposed any obligations,

---

[1] Of 7 July, in which Berchtold reports on the outcome of the Council of Ministers (9) on the same day; *Ö.D.* 10116.

[2] On 24 June; see *D.D.* 5.

he did not wish to deny that from time to time 'conversations' had taken place between the naval or the military authorities on both sides, the first of them as early as the year 1906, then again during the Morocco crisis, when they had believed here, he added, smiling, that we had intended to attack the French. But even these conversations, about which he knew in most cases nothing definite, had absolutely no aggressive intent, as English policy, now as before, was aimed toward the maintenance of peace, and would find itself in a very painful situation if a European war should break out.

I repeated to the Minister about the same sort of thing that I had recently told him, and gave him to understand that it would be desirable if such military conversations could be reduced to a minimum, as otherwise they might easily lead to serious consequences.

Since our previous conversation, added Sir Edward, he had informed himself thoroughly about the feeling toward us that existed in Russia, and had found no reason for a disquieting view of it; he also seemed quite ready, if we should so desire, to use his influence in any way on the attitude of Russia. He had also already been endeavouring, in case the Vienna Cabinet should find itself compelled as a result of the murder at Sarajevo to adopt a sterner attitude toward Serbia, to persuade the Russian Government to adopt a more peaceful view and to assume a more conciliatory attitude toward Austria. Very much would depend, as a matter of fact, Sir Edward thought, on the kind of measures that were under consideration, and on whether they might not arouse Slavic sentiment in such a fashion as to make it impossible for Mr Sazonov to remain passive under them.

In general, the Minister was in a thoroughly confident mood, and declared in cheerful tones that he saw no reason for taking a pessimistic view of the situation.

15 Chargé d'Affaires Schoen to Hertling

Report 373
Bayr. Dok. 8

Berlin, 9 July 1914

Yesterday in the early evening I went to see the Under-Secretary of State of the Auswärtiges Amt in order to introduce myself to him as the Chargé d'Affaires. . . .

The Auswärtiges Amt has been informed that the ministerial conferences which have taken place in Vienna in the last few days were solely concerned with internal matters relating to Bosnia and Herzegovina. The question as to whether and in what manner Austria might be disposed to act against Serbia if the inquiry into the assassination should reveal that official circles there were compromised was not touched upon in these discussions[1] and still awaits solution. Under-Secretary of State Zimmermann would consider the present moment as very favourable to Austria for undertaking what he termed a 'punitive expedition' against her southern neighbours and firmly believes that the war can be localised. However, he doubts that Vienna will decide to do this.[2]

If the Vienna Government were to make any inquiries in this matter, Berlin would do nothing to dissuade it from taking full measures against Serbia, but would rather intimate that, come what might, Austria would find her ally at her side. On the other hand, Berlin will carefully refrain from making any advance to Austria in this respect. The Auswärtiges Amt has emphasised to the representatives of the other Powers that it regards the situation without any trace of nervousness, and as evidence of this has pointed out that H.M. the Kaiser would otherwise not have left for his Scandinavian journey, that the Imperial Chancellor would not then have gone to Hohenfinow, and the Chief of the General Staff would not have gone on leave[3]. . . .

16   Tschirschky to Jagow

Telegram 85   Vienna, 10 July 1914
Absolutely confidential   D. 8.30 p.m.
D.D. 29   R. 10.32 p.m.

Count Berchtold gives me the following information concerning his yesterday's conference with His Majesty the Emperor Franz Joseph at Ischl:

His Majesty the Emperor discussed the state of

As His Majesty's affairs with great calmness. He first gave expression
memorandum is two of his warm gratitude for the attitude of our Most
weeks old, it is
taking a long time! Gracious Master and of the Imperial Government,[4] and stated that he was quite of our opinion that it was

---

[1] Contrast with 9 and 12. Tschirschky's telegram of 8 July only arrived late in the evening of the same day; see 12.

[2] See 28 and 33.   [3] See also 33.   [4] See 6, 8.

necessary *now* to come to some *determination,* in order to put an end to the intolerable conditions in connection with Serbia. His Majesty was quite clear as to the importance of such a determination, added Count Berchtold.

Of course, that was drafted as a foundation for the determination itself!

The Minister then informed the Emperor of the two methods under discussion here as to the approaching action against Serbia. His Majesty seemed to think that the difference between them might be bridged over. On the whole, however, His Majesty had shown himself more inclined to the view that *concrete demands should be levelled at Serbia.* Nor could he, the Minister,

Very much so! And unambiguous ones!

deny the advantages of such procedure. The odium of an unexpected attack on Serbia, which would otherwise fall upon the Monarchy, would thus be avoided and Serbia would be put in the wrong. This procedure would also make an attitude of neutrality at least, materially easier both for Roumania and for England.

They have had time enough for that.

At present the formulation of appropriate demands on Serbia constituted the principal source of anxiety here, and Count Berchtold said that he would be glad to know what they thought about it in Berlin.[1] He thought that among other things, it might be demanded that an agency of the Austro-Hungarian Government be established at Belgrade in order to keep an eye from there on the Greater Serbia machinations, perhaps, also, to insist upon the dissolution of the associations and the

All!

dismissal of *some compromised officers.*[2] The respite allowed for the reply must be made as brief as possible, say forty-eight hours. It is true, that even so short a respite would suffice to enable Belgrade to get advice

Hartwig is dead!

from St Petersburg. If the Serbs should accept all the demands made on them, it would prove a solution which would be 'very disagreeable' to him, and he was still considering what *demands* could *be put* that would be *wholly impossible for the Serbs to accept.*

Evacuate the Sanjac! Then the row would be on at once! Austria must absolutely get that back at once, in order to prevent the union of Serbia and Montenegro and the

Finally, the Minister complained again about the attitude of Count Tisza, which made energetic pro-

---

[1] Jagow's reply on this point on 11 July: 'We are unable to commit ourselves with respect to the formulation of the demands on Serbia, since this is Austria's concern' (*D.D.* 31).

[2] See **37**.

gaining of the
seacoast by the
Serbians! To act
like 'gentlemen' to
murderers, after
what has happened!
Idiocy!

cedure against Serbia difficult for him. Count Tisza
asserted that they must proceed 'like gentlemen,' but
that was scarcely possible to accomplish when such
important national interests were concerned and
especially against such an opponent as Serbia.

The Minister would be glad to follow the suggestion
of the Imperial Government about commencing even
now to set public opinion in England against Serbia
by means of the press—about which Count Szögyény
had telegraphed. But this must be done cautiously, in
his opinion, in order not to alarm Serbia prematurely.

The Minister of War is *going on his leave* tomorrow,
and Baron Conrad von Hötzendorf is also going to
leave Vienna for a time. This is being done, so Count

Childish!

Berchtold told me, *on purpose*, in order to *prevent any
disquiet.*

About as it was at the time of the Silesian War!

'I am against all councils of war and conferences, since the more timid party always has
the upper hand.'   Frederick the Great.

17   Tschirschky to Jagow

Private letter   Vienna, 11 July 1914
Absolutely confidential   R. 12 July
D.D. 34a

I took the opportunity again today to discuss the proceedings against
Serbia with Count Berchtold,[1] principally to impress upon the Minister
once more, emphatically, that quick action was called for.

The Minister expressed himself upon the matter as follows:

In order finally to obtain exact information as to what the investigation
at Sarajevo had so far brought to light, a confidential agent had been sent
from here to Sarajevo, whom he expected back Tuesday or Wednesday.[2]
Count Tisza had also been summoned to Vienna for Tuesday.[3] A closer
agreement had been arrived at since yesterday with the president of the
Hungarian Council concerning the note to be directed to Serbia, and he
hoped by Tuesday to be able to determine on the final version of this

[1] See 10.
[2] Sectional Adviser Wiesner. His report of 13 July, 19.
[3] I.e. on 14 July, *cf.* 20–22.

document. So far as he could say today, the principal demands on Serbia would consist of the requirement that the King should officially and publicly proclaim, in a formal declaration and through an order to the army, that Serbia discarded her Greater Serbia policy; secondly, the institution of an agency of the Austro-Hungarian Government to see to the strict keeping of this promise, would be required. The term granted for the answering of the note would be made as short as possible, say, perhaps, forty-eight hours.[1] If the reply is not regarded here as satisfactory, mobilisation will take place at once.

The question was now, at what time would it be best to deliver the note. He believed that it would not be advisable to deliver the note at the time when Mr Poincaré was in St Petersburg, and thus give the French and the Russians the opportunity of discussing their attitude together in St Petersburg.[2] The note should be delivered at Belgrade, if possible, before the departure of Mr Poincaré from Paris or after his departure from St Petersburg. Sometime, therefore, about 18, or on 24 July. The latter date might perhaps be preferable on account of the fact that at that time the harvest work in the Monarchy would be finished, lightening the difficulties of mobilisation and preventing great losses from an economic point of view.

With reference to the treatment of the foreign press, Count Berchtold told me, upon my asking him, that he had already entered upon concerted action with Berlin in the matter of exercising a united influence on the English press. He would now turn his attention toward the Roumanian and Italian press and see what could be done with money in Bucharest. The Minister is disturbed over the recent energetic efforts of the Russian Government to draw the Poles into a closer relation. These efforts would appear not to have been wholly unsuccessful, to judge by the attitude of some of the Polish papers.

I may conclude by saying that the Minister and Count Forgách, who was present at this conference, begged me *not* to telegraph in regard to the preceding and very confidential information, but to mention it only in private letters, in order that absolute secrecy may be assured. I got the impression that the gentlemen feared a leak *here in Austria* if I should telegraph in cipher.

Telegram 117 has this moment arrived.[3] I will inform the Minister of it at once.

---

[1] See **16** and **33**; also the ultimatum **37**. The first of the conditions named corresponds to the main clause of the ultimatum.

[2] See **20, 27** and **33**.

[3] See p. 107, note 1.

18   Szögyény to Berchtold

Report 60   Berlin, 12 July 1914
Ö.D. 10215   R. 13 July

My telegraphic reports during the last days and Count Hoyos' personal
impressions have informed your Excellency that not only His Majesty
Kaiser Wilhelm but all the other persons in authority, not only adhere
firmly to the allied Monarchy, but are encouraging us emphatically not
to neglect the present moment,[1] but to treat Serbia with full energy, so
as to clear out the conspirators' nest once for all, and are leaving the
choice of means for doing so to our judgment.[2] I never for a moment
doubted that Kaiser Wilhelm and all the German Empire would loyally
fulfil the duties of an ally, and I have been faithful to this conviction during
the whole period of my ambassadorship in Berlin. I was not in the least
surprised when in the present moment Germany assured us of its perfect
loyalty and assistance.

Still I think that the fact, that His Majesty Kaiser Wilhelm and with
him all persons in authority, urge us to undertake an action against Serbia,
which may eventually end in war, needs some explanation. It is clear that
after the late deplorable events, the monarchy must use all energy in its
dealings with Serbia, but the fact that the German Government from its
own point of view, considers the present moment politically opportune,
must be set in the right light. According to the German way of thinking,
entirely shared by myself, general political considerations, and special
ones, inspired by the murder of Sarajevo, form the conclusive argument.
Germany has recently found its conviction confirmed that Russia is
preparing for a war with its western neighbours, and does not regard war
as a possibility of the future, but positively includes it in the political
calculations of the future. This is important: it intends waging war, it is
preparing for it with all its might, but does not propose it for the present,
or we should rather say, is not prepared for it at the present time. It is
therefore anything but certain that if Serbia is engaged in a war with us,
Russia would lend an armed hand; and should the Czar's empire resolve
for war, it would not be ready from a military point of view, and not by any
means so strong, as it will be a few years hence.[3]

Moreover the German Government believes that it has proofs that
England would not take part in a war, caused by disturbances in the
Balkans, even if Russia and France were involved in it. Not only have the
relations between England and Germany improved so far, that Germany

---

[1] See 6, 8, 11, 15, 16 and 33.   [2] See p. 107, note 1.   [3] See also 30.

need no longer fear direct hostilities on England's part, but England just now desires anything rather than a war, and would certainly not expose itself to danger for Serbia's or even Russia's sake. When all is said, it must be admitted that the constellation is at present as favourable as it can be. In the past, a large portion of our population refused to believe in the separatist tendencies of our Serbians, hostile to the Monarchy and expressed doubts that Serbia's intrigues reached across the frontier; all are now convinced and there is a general outcry for an energetic treatment of Serbia, which will finally suppress all agitation for a Greater Serbia. In a similar manner the eyes of the whole world have been opened and there is no nation that does not condemn the bloody deed of Sarajevo and all admit that we must make Serbia responsible for it. If Serbia's foreign friends for political reasons do not openly blame Serbia, still we cannot believe that they will stand up for it at the present moment, at least not with armed forces. These I believe to be the political reasons why the German Empire with a clear perception of the opportunity offered, unreservedly encourages us to make clear our relations towards Serbia, which Germany also feels to be untenable, in such a manner, as to stop pan-slavist agitation for all time. In Kaiser Wilhelm's case these political grounds are, as I learn from a quarter, very much in His Majesty's confidence, enhanced by a purely personal circumstance, the infinite enthusiasm for our gracious Majesty, who as his letter to Kaiser Wilhelm proves is prepared to act with admirable energy, where the vital interests and the *prestige* of the countries, entrusted to his care, are at stake.

19 Wiesner[1] to Berchtold

Telegram (unnumbered)
Ö.D. 10252/53

Sarajevo, 13 July 1914
D. 1.10 p.m.; 2.00 p.m.
R. 5.00 p.m.; 5.40 p.m.

It is the firm belief of all persons in authority here, that Serbia is busily spreading propaganda for Greater Serbia—not to speak of the press—through societies and other organisations, and that everything is done with the knowledge and sanction of the Serbian Government.

Civil and military authorities have given me the material upon which they base their belief; it may be classified as follows. The material of the time before the assassination contains no proofs that the Serbian Govern-

[1] Sectional Adviser in the Imp. and Royal Foreign Ministry (17).

ment promoted propaganda. There is not much, but sufficient material to prove that the movement originates in Serbia and is tolerated by the Government.

Judicial inquiry on assassination.

There is nothing to prove or even to suppose that the Serbian Government is accessory to the inducement for the crime, its preparation or the furnishing of weapons. On the contrary, there are reasons to believe that this is altogether out of question.

From evidence of accused persons, ascertained almost indubitably that the crime was resolved upon in Belgrade and that preparations were made with the cooperation of Serbian state-officials Ciganović and Major Tankosić, who jointly provided bombs, Brownings, ammunition and prussic acid. Guilt of Pribicevic not ascertained; reports about him based on regrettable misunderstandings on part of examining police organs.

There can be no doubt that bombs came from army stores in Kragujevac, but there is no proof that they were obtained for the crime, as they might have been in the hands of the Komitadschis since the war.

Evidence of accused persons leaves scarcely a doubt that Princip, Čabrinović, Grabez, with bombs and weapons upon them, were secretly smuggled across the frontier to Bosnia by Serbian organs, under the direction of Ciganović. These organised transports were directed by the frontier-captains at Schabatz and Loznica and were contrived by frontier guards. Though it is not ascertained that they knew the purpose of the journey, still they must have realised secrecy of mission.

Other information gives insight into organisation of propaganda carried on by 'Narodna odbrana'. This is valuable material, which will be useful, but has not yet been sifted; will be delivered without loss of time.

If the demands put forth at the time I left, are still valid, the following might be added to what is demanded of Serbia:

A) Suppression of Government organs' cooperation in smuggling persons and goods across frontier.

B) Dismissal of Serbian frontier-captains at Schabatz and Loznica and the implicated frontier-guards.

C) Prosecution of Ciganović and Tankosić.[1]

I leave for Vienna this evening, arrive on Tuesday evening and go direct to the Foreign Ministry.

Verbal explanation necessary.

[1] See 37, points 7 and 8.

20 Berchtold to Franz Joseph

Ö.D. 10272   Vienna, 14 J

In today's conference, in which both premiers and the Hungarian minister at the court of Vienna took part, a perfect agreement was established
with regard to the demands to be addressed to Serbia. The text of the note
is at present being settled and will be submitted for approval in a conference of the Governments on Sunday, 19 inst.[1] When the text of the
note has been agreed upon, it will be presented in Belgrade on Saturday,
25 inst.,[2] and the Serbian Government will at the same time be informed
that the term for the answer to the note has been fixed at forty-eight
hours, within which space of time our demands must be conceded.

The date was selected out of consideration for the visit of the President
of the French Republic to the Czar, which is to last from 20 to 25 July.
All those present were of the same mind as myself, that if we sent the
ultimatum during the meeting in St Petersburg, this might be regarded as
an affront. Overmore, if the ambitious President of the Republic was to
discuss personally the new situation created by the ultimatum with the
Czar, there is more probability than otherwise, that France and Russia
may interfere.[3]

Count Tisza has given up his objections to an ultimatum with so short a
term, because I showed him the military difficulties, which would arise
from delayed action. I also argued that even after the mobilisation a
peaceful arrangement might be possible if Serbia gives way in good time.

Of course, if this happened, we should have to make Serbia pay the
costs of the mobilisation, and until payment is made we should have to
ask for a pledge in Serbia.

Count Tisza most decidedly declared that he would give his consent
to the intended action, if before the ultimatum is sent, a Council of the
Ministers of Austria and Hungary votes the resolution that the Monarchy
is not striving to acquire territory by the war, except what might accrue
from small regulations of the frontier lines.

The text of the note to be sent to Belgrade, as it was settled today, is
such that we must reckon with the probability of war. Should Serbia decide
upon conceding our demands, this incident would signify not only a downright humiliation for the kingdom, but *pari passu* a blow to Russian *prestige*
in the Balkans and it would no doubt procure for us certain guarantees
that Serbian intrigue and underground work on our territory will be
restrained.

[1] See 35.   [2] On 17 July the date was put forward to 23 July; see 27.
[3] See 17, 21 and 22; in fact the French state visit ended two days earlier, on 23 July.

21   Tschirschky to Bethmann Hollweg

Report 233   Vienna, 14 July 1914
Absolutely confidential   R. 15 July, afternoon
D.D. 49

Absolutely.

Count Tisza came to see me today after his conference with Count Berchtold.[1] The Count said that he had always been the one who had advised caution, but that every day had strengthened him in the conviction more and more *that the Monarchy would have to come to an energetic decision* in order to prove its vitality and *to put an end to the intolerable conditions in the south-east.* The tone of the Serbian press and of the Serbian diplomats was so *presumptuous as simply not to be borne.* 'It was very hard for me to come to the decision,' said the Minister, 'to give my advice for war, but I am now firmly *convinced of its necessity, and I* shall stand up for the greatness of the Monarchy to the utmost of my ability.'

Fortunately *full agreement and determination* prevail among the authorities here. His Majesty Franz Joseph judges very calmly of the situation, as Baron Burián, too, who has talked with His Majesty at Ischl during the last day or two, reports, and will certainly hold out to the bitter end. Count Tisza added that *Germany's* unconditional assumption of a stand *by the side of the Monarchy* had a great influence on the firm attitude of the Emperor.

Too bad.

The note to be forwarded to Serbia had not yet been completed today in its final wording. This will not be done before Sunday.[2] With regard to the time of its delivery to Serbia, it was decided today that it would be better to wait until Poincaré's departure from St Petersburg, that is until the twenty-fifth.[3] Then, however, immediately upon the expiration of the respite granted Serbia, in case the latter should not submit to all the demands, *mobilisation* would follow. The note is being composed so that the possibility of its acceptance is *practically excluded.* It was considered par-

[1] See 20.   [2] See 35.   [3] See p. 113, n. 2 and 3.

ticularly important that it should demand not only assurances and promises, *but deeds*. In the composition of the note it was necessary, according to his view, to take care that it should be intelligible to the great general public—particularly in England—and that it should put Serbia plainly and clearly in the wrong.

Baron *Conrad* had made a *very good impression* on him at the last conference. He had spoken with great decision and calmness. Within the next few days they must, it was true, be prepared to have the people begin complaining again that *indecision and delay held sway here*. But that mattered little, if they only knew in Berlin that such was not the case.

Well, a real man at last!

In conclusion Count Tisza pressed my hand warmly, and said: 'Together we shall now look the future calmly and firmly in the face.'

22   Tschirschky to Bethmann Hollweg

Report 234
Absolutely confidential
D.D. 50

Vienna, 14 July 1914
R. 15 July, afternoon

After Count Tisza had left me, Count Berchtold requested me to come and see him, so that he might inform me for his part of the results of today's conference.[1] To his great pleasure, a *general agreement* on the *tenor* of the note to be transmitted *to Serbia* had been arrived at. Count Tisza had agreed to his, the Minister's, views in a very pleasing way, and had even introduced a sharper tone at various places. However, the impossibility of delivering the note at Belgrade by the sixteenth or eighteenth had been demonstrated on technical grounds. The French text was to be gone over once again definitively at a ministerial conference next Sunday morning at nine o'clock.[2] Then he would presumably submit the note to the Emperor at Ischl Tuesday. He *would guarantee* that His Majesty *would give his approval to it.*

[1] See **20** and **21**.   [2] See **35**.

What a pity!

At today's conference it was unanimously agreed that it would be advisable in any case to await the departure of Mr Poincaré from St Petersburg before taking the step at Belgrade. For it was best to avoid if possible the celebration of a fraternization at St Petersburg, under the influence of champagne and of Messrs Poincaré, Iswolski and the Grand Dukes, which might have an effect on the assumption and possible fixation of an attitude on the part of both nations.[1] It would be much better to have the toasts over with before the delivery of the note. Thus the delivery could follow on 25 July.

Count Berchtold requested me, as Count Tisza had also done, expressly and repeatedly, not to leave my Government in the slightest doubt that the presence of Poincaré at St Petersburg was the sole reason for the delay in the delivery of the note at Belgrade, and that they could feel absolutely assured in Berlin that there was *not a thought of hesitation or uncertainty in existence* here.[2]

The Minister finally told me that after the final rendering of the text on Sunday, he would immediately forward the note to the Imperial Government for its absolutely confidential information, even before submitting it to his own Emperor.

23 Berchtold to Szögyény

Telegram 234   Vienna, 15 July 1914
Strictly confidential   D. 10.30 p.m.
Ö.D. 10276

I have already explained to Herr von Tschirschky the reasons of the delay in our forthcoming explication with Serbia,[3] but I am anxious that your Excellency should inform strictly in private the Imperial Chancellor and the Secretary of State of the following: Although the judicial inquiry in Sarajevo has furnished us with sufficient material,[4] still we believe that we should delay the exceedingly energetic step in Belgrade, until the President of the French Republic, just now on the way to St Petersburg,

[1] See 17, 20, 21, 23, 28 and 33.   [2] See 21, 23, 28, 31 and 33.
[3] See 22.   [4] See 19.

shall have left Russian territory. To begin the action we are proposing at the very moment, when the President as the guest of the Czar is being made much of, might naturally be regarded in the light of an intended affront, and this we should like to avoid. Besides, we should consider it unwise to undertake the threatening step in Belgrade at the very time when the peaceloving, reserved Czar Nicolas and undeniably cautious Herr Sazonov, are under the influence of the two, who are always for war, Isvolsky and Poincaré.[1] Under these circumstances we do not think that we ought to realise the plans we have already discussed with Herr von Tschirschky. This delay, which is in itself unwelcome, will explain the attitude of our official press. We are obliged to prevent public opinion in the Monarchy,[2] which favours our policy, from cooling in its enthusiasm, and yet we cannot allow the press to get up too much steam, so that other powers might think of mediation.[3]

24   Szögyény to Berchtold

Telegram 259   Berlin, 16 July 1914
Strictly confidential   D. 2.20 p.m.
Ö.D. 10296   R. 5.50 p.m.

Received your Excellency's telegram 234 strictly confidential of yesterday.[4] State Secretary understands perfectly that the intended energetic step in Belgrade cannot be undertaken before the President of the French Republic has left St Petersburg, but regrets this delay extremely. Herr von Jagow fears that the sympathetic approval for this step and the interest in it will be debilitated by this delay not only in the Monarchy, but in Germany as well. Herr von Tschirschky reports that Count Tisza came to see him during his last stay in Vienna and assured him that he had given up the scruples, which he had certainly at first entertained and that he now considered an energetic action necessary;[5] besides Count Tisza had said as much in his declaration in the Hungarian parliament the day before, as Herr von Jagow had learnt to his satisfaction.

My Italian colleague since a few days ago declares the situation fills him with alarm, but he sees a favourable symptom in the fact that the Imp. and Roy. War Minister and Chief of the General Staff have taken their summer leave.[6]

[1] See 16, 17, 20–22 and 33.   [2] See also 24 and 27.   [3] For Szögyény's reply see 24.
[4] See 23.   [5] See 21 and 22.   [6] See 16.

25 Bethmann Hollweg to Roedern[1]

Private letter   Hohenfinow, 16 July 1914
D.D. 56   D. 16 July

You will already have seen, from your reading of the papers, that the European situation is not at present free from dangers. In the event of an Austro-Serbian conflict it will be of the utmost importance to localise this difference.[2] We have reason for doubting, and sincerely trust that France, burdened at the present time with all sorts of troubles, will do everything she can to prevent Russia from intervening. This task will be made materially easier for the present authorities at Paris if the French nationalists find no cause for agitation of which to make capital during the next few weeks; I have therefore arranged at Berlin that all press polemics with France shall be cut out as far as possible during the next few weeks, and I would ask you to do the same thing at Strasbourg. It would also be advisable to postpone for a few weeks any administrative measures which have possibly been arranged for, which might be made use of in France for purposes of agitation. If we are successful not only in keeping France quiet but in having St Petersburg admonished to keep the peace, it would have what would be for us a most favourable effect on the Franco-Russian alliance.[3]

26 Jagow to Tschirschky

Decree 917   Berlin, 17 July 1914
Confidential
D.D. 61

As Your Excellency knows from having read the memorandum of Count Hoyos on his conference with the Under-Secretary of State, Count Hoyos stated here that Austria would have to proceed to a complete partition of Serbia.[4]

Count Berchtold and Count Tisza remarked in this connection that this declaration represented only the personal view of Count Hoyos, and that they therefore expressly did *not* identify themselves with it; but they have not apparently disclosed any further their own views as to territorial plans.

[1] Secretary of State for Alsace-Lorraine.   [2] See 15, 18, 28, 30, 33, 36 and 39.
[3] For Roedern's reply of 24 July, see *D.D.* 232.   [4] See 10.

For the benefit of the diplomatic handling of this conflict with Serbia, it would not be unimportant to know from the beginning what the ideas of the Austro-Hungarian statesmen concerning the future status of Serbia really are, as this question will have a material influence on the attitude of Italy and on the public opinion and attitude of England.

That the plans of the statesmen of the Danube Monarchy may be influenced and modified by the course of events is, of course, to be looked upon as self-evident; nevertheless, we must assume that the Vienna Cabinet has in mind some sort of a picture of the aims to be sought, even in the matter of territorial acquisition. Will Your Excellency kindly endeavour to get some information on this question in your talks with Count Berchtold, however, avoiding giving any impression, that we are attempting to put any obstructions in the path of Austrian activities or that we are trying to prescribe certain limits or aims. But it would be useful to us to be informed to a certain extent about where the road is likely to lead us.

27 Stolberg[1] to Bethmann Hollweg

Report 239
Confidential
D.D. 65

Vienna, 17 July 1914
R. 18 July

As Count Berchtold told me, the note containing the demands to be made on Serbia is to be presented at Belgrade on Thursday, 23 inst., in the afternoon. With the hope of hastening the occurrence as much as possible, the date has been advanced by a few days, and the day of Mr Poincaré's departure from St Petersburg has been set for it. They are counting on the fact that the President will already be aboard ship when the *démarche* at Belgrade becomes known at St Petersburg.

The wording of the note, the Minister tells me, has not yet been definitely established, and conferences with Count Tisza are still taking place; on Wednesday, 22 inst., it is to be laid before His Majesty the Emperor Franz Joseph for his final sanction.

Count Berchtold appeared to hope that Serbia would not agree to the Austro-Hungarian demands, as a mere diplomatic victory would put the country here again into a stagnant mood[2] for which they would have absolutely no use.[3]

---

[1] Counsellor at the German Embassy in Vienna. [2] See 24. [3] See also 31.

28   Biedermann[1] to Vitzthum[2]

Report 1076   Berlin, 17 July 1914
confidential
Bach no. 4

I have the honour most respectfully to report the following from a discussion which the Under-Secretary of State for the Auswärtiges Amt
accorded me today:

The development of the international political situation depends entirely upon the way in which the relations between Austria-Hungary and
Serbia take shape, in other words upon the demands posed by the Danube
Monarchy in her long-awaited note and the reply which it received from
Belgrade. The Government in Vienna seems only with some difficulty to
be summoning up the requisite energy for a *démarche*[3] and has now
definitely postponed until 25 July the delivery of the Note, originally
planned for 15 July.[4] It remains to be seen what form the demands will
take, but the possibility cannot be discounted that for Serbia they will be
'difficult to swallow'.

Although no attempt is being made to 'incite' our ally from this end,
there is an equal determination to avoid in any way 'discouraging' him;
indeed energetic measures would be welcomed[5] since it is held that this
would enhance the prestige of Austria-Hungary abroad, especially with
the Balkan States, and resolute action would be a suitable means of
retarding, for some time at least, the inner decomposition of the Monarchy.
Germany can only expect support from a strong, internally united ally.
As the well-known pro-Slav sympathies of the murdered Archduke
continue for the present to exercise a beneficially unifying after-effect,
Austria can now well afford to show a firmer hand. Efforts are therefore
being made over here to ensure that the press, too, presents the idea of an
Austrian intervention as a kind of mandate from Europe to perform the
praiseworthy task of clearing up the nest of anarchists in Belgrade.

Italy's co-operation in those unsettled questions is not taken for granted
here; consequently discussions are being conducted in strict secrecy
between Berlin and Vienna alone. On the whole I have the impression
that Italy is not regarded here as an especially reliable partner. Recently,
moreover, she officially informed the Imperial Government that the
calling up of reservists born in 1891 was to be attributed solely to domestic
reasons.

[1] Saxon Chargé d'Affaires in Berlin.   [2] Saxon Minister for Foreign Affairs
[3] See 15 and 33.
[4] The news of the antedating of the ultimatum to 23 July only reached Berlin on 18 July;
see 27.   [5] See 6, 8, 11, 15, 17 and 18.

If, contrary to expectations, Austria-Hungary should be compelled to take measures against Serbia, officials here count upon a localisation of the conflict, as England is altogether peacefully disposed, and France and Russia seem to be equally free from any belligerent inclinations.[1] Senator Humbert's disclosures on the state of the French army are seen as having come at a most opportune moment for the interests of world peace. To sum up, the Auswärtiges Amt does not take a pessimistic view of the situation and it has therefore also been decided not to upset the holiday and travelling arrangements of those in authority; nonetheless everyone is prepared for eventualities. . . .

29 Jagow to Wedel

Telegram 82
Confidential, private
D.D. 67

Berlin, 18 July 1914
D. 5.05 p.m.

Request exact particulars of the route of H.M.S. *Hohenzollern* from 23 inst. on. On that day, as we know, the Austrian *démarche* at Belgrade is to occur[2]—a forty-eight hour ultimatum appears to be planned—and it would depend on the development of events whether or when His Majesty's presence here might prove desirable. Kindly take Admiral von Müller into your confidence, if called for, but do not cause His Majesty any premature uneasiness.

As we wish to localise prospective conflict between Austria and Serbia, we cannot afford to alarm the world by the premature return of His Majesty, but on the other hand His Majesty must be within reach in case unforeseen circumstances should make important decisions (mobilisation) necessary for us also. Perhaps cruising about in the Baltic for the last few days of trip might be considered.

[1] See **4, 15, 18** and **25.**
[2] See **27.**

30 Jagow to Lichnowsky
Private letter   Berlin, 18 July 1914

D.D. 72   D. 19 July

Your opinion on our policy as contained in your Serbian report[1] is always
appreciated by me, and I am sure that the Imperial Chancellor feels the
same way about it. Nor do I hesitate to admit that many of your remarks
are justified. But after all, we are allied to Austria; *hic Rhodus, hic salta.*
There may also be different opinions as to whether we get all our money's
worth from an alliance with that ever increasingly distintegrating composition of nations beside the Danube, but there I say with the poet—
Busch, I think it was—'If no longer you like your company, look for
another, if any there be.' And, unfortunately, we have not yet been able
to arrive at a relationship with England that promises complete satisfaction,
nor could we, after all that has passed, arrive at it, if, indeed, we shall ever
be able to do so.

Austria, which has forfeited more and more prestige as the result of her
lack of vigour, hardly counts any longer as a really Great Power.[2] The
Balkan crisis weakened her position still further. Our alliance federation
has also been weakened by this retrogression of Austria's position as a
Power.

Austria no longer intends to tolerate the sapping activities of the
Serbians, and just as little does she intend to tolerate longer the con-
tinuously provocative attitude of her small neighbour at Belgrade—see
the talk in the Serbian press—and that of Mr Pašić. She fully realizes
that she has neglected many opportunities, and that she is still able to act,
though in a few years she may no longer be able to do so. Austria is
now going to force a showdown with Serbia, and has told us so.
During the whole Balkan crisis we mediated successfully in the interest
of peace, without forcing Austria to passivity at any of the critical mo-
ments. The fact that notwithstanding that we have often, with injustice,
been accused of trimming and shuffling, makes no difference to me. Nor
have we at the present time forced Austria to her decision. But we neither
could nor should attempt to stay her hand. If we should do that, Austria
would have the right to reproach us (and we ourselves) with having
deprived her of her last chance of political rehabilitation. And then the
process of her wasting away and of her internal decay would be still
further accelerated. Her standing in the Balkans would be gone forever.
You will undoubtedly agree with me that the absolute establishment of

[1] Of 16 July; *D.D.* 62.   [2] See **3, 11, 28, 31** and **33**.

the Russian hegemony in the Balkans is, indirectly, not perr
for us. The maintenance of Austria, and, in fact, of the n
Austria possible, is a necessity for us both for internal
reasons. That she cannot be maintained forever, I will wi
But in the meantime we may perhaps be able to arrang
binations.

We must attempt to localise the conflict between Austria and Serbia.[1]
Whether we shall succeed in this will depend first on Russia, and secondly
on the moderating influence of Russia's allies. The more determined
Austria shows herself, the more energetically we support her, so much the
more quiet will Russia remain. To be sure, there will be some agitation in
St Petersburg, but, on the whole, Russia is not ready to strike at present.[2]
Nor will France or England be anxious for war at the present time.
According to all competent observation, Russia will be prepared to fight
in a few years. Then she will crush us by the number of her soldiers;
then she will have built her Baltic Sea fleet and her strategic railroads.
Our group, in the meantime, will have become weaker right along. In
Russia this is well known, and they are therefore determined to have
peace for a few years yet. I readily believe your cousin Benckendorff
when he says that Russia wants no war with us at present.[3] Sazonov
assures us of the same thing, but the Government of Russia, which is
still attached to peace and half-way friendly to Germany today, is constantly growing weaker, while the feeling of the Slavic element is becoming
more and more hostile to Germany. Russia's fundamental treatment of us
was clearly indicated last fall. During the Balkan crisis she could not thank
us enough for our peaceful influence. But no sooner had the crisis passed,
than her unfriendly behaviour recommenced—on account of Liman, etc.
If we can not attain localisation (of the conflict) and Russia attacks Austria,
a *casus foederis* will then arise; we could not throw Austria over then.
We stand in the midst of an isolation that can scarcely be called 'proud.'
I desire no preventive war, but if war should come, we cannot hide behind
the fence.

I still hope and believe, even today, that the conflict can be localised.
In this matter the attitude of England will prove of great significance. I
am fully convinced that local opinion in that country will not be enthusiastic over Austria's procedure, and I admit that all your arguments
in this line are correct. But we must do all that is possible to prevent her
becoming too enthusiastic in the Serbian cause, for it is a long road from

---

[1] See **15, 18, 25, 28** and **29**. [2] See **3, 6, 8** and **33**.
[3] Benckendorff, the Russian Ambassador to London had assured his cousin Lichnowsky that
Russia had no desire for war; *D.D.* 62, 85.

either sympathy or antipathy to the fanning of the flames of a world-conflagration. Sir E. Grey is always talking of the balance of power represented by the two groups of Powers. It should, therefore, be perfectly obvious to him that this balance of power would be utterly destroyed if we should desert Austria and she should be demolished by Russia, and also that the balance of power would be made to totter considerably by a world conflagration. Therefore, if he is honest and logical, he must stand by us in attempting to localise the conflict. But now, *satis superque*; it is one o'clock in the morning. If these arguments in favour of our policy are, perhaps, not sufficient to convince you, I know, nevertheless, that you will stand behind them.[1]

July 19

I have just received your letter of 17 inst. In the main, it is answered by the above. First of all, leave of absence as a *cura posterior*; I will reply very soon as to the colonial agreement.

31 Stolberg to Jagow

Private letter   Vienna, 18 July 1914
D.D. 87   R. 20 July

Yesterday I saw Berchtold, who told me that the note in question is to be handed over at Belgrade on 23 inst. As I reported yesterday,[2] Berchtold hopes that the Austrian demands, about which he did not go into particulars, will not be accepted by Serbia. He is not, however, quite sure, and I gathered the impression from his statements as well as from those of Hoyos, that Serbia *can* accept the demands. To my question what would happen then, should the matter come to nothing in this fashion, Berchtold said that then they could exercise considerable latitude in the practical execution of the various demands. If they really want a final settlement of the relations with Serbia here, as Count Tisza claimed in a recent speech to be a peremptory necessity, it is certainly incomprehensible why they should not have preferred such demands as would make a breach unavoidable. If this action dies out like the shooting at Hornberg and remains nothing but a so-called diplomatic victory, then the view already taken here to the effect that the Monarchy is no longer capable of any

[1] Lichnowsky replied on 23 July; *D.D.* 161.
[2] See 27.

exercise of vigour, will be well confirmed. The results of such an action, both at home and abroad, are obvious.[1]

I also asked Berchtold whether he intended to get in touch with Italy before finally acting against Serbia, to which he replied that so far he had not uttered a single word, and that his intention was to place the Italian Government before a *fait accompli*, as it appeared to him not very reliable in the quality of secrecy, and as it might easily, in view of its Serbophile attitude, let something drop at Belgrade.[2] Even at Berlin they had agreed that Hoyos, with whom the matter was discussed, was right on this point. This was stated to me by Hoyos himself. At that, I explained at length to the Minister, according to the tenor of the secret despatch of 15 inst. (no. 911),[3] of what tremendous importance it appeared to us to be that the people here in Vienna should come to an understanding with Rome regarding the aims to be sought in case of war, and attempt to keep Italy on their side. Berchtold disclosed great optimism, and seemed to think that Italy could not possibly be so despicable an ally as to turn against the Monarchy. I said in reply that in case of a prospective conflict with Serbia only, the alliance would not come into question, and that Italy could very easily take a stand by the side of Serbia, if only morally; but even this might presage evil for the stability of the Triple Alliance, and it would unquestionably inflame Russia's lust for war. This struck the Minister as very evident, yet he would not of his own accord mention the question of compensation; even when Hoyos, who had been drawn into the conference, expressed the conviction that the Italians would have to be given something. As the Ambassador is to return early tomorrow morning, I thought it better for me [not] to go any more deeply into the details of this question, which will in any case necessitate a series of lengthy conferences.

On the other hand, I had a long conversation with Hoyos immediately afterward, during which he mentioned the subject of the Trentino of his own accord, and asked me whether this was the compensation that we had in mind, to which I replied in the affirmative. He did not by any means seem unfavourable to this, nor did he show himself in any way deaf to the argument that in this manner Irredentism could be done away with. I told him also that, if the occasion arose, it would be a question only of the comparatively small territory of the diocese of Trent. He listened to everything in very friendly fashion, and then mentioned as a possible compensation for Italy the ceding of the Dodecanese to her. He furthermore, however, advanced the point of view that, as a matter of fact, Italy had no right to claim compensation on the strength of the agreement, as it

[1] See 3, 11, 18, 28 and 33.   [2] See 28.   [3] *D.D.* 46.

referred only to Turkey. But I argued in reply that in this case the question could only be a political and not an equitable one, and that Austria would have to do everything possible, in consideration of the relation of alliance, to keep Italy in the traces. Finally, I advised him, in the event of the outbreak of any conflict with Serbia, to give Rome the assurance that they had no intention of making any territorial acquisitions but that, in case events should necessitate any such, they would compensate Italy in the most thorough manner.

I have just seen Berchtold again. He told me that tomorrow[1] the note is finally to be put into shape with the aid of Tisza, and that it still might be modified according to the happenings of the day (interview with Pašić, article in the *Samouprawa*, etc.). Hoyos has just told me that the demands were really of such a nature that no nation that still possessed self-respect and dignity could possibly accept them.[2] . . .

32   Kageneck to General Staff

Military Report 43   Vienna, 18 July 1914
A.A., *Der Weltkrieg*, Vol. 2[3]   R. 19 July

On the Situation

The *Pester Lloyd* brought news yesterday of the calling up of reservists in the Kingdom of Serbia. . . .

In an exchange of views on the military measures which might ensue after the *démarche* in Belgrade, Colonel von Hranilovic[4] surmised that in the event of a threat from Austria-Hungary the Serbs would undoubtedly transfer their fighting forces (2/3) from the new provinces to the north. The Imp. and Roy. General Staff allow 6 days for this. The Colonel considers that the Serbian Government could not surrender the whole of the old kingdom to an enemy's invasion without risking the outbreak of revolution. On the other hand, as soon as troops are withdrawn from the former Macedonia revolt will break out there. Bulgarian *Komitadschis* would see to that.

In the event of a possible bombardment of Belgrade the Imp. and Roy. officials concerned have been provided with exact sketches of the town,

[1] On 19 July; see 35.
[2] See 9, 12, 16, 17, 27 and 33.
[3] Duplicated copy.
[4] Head of the Imp. and Royal Bureau of Investigation (Military Information Service).

which show the sites of military installations, batteries and so on. The idea is to spare other buildings from the bombardment. Amongst these should presumably be included the buildings of foreign diplomatic missions in particular. The protection of constructions on the Austro-Hungarian railways has already been taken care of by the gendarmerie, as there is a real danger of attacks being perpetrated against the lines of advance, even by Austro-Hungarian Serbs. On the day the note is delivered in Belgrade the military occupation will immediately come into force, as provided for in the event of mobilisation. Only from this moment will the special military intelligence service also be put into effect . . .

33 Schoen[1] to Hertling

Report 386
D.D., App. IV, No. 2

Berlin, 18 July 1914

I have the honour most respectfully to report as follows to Your Excellency concerning the prospective settlement between the Austro-Hungarian Government and Serbia, on the basis of conversations I have had with Under-Secretary of State Zimmermann, and further with the Foreign Office reporter for the Balkans and the Triple Alliance, and with the counsellor of the Austro-Hungarian Embassy.[2]

The step which the Vienna Cabinet has decided to undertake at Belgrade, and which will consist in the presentation of a note, will take place on 25 inst.[3] The reason for the postponement of the action to that date is that they wish to await the departure of Messrs Poincaré and Viviani from St Petersburg, in order not to facilitate an agreement between the Dual Alliance Powers on any possible counter-action.[4] Until then, by the granting of leave of absence simultaneously to the Minister of War and the Chief of the General Staff, the Vienna authorities will have the appearance of being peacefully inclined;[5] and they have not failed of success in their attempts to influence the press and the exchange. It is recognised here that the Vienna Cabinet has been proceeding quite cleverly in this matter, and it is only regretted that Count Tisza, who at first is said to have been

---

[1] Chargé d'Affaires in Berlin.   [2] Gesandter von Bergen.
[3] Stolberg's notification on 17th of the antedating of the date of delivery to 23rd, only reached Auswärtiges Amt in the course of 18 July; see 27.
[4] See 17, 20–4 and 27.   [5] See 16.

against any severe action, has somewhat raised the veil of secrecy by his statement in the Hungarian House of Deputies.

As Mr Zimmermann told me, the note, so far as has yet been determined, will contain the following demands:

1 The issuing of a proclamation by the King of Serbia which shall state that the Serbian Government has nothing to do with the Greater-Serbia movement, and fully disapproves of it.

2 The initiation of an inquiry to discover those implicated in the murder of Sarajevo, and the participation of Austrian officials in this inquiry.

3 Proceedings against all who have participated in the Greater-Serbia movement.

A respite of forty-eight hours is to be granted for the acceptance of these demands.[1] It is perfectly plain that Serbia can not accept any such demands, which are incompatible with her dignity as a sovereign state.[2] Thus the result would be war. Here they are absolutely willing that Austria should take advantage of this favourable opportunity, even at the risk of further complications.[3] But whether they will actually rise to the occasion in Vienna, still seems doubtful to Mr von Jagow, as it does to Mr Zimmermann.[4] The Under-Secretary of State made the statement that Austria-Hungary, thanks to her indecision and her desultoriness, had really become the Sick Man of Europe as Turkey had once been, upon the partition of which, the Russians, Italians, Roumanians, Serbians and Montenegrins were now waiting. A powerful and successful move against Serbia would make it possible for the Austrians and Hungarians to feel themselves once more to be a national power, would again revive the country's collapsed economic life, and would set foreign aspirations back for years. To judge from the indignation at the bloody deed that was now dominant over the entire Monarchy, it looked as if they could even be sure of the Slav troops. In a few years, with the continuance of the operation of the Slavic propaganda, this would no longer be the case, as even General Conrad von Hötzendorf himself had admitted.

So they are of the opinion here that Austria is face to face with an hour of fate, and for this reason they declared here without hesitation, in reply to an inquiry from Vienna, that we would agree to any method of procedure which they might determine on there, even at the risk of a war with Russia.[3] The blank power of full authority that was given to Count Berchtold's Chief of the Cabinet, Count Hoyos, who came here to deliver a personal letter from the Emperor together with a detailed memorial,

[1] See 16 and 17.   [2] See 9, 12, 16, 17, 27 and 31.
[3] See 15, 18, 28 and 30.   [4] See 11, 15, 28 and 31.

went so far that the Austro-Hungarian Government was empowered to deal with Bulgaria concerning her entrance into the Triple Alliance.

In Vienna they do not seem to have expected such an unconditional support of the Danube Monarchy by Germany, and Mr Zimmermann has the impression that it is almost embarrassing to the always timid and undecided authorities at Vienna not to be admonished by Germany to caution and self-restraint. To what extent they waver in their decisions at Vienna is shown by the circumstance that Count Berchtold, three days after he had had enquiries made here concerning the alliance with Bulgaria, telegraphed that he still had scruples about closing with Bulgaria.[1]

So it would have been liked even better here, if they had not waited so long with their action against Serbia, and the Serbian Government had not been given time to make an offer of satisfaction on its own account, perhaps acting under Russo-French pressure.[2]

What attitude the other Powers will take toward an armed conflict between Austria and Serbia will chiefly depend, according to the opinion here, on whether Austria will content herself with a chastisement of Serbia, or will demand territorial compensation for herself. In the first case, it might be possible to localise the war; in the other case, on the other hand, more serious complications would probably be inevitable.

The administration will, immediately upon the presentation of the Austrian note at Belgrade, initiate diplomatic action with the Powers, in the interest of the localisation of the war.[3] It will claim[4] that the Austrian action has been just as much of a surprise to it as to the other Powers, pointing out the fact that the Emperor is on his northern journey and that the Prussian Minister of War, as well as the Chief of the Grand General Staff are away on leave of absence.[5] (As I take the liberty to insert here, not even the Italian Government has been taken into confidence.) It will lay stress upon the fact that it is a matter of interest for all the monarchical Governments that 'the Belgrade nest of anarchists' be once and for all rooted out; and it will make use of its influence to get all the Powers to take the view that the settlement between Austria and Serbia is a matter concerning those two nations alone. The mobilisation of the German Army is to be refrained from, and they are also going to work through the military authorities to prevent Austria from mobilising her entire Army,

[1] *Ö.D.* 10126.

[2] A war between Austria and Serbia would thus have been rendered superfluous (6 and 8). In contrast the German statesmen subsequently asserted that they had only urged a precipitation of the 'action' in order to ensure localisation (*U.A.*, p. 27; Bethmann Hollweg, *Betrachtungen*, I, p. 135).

[3] See **39**.   [4] See pp. 93–7.   [5] See **15** and **29**.

and especially not those troops stationed in Galicia, in order to avoid bringing about automatically a counter-mobilisation on the part of Russia, which would force, first ourselves, and then France, to take similar measures and thereby conjure up a European war.[1]

The attitude of *Russia* will, above all else, determine the question whether the attempt to localise the war will succeed.

If Russia is not determined on war against Austria and Germany, in any case, she can, in that event—and that is the most favourable factor in the present situation—very well remain inactive, and justify herself toward the Serbs by announcing that she approves of the kind of fighting that goes to work with the throwing of bombs and with revolver shots just as little as any of the other civilised nations; this, especially, so long as Austria does not render doubtful Serbia's national independence. Mr Zimmermann assumes that both England and France, to neither of whom a war would be acceptable at the present moment, will try to exert a pacifying influence on Russia; besides that, he is counting on the fact that 'bluffing' constitutes one of the most favoured requisites of Russian policy, and that while the Russian likes to threaten with the sword, he still does not like so very much to draw it in behalf of others at the critical moment.[2]

England will not prevent Austria from calling Serbia to account; it is only the destruction of the nation that she would scarcely permit, being far more likely—true to her traditions—presumably to take a stand, even in this case, for the principles of nationality. A war between the Dual Alliance and the Triple Alliance would be unwelcome to England at the present time, if only in consideration of the situation in Ireland. Should it, however, come to that, according to all opinion here, we should find our English cousins on the side of our enemies, inasmuch as England fears that France, in the event of a new defeat, would sink to the level of a Power of the second class, and that the 'balance of power,' the maintenance of which England considers to be necessary for her own interests, would be upset thereby. . . .

---

[1] Thus Berlin, now as ever, was perfectly aware of the mechanics of the various treaty obligations and plans for mobilisation (4).

[2] See 30.

34 Memorandum of the Russian Ministry for Foreign Affairs

Int. Bez. I, 4, 272   St Petersburg, 18 July 1914

S. D. Sazonov returned from a short country excursion. Wishing to render himself *au fait* as to the state of affairs prior to his meeting with the Austrian Ambassador, Baron Schilling went to meet him at the terminus, and on the way from thence to the Ministry acquainted him with the contents of a telegram (no. 88)[1] received from N. N. Schebeko in Vienna on the preceding evening, and also with his conversation with the Italian Ambassador on July 16.[2] The Minister was troubled by this information, and agreed with Baron Schilling as to the necessity of forewarning Austria regarding the determination of Russia on no account to permit any attempts against the independence of Serbia. The Minister formed the resolve to express himself in the most decided manner to the Austro-Hungarian Ambassador regarding this matter.

Soon after reaching the Ministry, S. D. Sazonov received Count Szápáry, who spoke in the most peaceable manner of an entire absence in Austria of any intention of rendering relations with Serbia more acute. His assurances were so positive that they completely quieted the Minister's apprehensions, so much so that after this interview he said to Baron Schilling that he had had no need to resort to threats, as the Austro-Hungarian Ambassador had sufficiently emphatically assured him of the love of peace of his Government. 'Il a été doux comme un agneau.'[3]

[1] Of 16 July (*Int. Bez.* I, 4, 247). Schebeko announced that the Imp. and Royal Government intended 'to make certain demands'.

[2] See p. 101.

[3] 'He was as gentle as a lamb.'

4 The First Danger Signals
19 – 22 July

On Sunday 19 July there appeared in the quasi-official *North German Gazette* a brief notice, in tortuous official language, which for the first time lifted a corner of the veil of secrecy; it spoke of the 'settlement of differences which might arise between Austria-Hungary and Serbia' and expressed the hope that they might 'remain localised' (36). The author of the article was Secretary of State von Jagow himself. Evidently his intention was cautiously to introduce the German policy of localisation in conjunction with a warning of the approaching conflict. The overall effect however was the opposite of that envisaged by Jagow, for it alarmed the European Governments, and it was only now that French diplomacy began to be more seriously concerned with the prospect of a possible crisis.[1]

At all events, the architects of the German policy of localisation were from the very beginning faced with a serious dilemma: on the one hand, even before delivery of the ultimatum, they wanted to pave the way for a 'localisation' of the still only imminent conflict, and on the other they sought to avoid giving the impression that they were informed of Austria's intentions, as if they were accomplices with Vienna, or were even 'inciting the Austrians to war'.[2] In this dilemma Jagow threw out his first (still guarded) threat to the other Powers that they should at all events leave Austria a free hand in her dealings with little Serbia. With this in mind he had tried to ensure that his remarks in the *North German Gazette* were 'intentionally written in a mild tone with an eye to European diplomacy',

[1] See *D.F.X.*, p. V.   [2] See above, p. 99.

for 'this markedly official paper was not to give alarm prematurely', as he himself put it in a telegram to Tschirschky on 18 July.

On the other hand this cautious formulation might have given grounds for misunderstanding in Vienna; therefore Tschirschky was to 'take care that this is not wrongly interpreted there as German deprecation of Vienna's determination.'[1] Thus the Auswärtiges Amt was still anxious that Austria should show 'determination'. Yet it was most improbable that the feared misunderstanding would occur; only the previous day Jagow had instructed the German Ambassador in Vienna, when asking for Austrian territorial aims, to avoid 'giving any impression that we are attempting to put any obstructions in the path of Austrian activities or that we are trying to prescribe certain limits or aims' (26).

As a further preliminary to localising the conflict, the Auswärtiges Amt prepared a circular note to the three Entente Powers. This was to be delivered on 24 July by the German Ambassadors in London, Paris and St Petersburg and was intended to give diplomatic support for the Austrian ultimatum. The note presented Austria's case against Serbia in a somewhat long-winded manner, and only reached the heart of the matter near the end: 'We urgently desire the localisation of the conflict, as the intervention of any other Power would, as a result of the various alliance obligations, bring about inestimable consequences' (39). In a firmer and more open manner than the notice in the *North German Gazette* (36) the German Government threatened a general war if the other Powers failed to endorse the German view 'that the matter in question is an issue to be determined between Austria-Hungary and Serbia alone'. The diplomatic escalation, which was to culminate in World War less than a fortnight later, was clearly under way. The circular was despatched to the various diplomatic missions on 21 July, but the German White Book gave the later date of 23 July, probably in an attempt to mitigate the unfortunate impression of German complicity with Vienna created after the delivery of the ultimatum to Serbia.

Meanwhile, the remaining German preliminaries for a localisation of the imminent conflict progressed with all discretion and thoroughness. When Szögyény, on Berchtold's instructions, reminded Jagow on 21 July of his earlier promise that the German Chargé d'Affaires in Belgrade would act as diplomatic representative of the Danube Monarchy after the rupture of relations with Serbia, the Secretary of State immediately consented to give the German Minister the relevant instructions.[2]

---

[1] *D.D.* 70.
[2] *Ö.D.* 10442; Berchtold's corresponding instructions on 20 July in *Ö.D.* 10397; see also above, p. 96.

On 19 July the Kaiser on his Scandinavian journey was rudely brought to his senses by the warning telegram of 18 July (29) and cabled the Auswärtiges Amt that he desired Ballin and Plettenberg (of *Hapag* and *Norddeutsche Lloyd*[1] respectively) to be discreetly informed. In addition he ordered the High Seas Fleet to remain together until 25 July in a state of readiness for immediate departure.[2] Jagow telegraphed Plettenberg and informed Ballin by word of mouth, as the latter happened to be in Berlin at the time.[3] The Kaiser's command with regard to the Fleet was more complicated. The Chancellor set no store by keeping the Fleet together as he was afraid that after rejection of the ultimatum (he clearly did not reckon with an acceptance), the Kaiser would 'prematurely' order 'conspicuous movements of the Fleet'.[4]

The German Government, whilst taking great pains to avoid too striking a synchronisation of its measures with the developing crisis between Vienna and Belgrade was taking equal pains to ensure that Austria's action against Serbia should coincide exactly with Poincaré's departure from St Petersburg. To this end on 20 July Jagow directed Tschirschky to inform him not only of the contents of the ultimatum 'in order to facilitate the handling of our public' but also of the day and hour of its delivery in Belgrade.[5] Jagow had clearly thought of everything; on the 21 July he enquired of St Petersburg the exact time of the French President's departure from Kronstadt. The answer came back on the following day: 11.00 p.m. St Petersburg time[6]—hence considerably later than 5.00 p.m. Central European Time, the hour arranged for delivery of the ultimatum in Belgrade. The Secretary of State instantly sent a telegram 'for immediate attention' to Tschirschky, in which he pointed out the technical error which would mean that the Note would 'be made known while Poincaré is still in St Petersburg'.[7] This could not be allowed to happen. Berchtold immediately took the point and instructed Baron Giesl, the Austro-Hungarian Minister in Belgrade, if possible to delay his *démarche* at the Serbian Foreign Ministry by an hour, until 6.00 p.m.[8] The telegram from Vienna reached Belgrade in the nick of time and enabled Giesl to defer his action by an hour (45). The piece of precision diplomacy was saved literally in the last hour by the German Secretary of State.

In the meantime the notice in the *North German Gazette* (36) had had its effect on the Entente Powers. On 21 July their diplomatic representatives came to the Auswärtiges Amt to question the Secretary of State

[1] The two largest German steamship companies.
[2] Wedel to Jagow, 19 July; *D.D.* 80.   [3] *D.D.* 90.
[4] Bethmann Hollweg to Jagow, 21 July; *D.D.* 101.
[5] *D.D.* 83.   [6] *D.D.* 93; *D.D.* 108.
[7] *D.D.* 112.   [8] *Ö.D.* 10518.

about the meaning of the article. Jules Cambon, the French Ambassador, even made a direct enquiry as to the contents of the forthcoming Austrian Note. Jagow denied all knowledge of the matter (41). With feigned or genuine naivety Bronevski, the Russian Chargé d'Affaires, stalked the same quarry, save that he trod more gingerly. Again Jagow asserted that he knew nothing. When Bronevski thereupon drew the conclusion from his ostensible ignorance 'that if this were the case he would, so to speak, have set his signature to a blank cheque which he would have left for Vienna to fill in at her own discretion', Jagow had recourse to an excuse which was not exactly convincing. When Bronevski drew his attention to the panic on the Stock Exchange, the Secretary of State replied imperturbably: 'Well, it is rather a different matter if you are asking me if that is clever of the Austrians! But they have never before been very clever' (43). Jagow, however, clearly fancied himself to be very clever, when he subsequently revealed to the British Chargé d'Affaires, Rumbold, that he himself had written the article in question, while at the same time emphasising 'that the question at issue between Austria-Hungary and Serbia was one for discussion and settlement by these two countries alone without interference from outside' (44).

In his dilemma Jagow naturally cut rather a sorry figure. Neither Cambon nor Bronevski was particularly convinced by his assurances that he had no foreknowledge of the coming Austrian Note. Rumbold wrote at the close of his account: 'The impression left on me by this conversation was that Herr von Jagow would approve prompt and vigorous action on the part of Austria-Hungary at the present juncture, and that he is aware of the general character of the *démarche* to be made at Belgrade'.[1] In this Rumbold was only too correct.

The news reaching Berlin of the state of the preparations for action against Serbia, the dynamic thrust injected by the Germans into their Austrian allies and the information which the Wilhelmstrasse divulged to at least some of the Governments of Bavaria, Saxony and Baden, all clearly indicated that Berlin was fully aware of Austria's intentions and as much as ever retained a lively interest in the use of force against Serbia. The events of 22 July in Berlin once more corroborate the assumption of the Entente diplomats that the German Government had been fully taken into confidence on essentials. That afternoon Jagow had definite information that Giesl's instructions were to break off relations with Serbia if her reply 'should not be satisfactory or should not be given in time'.[2] He subsequently contributed towards ensuring that the delivery of the ultimatum dove-tailed with Poincaré's departure from St Petersburg,[3]

---

[1] *B.D.* 158.   [2] Tschirschky to Jagow, 22 July; *D.D.* 110.   [3] See above, p. 134.

and shortly afterwards he directed the German Chargé d'Affaires in Belgrade to 'take over the affairs and the protection of the subjects of Austria-Hungary'[1] on the departure of the Austrian Minister. At about the same time a telegram arrived from Tschirschky: 'The note to be delivered to Serbia has received the sanction of His Majesty the Emperor Franz Joseph without alteration'.[2]

Immediately afterwards Szögyény presented himself at the Auswärtiges Amt and handed to the Secretary of State the complete text of the ultimatum to Serbia. After the war Jagow asserted in his evidence to the Committee of Inquiry that he had been startled at the harshness of the conditions and had expressed to Szögyény his 'great surprise that the information arrived so late, that no opportunity was offered us to act upon it'. Szögyény allegedly replied that the Note was to be delivered in Belgrade the very next morning, so that it was too late to do anything.[3]

There is almost certainly no truth in this. For one thing it is scarcely credible that the alert Jagow would have allowed Szögyény to bluff him with false time for the delivery of the ultimatum. Jagow knew very well that the Note was not to be handed over in Belgrade until the late afternoon, as only one hour previously he had indirectly advised Vienna not to carry out the *démarche* as early as 5.00 p.m.[4] Moreover, the documents provide no shred of evidence that the German Government lodged a protest or even expressed its misgivings—Jagow did not even leave a modest record of his conversation with Szögyény. In any case, a German protest would have been totally illogical and even contradictory, after the Auswärtiges Amt had not only been familiar with the contents and the tenor of the Note for nearly two weeks, but had fervently hoped that the Austrians would in fact finally attack. Basically, the Germans in their impatience had already come to regard the ultimatum as a troublesome and time-consuming formality and they feared that the stipulations would not be sufficiently unacceptable, so that the Austrians would let slip the chance of a war against Serbia.[5] It is much more plausible that Szögyény's report of 24 July corresponds to the historical truth. According to him, Jagow assured him 'that the German Government is naturally in agreement with the contents of the Note'.[6] In view of Germany's previous and subsequent policy in the July crisis, her assent would indeed have been 'natural', whilst nothing could serve to explain why the Germans should have suddenly raised any objections, let alone prove that they actually did.

---

[1] *D.D.* 114.   [2] *D.D.* 113.
[3] *Official Documents Relating to the World War*, vol. II (New York/London, 1923), 30, 31.
[4] See above, p. 134.   [5] See above, pp. 96f.
[6] Szögyény to Berchtold 24 July; *Ö.D.* 10582.

In Vienna, too, all the preparations for the 'action' had meanwhile been completed. On 20 July the ultimatum (37), together with detailed instructions, was forwarded to Giesl in Belgrade.[1] At the same time the Ambassadors to the Great Powers received a copy of the ultimatum with a carefully slanted commentary for each individual country (38). The copy of the Note and accompanying commentary were to be delivered by hand on the morning of 24 July.

Shortly before the 'action' began the moment dreaded by Berlin really looked like coming to pass: Berchtold apparently took fright at his own bravado. On the 23 July he told Conrad of his misgivings about Italy's attitude; the General replied: 'We must not mobilise if we also have Italy to fear' as he maintained that a war on three fronts would be impossible for Austria-Hungary. Earlier Berchtold had expressed his doubts: 'But if Serbia yields on the second day of mobilisation?' Conrad's answer: 'Then Serbia must pay the price'.[2] Vienna was still not unshakeable in her decision for a war at all costs.

Meanwhile the already advanced preparations had gained such momentum that any belated scruples were overridden. The Austrian diplomatic missions were given a final briefing on the official line[3] and on the 22 July Berchtold was already worrying as to the best means of delivering the declaration of war to the Serbian Government (42).

The European Powers had become increasingly anxious in the final days before the delivery of the ultimatum. The *démarches* of the Entente diplomats at the Wilhelmstrasse on 21 July had already indicated their uneasiness.[4] On the other hand, the subsequent attitude of the Entente in the crisis was gradually becoming clarified: Russia was certainly prepared for the present to appease in Belgrade,[5] in other words to intercede for the satisfaction of Austria-Hungary so long as Serbian sovereignty was unmolested. But equally, on 21 July, Sazonov told Count Pourtalès, the German Ambassador in St Petersburg, of his suspicion that those elements 'which did not hesitate at the idea of plunging Austria into a war, even at the risk of starting a general world conflagration' were constantly gaining ground in Austria-Hungary. More specifically Sazonov warned against an ultimatum to Serbia (40).

France also adopted a similar attitude. Poincaré, during his state visit to St Petersburg, took advantage of a diplomatic reception on 21 July to deliver a clear warning to Austria-Hungary. He told Szápáry that the

[1] Berchtold to Giesl (private letter), 20 July; *Ö.D.* 10396.

[2] L. Albertini, *Origins*, II, p. 377 n. (Conrad, *Dienstzeit*, IV, p. 108).

[3] *Ö.D.* 10536.

[4] See above, pp. 134f.

[5] Thus Lichnowsky on 20 July, in a conversation he had with Benckendorff; *D.D.* 85.

Danube Monarchy could not hold the Serbian Government responsible for the assassination unless she produced concrete evidence, 'otherwise a *démarche* of this kind would be a mere pretext'. He added: 'At any rate, one must not forget that Serbia has friends and that a situation might be created, which might become dangerous to peace'.[1]

The tensions between Belgrade and Vienna and the possibility of an Austrian move naturally provided the subject of the consultations between Poincaré and Sazonov. But there can be no question of France having at that time given Russia an 'authorisation similar to that which Germany gave Austria'. Yet more implausible is the further argument that 'the main difference was admittedly that there could no longer be any hope of localising the conflict in the event of an Austrian attack on Serbia'.[2] Although no official minutes of the St Petersburg discussions of 20–23 July exist, a moment's reflection will suffice to show that such a sweeping assertion could not be correct: neither France nor Russia at that time knew whether or how Austria could proceed against Serbia and all existing agreements could only come into force in the event of an Austrian war against Serbia; therefore it was up to both Vienna and Berlin to prevent any such clear breach of the peace. However Russia and France were not disposed to tolerate a violation of Serbian sovereignty, let alone a war against Serbia (47) and further evidence for this is provided by the instructions sent to the Russian and French Ambassadors in Vienna in connection with the French state visit. It does, then, seem problematic to place Germany's pressure tactics ('blank cheque') on a par with the agreement between Russia and France to counter the possibility of a crisis over Serbia with a show of solidarity as allies.

Finally, Grey repeatedly made only too clear to the German Government what it so badly needed to know—the limits to England's passive forbearance. He insisted that 'everything would depend on the form of the satisfaction demanded, and whether moderation would be exercised, but especially on whether the accusations raised against Serbia could be made on convincing grounds'.[3] As late as 22 July the British Foreign Secretary declared that England would be prepared to exert influence on Serbia to accept the Austrian conditions, 'in case they are moderate and are made reconcilable with the independence of the Serbian nation' (46). Italy hinted in London that she did not intend to take part in a war provoked by Austria-Hungary.[4]

[1] Szápáry to Berchtold, 21 July; *A.R.B.* I, 45, *Ö.D.* 10461; also Pourtalès to Jagow, 23 July; *D.D.* 134.
[2] See K.-D. Erdmann, *Die Zeit der Weltkriege*, p. 17.
[3] Lichnowsky to Jagow, 20 July; *D.D.* 92.
[4] Rodd to Grey, 22 July; *B.D.* 161.

35 Protocol of the Council of Ministers for Common Affairs held in Vienna, 19 July 1914

Ö.D. 10393

Present: the Imp. Royal Premier Count Stürgkh; the Royal Hung. Premier Count Tisza; the Imp. and Royal Common Finance Minister Dr von Biliński; the Imp. and Royal War Minister F. Z. M. von Krobatin; the Imp. and Royal Chief of the General Staff G. of I. Baron Conrad von Hötzendorf; the Deputy Chief of the Naval Staff Vice-Admiral von Kailer. Secretary: Councillor of Legation Count Hoyos.

Subject under discussion: the forthcoming diplomatic action against Serbia.

Before the Council of Common Ministers was constituted and the sitting was opened by the Minister in the chair, an informal discussion on the text of the note to be presented to the Serbian government, took place and the text was definitely settled.

The *Presiding Minister* then opened the Council of Ministers and proposed that the note should be presented to the Royal Serbian Government on 23 July at five in the afternoon, so that the term of 48 hours would expire on Saturday, 25 inst. at five in the afternoon and the order for mobilisation could be published, in the night from Saturday to Sunday. It was Count Berchtold's belief that it is improbable that the news of our step would be publicly known before the President of the French Republic had left St Petersburg: but even if this were the case, he did not think that it would do any harm, since we had fully considered the duties of etiquette and had waited until the visit was over.[1] To a prolongation of the delay he must object on diplomatic grounds. Berlin was beginning to get nervous[2] and news of our intentions had already transpired in Rome,[3] so that untoward incidents could not be guarded against, if action were again postponed.

Under the prompting of this declaration, made by the Presiding Minister, the Council voted by common assent that the note should be presented on the 23 inst. at five in the afternoon.

The *Royal Hungarian Premier* (Count Tisza) declares that if the news of the presenting of the ultimatum should reach Budapest from Belgrade on the Thursday, he would speak on the subject in the Hungarian House of Deputies. This was taken into account.

The *Chief of the General Staff* (Baron Conrad) remarked that for military reasons he was in favour of a speedy beginning of the impending action.

[1] See 17, 20–4, 27 and 33.   [2] See 15, 28, 31 and 33.   [3] See p. 101.

The news he had lately received from Serbia showed that three situations had by degrees been created.

First large numbers of troops had been collected along the Bulgarian and Albanian frontiers; next there were reports of great numbers of soldiers having been transported to Old Serbia. Of these he had taken no account, because it was shown that they were merely exchanged for reserves. During the last three days, however, he had received more serious news. First he was informed that two regiments, the 6th and the 17th, had been transferred from New Serbia to Old Serbia, and yesterday he heard from a very trustworthy confidential person in Bulgaria, that three divisions had been ordered north. Of course he would have to get these reports verified. If they proved true, he must ask to be allowed to take speedy counter-measures.

Next the question of proclaiming the state of siege in all the territory of the monarchy inhabited by South Slavs was discussed and after a long debate, it was unanimously resolved that the state of siege would not be proclaimed before the mobilisation was published, not only to avoid a bad impression in foreign countries, but also among our own population. The same was resolved for Bosnia and Herzegovina, where the state of siege was also to be put in force at the same time as the mobilisation.

The *Imp. and Royal War Minister* (Krobatin) then communicated the diverse measures for the mobilisation, which he had caused to be prepared. His explanations showed that everything necessary could be completed for the Imperial sanction on Wednesday, 22 inst. and that arrangements had been made with both Governments with regard to the measures to be taken by the administrative authorities in both countries.

The Council of Ministers then resolved to send a private letter to the chief commander of Bosnia and Herzegovina through the Common Finance Minister, informing him of the intentions of the Imp. and Royal Government with regard to Serbia.

At the express desire of the Royal Hungarian Premier (Tisza) the *Chief of the General Staff* gives private information on the mobilisation, and answers in the affirmative Count Tisza's question whether, in the case of a general mobilisation, the garrisons remaining in Transylvania for its safety were sufficiently strong to ensure order in case of internal disturbances. The garrisons were *Landsturm*-formations, commanded by officers. An experienced general would take the command. These troops would certainly not be sufficiently strong to resist an attack on the part of the Roumanian army, but they could retard the advance of the Roumanian army. These troops were recruited in such a manner, that there were very few Hungarian Roumanians among them. . . .

The *Royal Hungarian Premier* (Tisza) then begged the Council to vote the resolution, of which he had spoken at their last meeting,[1] and from which the Royal Hungarian Government made the whole action depend. The Council of Ministers must declare unanimously that the action against Serbia was not in any way connected with plans of aggrandisement on the part of the Monarchy, and that not any portion of Serbia should be annexed, except slight frontier regulations, imposed by military considerations. He must absolutely insist that such a resolution be voted unanimously by the council.

The *Presiding Minister* (Berchtold) declared that he could not accept the Royal Hungarian Premier's point of view without certain reservations. In the present political situation, he was also of opinion that, should it come to war with Serbia and we were the victors, we should annex no part of this country, but by making it surrender large portions of its territory to Bulgaria, Greece and Albania, eventually to Roumania, reduce its size so much, that it would cease to be dangerous. The situation in the Balkans might change; it is not impossible that Russia should succeed in overthrowing the present Cabinet in Sofia and appointing a government hostile towards us; Albania is no reliable factor as yet; he must, as manager of the foreign affairs of Austria-Hungary reckon with the possibility that after the war there might be circumstances which would make it impossible for us to renounce all annexation, if we are to improve our frontiers.

The *Royal Hungarian Premier* (Tisza) declared that he could not accept these reservations of Count Berchtold and must, in consideration of his responsibility as Hungarian Premier ask the conference to vote his point of view unanimously. He asks this not only from reasons basing on our home politics, but more particularly, because he is firmly convinced that Russia would resist *à outrance* if we were to insist upon the complete annihilation of Serbia, and because he believes that the best card we hold for improving our international situation is to declare to the Powers as early as possible that we have no intention of annexing any territory whatever.[2]

The *Presiding Minister* (Berchtold) declares that even before this discussion he had the intention of declaring as much in Rome.

The *Imp. and Royal Premier* (Stürgkh) expressed his belief that even if the annexation of Serbian territory remained out of the question, Serbia might be made dependent upon the Monarchy by the deposition of the dynasty by a military convention and by other corresponding measures. Certainly the resolution of the Council of Ministers must not be voted in such a manner that corrections of the frontier lines, which might

[1] See 9.   [2] See 31.

become necessary from a strategic point of view would have to be renounced.

The *Imp. and Royal War Minister* (Krobatin) declared that he would vote the resolution on the condition that besides corrections of the frontier lines the occupation of a bridgehead on the other side of the River Save, for instance in the Schabatz district, would be allowed. After this the following resolution was unanimously voted:

The Common Council of Ministers at the proposition of the Royal Hungarian Premier (Tisza) votes that as soon as the war begins, the Monarchy declares to the foreign Powers that no war for conquest is intended, nor is the annexation of the kingdom contemplated. Of course the strategically necessary corrections of the frontier lines, or the reduction of Serbia's territory to the advantage of other states or the unavoidable temporary occupation of Serbian territory is not precluded by this resolution.

The *Presiding Minister* (Berchtold) mentions with gratification that on all points the council is perfectly agreed and closes the conference.

36 Statement in the *North German Gazette* of 19 July 1914

In the utterances of the European press in regard to the existing tension between Austria-Hungary and Serbia it is increasingly recognised that Austria-Hungary's desire to clear up her relations with Serbia is justified. In this connection we share the hope expressed in more than one quarter that a serious crisis will be avoided by the Serbian Government giving way in time. In any event the solidarity of Europe, which made itself felt during the long Balkan crisis in maintaining peace among the great Powers, demands and requires that the settlement of differences which may arise between Austria-Hungary and Serbia should remain localised.[1]

37 Berchtold to Giesl

Decree 3400   Vienna, 20 July 1914
Ö.D. 10395

You are asked to present the following note to the Royal Government on the afternoon of 23 July, not later than between four and five o'clock.

[1] See **39**. The notice was drafted by Jagow himself (see **44**).

'On 31 March 1909 the Royal Serbian Minister at the court of Vienna by order of his Government made the following declaration before the Imp. and Royal Government:

'Serbia acknowledges that none of its rights have been touched by the situation created in Bosnia and Herzegovina and that it will therefore accommodate itself to the decisions which the powers will resolve with regard to the article XXV of the Treaty of Berlin. Serbia, in following the advice of the Great Powers, pledges itself to give up the attitude of protest and resistance which it adopted since last October with regard to the annexation, and it pledges itself furthermore to change the course of its present policy towards Austria-Hungary and to live in future on terms of friendly and neighbourly relations.'

The history of latter years and especially the grievous events of 28 June have given proofs of a subversive movement in Serbia, whose ultimate aim it is to disjoin certain portions from the territory of Austria-Hungary. This movement, which has developed under the eyes of the Serbian Government, has resulted in acts of terrorism outside the frontier lines of the kingdom, in a series of attempts at murder and in murders.

Far from keeping the formal promises given in the declaration of 31 March 1909, the Royal Serbian Government has done nothing to suppress this movement. It tolerated the criminal doings of the diverse societies and associations directed against the Monarchy, the outrageous language of the press, the glorification of the instigators of plots; it allowed officers and officials to take part in subversive plans, tolerated a most unhealthy propaganda in public instruction and gave permission for manifestations, which caused the Serbian population to hate the Monarchy and despise its institutions.

The toleration, of which the Serbian Government was guilty, lasted until the very moment when the events of 28 June showed all the world the horrible consequences of such toleration.

The depositions and confessions of the criminal perpetrators of the plot of 28 June prove, that the murder of Sarajevo was prepared in Belgrade, that the murderers had received the weapons and bombs, with which they were armed, from officers and officials, belonging to the *Narodna odbrana* and that the conveyance of criminals and weapons to Bosnia had been prepared and carried through by Serbian frontier organs.

The above-quoted results of the judicial enquiry do not permit the Imp. and Royal Government to keep up its attitude of patient observation, maintained for years in the face of criminal dealings, which emanate from Belgrade and thence spread to the territory of the Monarchy. These results make it the duty of the Imp. and Royal Government to put an end to such doings, which are constantly threatening the peace of the Monarchy.

To attain this end, the Imp. and Royal Government finds itself obliged to demand from the Serbian Government an official assurance that it condemns the propaganda directed against Austria-Hungary and in their entirety the dealings whose ultimate aim it is to disjoin parts of the territory belonging to the Monarchy and that it pledges itself to suppress with all the means in its power this criminal and terrorist propaganda.

With a view to giving these assurances a solemn character, the Royal Serbian Government will publish the following declaration on the first page of its official press-organ of 26/13 July:

'The Royal Serbian Government condemns the propaganda directed against Austria-Hungary, that is the entirety of the ambitions, whose ultimate aim it is to disjoin parts of the territory belonging to the Austrian-Hungarian Monarchy and regrets sincerely the horrible consequences of these criminal ambitions.

The Royal Serbian Government regrets that Serbian officers and officials have taken part in the propaganda above-mentioned and thereby imperilled the friendly and neighbourly relations, which the Royal Government had solemnly promised to cultivate in its declaration of 31 March 1909.

The Royal Government, which condemns and rejects every thought and every attempt to interfere in behalf of the inhabitants of any part of Austria-Hungary, considers it a duty to warn officers, officials and indeed all the inhabitants of the kingdom, that it will in future use great severity against such persons, as will be found guilty of similar doings, which the Government will make every effort to suppress.'

This declaration will at the same time be communicated to the Royal army by an order of His Majesty the King, and will besides be published in the official organ of the army.

The Royal Serbian Government will overmore pledge itself to the following:

1 To suppress every publication likely to inspire hatred and contempt against the Monarchy or whose general tendencies are directed against the integrity of the latter;

2 to begin immediately dissolving the society called *Narodna odbrana*; to seize all its means of propaganda and to act in the same way against all the societies and associations in Serbia, which are busy with the propaganda against Austria-Hungary; the Royal Government will take the

necessary measures to prevent these societies continuing their efforts under another name or in another form;

3 to eliminate without delay from public instruction everything that serves or might serve the propaganda against Austria-Hungary, both where teachers or books are concerned;

4 to remove from military service and from the administration all officers and officials who are guilty of having taken part in the propaganda against Austria-Hungary, whose names and the proofs of whose guilt the Imp. and Royal Government will communicate to the Royal Government;

5 to consent that Imp. and Royal Officials assist in Serbia in the suppressing of the subversive movement directed against the territorial integrity of the Monarchy;

6 to have a judicial enquiry instituted against all those who took part in the plot of 28 June, if they are to be found on Serbian territory; the Imp. and Royal Government will delegate organs who will take an active part in these enquiries;

7 to arrest without delay Major Voija Tankosić and a certain Milan Ciganović, a Serbian government official, both compromised by the results of the enquiry;

8 to take effective measures so as to prevent the Serbian authorities from taking part in the smuggling of weapons and explosives across the frontier; to dismiss from service and severely punish those organs of the frontier service at Schabatz and Loznica, who helped the perpetrators of the crime of Sarajevo to reach Bosnia in safety;

9 to give the Imp. and Royal Government an explanation of the un-justified remarks of high Serbian functionaries in Serbia as well as in foreign countries, who, notwithstanding their official positions, did not hesitate to speak in hostile terms of Austria-Hungary in interviews given just after the event of 28 June;

10 to inform the Imp. and Royal Government without delay that the measures summed up in the above points have been carried out.

The Imp. and Royal Government expects the answer of the Royal Government to reach it not later than Saturday, 25 inst., at six in the afternoon.[1]

A memorandum on the results of the investigation of Sarajevo, inas-much as they refer to the functionaries mentioned in points 7 and 8 will be found enclosed.'

---

[1] Originally 5.00 p.m. had been the deadline envisaged; for the postponement by an hour, see p. 134.

Supplement

The enquiry set on foot by the court of justice in Sarajevo against Gavrilo
Princip and accomplices, guilty of and accessory to the murder committed on 28 June, has up to the present time led to the following
conclusions:

1 The plan of murdering Archduke Francis Ferdinand during his stay
in Sarajevo was devised in Belgrade by Gavrilo Princip, Nedeljko
Čabrinović, a certain Milan Ciganović and Trifko Grabez with the
assistance of Major Voija Tankosić.

2 The six bombs and four Browning pistols with their ammunition,
which were the tools used by the murderers, were procured in Belgrade
by a certain Milan Ciganović and by Major Voija Tankosić and there
handed to Princip, Čabrinović and Grabez.

3 The bombs are hand-grenades, which come from the arms-depôt of
the Serbian army in Kragujevac.

4 To make sure that the plot would succeed, Ciganović taught Princip,
Čabrinović and Grabez the use of the grenades and in a wood near the
rifle grounds of Topschider he taught Princip and Grabez the use of the
Browning pistols.

5 To make it easy for Princip, Čabrinović and Grabez to cross the
frontier of Bosnia-Herzegovina, and to get their weapons through,
Ciganović organised a system of transports. The frontier-captains of
Schabatz (Rade Popović) and of Loznica, the customs officer Radivoj
Grbić of Loznica and several other persons were all implicated in the
transport of the criminals and their weapons to Bosnia and Herzegovina.

At the same time as delivering the above would Your Honour kindly
add by word of mouth that you have been instructed—in the event of
your not having meanwhile received a reply of unconditional acceptance
from the Serbian Government—to leave the Imp. and Royal Legation in
Belgrade, together with the personnel, on expiry of the 48 hour time limit
provided for in the Note, and this to be calculated from the day and hour
of delivery.

38 Berchtold to the Imp. and Royal Ambassadors in Berlin, Rome, Paris, London, St Petersburg and Constantinople

Decrees 3426–3431   Vienna, 20 July 1914
Confidential   D. 20 July
Ö.D. 10400

1 *Berlin* When Your Excellency, on Friday 24 inst., personally informs the Government of the enclosed official decree,[1] you will remark that the perfect political understanding with the German Government already achieved, saves you the trouble of a confidential verbal explanation of our step in Belgrade. The reasons why we could not undertake the *démarche* in Belgrade before yesterday have been told Herr von Tschirschky verbally at the time,[2] and Your Excellency has communicated them[3] to the German Government from my telegram 234 of 15 July.[4]

2 *Rome* Your Excellency will tender the enclosed official decree[5] to the Royal Italian Government; should Marquis di San Giuliano still be absent from Rome, to his representative, on Friday 24 inst. in the forenoon. Your Excellency will not find verbal explanations necessary, since you will have seen the Marquis shortly before, and will have prepared him. But perhaps your Excellency will think it useful to call attention to the fact that the society *Narodna odbrana*, to which all the persons compromised in the plot of 28 June belong as members, is a combative organisation spread all over Serbia, whose activity, according to the authentic programme in our possession, now that Turkey no longer counts, is exclusively directed against our Monarchy.

3 *Paris* The enclosed official decree which is to be communicated to the Government, refers to the demands, which we are compelled to address to the Royal Serbian Government, to confine the movement in favour of Greater Serbia. Your Excellency will tender the document to the Government on Friday 24 inst. in the forenoon. The exposition of this document is so clear that it saves me the trouble to ask Your Excellency to add a verbal explanation of the step we are taking with regard to Serbia. Still it will be useful if Your Excellency, in tendering this document, reminds the French Government, that in all difficulties which have arisen in European policy during latter years, France has always played the grateful part of a mediator between the discordant groups of Powers.

4 *London* Your Excellency will be good enough to tender the enclosed official decree[5] to the State Secretary or his representative on Friday,

---

[1] Ultimatum 37, together with official commentary; *Ö.D.* 10399.
[2] See 22.   [3] See 24.   [4] See 23.
[5] Ultimatum 37, together with official commentary; *Ö.D.* 10399.

24 inst., in the forenoon. Your Excellency might verbally explain upon this occasion that English policy and that of the Monarchy in the near East, have during latter years most satisfactorily shown a converging tendency; reciprocal confidence has been re-established and the British public (after a short period of vacillation, which is over), takes interest in the position of Austria-Hungary as a Great Power and gives its attention to life in the Monarchy. The assassination of the Archduke-heir to the throne (of which the *dossier* is at the disposition of the Powers), has shown plainly what may be expected if Serbia is not compelled to break off all relations with political conspirators (such as the *Narodna odbrana*), whose threads reach to all the countries and territories of the Monarchy. England, where so much indignation was shown when the Serbian King and his Queen were murdered, will certainly understand that public opinion in the Monarchy is crying out for atonement of the moral complicity and the criminal toleration of the Belgrade authorities. The enunciations of Serbian diplomatists and officers prove that Serbia does not as yet conceive the degree of abomination of the Sarajevo plot; every line printed on the subject in Belgrade papers proves the same, and more than anything, the fact that the Serbian Government has not yet moved a finger to seize the accomplices of the crime of 28 June, who are still on Serbian territory.

5 *St Petersburg* Your Excellency will forward the enclosed official decree[1] to the Minister of Foreign Affairs or to his representative on Friday, 24 inst., in the forenoon. I beg Your Excellency to add to the explanations of the document, the following verbal elucidations: The Imp. and Royal Government feels no ill-will or grudge against Serbia; as lately as 1912 the Imp. and Royal Government by its loyal and territorially disinterested attitude gave Serbia a chance to become nearly twice the size it was before. Even now the Monarchy is undertaking this serious step in Belgrade only because its self-preservation and its self-defence demand as much. All the Imp. and Royal Government asks, is to preserve its territory from the insurrectional miasma spreading from across the neighbouring kingdom and to put a stop to the indulgent toleration, with which the Royal Serbian Government has hitherto treated the efforts, which by word, script and deed were in Serbia directed against the integrity of the Monarchy. The assassination of the Archduke-heir to the throne naturally exhausted the patience of the Imp. and Royal Government with regard to Serbian plotting. (The *dossier* on the crime, which is at the disposition of the Imperial Government, shows the connection of the criminals with the society *Narodna odbrana*.) The murder at Sarajevo must at the same time strengthen the feeling of solidarity between the great Monarchies whose

[1] Ultimatum 37 together with official commentary; *Ö.D.* 10399.

common interest it is to defend themselves against the murder of Monarchs, from whatever quarter it may come, or whoever suffers by it. 6 *Constantinople* Your Excellency will tender the enclosed official decree[1] to the Minister of Foreign Affairs or to his representative on Friday, 24 inst., in the forenoon.[2]

39 Bethmann Hollweg to the Ambassadors at St Petersburg, Paris and London

Decrees 592, 918, 1055 Berlin, 21 July 1914
D.D. 100

The public statements of the Austro-Hungarian Government relating to the circumstances under which the assassination of the heir to the Austrian throne and of his wife took place, fully disclose the aims which the Greater Serbia propaganda had set for itself, and the means of which it availed itself towards the realisation of these aims. The facts that have been made public must also do away with the last doubt that the centre of the activities that were to result in the separation of the southern Slav provinces from the Austro-Hungarian Monarchy and in their union with the Kingdom of Serbia, is to be found at Belgrade, and were developed there at least with the connivance of members of the Government and of the army.

The Serbian mischief-making goes back over a long term of years. The Greater Serbia chauvinism appeared in particularly marked form during the Bosnian crisis. Only the extreme moderation and self-command of the Austro-Hungarian Government and the energetic intervention of the Great Powers can be credited with the fact that the provocations to which Austria-Hungary was at that time exposed by Serbia did not lead to war. The Serbian Government has not made good the assurances of future good conduct which she gave at that time. The Greater Serbia propaganda has since been continually increasing in extent and intensity under the very eyes of official Serbia, and, at least, with its tacit consent. It is to the account of that propaganda that the latest outrage, the trail of which leads to Belgrade, can be charged. It has become unmistakably evident that it would no longer comport either with the dignity or with the self-preservation of the Austro-Hungarian Monarchy to regard inactively any longer the mischief-making on the other side of the border—mischief-

[1] Ultimatum 37, together with official commentary; *Ö.D.* 10399.
[2] The reports of the respective Ambassadors, **49–52**.

making by which the security and integrity of its dominions are lastingly menaced. In such a state of affairs, neither the procedure nor the demands of the Austro-Hungarian Government can be regarded as otherwise than moderate and proper. Nevertheless, the attitude adopted of late by public opinion as well as by the Government in Serbia does not exclude the fear that the Serbian Government may refuse to satisfy these demands, and that it is allowing itself to be driven into a provocatory attitude toward Austria-Hungary. In such a case there would remain for the Austro-Hungarian Government, unless it wishes to dispense forever with its standing as a Great Power,[1] no other course than to enforce its demands upon the Serbian Government by strong pressure, and if necessary, to take military measures—a situation in which the choice of means must be left to itself.

I have the honour of requesting Your Excellency to express the tenor of the foregoing argument to Mr Sazonov,[2] and in so doing to emphasise particularly the view that the problem under discussion is one which it is solely for Austria-Hungary and Serbia to solve, and one which it should be the earnest endeavour of the Powers to confine to the two immediate participants. We urgently desire the localisation of the conflict,[3] as the intervention of any other Power would, as a result of the various alliance obligations, bring about inestimable consequences.

Your Excellency will furthermore call Mr Sazonov's attention[4] to the serious consequences which might ensue for the Monarchical idea, if, in the case suggested above, the Monarchical Powers should not stand solidly by the side of Austria-Hungary, setting aside for the moment any possible national prejudices or political points of view, inasmuch as it is a question of dealing the death-blow to a political radicalism, now reigning in Serbia, which does not hesitate at making even members of its own rulers' families the victims of its criminal tendencies. Russia is fully as interested in such a task as is Germany. I venture to hope that Mr Sazonov will not be blind to this fact.

I shall await with interest a telegraphic report of your conference at your earliest convenience.[5]

---

[1] See 3, 11, 28 and 31.
[2] The relevant name was substituted in the case of London and Paris.
[3] See 6, 8, 11, 15, 17, 18, 25, 28–30, 33 and 36.
[4] This paragraph was only included in the instructions to St Petersburg.
[5] See 55, 57 and 58.

40 Pourtalès to Bethmann Hollweg

D.D. 120

St Petersburg, 21 July 1914
R. 23 July, morning

Mr Sazonov, who spent several days last week at his country estate in the Government of Grodno, has been quite anxious since his return from there on account of the relations between Austria-Hungary and Serbia. He told me that he had received very alarming reports from London, Paris and Rome, and that Austria-Hungary's attitude was inspiring an increasing worry everywhere. Mr Schebeko, too, who was in general a calm observer, reported that the feeling in Vienna against Serbia was constantly growing more bitter.

The Minister took the opportunity of giving his wrath at the Austro-Hungarian policy free rein, as usual. That the Emperor Franz Joseph and even Count Berchtold were friends of peace, Mr Sazonov was, it is true, willing to admit, but he said that there were very powerful and dangerous influences at work, which were constantly gaining ground in both halves of the Empire, and which did not hesitate at the idea of plunging Austria into a war, even at the risk of starting a general world conflagration.[1] One anxiously asked oneself the question whether the aged Monarch and his weak Foreign Minister would always be able to oppose these influences successfully.

The picture fits St Petersburg much better!

Previously the belligerent elements, among which clerical intrigues also played an especially important role, had set their hopes on the dead Archduke, Franz Ferdinand. The death of the Archduke had in no way discouraged them; on the other hand, they were the very ones who were inspiring the dangerous policy which Austria-Hungary was pursuing at the present moment. The actual leaders in this policy were two men, particularly, whose increasing influence appeared to the highest degree dubious—namely, Count Forgách, who is 'an intriguer of the basest sort,' and Count Tisza, who 'is half a fool'.

Fool yourself, Mr Sazonov!

[1] See also Hoyos' remark to Redlich on 15 July: 'If world war ensues [i.e. from the proceedings against Serbia], it need make no difference to us.' J. Redlich, *Tagebuch*, I, p. 237.

I replied to Mr Sazonov that his unmeasured reproaches against Austro-Hungarian policy appeared to
me to be strongly influenced by his too great sympathy
for the Serbs, and to be utterly unjustified. No sensible
man could refuse to recognise the complete restraint
observed by the Vienna Cabinet since the assassination
at Sarajevo. It seemed to me that to decide just how
far Austria-Hungary was justified in holding the
Serbian Government responsible for the Greater Serbia
agitations, as early as this, before the result of the
inquiry concerning the assassination was known, was
absolutely premature. But according to everything that
was already known, one could scarcely doubt *that the
Greater Serbia agitation was stirred up under the very
eyes of the Serbian Government, and that even the shame-
less assassination itself had been planned in Serbia.* No
great nation, however, could possibly tolerate permanently the existence along its borders of a propaganda which directly threatened its own security.
Should, therefore, as appearances now seemed to
indicate, traces be discovered at the inquiry into the
origin of the crime which pointed back to Serbia, and
should it be proved that the Serbian Government had
regrettably connived at the intrigues directed against
Austria, then the Austro-Hungarian Government
would unquestionably be justified in using strong
language at Belgrade. I could not conceive that in such
a case the representations of the Vienna Cabinet to the
Serbian Government could meet with the objection of
any Power whatsoever.

The Minister met these arguments with the assertion
that the support of the Greater Serbia propaganda in
Austria-Hungary by Serbia or by the Serbian Government in any way, *had in no wise been proved.* A whole
country *could not be held responsible* for *the acts of
individuals.* Furthermore, the murderer of the Archduke was not even a Serbian subject. There *certainly*
was a Greater Serbia propaganda *in Austria,* but it was
the result of the *bad* methods of government by which
Austria had distinguished herself for ages back. Just
as there was a Greater Serbia propaganda, one heard

Yes.

Right.

Yes.

Good.

Genuinely Russian.

talk also of the Italian Irredenta and of the Free-from-Rome movement. The Vienna Cabinet had not the slightest reason for complaining of the *attitude of the Serbian Government*, which, on the contrary, *was behaving itself with entire propriety*.

Damnation!

I interjected here that it did not suffice for members of the Serbian Government themselves to refrain from participation in the anti-Austrian propaganda. Austria-Hungary had far more reason to require that the Serbian authorities should proceed actively against the anti-Austrian propaganda, for it was impossible that the Government should refuse responsibility for everything that was going on in the country.

Right.

According to that principle, returned Mr Sazonov, Russia ought to hold the Swedish Government responsible for the *anti-Russian agitation* that has been *going on in Sweden* for about a year and a half.

And Russia for her spies that are being apprehended everywhere!

I pointed out that in Sweden the matter merely concerned a political agitation, and not, as in Serbia, a propaganda of action.

Mr Sazonov remarked in reply that those people in Austria who were advocating proceeding against Serbia would apparently not content themselves with making representations at Belgrade, but that their object was the annihilation of Serbia. I answered that I had never heard of any object but one, namely, the 'clarification' of Austria-Hungary's relations with Serbia.

And the best thing, too.

The Minister continued excitedly, saying that in any case, Austria-Hungary, if she was absolutely determined to disturb the peace, ought not to forget that in that event she would *have to reckon with Europe*. Russia could not look indifferently on at a move at Belgrade which aimed at the humiliation of Serbia. I remarked that I was able to *see no humiliation* in serious representations by which Serbia was reminded of her international obligations. Mr Sazonov answered that it would all depend on how the move was carried out; that in no case *should there be any talk of an ultimatum*.

No! with Russia, yes! as the perpetrator and advocate of regicide!!

Right.

It's already there!

The Minister repeatedly called attention in the course of the conversation to the fact that, according to information he had received, the situation was being very

He is wrong!

seriously regarded in Paris and London also, and he was visibly attempting to give me the impression that even in England Austria's attitude was strongly disapproved of.

At the conclusion of our conversation I asked Mr Sazonov what there was, in his opinion, to the alleged plan for the union of Serbia and Montenegro, lately so much discussed in the papers. The Minister remarked that such a union was desired only by Montenegro, which would of course benefit most by it. Such a union was not being considered at all in Serbia, as the late Mr Hartwig had specifically emphasised in one of his last reports.[1] At the most, all that was wanted was a closer economic relation with Montenegro, but a personal union was not in any way desired.

Qui vivra verra!

Mr Sazonov had also expressed to my Italian colleague his anxiety about the Austro-Serbian tension, and remarked at the time that Russia would *not be able to permit* Austria-Hungary to *make any threats against Serbia* or to *take any military measures*. '*La politique de la Russie*,' said Mr Sazonov, '*est pacifique, mais pas passive*.'[2]

41   Jules Cambon to Bienvenu-Martin

Telegram 181   Berlin, 22 July 1914
Confidential   D. 00.10 a.m.
D.F. X. 551   R. 2.10 a.m.

Further to my telegram 178.[3] The Stock Exchange continues to fall. The Chargé d'Affaires and I have held separate discussions with the Secretary of State about the article in the *North German Gazette*[4] which expresses the hope that the Austro-Serbian tensions will be localised. I questioned Herr von Jagow as to the contents of the Austrian Note. He assured me that he knew nothing about it.[5] I was all the more astonished at this since Germany is about to take her stand at Austria's side with particular vigour.

[1] Of 9 July; *Int. Bez.* I, 4, 148.
[2] 'Russia's policy is peaceful but not passive.'
[3] Of 21 July; *D.F.* X, 539.   [4] See 36.   [5] See 16, 17, 28 and 33.

Most confidential. I have been assured that, as in the periods of tension in 1911 and at the time of the Serbian crisis in 1912, the first warnings prior to mobilisation have been issued in Germany. I am communicating this information to the Ministry with all reserve.

42 Tschirschky to Jagow

Report 247
Confidential
D.D. 138

Vienna, 22 July 1914
R. 24 July, morning

Baron Macchio requests me to submit the following to Your Excellency:
According to the Hague Conventions, the Monarchy would be bound eventually to serve Serbia with a formal declaration of war. This declaration of war would follow the completion of mobilisation, immediately before the commencement of military operations.[1] Inasmuch as the Imperial and Royal representative in Serbia has received orders to leave Belgrade at once with his entire personnel in case of an unsatisfactory answer to the note,[2] the Monarchy would possess no official organ later, at the time of the declaration of war, through which to bring the declaration to the attention of the Serbian Government in correct and secure fashion. It would also have to be assumed that at that time telegraphic connection between Austria-Hungary and Serbia would be broken off; to send it through the mails would also be unsafe, and the due receipt of the declaration of war might be contested on the part of Serbia. Likewise, the delivery of the declaration of war at Belgrade by an official to be specially sent would hardly be possible, as it is not likely that the Serbs would let such a person cross the border, and as the sending of an officer with a flag of truce *before* an actual declaration of war would not be proper according to international law.

The Imperial and Royal Government therefore enquires of Your Excellency whether the Imperial Government would perhaps be willing to undertake to transmit to the Serbian Government the declaration of war signed by Count Berchtold by way of Berlin through the German Minister. Should the Imperial Government, however, have any scruple about undertaking its transmission in this way, some other sure means must be discovered.[3]

[1] Jagow's reply on this point see 53.
[2] See Berchtold to Giesl, 20 July; *Ö.D.* 10396.
[3] For Jagow's reply, see 53.

43 Chargé d'Affaires Bronevski to Sazonov

Letter   Berlin, 22 July 1914
Confidential
Int. Bez. I, 4, 332

In the secret telegram of 20 and 22 July of this year, nos. 114[1] and 116,[2] I
had the honour of bringing to Your Excellency's attention both the enclosed cutting of the text of the semi-official notice in the *North German
Gazette* setting out the German Government's standpoint on the question
of the impending move by the Austro-Hungarian Government with
regard to Serbia in connection with the investigation into the circumstances of the Sarajevo tragedy,[3] and the explanations relating to this
matter which I received from the Secretary of State at the Auswärtiges
Amt.

At yesterday's meeting with Herr von Jagow I opened the discussion
by indicating that it was not without a certain satisfaction that I had read
the article in the *North German Gazette*, as I detected in the attitude
which Germany took to this question a guarantee for the justice and
moderation of the Austrian demands; probably Germany would only fully
and wholly support her ally under these conditions and likewise only
under these circumstances could one be certain that Austria's impending
'dialogue' with Serbia would remain localised in accordance with the
wish expressed in the article.

Herr von Jagow replied that for all that he did not know what the
Austrian demands would comprise,[4] although he for his part had no reason
for supposing that they would be excessive. On my observing that in that
case he would so to speak have set his signature to a blank cheque which
he would have left for Vienna to fill in at her own discretion, Herr von
Jagow replied that he had not wanted to make a preliminary examination
of the Austrian demands and so take upon himself any subsequent reproaches and criticism either because the demands were exaggerated or
because of their weakness and inadequacy. In his opinion he had acted
absolutely correctly in leaving the allied Great Power to herself to find her
own solution to a question which was bound up with her vital interests.

My only comment on this was that the edginess which Vienna had so
frequently displayed whenever its relations with Serbia were concerned
regrettably gave grounds for fearing certain changes meant to dishonour
Serbia which would be irreconcilable with the dignity of a certainly not
large but nonetheless independent state. At this the Secretary of State

[1] *Int. Bez.* I, 4, 296.   [2] *Int. Bez.* I, 4, 330.
[3] See 36.   [4] In contrast see 16, 17, 28 and 33.

with a certain agitation on his part recalled the lack of restraint in Mr Pašić's speeches and cited as an illustration his address at the funeral of Hartwig, when Mr Pašić allegedly glorified Pan-Slavism ('c'était une glorification du panslavisme'). As an illustration of the Serbian Prime Minister's hostility towards Austria he did not fail in addition to quote his discussion with a correspondent of the *Leipziger Neueste Nachrichten* of which I enclose a cutting.[1] Moreover, the remarks which Mr Pašić is alleged to have made in this interview about Serbia's relations with Greece—which he described as not particularly cordial—are somewhat incomprehensible from the Serbian point of view. As the Greek Minister told me, these words of Mr Pašić have made a very unfavourable impression on Athens and, in view of the gravity of the present situation for Serbia, it would have seemed to me indispensable to make a categorical refutation of these remarks, if this has not already been done. For if voices could be heard in time from Bucharest and Athens that the turn which the Austro-Serbian 'dialogue' might take would not altogether leave unaffected the interests of the two states, this could not but probably have a moderating effect on Vienna.

When at the close of our conversation I alluded to the panic which broke out a few days ago on the Berlin Stock Exchange and the substantial fall in value of most of the shares[2] and enquired what he thought about German shareholders having to pay the price with their own securities for the methods of the Austrian politicians which in the course of three weeks had been nervously heralding a secret move, Herr von Jagow merely remarked: 'Well it is rather a different matter if you are asking me whether that is clever of the Austrians! But they have never before been very clever.'

The Secretary of State also expressed himself in the same vein to the French Ambassador, to whom he likewise repeated the assurance that he was completely ignorant of the substance of the forthcoming Austrian remonstrances to Belgrade.[3]

In addition to bringing the above to the attention of Your Excellency, for the present I merely take the liberty of adding that neither M. Cambon nor I are particularly convinced that Herr Jagow is not acquainted with the substance of the forthcoming Austrian demands. As I have already mentioned in my secret telegram of today, the French Ambassador inclines rather to be pessimistic; he regards as a disquieting symptom the simultaneous calling up of 60,000 reservists in Italy, a still greater number (about 100,000) in Austria and, finally, the increase of the peace-

---

[1] Not among the documents.   [2] See also **41**.
[3] See *D.F.*, X, 551.

time strength of the army to 450,000 in Germany,[1] on account of the large manoeuvres in the middle of August; initially he even thought that Austria would postpone the delivery of its demands until just this favourable moment. Yesterday in confidential private discussion he told me that he himself wondered whether Austria might not require Serbia to renounce all future attempts at unification with Montenegro. Even if Serbia were to give such a promise she would certainly not keep it afterwards because it would conflict with the natural course of events. In the opinion of M. Cambon this promise would have the same validity as the pledge which Greece gave some time ago in answer to the Great Powers' demand that she should abandon the efforts and intrigue which she was employing in Crete in order to annex that island in the shortest possible time.

44 Rumbold to Grey
Telegram 88   Berlin, 22 July 1914
Confidential   D. 2.20 p.m.
B.D. 77   R. 4.00 p.m.

Austria-Hungary and Serbia

Secretary of State for Foreign Affairs spoke to me last night about forthcoming Austro-Hungarian *démarche* at Belgrade, which he evidently expected would have been made before now. He said that attitude of German Government was as described in semi-official statement published in *North German Gazette* of 19 July, and admitted that he had practically drafted this statement himself.[2] He insisted that question at issue between Austria and Serbia was one for discussion and settlement by those two countries alone without interference from outside. That being his view, he had not considered it opportune to say anything to Austro-Hungarian Government. He added, however, that he had repeatedly impressed on Serbian Minister necessity of putting Serbia's relations with Austria-Hungary on a proper footing. Serbian Minister had said that his Government could not control Serbian press, which was free to publish what it liked.

[1] A mistake must have crept in somewhere, for the normal peace-time strength of the German Army in July 1914 stood well above 450,000 men, in fact around 750,000. It is a moot question what Cambon may have meant by this figure.
[2] See **36**.

Secretary for Foreign Affairs observed, with regard to this point, that if a person would or could do nothing to put a stop to a nuisance the complainant must take remedy into his own hands. He said that, in his opinion, Austro-Hungarian Government had shown great forbearance towards Serbia for a long time past.

Minutes

It is difficult to understand the attitude of the German Government. On the face of it, it does not bear the stamp of straightforwardness. If they really are anxious to see Austria kept reasonably in check, they are in the best position to speak at Vienna. All they are doing is to inflame the passions at Belgrade and it looks very much like egging on the Austrians when they openly and persistently threaten the Serbian Government through their official newspapers.

It may be presumed that the German Government do not believe that there is any real danger of war. They appear to rely on the British Government to reinforce the German and Austrian threats at Belgrade; it is clear that if the British Government did intervene in this sense, or by addressing admonitions to St Petersburg, the much desired breach between England and Russia would be brought one step nearer realisation.

But I admit that all this is speculation. We do not know the facts. The German Government clearly do know. They know what the Austrian Government is going to demand, they are aware that those demands will raise a grave issue, and I think we may say with some assurance that they have expressed approval of those demands and promised support, should dangerous complications ensue. So much can, I think, be read in the present telegram.

Prince Lichnowsky's vague hints and apprehensions do not quite correspond to the actual situation which his Government is helping to create.—E. A. C. 22 July.

I will answer this telegram to-morrow after I have seen Count Mensdorff.—E. G. 22 July 1914.

This telegram is now not worth answering separately.—E. G. 24 July 1914.

5 Ultimatum and Breaking-off of Relations
23 – 25 July

At 6.00 p.m. on 23 July Giesl, the Austrian Minister at Belgrade, delivered the Austro-Hungarian ultimatum (37) to the acting Serbian Prime Minister, Finance Minister Paču (45). Thus, the 48-hour time-limit was due to expire at 6.00 p.m. on Saturday, 25 July. As the remaining Governments, with the exception of Germany, were officially informed of the ultimatum only on the morning of 24 July, Austrian diplomacy had reduced the already brief time available for mediatory efforts by at least 15 hours.

The note was deliberately intended to be unacceptable and unacceptable it certainly was by the standards of the time. It burst on Belgrade like a bombshell. Pašić broke off his electoral campaign and hurried back to Belgrade. There the Serbian reaction was unanimous: unacceptable (56). Pašić immediately turned to Russia, Italy and England in an effort to obtain a mitigation of the conditions (65).[1]

The Entente Powers were also in general agreement that the Note was unacceptable. For the European Powers, the July crisis proper only really began with the ultimatum and the parallel German measures. Sazonov's reaction was the most extreme: he reproached the Austrians with setting Europe ablaze and predicted European war as the consequence (49, 51, 68). However, he did not desire this. On 24 July the Russian Council of Ministers decided on two courses of action. On the one hand,

[1] Also Crackanthorpe to Grey, 24 July; *B.D.* 92. For further details, see especially L. Albertini, *Origins*, II, pp. 346ff.

with the help of the Entente Allies, they would exert pressure on Vienna to extend the time-limit and advise Serbia to offer the minimum of resistance in the event of Austrian aggression. On the other they would obtain the Czar's agreement in principle to a partial mobilisation, which would afford protection against all eventualities (59).

On 25 July, after a survey given by Sazonov, the Council, presided over by the Czar, endorsed the resolutions drawn up the previous day (76, 77). At a meeting of the General Staff on the same day the Czar spoke out in support of Serbia 'even if it should prove necessary to proclaim mobilisation and open hostilities'.[1] At the same time the order was given to begin the phase preparatory to mobilisation. In an official announcement the Russian Government made it known that 'the despatch of an ultimatum to Serbia by Austria-Hungary is causing . . . the greatest anxiety' and it was 'closely following the course of the dispute between the two countries, to which Russia cannot remain indifferent'.[2] However, it appears that the warning either was not heeded or was not taken sufficiently seriously in Vienna and Berlin.

Grey characterised the note as 'the most formidable document that was ever addressed from one State to another', and in particular criticised its ultimative character. He undoubtedly feared repercussions for the general peace, but appeared disinterested in an Austro-Serbian conflict so long as it did not lead to a war between Austria and Russia (50). In his ensuing discussion with Lichnowsky, Grey referred even more forcibly to the danger of such a war, since all the Great Powers would become involved. Grey, then, recognised and declared that a war between Austria and Russia could no longer be localised, but spoke only vaguely of mediation between Vienna and St Petersburg (57), rather than between Vienna and Belgrade, as Paul Cambon, the French Ambassador in London had recommended.[3] The German gesture of support for the Austrian ultimatum made a particularly bad impression on Whitehall (39).

As the first British attempt at mediation in the July crisis, Grey spontaneously suggested to Lichnowsky an extension of the 48-hour time-limit as also did Sazonov, at the same time and quite independently (57, 60).

Circumstances did not yet seem to have evolved sufficiently far to justify dramatic measures. On the contrary, Berchtold's protestation that the *démarche* at Belgrade in no way amounted to an ultimatum[4] and the news of the probable contents of the Serbian reply (79) went a considerable

[1] *Int. Bez.* I, 5, 79.
[2] *Int. Bez.* I, 5, 43.
[3] Paul Cambon to Bienvenu-Martin, 24 July; *D.F.* XI, 23.
[4] Berchtold to Mensdorff, 24 July; *Ö.D.* 10599.

way towards reassuring Grey on 25 July.[1] The preceding day he had strongly advised the Serbs 'to express concern and regret that any officials, however subordinate, should have been accomplices in the murder of the Archduke, and promise, if this is proved, to give fullest satisfaction,' furthermore, 'to give a favourable reply on as many points as possible within the limit of time, and not to meet Austrian demands with a blank negative.'[2] Vienna's assurance gave grounds for hopes of a reconciliation, which would certainly be honoured by Belgrade, in its anxiety to show a willingness to comply with the Austrian demands. Accordingly, on 25 July Grey still clung to his original distinction between an Austro-Serbian and an Austro-Russian conflict, although even at this early stage he very definitely took into his calculations the possibility of Austria and Russia mobilising against each other (80, 82, 85).

However, one man in the British Foreign Office saw farther: Sir Eyre A. Crowe. From the beginning he had recognised the difficulty of localising the Austro-Serbian conflict, and he must have felt borne out by a telegram reaching London from Berlin in the late evening of 25 July which touched upon the inner connection between the success of localisation and England's commitment on the side of Russia and France.[3] Crowe in a detailed note drew attention to the central point to be ascertained: 'whether Germany is or is not determined to have this war now'. He continued, 'There is still the chance that she can be made to hesitate if she can be induced to apprehend that the war will find England by the side of France and Russia' (68, Minutes). Crowe held an open avowal of British commitment on the side of France and Russia in the event of a Continental war to be the only, or at least the best, means of preserving general peace.

French diplomacy was inevitably the most passive of all three Entente Powers, as Poincaré and Viviani while aboard the *France* in the Baltic and on their brief state visit to Stockholm could virtually be left out of account; Viviani's Deputy, Finance Minister Bienvenu-Martin, had no experience in foreign affairs. The dilemma in which the French were placed by Vienna's split-second timing in starting the July crisis is illustrated by Paul Cambon's return to Paris on the evening of 24 July in order to give his support to Bienvenu-Martin until Viviani should arrive. On 24 July, Bienvenu-Martin had been mainly non-committal in his attitude to the joint action by Germany and Austria (52, 55). Nevertheless, to judge from his own account, he seems to have laid greater

---

[1] *B.D.* 105, 118.
[2] Grey to Crackanthorpe, 24 July; *B.D.* 102.
[3] Rumbold to Grey, 25 July; *B.D.* 128.

stress on the prevention of conditions unacceptable to Serbia[1] than the German and Austro-Hungarian Ambassadors suggest in their versions of the discussions which they held with him on that day. But this discrepancy is not otherwise significant, in view of the general paralysis of French foreign policy. More important is the fact that Jules Cambon, while still in London, on 24 July proposed a conference of the Great Powers with the aim of further delaying Austria from putting the ultimatum into effect;[2] and that in addition Paléologue, the French Ambassador in St Petersburg, of his own accord and without instructions from his Government, gave the Russian Foreign Minister a pledge of France's unconditional solidarity (68). On July 25 in a joint conversation with Buchanan and Sazonov Paléologue repeated his personal pledge (83) and also communicated his view to Carlotti, the Italian Ambassador in St Petersburg.[3]

A symptom of the forced tempo which the Austrians had set with their tight limit of 48 hours was the fact that Dumaine, the French Ambassador in Vienna, could not even attempt to carry out his Government's instructions to support the Russian *démarche* at Vienna and so gain an extension of the time-limit (47), as the deadline had already expired by the time the order reached him from Paris.[4] Dumaine held Austria's resolve to demonstrate her might against Serbia to be unshakeable, but he still believed that the Monarchy would prove amenable to subsequent attempts at mediation.[5] Jules Cambon, in contrast, was more pessimistic. On the basis of his observations in Berlin, he felt that the situation had already gone so far that as early as 25 July he recommended to his Government that it should make discreet military preparations.[6]

With these concurrent attempts at mediation, the preservation of peace now depended on whether or not Vienna and Berlin repudiated the efforts of the Great Powers to extend the time limit and effect a reconciliation. Austria-Hungary, seconded by Germany, brusquely rejected the proposal for an extension of the time-limit (69, 70). Both Governments resisted with all their might any attempts at mediation between Vienna and Belgrade and would only consider mediation between Vienna and St Petersburg. The first form of diplomatic intervention was regarded by Berlin as unwarranted interference (53)[7] as it would in fact have stood

---

[1] Bienvenu-Martin to Viviani, 24 July; *D.F.* XI, 7.
[2] Paul Cambon to Bienvenu-Martin, 24 July; *D.F.* XI, 12.
[3] Carlotti to San Giuliano, 25 July; *Kriegsschuldfrage*, I, p. 164.
[4] *D.F.* XI, 55.   [5] *D.F.* XI, 52.   [6] *D.F.* XI, 49.
[7] Thus still G. Ritter, *Staatskunst*, II, p. 313: 'there it was taken for granted that the use of force, in other words, the declaration of war which had so frequently been declared to be urgently necessary, would immediately follow on Serbia's note of rejection, and to that end

in the way of an essential goal of Reich policy—a small *blitzkrieg* against Serbia as a remedy to Austria-Hungary's internal troubles. The second form would have averted a *European* war and realised the German concept of localisation, but it would also have resulted in a considerable strengthening in the power of the Triple Alliance, and this would have been unacceptable to the Entente.

After the ultimatum Berchtold outwardly protested his peaceful intentions (48, 54, 63, 64), and indeed achieved a certain success in this,[1] as Grey's reaction to the official deprecation of the ultimative character of the *démarche* at Belgrade demonstrates. Yet on 24 July Tisza and Conrad reaffirmed their fixed determination to mobilise, should the Serbian reply turn out to be unsatisfactory,[2] and on 25 July the once so cautious Tisza insisted to Emperor Franz Joseph that, on expiry of the time-limit, Austria should immediately break off relations with Serbia and order mobilisation.[3]

On the day after the ultimatum Secretary of State Jagow had to face a second assault by the Entente diplomats. In accordance with pre-established tactics (33) he tried to the best of his ability to sustain the fiction that the German Government had had no foreknowledge of the Austrian ultimatum—an assertion which he never tired of repeating, with all the variations imaginable. Jagow diligently gave currency to an identical story in Rome through Flotow, the German Ambassador, and through Bollati, the Italian Ambassador in Berlin,[4] in order to reassure Italy, who although an ally, had been deliberately kept in the dark. In all these discussions the Secretary of State stoutly defended the contents of the note in principle but tried to ease his position by conceding to Cambon on 24 July and Rumbold on 25 July that the note was nevertheless somewhat sharp (66, 81).

The German Government, unmoved by Europe's stern reaction to the Austrian ultimatum to Serbia, continued with its secret preparations for the large-scale conflict which was becoming ever more likely. The Austrian enquiry of 22 July as to the most appropriate way of delivering the declaration of war to Serbia only reached Berlin on 24 July (42). Jagow replied immediately without raising any objection to this fresh evidence of Austria's belligerent intentions, although this might reasonably have

---

Berlin (still without knowing the Serbian reply) advised that this should be carried out as soon as possible in order to forestall the longing of the Triple Entente to interfere.'
  [1] See above, p. 161.
  [2] *Ö.D.* 10637, 10633.
  [3] *Ö.D.* 10708.
  [4] Jagow to Flotow, 24 July; *D.D.* 145; Szögyény to Berchtold, 25 July; *Ö.D.* 10655.

been expected after his alleged protest to Szögyény at the severity of Austria's conditions to Serbia.[1] It was for tactical reasons alone that the German Secretary of State declined to accede to the Austrian request for the German Minister in Belgrade to undertake the delivery of the ultimatum to the Serbian Government, for he sought to avoid making it 'appear as though we have harried Austria-Hungary into the war' (53).

Meanwhile administrative preparations for war went ahead in Berlin. As early as 24 July a meeting which included Delbrück, who had returned early from his holiday, was held at the War Ministry to consider domestic measures for the treatment of national minorities (Poles, Danes, French), and members of the German Social Democratic Party. At this meeting Delbrück successfully used his influence to secure a greater flexibility than had originally been planned;[2] the leaders of the national minorities and of the Socialists were not to be automatically thrown into prison immediately war broke out.

Meanwhile, leaving the Entente to worry over world peace, in the hope that they would persuade Serbia to submit to Austria's conditions, the German Government did everything in its power to provide a political and diplomatic screen for Austria's action against Serbia. Berlin therefore consistently thwarted all attempts by the other Powers to avert a local war by mediation between Vienna and Belgrade. At the same time Jagow urged Austria to begin the war as soon as possible in order to knock the bottom out of the attempts at reconciliation (71). Although, as so often in the course of these weeks,[3] there came a further warning from Lichnowsky in London urgently advising Austria to accept the British proposals for conciliation (73, 74), Jagow failed to treat Grey's initiative with any degree of urgency and held it back for the time being. Only two hours after the time-limit had expired did he forward these proposals to Vienna, without giving any indication of his support.[4] As Vienna knew the German viewpoint, such a curt treatment of Grey's initiative must have amounted to an indirect and tacit invitation to refuse. However, Jagow tried to impress upon the British that he had given the Austrians immediate and positive indication that he supported the British initiative (81).

Jagow used the same delaying tactics with the Russians. He allowed plenty of time before acceding (on 25 July) to Bronevski's request for an appointment, and only received the Chargé d'Affaires an hour and ten minutes before expiry of the time-limit imposed on Serbia, so that the

[1] See above, p. 126.
[2] C. v. Delbrück, *Mobilmachung*, p. 98.
[3] See 97, 98 and 99; also *D.D.* 43, 52, 55, 62, 152, 161, 163, 165, 218, 237 and 447.
[4] Jagow to Tschirschky, 25 July; *D.D.* 171.

Russian move to obtain German support for an extension of the time-limit never got off the ground. To cap his diplomatic slight Jagow rejected the Russian plea and merely tried to console the Russians by referring them to Austria's declaration of territorial *désintéressement* (78).[1]

In the interests of a successful localisation of the conflict the Auswärtiges Amt remained, as before, opposed to all premature movements of the German Fleet of the kind envisaged by the Kaiser's command, as it was afraid of startling England into taking sides with Russia and France.[2] For this reason Jagow preferred to encourage Grey in the distinction he drew between an Austro-Serbian and an Austro-Russian conflict (75); for, if England acquiesced, the Auswärtiges Amt would have achieved the full objective of its policy of localisation.

The decision on Serbia's reply was taken in Belgrade on the 24–25 July. So far there is virtually no documentary evidence of proceedings either on the Serbian side or between St Petersburg and Belgrade, as the Russian files here show considerable lacunae and those of the Serbians have yet to be published.[3] This unsatisfactory archival situation has led to the view that the Serbian Government had initially wanted to submit and had only decided to give an intransigent reply under the influence of promises from Russia.

In a penetrating analysis, Albertini has pointed out that it was clear to the Serbs that they would have to comply with the ultimatum because of their own weakness and Russia's hesitant attitude in the past. Only Russia's attitude to the ultimatum could have subsequently given the Serbs courage to resist, whereas talk in Serbian Government circles, before and after the ultimatum, of wanting to reject unacceptable conditions amounted to little more than the customary Balkan tactics.[4]

Nevertheless, the most recent authoritative opinion that 'Serbia received every conceivable encouragement from Russia'[5] begins to look questionable. The Russian Government in no wise gave Serbia a blank cheque for unconditional resistance to the Austrian demands. Before and after the ultimatum it indicated separately to Vienna and Berlin that it was in favour of Austria obtaining satisfaction from Serbia—in other words, Serbia should accept such conditions as were acceptable; in the last days of the July crisis, Sazonov even went so far as to admit that Serbia had

[1] See also Bronevski to Jagow, 25 July, *D.D.* 172, as well as Jules Cambon to Bienvenu-Martin, 25 July, *D.F.* XI, 49.

[2] Bethmann Hollweg to Wilhelm II, 25 July; *D.D.* 182.

[3] Vladimir Dedijer is now at the head of a commission to publish the Serbian Documents on the First World War.

[4] L. Albertini, *Origins*, II, pp. 350ff.

[5] K.-D. Erdmann, *Die Zeit der Weltkriege*, p. 17.

deserved a 'lesson'.[1] In the only surviving instructions to Belgrade during those crucial days of 24–25 July Sazonov in no sense spoke of resistance, nor did he encourage the Serbian Government to reject the conditions; rather he advised it to renounce the idea of military resistance in the event of an Austrian invasion and to appeal to the other Powers for arbitration (60). Accordingly St Petersburg only opposed those conditions which were unacceptable and to the end advocated that these should be mitigated.[2]

The attitude of the Serbian Government was wholly analogous: before the ultimatum it repeatedly stressed that it was prepared to accept conditions which were not injurious to Serbian sovereignty: on 20 July it dispatched a circular informing the other Powers that it would 'agree to the demands of the Imperial and Royal Government relating to the prosecution of the accomplices of the Sarajevo criminals if any such should be discovered'. But—and now follows the crucial sentence—'It would only be unable to comply with such demands as were inconsistent with the dignity and independence of the Serbian nation'.[3] Two days later Dumaine notified Paris that Jovanović, the Serbian Minister in Vienna, believed that the Austrian conditions would be accepted. The grounds for such an acceptance can be deduced from the context: 'The demands of the Austro-Hungarian Government relating to the punishment of the assassins and specific guarantees for supervision and policing seem acceptable to the dignity of Serbia'.[4] As Dumaine on the other hand also reported Serbian determination to resist, it may be assumed that he was taking into account the possibility that Vienna would pose unacceptable conditions, which in fact, was precisely what happened. As late as 23 July, in an exhaustive analysis of the Serbian situation immediately prior to the ultimatum, Strandtmann, the Russian Chargé d'Affaires, reported that the Serbian Government would certainly 'meet all demands if they are in the slightest degree compatible with the dignity of an independent state'.[5]

The Serbian Government, in its spontaneous reaction to the ultimatum, also gave no evidence that it was considering an unconditional submission, in other words, a complete and unqualified acceptance of all demands. Here, one repeatedly comes up against the distinction between acceptable and unacceptable demands, made by those actually involved in the situation. Thus, immediately after receiving the ultimatum on the evening of July 23 Pašić, the acting Prime Minister, sought out the Russian

[1] See 100.   [2] See 90, 107, 123, 141a and 168.
[3] Jagow to Tschirschky, 20 July; *D.D.* 91.   [4] *D.F.* X, 554.
[5] *Int. Bez.* I, 5, 9.

Chargé d'Affaires, implored Russia's protection and declared that 'no Serbian Government could accept the demands of Austria'.[1] On the following day, in its first commentary on the ultimatum, the Serbian press adopted the line previously taken by Serbian diplomacy. As Giesl telegraphed to Vienna on 24 July, it was unanimously reported that Serbia could only comply with demands which were not detrimental to her independence.[2] The German Minister in Belgrade telegraphed the same day that in the Serbian capital 'it is said to be impossible to carry out the demands set forth within 48 hours, especially points 2, 4, 5 and 6 (paragraph 2), in which a direct attack upon Serbia's sovereignty is seen'.[3]

On 24 July Strandtmann reported his first conversation with Pašić after the ultimatum: the Prime Minister's 'first impression is that it is neither possible to accept the Austrian Note nor to reject it; time must be gained at all costs.' Apparently Pašić intended 'to give an answer to Austria within the prescribed time limit . . . showing the points which are acceptable or unacceptable'.[4] Jovanović in Vienna took the same standpoint in naming to Dumaine the unacceptable points whilst predicting broad satisfaction on the remainder (66). Likewise Crackanthorpe, British Chargé d'Affaires in Belgrade, reported that Pašić responded with a request for British mediation 'to soften those Austrian demands which he described as impossible'.[5]

To sum up, it can be ascertained from the available documents that from the very beginning the Serbs only intended to make a qualified rather than an outright rejection of the ultimatum. Subsequently the pressure which the Entente Powers brought to bear on Serbia to give the most conciliatory reply possible seems to have been so effective that at about midday on 25 July the Serbian Government was able to give the British and French delegates a résumé of the envisaged reply containing an acceptance of all the points with but a few minor reservations (79). The cause of the alteration of a qualified acceptance of Point 6 into a rejection in the final reply (72) is generally attributed to a telegram from St Petersburg promising Russian assistance in the event of an attack on Serbia.[6] The deplorable lack of documents on this point renders such an explanation plausible, but before going on to conclude that *therefore* a large burden of the responsibility for the First World War should fall upon Russia and Serbia, one would first still have to prove that the Austrians (and the Germans) would have been satisfied with the provisos foreshadowed in the Serbian reply. After all, Giesl had received instruc-

[1] *Int. Bez.* I, 5, 10.   [2] *A.R.B.* II, 3 (Ö.D. 10577).
[3] *D.D.* 159.   [4] *Int. Bez.* I, 5, 35.
[5] *B.D.* 92.   [6] See L. Albertini, *Origins*, II, pp. 357f.

tions to treat even reservations as unsatisfactory;[1] moreover, the Austrians did, in actual fact, denounce these reservations as unsatisfactory.[2] Further, the Russians' pledge not to countenance an attack on Serbia fully accorded with the line they had taken *before* the ultimatum,[3] and finally, the Austrians could have been content with the astonishing compliance of Serbia if they had not needed a pretext for war.

Thus Serbian mobilisation at 3 p.m. on 23 July, three hours before delivery of the Serbian reply, cannot in itself be regarded as provocative. In the last analysis, it was a purely defensive move entailing, for instance, a military withdrawal from Belgrade, which lay directly on the frontier, and was only separated from Austria-Hungary by the Danube. It was no more than a straightforward precautionary measure. As the secret intention to launch a surprise attack on Serbia proves, Serbian suspicions were not without foundation in view of the small size of the country. The bombardment of Belgrade by the Austrian artillery, which began on the day immediately following the declaration of war, merely furnished fresh evidence in support of Serbian fears.

When Baron Giesl received the Serbian reply (72), he simply glanced through the long document. He was quick to grasp that it did not contain a total and unconditional submission, and he immediately broke off diplomatic relations with Serbia. The embassy staff had already packed and left Belgrade by a regular train only half an hour after relations had been severed. A ten minutes' journey brought Giesl across the bridge over the Danube and into Semlin, on Austro-Hungarian soil, and from there he telegraphed news of the rupture to Budapest and Vienna. Even before the information arrived Vienna had proclaimed partial mobilisation against Serbia.

45 Giesl to Berchtold

Telegram 175
Ö.D. 10526

Belgrade, 23 July 1914
D. 8.00 p.m.
R. 24 July, 2.15 a.m.

Ultimatum.

Premier *ad interim* Paču after some hesitation conceded a conversation for six o'clock, and received me at the striking of the clock. Secretary-

[1] Ö.D. 10396.
[2] In the official commentary of 28 July to the Serbian Note of reply; Ö.D. 10860.
[3] See above, p. 137.

General Gruic was with him, because Paču does not know French. I gave him the note and added that the term for the answer had been fixed for Saturday at 6 p.m. and that if by that time I had received no answer or an unsatisfactory one, I should leave Belgrade with the entire legation; that at the same time as the answer, I wished to receive the Serbian translation of both enunciations, which we were desirous to compare. Paču, without reading the note, answered that the elections were being carried on and some of the Ministers were absent from Belgrade. He feared it would be physically impossible to assemble a complete Council of Ministers in time for taking, what he must believe to be an important decision. The Council of Ministers had been assembled ever since five o'clock. I answered that in our age of railways, telegraphs and telephones and the diminutive size of the country, it could only be a question of a few hours to assemble the Ministers, and that in the forenoon I had advised to inform Herr Pašić. But this was an internal Serbian concern, that I had no right to judge. Nothing more was discussed.

46　Jagow to Wilhelm II

Telegram 116
D.D. 121

Berlin, 23 July 1914
D. 1.40 p.m.
R. 8.30 p.m.

Your Majesty's Ambassador in London telegraphs:[1]
Sir Edward Grey, as I am confidentially informed, is going to state to Count Mensdorff tomorrow that the British Government will exert itself to influence the Serbian Government to accept the Austro-Hungarian demands, in case they are *moderate* and are *made reconcilable with the independence of the Serbian nation.* He also believes that Sazonov will use his influence at Belgrade toward the same end. But the condition precedent to this attitude would be that Vienna should bring no unprovable accusations *à la* Friedjung, and that the Austro-Hungarian Government should be in a position to demonstrate indubitably the connection between the murder at Sarajevo and the political circles in Belgrade. Everything will depend on the

It's not for him to decide as to this; that is the business of His Majesty the Emperor Franz Joseph!

That's their business!

[1] Lichnowsky's telegram was dated 22 July; *D.D.* 118.

manner in which the note is drawn at Vienna and on the results of the inquiry up to date. But it will be *impossible*, however, to make representations *at Belgrade* on the strength of *frivolous* assertions. I am in the meantime endeavouring to influence matters here so that, in view of Austria's justifiable desire for satisfaction and for the final termination of the long disturbances, they may advocate the unconditional acceptance of the Austrian demands, even if the latter should not fully respect *Serbia's national dignity*. In so doing I meet with the expectation that our influence at Vienna has been successful in suppressing demands that cannot be met. They are counting with certainty on the fact that we shall not identify ourselves with demands that are plainly intended to bring on war, and that we will not support any policy which makes use of the murder at Sarajevo merely as an excuse for carrying out Austrian desires in the Balkans, and for the annulment of the peace of Bucharest. Furthermore, Sir Edward Grey let me know again today that he was trying to use his influence at St Petersburg on behalf of the Austrian point of view. But the fact that Count Berchtold has so far very noticeably avoided discussing the Serbian question with Sir Maurice de Bunsen has not created a pleasant impression here.

Your Majesty's Ambassador at London is in receipt of instructions, for the benefit of his conferences, to the effect that we do not know what the Austrian demands are, *but that we regarded them as part of Austria-Hungary's internal affairs, which it would not become us to attempt to influence.*[1]

Marginal notes by Wilhelm:

What does he mean, frivolous? How can Grey use such a word about that old and honoured sovereign?

There isn't any such thing!

Why should I do any such thing? None of my business! What does 'cannot be met' mean? The rascals have added murder to agitation and must be humbled. That is a tremendous piece of British insolence. I am not called upon to prescribe à la Grey to His Majesty the Emperor how to preserve his honour!

Right! Grey must be told this plainly and seriously! So that he will see that I am not fooling. Grey is committing the error of setting Serbia on the same plane with Austria and other Great Powers! That is unheard of! Serbia is nothing but a band of robbers that must be seized for its crimes! I will meddle in nothing of which the Emperor is alone competent to judge! I expected this despatch, and am not surprised by it! Real British reasoning and condescending way of giving orders, which I insist on having rebuffed!   Wilhelm I. R.

[1] Jagow's instruction to Lichnowsky of 23 July; *D.D.* 126.

47 Viviani to Bienvenu-Martin

Telegram (unnumbered)   St Petersburg, 24 July 1914
D.F. XI, 1   D. 2.05 a.m.
                                                             R. 5.30 a.m.

I should be obliged if you would urgently send on to M. Dumaine the
following information and instructions:

In the course of my conversations with the Russian Minister for Foreign
Affairs we had to take into consideration the dangers which might result
from any step taken by Austria-Hungary in relation to Serbia in connection
with the crime of which the Hereditary Archduke has been a victim. We
found ourselves in agreement in thinking that we should not leave anything undone to prevent a request for an explanation or some *mise en
demeure* which would be equivalent to intervention in the internal affairs
of Serbia, of such a kind that Serbia might consider it as an attack on her
sovereignty and independence.

We have in consequence come to the opinion that we might, by means
of a friendly conversation with Count Berchtold, give him counsels of
moderation, of such a kind as to make him understand how undesirable
would be any intervention at Belgrade which would appear to be a threat
on the part of the Cabinet at Vienna.

The British Ambassador, who was kept informed by M. Sazonov,
expressed the idea that his Government would doubtless associate itself
with a *démarche* for removing any danger which might threaten general
peace, and he has telegraphed to his Government to this effect.[1]

M. Sazonov has addressed instructions to this effect to M. Schebeko.[2]
While there is no question in this of collective or concerted action at
Vienna on the part of the representatives of the Triple Entente, I ask you
to discuss the matter with the Russian and British Ambassadors, and to
come to an agreement with them as to the best means by which each of you
can make Count Berchtold understand without delay the moderation that
the present situation appears to us to require.

Further, it would be desirable to ask M. Paul Cambon to bring the
advantages of this procedure to the notice of Sir Edward Grey, and to
support the suggestion that the British Ambassador in Russia will have
made to this effect to the Foreign Office. Count Benckendorff is instructed
to make a similar recommendation.

[1] On 22 July; *B.D.* 76.
[2] On 22 July; *Int. Bez.* I, 4, 322.

48 Conversation between Berchtold and the Russian Chargé d'Affaires

Daily Report 3578   Vienna, 24 July 1914
Ö.D. 10615

I received the Russian Chargé d'Affaires in the forenoon of 24 July and assured him that I was particularly anxious to inform him as soon as possible of our step in Belgrade and to explain to him how we stand.

While thanking me for this kind intention, Prince Kudachev did not conceal his apprehension over our categorical way of treating Serbia, remarking that in St Petersburg the Government was all along preoccupied whether our *démarche* would not take the form of much humiliation for Serbia, in which case a repercussion would be unavoidable in Russia.

I took great pains to reassure the Russian Chargé d'Affaires. There was nothing further from our mind than to humiliate Serbia, a proceeding which would be against our interests. It had been my particular care to eliminate from the Note everything which could have been interpreted in this sense.[1] The only aim we had in view was to clear up the intolerable situation between Serbia and the Monarchy, and this we hoped to accomplish by causing the Serbian Government to deny having anything to do with the tendencies directed against our Monarchy and stopping the movement by administrative measures. On the other hand we asked to be allowed to convince ourselves that these measures were being conscientiously applied. I explained fully what a serious danger to the integrity of the Monarchy the continuation of the movement in favour of Greater Serbia must become, and that it might even endanger the equilibrium of Europe, its peace and the safety of its dynasties, not excepting the Russian, if the conviction gained ground that doings which counted murder among their weapons remained unpunished. I concluded by assuring him that we had no intention of increasing the size of our territory, but wished to maintain it intact, a point of view which Russia must applaud, as much as we think it natural, that Russia would never tolerate an attack upon its own integrity.

Prince Kudaschev said that he was not acquainted with his Government's point of view and had no idea what Serbia would say to the different demands addressed to it. His personal impression was, that we were asking the impossible from a constitutionally governed state. He felt as if somebody had been asked to jump out of the window first and come back over the stairs afterwards. We are prescribing the text of the Government's declaration and the army order, and this he thinks Serbia will

[1] See in contrast 9, 12, 16, 20, 27, 31 and 35.

regard in the light of a deep humiliation. Then he was thinking of the point, in which we asked to be allowed to let our organs help in the repression of propaganda, and this was a violation of international law. It is true Russia has made arrangements for establishing Russian secret services in France and Germany. But this is regarded as a 'privilege' and not a 'right'. Nor does it agree with international law that the guilty persons are to undergo punishment in Serbia; their extradition might be demanded. (It is not clear what Prince Kudaschev meant by this, and when I contradicted him, he changed the conversation.) The short term of the ultimatum also caused anxiety to the Russian representative. He asked: What will happen, if the term expires and no satisfactory answer comes from Serbia?

When I told him that in this case our Minister would leave Belgrade with the personnel of the legation, he reflected some time and then said: 'Alors, c'est la guerre!'

Before leaving, the Russian representative said that he would not fail to give his Government all the information he had received from me, and most especially the assurance that we did not intend to humiliate Serbia in any way.[1]

49   Szápáry to Berchtold

Telegram 156   St Petersburg 24 July 1914
Ö.D. 10616   D. 3.35 p.m.
                                                             R. 11.00 p.m.

Instructions contained in no. 3405 and 3430 carried[2] out this morning. I take the liberty of reporting provisionally that the Minister from the very first said that he would not take sides with regard to the *démarche* and also to some occasionally violent discussions, listened to my reading of the note and to my comments in comparative quiet.

He avoided saying anything that could be construed into an understanding what Russia would do, but from time to time he said: 'I know what it is. You want to go to war with Serbia! I can see what is going on, the German papers are adding fuel to the fire! You are setting fire to Europe! It is a great responsibility you are assuming, you will see what sort of an impression you will make in London and in Paris and perhaps elsewhere. It will be considered as an unjustified aggression.' But he never mentioned Russia directly. . . .[3]

[1] See also **54, 63** and **64**.   [2] See **38**.   [3] Cipher mutilated.

In his arguments, he tried to deny any responsibility on the part of the Serbian Government, called our demands simply unacceptable, and referring to the dissolution of the *Narodna odbrana* said that Serbia never would allow this. He found fault with the form of an ultimatum, which prevented Serbia from justifying herself, and finally repeated that he was taking nobody's part, and would vouchsafe no answer. As a last word he added that certainly a grave situation had been created. However an inevitable discussion followed, in the course of which, he asserted that it was all Count Forgách's doing, and tried to depreciate our proofs, by saying he doubted them. To my repeated warnings[1] that all monarchical interests were at stake[2] he lent a deaf ear. The personal impression I received, was that the Minister was more saddened and depressed than excited; the tactics he followed were not to commit himself with regard to Russia's future attitude. A detailed telegraphic report will follow.[3]

50 Mensdorff to Berchtold

Telegram 108
Ö.D. 10600

London, 24 July 1914
D. 2.50 p.m.
R. 25 July, 9.00 a.m.

In addition to the telegram 107 of yesterday.[4]

Just presented the circular note to Sir Edward Grey, who read it through attentively. Arrived at Point 5 he asked how the following was to be understood? 'Organs of our Government to be placed in Serbia'. This would put an end to Serbia's independence as a State. I answered that the collaboration of police-organs, for instance, does not touch a State's sovereignty.

The Secretary of State repeated the objections he raised yesterday on account of the shortness of the term, which does not allow other States time to use their influence. He called our Note to Serbia the most formidable document that was ever addressed from one State to another, but at the same time admitted, that what it said on the guilt of Serbia in the crime of Sarajevo and some of our demands were fully justified.

What appear to be his objections are: Point 5, the shortness of the term, and the fact that the Note, so to speak, dictates the answer.

[1] Cipher mutilated.   [2] See 38 and 39.   [3] See 51.
[4] *Ö.D.* 10537; in this Mensdorff reports that he has unofficially and in confidence informed Grey of the contents of the Note.

What makes him seriously anxious is the possible effect upon the peace of Europe. If there was no danger to that, he would be quite prepared to consider the affair as solely regarding Austria-Hungary and Serbia. But he confesses to being most 'apprehensive' that several Great Powers might become involved in a war. Speaking of Russia, Germany and France, he remarked, that he believed the conditions of the alliance between France and Russia were very much the same as those between the Powers of the Triple Alliance.

I laid our point of view before him very explicitly, used all the arguments of telegram 159 of 23 inst.[1] and repeated that we must remain firm, to obtain some guarantees of good faith, since in the past Serbian promises had never been kept. I told him that I perfectly understood that to him the whole question appeared in the light of danger to Europe's peace, but that I must ask him to consider our point of view also and put himself in our place.

He would not continue to discuss this theme, promised to study the Note more closely and to attempt whatever could be done to avert the threatening danger. He began by calling to his presence the German and French Ambassadors. He said that he must first of all speak to the allies of Austria-Hungary and Russia, who have no interests of their own in Serbia.

He repeated several times in the course of conversation, that he was very anxious about the maintaining of the peace between the Great Powers.

51   Szápáry to Berchtold

Telegrams 157, 159   St Petersburg, 24 July 1914
Ö.D. 10617, 10619   D. 8.00, 8.25 p.m.
                                        R. 25 July, 0.50 a.m., 7.00 a.m.
My telegram of today 156[2] continued.

The Minister received me with the words: he knew already what brought me, and he must declare from the very first that he would take no sides in the *démarche* I was about to lay before him. I began by reading the decree to him as instructed. He interrupted me the first time, when the series of attempted murders was mentioned, and asked if there were any proofs that these originated in Belgrade? I answered that they were certainly the result of Serbian agitation.

[1] *Ö.D.* 10536.   [2] See 49.

In the course of the reading he said, he knew how it was, we wanted to make war with Serbia and here was the pretext.[1] I replied rather sharply, that our attitude during the last years was a sufficient proof, that with regard to Serbia we neither sought nor required pretexts. Strange to say, the Minister had nothing to say against the demanded solemn enunciations, only he repeatedly asserted that Pašić had already said things to the same effect and of course I contradicted this. 'He will repeat that twenty-five times if you wish to hear it as often!' he said. When the publications were mentioned, he asked if this would be reciprocal? I told him that in our country no one was doing anything against the Serbian integrity or dynasty.[2] To my surprise, Herr Sazonov protested most vividly against the dissolution of the society *Narodna odbrana*, a condition Serbia would never accept. The Minister was also very much against Imperial and Royal functionaries taking an active part in the suppression of the subversive movement. Serbia would no longer be its own master in its own house! 'You will be always wanting to interfere and what sort of a life will you make Europe lead!' I answered it will be a more quiet life than in the past, if only Serbia shows good will.

Herr Sazonov then tried to pull to pieces the appendage with the results of the enquiry, and to throw doubt on the correctness of the conclusions drawn. Why did one not allow the Serbians to speak for themselves? Why this form of an ultimatum? Possibly Serbia could prove the falseness of the accusations? I protested in fitting form.

The Minister listened pretty quietly to the comments accompanying the communication of the Note; but when I came to the words, that we know that our feelings are shared by all civilised nations, he said: that was a mistake. To this I replied, as impressively as I could, that it would be sad indeed, if in what we hold most sacred, and whatever he might say, was held sacred in Russia as well, we found no sympathy in that country. The Minister tried to make little of the Monarchical part of the whole affair, saying: 'the Monarchical idea has nothing to do with this affair at all'.

As to the *dossier* which the Government is prepared to furnish to the Powers, Herr Sazonov remarked that we need not have given ourselves the trouble, when we had sent out an ultimatum. This fact alone proves that we were not anxious for an impartial judgment on our case. I told him that in this affair, which exclusively concerned Austria-Hungary and Serbia, the results achieved by our enquiry must be sufficient to justify our action, but that we were prepared to give the Powers fullest explanations, if these interested them, because we had nothing to conceal.

[1] See 9, 11, 15, 16, 18, 22, 28, 30, 31, 33 and 35.   [2] See in contrast 35.

Herr Sazonov said that after the ultimatum he felt no curiosity about the case. 'What you want is war, and you have burnt your bridges behind you.'

I answered that we were the most pacific power in the world; what we wanted was to preserve our territory from revolution and our dynasty from bombs.

'One can see how pacific you are, since you are setting fire to Europe!' said Sazonov.

What we wish, I replied, is to be left in peace, and my Government has taken the necessary measures for obtaining this result.

The comments I was instructed to give by word of mouth, he listened to without protesting, only refuting the last sentence, that concerned the murder of Royal personages.

A protracted discussion followed the execution of my instructions, during which Herr Sazonov attempted to attribute our policy entirely to Count Forgách. I seized the opportunity for vindicating the conciliatory part played by that functionary while he was Minister at Belgrade. I also tried to convince the minister of the truth, with regard to the Friedjung trial,[1] which has lately been again brought forward here. In the course of conversation Sazonov once more remarked that we had most certainly created a serious situation. He never once mentioned Russia, Slavdom, orthodoxy; but he was continually referring to England, France, Europe and the impression, which our step would make in these parts of the world and elsewhere.

Notwithstanding the comparative serenity of the Minister, his whole attitude, as was to be expected, was from first to last noncompliant and hostile. The discourse had lasted an hour and a half when I left the Minister's study.[2]

---

[1] The Friedjung Trial in 1909 had been a vain attempt to prove that the Serbian Government was connected with the Pan-Serbian agitations in Bosnia-Herzegovina. For details see Hans Uebersberger, *Österreich zwischen Russland und Serbien*, pp. 50ff.

[2] Berchtold replied on 25 July (*Ö.D.* 10682). See also **50** and **52**.

52 Szécsen to Berchtold

Telegram 119
Ö.D. 10606

Paris, 24 July 1914
D. 4.55 p.m.
R. 25 July, 9.00 a.m.

Serbia. Referring to decree 3428 of the 20 inst.[1]

Have just read the decree 3428 to the Minister of Justice, representing the absent Minister of Foreign Affairs, and have left him a copy. Monsieur Bienvenu-Martin, who had learnt part of our *démarche* through the morning papers, seemed rather impressed by my communication. He would not discuss the text, but admitted freely that the events of recent times and the attitude of the Serbian Government had made energetic action on our part, a matter that could be understood.

The Minister seemed most surprised at Point 5 of the Note presented in Belgrade; I had to read it to him twice.

The Minister thanked me for my communication, which, he said would be thoroughly considered. I seized this opportunity for saying that here was a question which must find its direct solution between us and Serbia, but that it is certainly in the interest of Europe, if the disquiet, which has for many years been kept up in our country by Serbian intrigue, is replaced by a normal state of affairs.

All friends of peace and order, and among these I range France in the first place, should seriously advise Serbia to alter its attitude and to accede to our justified demands.

The Minister admitted that it was Serbia's duty to take energetic steps against possible accomplices of the murderer of Sarajevo, a duty from which it could not well shrink. Referring most impressively to the sympathies of France for Austria-Hungary, and to the good relations between the two countries, the Minister expressed the hope that the present dispute would end peaceably, in a manner to satisfy our wishes.

The Minister visibly refused to defend or condone the attitude of Serbia in any way whatever.

Monsieur Bienvenu-Martin has of course no influence whatever on the course of foreign policy in France.

[1] See **38**.

53 Jagow to Tschirschky

Telegram 134   Berlin, 24 July 1914
D.D. 142   D. 2.05 p.m.
                                                            R. 6.15 p.m.

We consider it desirable to have the declaration of war on Serbia sent
directly, and not through our Legation.[1] Our standpoint has to be that
the quarrel with Serbia is an Austro-Hungarian internal affair, in which it
would no more become us to mix than it would others, and for that reason
we are advocating the localisation of the conflict. Only if Russia should
intervene would we be drawn into the conflict. Declaration of war through
our Legation would in general, especially to that portion of the public
not acquainted with diplomatic customs, appear as though we had *harried*
Austria-Hungary into the war.[2]

54 Tschirschky to Jagow

Telegram 101   Vienna, 24 July 1914
D.D. 155   D. 8.50 p.m.
                                                            R. 11.23 p.m.

Absolutely superfluous! Will give the impression of weakness and the impression of an apology, which, in connection with Russia is absolutely false and must be avoided. Austria has her good reasons, has made a move on the strength of them; now it cannot later be made the subject of a quasi-discussion!

Ass! She must take back the Sanjac, else the Serbians will reach the Adriatic.

In order to *prove by documentary evidence his good
intentions* toward Russia, Count Berchtold requested
the Russian Chargé d'Affaires to call on him this
morning, in order to make him an exhaustive explanation of Austria-Hungary's position with regard to
Serbia. After recapitulating the historical developments
of the last few years, he emphasised the fact that the
Monarchy was far from wishing to oppose Serbia in the
role of a conqueror. Austria would not lay the *least claim
to any Serbian territory*. In like manner there had been
a careful avoidance in the note directed to Serbia of any
humiliation of Serbia. Austria strictly insisted that the
step was purely a defensive measure with the aim of
opposing the Serbian intrigues, but was compelled by
necessity to demand guaranties for a subsequent more
friendly attitude on the part of Serbia toward the

[1] See 42.   [2] See p. 99.

That will come entirely of its own accord, and must come. Austria must become preponderant in the Balkans as compared with the little ones, and at Russia's expense; otherwise there will be no peace.

Monarchy. He was far from wishing to upset the balance of power either in the Balkans or in Europe. On the contrary, he regarded the unaffected stability of Russia as a necessary factor of European policy. It should believe that it was in the interest of Europe in general to put an end to the Serbian intrigues that were continually disturbing Europe; and particularly the monarchically ruled nations of Europe should show a solid front in their united opposition to the Serbian policy conducted with revolver and with bomb.

Prince Kudaschev, who has as yet received no instructions of any kind from St Petersburg, took the arguments of the Minister under consideration, with the promise that he would submit them at once to Sazonov.[1]

I have informed the Duke d'Avarna of the above; he thought this move of Count Berchtold's with regard to Russia excellent, and felt assured that it would have an especially good effect on the Marquis di San Giuliano.

Feeble!

55 Schoen to Jagow

Telegram 210
D.D. 154

Paris, 24 July 1914
D. 8.05 p.m.
R. 10.35 p.m.

The Minister of Justice, representing the Premier, to whom I expressed myself along the lines of despatch 918,[2] was visibly relieved at our idea that Austro-Serbian conflict was one to be settled exclusively by the two participants. French Government sincerely shares the wish that conflict remain localised, and will labour along this line in the interest of the maintenance of European peace. It does not conceal from itself, however, that such a Power as Russia, which has to reckon with the current of Pan-Slavism, would find it difficult to maintain an entirely disinterested attitude,

Rot.

[1] See also 48, 63 and 64.   [2] See 39.

especially should Austria-Hungary insist upon the immediate fulfilment of all demands, even those which are scarcely compatible with Serbian sovereignty, or are impracticable to carry out at once. French Government feels that it goes without saying that Serbia should give satisfaction in a convincing manner, and should be obliged to assure the punishment of criminals and the prevention of conspiracies against Austria-Hungary. Here, too, advice has been given the Serbians to make all the concessions possible. But the view is held here that Austria-Hungary would do well, in case Serbia might not agree to all the demands at once but should wish to discuss individual points, not to refuse such requests without further ado, provided that on the whole Serbia's good-will was not *questionable*.

Ultimata are accepted or not! But one does not *discuss* any longer! Thence the name!

It is. Rubbish clad in stately phrases!

56   Griesinger to Jagow

Telegram 31
D.D. 159

Belgrade, 24 July 1914
D. 9.45 p.m.
R. 25 July, 2.33 a.m.

The energetic tone and the detailed demands of the Austrian note were *absolutely unexpected by the Serbian Government*. The Ministerial Council has been deliberating since early this morning with the *Crown Prince as Regent in the chair*, but is *unable to arrive at any decision*. It is said to be impossible to carry out the demands set forth within forty-eight hours, especially points 2, 4, 5, and 6, paragraph 2, in which a direct attack upon Serbian sovereignty is seen. In case of the proclamation of the Order of the Day, a *military uprising is feared*.

As I am informed, the removal of the Government to Nish is being considered.

Bravo! one would not have believed it of the Viennese! It looks as if His Majesty had made himself scarce. The proud Slavs!

How hollow the whole so-called Serbian power is proving itself to be; thus it is seen to be with all the Slav nations! Just tread hard on the heels of that rabble!

57 Lichnowsky to Jagow

Telegram 151
D.D. 157

London, 24 July 1914
D. 9.12 p.m.
R. 25 July, 1.16 a.m.

Sir E. Grey asked me to call on him just now. The Minister was evidently greatly affected by the Austrian note, which, according to his view, exceeded anything he had ever seen of this sort before. He said that he had so far had no news from St Petersburg, and consequently did not know what they thought of the matter there. But he very much doubted whether it would be possible for the Russian Government to recommend to the Serbian Government the unconditional acceptance of the Austrian demands. Any nation that accepted conditions like that would really cease to count as an independent nation.[1] It was very difficult for him, Sir E. Grey, to offer advice of any sort to St Petersburg at the present moment. He could only *hope* that a *mild* and pacific view of the situation would gain ground there. As long as the matter concerned a localised quarrel between Austria and Serbia, such as Your Excellency laid stress on in despatch 1055[2] which I employed in talking to Sir E. Grey, he, Sir E. Grey, had nothing to do with it; but it would be a different matter should public opinion in Russia force the Government to proceed against Austria.

To my remark that one could not measure the Balkan peoples by the same standard as the *civilised nations* of Europe, and that therefore one had to use another kind of language with them—that had been proved by their barbaric manner of warfare—than one used, say, towards Britons or Germans, the Minister replied that even if he were able to share this opinion, he did not believe that it would be accepted in Russia. The danger of a European war, should Austria *invade Serbian territory*, would become immediate. The results of such a war between *four* nations—he expressly emphasised the *number four*, and meant by it Russia,

This would be very desirable. It is not a nation in the European sense, but a band of robbers!

Right.

Right for they aren't!

Right.

Then the Russians are not any better themselves.

Which will certainly happen.
He forgets Italy.

[1] See 31.   [2] See 39.

Austria-Hungary, Germany and France—would be absolutely incalculable. However the affair might come out, one thing would be certain: that would be total exhaustion and impoverishment; industry and trade would be ruined, and the power of capital destroyed. Revolutionary movements, like those of the year 1848, due to the collapse of industrial activities would be the result. What Sir Edward Grey most deplored, beside the tone of the note, was the brief time-limit, which made war almost unavoidable. He told me that he would be willing to join with us in pleading for a prolongation of the time-limit at Vienna, as in that way *perhaps a way out* might be found. He requested me to transmit this proposal to your Excellency. He further suggested that in the event of a dangerous tension between Russia and Austria, the four nations not immediately concerned—England, Germany, France and Italy—should undertake to mediate between Russia and Austria. This proposal, also, he requested me to submit to Your Excellency.

The Minister is evidently endeavouring to do everything to avoid European complications, and could not conceal his great regret at the challenging tone of the Austrian note and at the brief time-limit.

I am told from another quarter in the Foreign Office that there is reason for the assumption that Austria is very much under-estimating Serbia's power of self-defence. In any event it will be a long and desperate fight, in which Austria will be excessively weakened and in which she will be *bled white*. They also claim to know that Roumania's attitude is more than uncertain, and that they were saying in Bucharest that they would be against anybody who attacked.

Marginal notes:

Useless.

This is superfluous, as Austria has already made matters plain to Russia, and Grey has nothing else to propose. I will not join in it unless Austria expressly asks me to, which is not likely. In *vital* questions and those of honour, one does not consult with others.

Nonsense.

It may give Persia to England.

58 Pourtalès to Jagow

Telegram 149   St Petersburg, 25 July 1914
D.D. 160   D. 1.08 a.m.
                                                         R. 3.45 a.m.

Have just had long interview[1] with Sazonov at which
subject of despatch 592[2] figured exhaustively. Minister,

Good.

who was *very much excited* and gave vent to boundless
reproaches against Austria-Hungary, stated in the
most determined manner that it would be impossible
for Russia to admit that the Austro-Serbian quarrel
could be settled between the two parties concerned. The
obligations which Serbia had assumed after the Bosnian
crisis and to which the Austrian note refers, were
assumed toward Europe, consequently the affair was a

Rot!

European affair, and it was for *Europe* to investigate as
to whether Serbia had lived up to these obligations. He
therefore proposes that the documents in relation to the
inquiry be laid before the Cabinets of the six Powers.

That's a question of
the point of view!

Austria could not be both accuser and judge in her own
case. Sazonov announced that he could in no way
consider as proven the facts alleged by Austria in her
note, that the inquiry, on the other hand, inspired him
with the greatest suspicion. He continued by saying that,
in case the facts asserted should be proved to be true,
Serbia could give Austria satisfaction in the purely legal
questions, but not, on the other hand, in the matter
of the demands of a political nature. I called attention

Cannot be separated.

to the fact that it was impossible to separate the legal
from the political side of the matter, as the assassination

Right. Pan-Slavistic.

was inseparably connected with the Greater Serbia
propaganda.

I promised to lay his ideas before my Government,
but did not believe that we would suggest to our ally
to submit the results of an inquiry conducted by her

Most certainly not!

once more to a European tribunal. Austria would object
to this suggestion just as any Great Power would have

Bravo! Well said!

to refuse to submit itself to a court of arbitration in a
case in which its vital interests were at stake.

[1] I.e. on 24 July about 7.00 p.m.; see **62**.   [2] See **39**.

My references to the Monarchical principle made
little impression on the Minister. Russia *knew* what she
owed to the monarchical principle, with which, however,
this case had nothing to do. I requested Sazonov very
seriously, avoiding everything that might have the
appearance of a threat, not to let himself be led astray
by his hatred of Austria and '*not to defend a bad cause.*'
Russia could not possibly constitute herself the advocate
of regicides.

In the course of the conversation Sazonov exclaimed:
'If Austria-Hungary devours Serbia, we will go to war
with her.' From this it may perhaps be concluded that
Russia will only take up arms in the event of Austria's
attempting to acquire territory at the expense of Serbia.
The expressed desire to Europeanise the question also
seems to point to the fact that immediate intervention
on the part of Russia is not to be anticipated.

[marginal notes:]

Not since her
fraternising with the
French socialist
republic!

Regicide.
Very good.

Well, go to it!

That it does not want
to do, it seems.

Correct.

59 Special Journal of the Russian Council of Ministers

Int. Bez. I, 5, 19   St Petersburg, 24 July 1914

*Concerning the communication of the Foreign Minister about the latest
measures of the Austro-Hungarian Government in relation to Serbia.*

The Foreign Minister told the Council of Ministers that, according to
information he had received, and the note delivered by the Austro-
Hungarian Ambassador at the Imperial Court, the Austro-Hungarian
Government had issued demands to the Serbian Government which were
in essence wholly unacceptable to the Kingdom of Serbia as a sovereign
state, and were expressed in the form of an ultimatum imposing a deadline of 6.00 tomorrow evening, 25 July for the reply. As it was likely that
Serbia would seek our advice and perhaps also request our assistance the
need arose immediately to prepare an answer which we could give
Serbia.

After discussing the statement submitted by Sazonov, the Council
of Ministers passed the following resolutions, in conjunction with the
commentaries on the present political and military situation made before
the Council by the War Minister, Naval Minister and Finance Minister:

I. To endorse the proposal of the Foreign Minister that he should make contact with the Cabinets of the Great Powers in an effort to persuade the Austro-Hungarian Government to grant Serbia a temporary postponement of her reply to the ultimative demands set by the Austro-Hungarian Government in order to give the Governments of the Great Powers the opportunity to inspect and study the documents on the crime committed in Sarajevo that the Austro-Hungarian Government has at its disposal and which, as the Austro-Hungarian Ambassador confirms, it is willing to communicate to the Russian Government.[1]

II. To endorse the proposal of the Foreign Minister that the Serbian Government should be advised that, in the event of Serbia's position being such that she is not strong enough to defend herself unaided against a possible Austrian attack, it should offer no resistance to armed invasion of Serbian territory, if a sudden attack of this kind were to take place. Rather should it declare that Serbia would yield to superior force and entrust her fate to the judgment of the Great Powers.[2]

III. To charge the War and Naval Ministers, as may be most appropriate, with the task of entreating the most gracious assent of Your Imperial Majesty to a proclamation of mobilisation of the four military districts of Kiev, Odessa, Moscow and Kazan, and of the Baltic and Black Sea Fleets, should the subsequent course of events so require.

IV. To charge the War Minister without delay to speed up the stock-piling of war materials for the army.

V. To charge the Finance Minister to take measures for the immediate reduction of sums belonging to the Finance Department at present deposited in Germany and Austria-Hungary.

The Council of Ministers considers it to be its most humble and obedient duty to bring these its resolutions to the most exalted attention of Your Imperial Majesty.

60 Sazonov to Chargé d'Affaires Strandtmann

Telegram 1487   St Petersburg, 24 July 1914
Urgent
Int. Bez. I, 5, 22

Personal. Please decipher yourself.

If Serbia is really in such a helpless condition as to leave no doubt regarding the result of an armed struggle with Austria, it would perhaps be

[1] See **61**.   [2] See **60**.

better that in the event of an invasion by Austria the Serbs should make
no attempt whatever to offer resistance, but should retire and, allowing
the enemy to occupy their territory without fighting, appeal to the Powers.
In this appeal the Serbs, after pointing out the difficulty of their position
after the recent war during which they gained the recognition of Europe
by their moderation, might allude to the impossibility of their maintaining
an unequal struggle, and ask for the protection of the Powers based upon
a sense of justice.[1]

61 Sazonov to the missions in Vienna, Berlin, Paris, London, Rome and
Bucharest

Telegram 1488   St Petersburg, 24 July 1914
Urgent
Int. Bez. I, 5, 23

Communicated to Belgrade.

As Austria-Hungary has only addressed herself to the Powers twelve
hours after the delivery of her ultimatum to Belgrade[2] it is impossible for
the Powers in the short time remaining to undertake anything useful
towards the settlement of the complications that have arisen. Therefore,
in order to avoid the innumerable and universally undesirable consequences to which Austria's course of action could lead, we should think
it necessary that she should first of all extend the time limit which she has
set Serbia for a reply. Since Austria has declared her readiness to acquaint
the Powers with the results of the enquiry on which the accusations are
based, the Powers should be given the opportunity to form an opinion
on the matter. If the Powers were to convince themselves of the legitimacy
of some of the Austrian demands, they could accordingly give advice to
Serbia. The rejection by Austria of our proposal for dealing with the
matter would rob the declaration made by her today of all meaning and be
openly at variance with international ethics.

Vienna:

Kindly inform the Foreign Minister to this effect.

For the others:

Whilst instructing Kudaschev to express his opinion to this effect, we
hope that the Governments to which you are accredited will concur with
our view and will urgently instruct their representatives in Vienna for
their part to adopt a parallel procedure.

[1] See 59.   [2] See 38.

62 Memorandum of the day of the Russian Ministry for Foreign Affairs

Int. Bez. I, 5, 25   St Petersburg, 24 July 1914

Early this morning a telegram[1] was received at the Foreign Ministry from Belgrade confirming the information[2] given yesterday by the Councillor of the Italian Embassy. Baron Schilling immediately warned the Ambassadors Isvolsky and Schebeko of the necessity of their returning immediately to their posts.

Towards 10 a.m. S. D. Sazonov arrived from Tzarskoe Selo, when Baron Schilling immediately communicated the above-mentioned information to him, which created a very strong impression upon the Minister, who at once exclaimed: 'C'est la guerre européenne.'[3] The Austro-Hungarian Ambassador was at once called to the Ministry by telephone, and while awaiting him S. D. Sazonov reported to the Czar by telephone from Baron Schilling's office regarding Austria's ultimatum to Serbia. His Majesty exclaimed, 'This is disturbing,' and gave orders to keep him informed as to the further course of events.

Meanwhile the Austro-Hungarian Ambassador arrived and handed to the Minister a copy of the Austrian note to Serbia. At the same time Baron Schilling, in the name of the Minister, informed the Ministers for War, Marine and Finance of the course of affairs and, on the instruction of S. D. Sazonov, warned them to attend the sitting of the Council of Ministers without fail. At the request of Admiral Grigorovich, Baron Schilling sent a similar communication to Admiral Rusin, the Chief of the Naval General Staff. The Minister of Finance had only just returned from reporting to the Czar, from whom he had already learned of the step taken by Austria in Belgrade. Baron Schilling pointed out to P. L. Barck the necessity in any case of at once withdrawing as far as possible all our State deposits in Germany.

A. A. Neratov, Prince Troubetzkoi and all the officials of the Ministers' Chancellery and of the Near East Section, were at once recalled from leave by telegraph.

The French Ambassador after breakfast called together for an exchange of opinions S. D. Sazonov, and the English Ambassador and the Roumanian Minister. The Minister pressed these representatives to communicate to their respective Governments his request that they would immediately elaborate with us a plan of action. This request was naturally

[1] Strandtmann's telegram of 23 July; *Int. Bez.* I, 5, 10.
[2] I.e. on the subject of the delivery of the ultimatum in Belgrade; entry of 23 July, *Int. Bez.* I, 5, 5.
[3] 'That means European war'; see also 68.

addressed to the Roumanian Minister as well, so that Roumania was thereby drawn into this matter of general concern. It was of the greatest advantage for us that Roumania should be drawn in on our side, while for Roumania it was manifestly flattering to participate as an equal in the diplomatic steps taken by the Great Powers.

The Council of Ministers met at 3 p.m.,[1] at which S. D. Sazonov reported regarding the course of the negotiations arising from the handing of the threatening note to Serbia on the previous day by Austria-Hungary. The Council of Ministers expressed approval of the proposals of the Foreign Minister, viz. (1) In conjunction with the other Powers to request Austria to prolong the period which she had fixed for the receipt of a reply from Serbia in order to afford the Powers time in which to acquaint themselves, in accordance with the proposal of Austria herself with the results of the judicial enquiry into the Sarajevo assassination; and (2) to advise Serbia not to enter into hostilities with Austro-Hungarian troops, but, withdrawing her own forces, to request the Powers to compose the quarrel that had arisen. At the same time it was decided in principle to mobilise four military districts (Odessa, Kiev, Moscow, Kazan) and the two fleets (Baltic and Black Sea) and to take other military measures should circumstances so require. In this connection attention was turned to the fact that all military preparations must be clearly and exclusively directed with a view to the possibility of a conflict with Austria-Hungary, and could not be represented as unfriendly actions with regard to Germany.

After the Council meeting there was an interview between S. D. Sazonov and the Serbian Minister, during which the former advised extreme moderation in respect of the Serbian reply to the Austrian note.[2]

At 7 p.m. the German Ambassador came to the Foreign Office. He endeavoured to justify Austria's action on the grounds that the investigation with regard to the Sarajevo assassination established the guilt of the Serbian Government. In addition, he endeavoured to establish the correctness of the Austrian procedure by reason of the necessity for protecting the 'Monarchical principle'. S. D. Sazonov addressed Count Pourtalès in a very firm manner, and sharply criticized the Vienna Cabinet, insisting upon the unacceptable nature of the Note to Serbia and the lack of courtesy towards the Great Powers in that Austria, in turning to them at the same time accorded to Serbia so short a period wherein to meet her demands that the Powers were not afforded a possibility of considering the matter and giving their observations in time to be of avail.[3]

Those who saw Count Pourtalès as he left the Ministry state that he

[1] See **59**.   [2] See also **60**.   [3] See also **58**.

was very agitated, and did not conceal the fact that S. D. Sazonov's words, and especially his firm determination to resist the Austrian demands, had made a strong impression upon him.

While the German Ambassador was with the Minister the French Ambassador arrived at the Foreign Office and, not wishing to meet his German colleague, went to Baron Schilling and waited with him in his cabinet until the Minister was free, as Count Pourtalès could not pass through there. The French Ambassador meanwhile expressed the opinion that despite the events which had occurred he considered that the President of the French Republic ought not to change in any respect the programme for his journey to the Scandinavian capitals, but should return quietly to France, as previously proposed, after making halts at Stockholm and Copenhagen. Otherwise, in the opinion of the Ambassador a general panic might arise, because there would be an impression that the head of the French Republic regarded the political situation as threatening. Meanwhile the Ambassador considered the situation as by no means hopeless. He founded his optimism upon the supposition that Germany would scarcely decide to support Austria since she knew to what serious consequences this would inevitably lead at the present moment. 'We have never been in a better position', he said, 'for we are in perfect agreement. This is not the appreciation of an Ambassador, but we have four recent documents of great importance to prove it.' Baron Schilling, somewhat astonished, asked the Ambassador what was the nature of these four, apparently to him, unknown documents which were of such great importance that in presence of them Germany would have to call a halt even if she desired to go to war for the purpose of supporting her ally Austria. It appeared that M. Paléologue regarded as such documents the speeches recently exchanged by the Emperor and the President of the French Republic at Peterhof and on board the battleship *France*.[1]

Immediately after the departure of Count Pourtalès the French Ambassador was received by the Minister, who promptly informed him of the decisions reached by the Council of Ministers, and also concerning his conversations with the Serbian Minister and the German Ambassador.

[1] *Int. Bez.* I, 4, 294, 293, and *Int. Bez.* I, 5, 1, 2.

63 Chargé d'Affaires Kudaschev to Sazonov

Telegram 90   Vienna, 24 July 1914
Int. Bez. I, 5, 31

Berchtold has just told me that, in composing the ultimatum which Baron
Giesl delivered to the Serbian Government yesterday, he had not been
guided by the wish to humiliate Serbia but by the unanimous conviction
of all the Ministers and of the Emperor himself that it was necessary to
have recourse to radical measures to put an end to the continuation of
Pan-Serbian propaganda which was intolerable to the Monarchy as it
directly undermined its structure and the dynasty. On my enquiring
what would happen if Serbia could not reply within the time-limit imposed, the Minister replied: the entire legation has been instructed to
leave Belgrade. The Austro-Hungarian Government plainly considers
that her demands can be met and is prepared to risk armed conflict in the
event of a rejection.[1]

64 Chargé d'Affaires Kudaschev to Sazonov

Telegram 91   Vienna, 24 July 1914
Int. Bez. I, 5, 32

In my conversation with Berchtold today[2] the latter, without denying
that the ultimatum was couched in severe terms, insisted upon the view
both that it was acceptable and that it could be complied with by Serbia.
Touching upon the problem of Austro-Serbian relations in general, he
declared that the very existence of Austria-Hungary as a Great Power
depended upon the absolute clarification of those relations. Austria-
Hungary had to give proof of her stature as a Great Power, essential to
the balance of power in Europe, by an outright *coup de force*. He estimated
that Russia, who had an interest in the maintenance of this balance of
power and of monarchist principles,[3] could not desire the collapse of
Austria-Hungary; yet the propaganda of the southern Slavs would inevitably lead to just such a collapse. Not wishing to anticipate your
Excellency's assessment of the Austrian ultimatum, still less the reply of
the Serbian Government, I confined myself to an expression of my
personal reflections as to the form and content of this document, in
connection with which I mentioned that, in view of the expected move

[1] See 48 and 64.   [2] See 48 and 63.   [3] See also 38 and 39.

by Austria-Hungary, you attached great importance to ensuring that Serbian dignity was left intact. Only in this fashion could I profit by Your Excellency's Instruction no. 1475,[1] which arrived too late to be implemented in time.

65   Chargé d'Affaires Strandtmann to Sazonov

Telegram 214   Belgrade, 24 July 1914
Most urgent
Int. Bez. I, 5, 36

In no. 215, at the request of the Crown Prince and Regent, I am conveying his personal request to His Majesty the Emperor.[2] The Council of Ministers has resolved on sending a telegram from the Heir Apparent to the King of Italy with the request that he should use his good offices at Vienna in favour of an extension of the time limit laid down in the ultimatum and a mitigation of those conditions which are incompatible with Serbian legislation. Moreover Pašić informed me that despite the concentration of Austrian troops on the frontier it has been decided here that initially only the first line of the reserve should be called up. He will inform the party leaders of the situation today and hopes to obtain their consent to reconvening the Skupština in its former composition and an adjournment of the elections. The Government will move to Krushevatz if the need should arise. The political files of the legation have been packed.

66   Dumaine to Bienvenu-Martin

Telegram 105   Vienna, 24 July 1914
D.F. XI, 16   D. 4.45 p.m.
                                                         R. 6.15 p.m.

The suddenness and the excessive sharpness of the demands of Austria-Hungary's note or ultimatum to Belgrade have, with the exception of military circles, surprised even the most bitter adversaries of Serbia. One of them admitted that he had no other fear but that the Serbian

---

[1] See 22 July; the instructions were aimed at the exercise of restraint in Vienna; *Int. Bez.* I, 4, 322.
[2] *Int. Bez.* I, 5, 37.

Government might yield to the stringency of the conditions.[1] There is speculation that an early and swift military campaign may be launched: there would be glory in having inflicted a well-deserved chastisement on the little kingdom.

Mr Jovanović assumes that his Government, despite its willingness to meet the Austrian demands to a very considerable degree, would regard as totally unacceptable:

First, the humiliation for the King of having to sign an order to the Army the wording of which had been imposed upon him. This text could only appear in the official journal after modification by the Royal Government;

Secondly, the compulsion to dismiss officers and functionaries suspicious to the Austrians;

Thirdly the interference by Austro-Hungarian judicial and police authorities with the enquiry on Serbian territory.

However, one would promise broad satisfaction relating to the prosecution and punishment of the accomplices to the crime in addition to measures for suppressing and supervising those associations which conducted anti-Austrian propaganda.

If it were possible to enter into negotiations, my Serbian colleague believes that the acute conflict could nonetheless still be settled with the assistance of the friendly Powers. But that is what Austria seems to be seeking to avoid, in preventing any outside interference by the brevity of the term fixed for the reply. Public opinion, which has been artificially inflamed, is invoked to prove the necessity for this harsh measure.

67 Jules Cambon to Bienvenu-Martin

Telegram 185   Berlin, 25 July 1914
Confidential. Top secret   D. 1.15 a.m.
D.F. XI, 33 (F.Y.B. 30)   R. 2.50 a.m.

I *asked* the Secretary of State today, in the interview which I had with him,[2] if it was correct, as announced in the newspapers, that Austria had

---

[1] See also 31; further, Kageneck's entry in his diary on 25 July 1914: 'This afternoon I go to the War Ministry, meet Conrad and accompany him back to his house; we are both despondent, since special editions with the acceptance of all the conditions (of A.-H. to Serbia) have been distributed in Frankfurt; it is said to be all over once more and we already discuss the domestic measures which will now be necessary.' (G. Ritter, *Staatskunst*, II, p. 381, n. 13); likewise Redlich's entry in his diary on 26 July; J. Redlich, *Tagebuch*, I, p. 229.

[2] I.e. on 24 July.

presented a note to the Powers on her dispute with Serbia; if he had received it; and what view he took of it.

Herr von Jagow answered me in the affirmative, adding that the note was forcible, and that he approved it,[1] the Serbian Government having for a long time past wearied the patience of Austria. Moreover, he considers this question to be a domestic one for Austria, and he hopes that it will be localised.

I then said to him that not having as yet received any instructions, the views which I wished to exchange with him were strictly personal. Thereupon I asked him if the Berlin Cabinet had really been entirely ignorant of Austria's requirements before they were communicated to Belgrade, and as he told me that that was so, I showed him my surprise at seeing him thus undertake to support claims, of whose limit and scope he was ignorant.[2]

Herr von Jagow interrupted me, and said, 'It is only because we are having a personal conversation that I allow you to say that to me'.

'Certainly,' I replied, 'but if Peter I humiliates himself, domestic trouble will probably break out in Serbia; that will open the door to fresh possibilities, and do you know where you will be led by Vienna?' I added that the language of the German newspapers was not the language of persons who were indifferent to, and unacquainted with, the question, but betokened an active support. Finally, I remarked that the shortness of the time limit given to Serbia for submission would make an unpleasant impression in Europe.

Herr von Jagow answered that he quite expected a little excitement (*un peu d'émotion*) on the part of Serbia's friends, but that he was counting on their giving her wise advice.

'I have no doubt,' I then said to him, 'that Russia would endeavour to persuade the Cabinet of Belgrade to make acceptable concessions; but why not ask from one what is being asked from the other, and if reliance is being placed on advice being given at Belgrade, is it not also legitimate to rely on advice being given at Vienna from another quarter?'

The Secretary of State went so far as to say that that depended on circumstances; but immediately checked himself; he repeated that the difficulty must be localised. He asked me if I really thought the situation serious. 'Certainly,' I answered, 'because if what is happening is the result of due reflection, I do not understand why all means of retreat have been cut off.'

[1] See p. 136.
[2] See in contrast 16, 17, 28, 33, 41 and 43.

68 Buchanan to Grey

Telegram 166   St Petersburg, 24 July
Urgent   D. 5.40 p.m.
B.D. 101   R. 8.00 p.m.

My immediately preceding telegram.[1]

Minister for Foreign Affairs telephoned to me this morning saying that he had just received text of ultimatum presented by Austria at Belgrade yesterday that demands a reply in forty-eight hours. Step thus taken by Austria meant war, and he begged me to meet him at the French Embassy.

Minister for Foreign Affairs and French Ambassador[2] told me confidentially that result of the visit of the President of the French Republic had been to establish the following points:

1 Perfect community of views on the various problems with which the Powers are confronted as regards the maintenance of general peace and balance of power in Europe, more especially in the East.

2 Decision to take action at Vienna with a view to the prevention of a demand for explanations or any summons equivalent to an intervention in the internal affairs of Serbia which the latter would be justified in regarding as an attack on her sovereignty and independence.[3]

3 Solemn affirmation of obligations imposed by the alliance of the two countries.

Minister for Foreign Affairs expressed the hope that His Majesty's Government would proclaim their solidarity with France and Russia. He characterised Austria's conduct as immoral and provocative. Some of the demands which she had presented were absolutely inacceptable, and she would never have acted as she had done without having first consulted Germany. The French Ambassador gave me to understand that France would not only give Russia strong diplomatic support, but would, if necessary, fulfil all the obligations imposed on her by the alliance.

I said that I could not speak in the name of His Majesty's Government, but that I would telegraph all that they had said. I could personally hold out no hope that His Majesty's Government would make any declaration of solidarity that would entail engagement to support France and Russia by force of arms. We had no direct interests in Serbia, and public opinion in England would never sanction a war on her behalf. Minister for Foreign Affairs replied that the Serbian question was but part of general European question and that we could not efface ourselves.

I said that I gathered that His Excellency wished us to join in telling

---

[1] Of 23 July (*B.D.* 84).   [2] See **62**.   [3] See **47**.

Austria that we could not tolerate her active intervention in Serbian internal affairs. If she paid no attention to our representations and took military action against Serbia, did Russia propose to declare war upon her? Minister for Foreign Affairs said that the whole question would be considered by a Council of Ministers to be held this afternoon, but that no decision would be taken till a further Council of Ministers had been held under the presidency of the Emperor,[1] probably tomorrow. He personally thought that Russia would at any rate have to mobilise.

I suggested that the first thing to be done was to try to gain time by bringing our influence to bear to induce Austria to extend term of delay accorded to Serbia. The French Ambassador replied that time did not permit of this; either Austria was bluffing or had made up her mind to act at once. In either case a firm and united attitude was our only chance of averting war. I then asked whether it would not be advisable to urge Serbian Government to state precisely how far they were prepared to go to meet Austria's wishes. Minister for Foreign Affairs said that some of the demands contained in ultimatum might no doubt be accepted, but that he must first consult his colleagues.

As they both continued to press me to declare our complete solidarity with them, I said that I thought you might be prepared to represent strongly at Vienna and Berlin danger to European peace of an Austrian attack on Serbia. You might perhaps point out that it would in all probability force Russia to intervene, that this would bring Germany and [? France] into the field, and that if war became general, it would be difficult for England to remain neutral. Minister for Foreign Affairs said that he hoped that we would in any case express strong reprobation of Austria's action. If war did break out, we would sooner or later be dragged into it, but if we did not make common cause with France and Russia from the outset we should have rendered war more likely, and should not have played a 'beau rôle'.

From French Ambassador's language it almost looked as if France and Russia were determined to make a strong stand even if we declined to join them. Language of Minister for Foreign Affairs, however, was not so [? decided] on this subject.

Austrian Government seemed purposely to have presented their ultimatum at moment when President of the French Republic and President of the Council were leaving Russia on their return to France, where they cannot arrive for four or five days.[2]

Towards the close of our interview we were joined by Roumanian Minister,[3] with whom Minister for Foreign Affairs had a private

[1] See 59 and 76.   [2] See 17, 20–4, 27, 33 and 35.   [3] See 62.

conversation in which His Excellency invited also Roumanian Government to make representations at Vienna.

Minutes

The moment has passed when it might have been possible to enlist French support in an effort to hold back Russia.

It is clear that France and Russia are decided to accept the challenge thrown out to them. Whatever we may think of the merits of the Austrian charges against Serbia, France and Russia consider that these are the pretexts, and that the bigger cause of Triple Alliance versus Triple Entente is definitely engaged.

I think it would be impolitic, not to say dangerous, for England to attempt to controvert this opinion, or to endeavour to obscure the plain issue, by any representation at St Petersburg and Paris.

The point that matters is whether Germany is or is not absolutely determined to have this war now.

There is still the chance that she can be made to hesitate, if she can be induced to apprehend that the war will find England by the side of France and Russia.

I can suggest only one effective way of bringing this home to the German Government without absolutely committing us definitely at this stage. If, the moment either Austria or Russia begin to mobilise, His Majesty's Government give orders to put our whole fleet on an immediate war footing, this may conceivably make Germany realise the seriousness of the danger to which she would be exposed if England took part in the war.

It would be right, supposing this decision could be taken now, to inform the French and Russian Governments of it, and this again would be the best thing we could do to prevent a very grave situation arising as between England and Russia.

It is difficult not to agree with M. Sazonov that sooner or later England will be dragged into the war if it does come. We shall gain nothing by not making up our minds what we can do in circumstances that may arise to-morrow.

Should the war come, and England stands aside, one of two things must happen:

(*a*) Either Germany and Austria win, crush France, and humiliate Russia. With the French fleet gone, Germany in occupation of the Channel, with the willing or unwilling co-operation of Holland and Belgium, what will be the position of a friendless England?

(*b*) Or France and Russia win. What would then be their attitude towards England? What about India and the Mediterranean?

Our interests are tied up with those of France and Russia in this struggle, which is not for the possession of Serbia, but one between Germany aiming at a political dictatorship in Europe and the Powers who desire to retain individual freedom. If we can help to avoid the conflict by showing our naval strength, ready to be instantly used, it would be wrong not to make the effort.

Whatever therefore our ultimate decision, I consider we should decide *now* to mobilise the fleet as soon as any other Great Power mobilises, and that we should announce this decision without delay to the French and Russian Governments.—E. A. C. 25 July.

The points raised by Sir Eyre Crowe merit serious consideration, and doubtless the Cabinet will review the situation. Our attitude during the crisis will be regarded by Russia as a test and we must be most careful not to alienate her.—A. N.

Mr Churchill told me to-day that the fleet can be mobilised in twenty-four hours, but I think it is premature to make any statement to France and Russia yet.—E. G.

69 Macchio to Berchtold

Telegram (unnumbered)   Vienna, 25 July 1914
Ö.D. 10703   D. 1.45 p.m.

The Russian representative came to see me in the forenoon, and in the name of his government expressed the wish that the term of our Note to Serbia might be prolonged.[1] This wish was based on the fact, that the Powers had been completely taken by surprise by our step and that the Russian Government would consider it but as a natural sign of regard from the Vienna cabinet to the cabinets of the Powers, to give them an opportunity for studying the communication to them and also the *dossier*, the insight into which was offered.[2]

I answered the representative that I would immediately communicate what he had told me, to Your Excellency, but that I could already tell him, that there was no chance of our consenting to prolong the term which had been fixed. As to the reasons which the Russian Government gave for justifying its demand, they seemed to be based on a mistaken idea, as though the Note to the Powers had been sent out with a view to learning their opinion of the case. All we intended was to inform the Powers on

[1] See 70.   [2] See 61.

our step and thus comply with a duty of international etiquette. We consider our action as an affair, which concerns exclusively us and Serbia, and to which we were compelled against our will by the development of circumstances, which are threatening our most vital interests and which the patience and toleration we have shown for years, could not change.

I promised the Russian representative that I would let him have your answer as soon as ever I could, and I therefore beg for telegraphic information whether your Excellency approves the answer I gave.[1]

70 Berchtold to Macchio

Telegram (unnumbered)	Lambach, 25 July 1914
Confidential	D. 2.00 p.m.
Ö.D. 10704	R. 4.00 p.m.

For Baron Macchio. Russian representative telegraphs me that he has been urgently instructed by his Government to demand a prolongation of the term for the ultimatum to Serbia.[2] I beg Your Excellency to answer him in my name that we cannot concede a prolongation of the term. Your Excellency will add moreover that even after the breaking off of diplomatic relations the unconditional acceptance of our demands could bring about a peaceful solution, but that in this case we should be obliged to demand reimbursement for the expenses incurred by military measures.[3]

I beg Your Excellency to inform the German Ambassador of the above.[4]

71 Szögyény to Berchtold

Telegram 285	Berlin, 25 July 1914
Confidential	D. 2.15 p.m.
Ö.D. 10656	R. 8.00 p.m.

With regard to the concluding words in Your Excellency's telegram 258 of yesterday (Count Mensdorff's answer to Sir Edward Grey)[5] I should

---

[1] Berchtold telegraphed his approval on the self-same day; *Ö.D.* 10705.

[2] See **61** and **69**.

[3] See also p. 137.

[4] Tschirschky's corresponding telegram of 25 July (*D.D.* 178) did not, however, mention the last point (possible repayment of the costs of mobilisation).

[5] *Ö.D.* 10580; Berchtold added a decisive sentence to the telegram from London, which read as follows: 'The state of war will only arise after a declaration of war'.

like to remark that here the general belief is, that if Serbia gives an unsatisfactory answer our declaration of war and war operations will follow immediately. Here every delay in the beginning of war operations is regarded as signifying the danger, that foreign powers might interfere. We are urgently advised to proceed without delay[1] and to place the world before a *fait accompli*. I am completely of the same mind as the Auswärtiges Amt.

72 Serbian Government to Giesl

Ö.D. 10648[2]   Belgrade, 25 July 1914

The Royal Serbian Government have received the communication of the Imperial and Royal Government of the 10th inst., and are convinced that their reply will remove any misunderstanding which may threaten to impair the good neighbourly relations between the Austro-Hungarian Monarchy and the Kingdom of Serbia.

Conscious of the fact that the protests which were made both from the tribune of the national Skupština and in the declarations and actions of the responsible representatives of the State—protests which were cut short by the declarations made by the Serbian Government on 31 March 1909—have not been renewed on any occasion as regards the great neighbouring Monarchy, and that no attempt has been made since that time either by the successive Royal Governments or by their organs, to change the political and legal state of affairs created in Bosnia and Herzegovina, the Royal Government draw attention to the fact that in this connection the Imperial and Royal Government have made no representation except one concerning a school book, and that on that occasion the Imperial and Royal Government received an entirely satisfactory explanation. Serbia has several times given proofs of her pacific and moderate policy during the Balkan crisis, and it is thanks to Serbia and to the sacrifice that she has made in the exclusive interest of European peace that that peace has been preserved. The Royal Government cannot be held responsible for manifestations of a private character, such as articles in the press and the peaceable work of societies—manifestations which take place in nearly all countries in the ordinary course of events, and which, as a general rule, escape official control. The Royal Government are all the less responsible, in view of the fact that at the time of the

[1] See in contrast 42.   [2] Original in French, German text from *Ö.D.* 10860.

solution of a series of questions which arose between Serbia and Austria-Hungary they gave proof of a great readiness to oblige, and thus succeeded in settling the majority of these questions to the advantage of the two neighbouring countries.

For these reasons the Royal Government have been pained and surprised at the statements, according to which members of the Kingdom of Serbia are supposed to have participated in the preparations for the crime committed at Sarajevo; the Royal Government expected to be invited to collaborate in an investigation of all that concerns this crime, and they were ready, in order to prove the entire correctness of their attitude, to take measures against any persons concerning whom representations were made to them. Falling in, therefore, with the desire of the Imperial and Royal Government, they are prepared to hand over for trial any Serbian subject, without regard to his situation or rank, of whose complicity in the crime of Sarajevo proofs are forthcoming, and more especially they undertake to cause to be published on the first page of the *Journal officiel*, on the date of 26 July, the following declaration:

'The Royal Government of Serbia condemn all propaganda which may be directed against Austria-Hungary, that is to say, all such tendencies as aim at ultimately detaching from the Austro-Hungarian Monarchy territories which form part thereof, and they sincerely deplore the baneful consequences of these criminal movements. The Royal Government regret that, according to the communication from the Imperial and Royal Government, certain Serbian officers and officials should have taken part in the above-mentioned propaganda, and thus compromised the good neighbourly relations to which the Royal Serbian Government was solemnly engaged by the declaration of 31 March 1909, which declaration disapproves and repudiates all idea or attempt at interference with the destiny of the inhabitants of any part whatsoever of Austria-Hungary, and they consider it their duty formally to warn the officers, officials and entire population of the kingdom that henceforth they will take the most rigorous steps against all such persons as are guilty of such acts, to prevent and to repress which they will use their utmost endeavour.'

This declaration will be brought to the knowledge of the Royal Army in an order of the day, in the name of His Majesty the King, by his Royal Highness the Crown Prince Alexander, and will be published in the next official army bulletin.

The Royal Government further undertake:

1 To introduce at the first regular convocation of the Skupština, a provision into the press law providing for the most severe punishment of incitement to hatred or contempt of the Austro-Hungarian Monarchy,

and for taking action against any publication the general tendency of which is directed against the territorial integrity of Austria-Hungary. The Government engage at the approaching revision of the Constitution to cause an amendment to be introduced into article XXII of the Constitution of such a nature that such publication may be confiscated, a proceeding at present impossible under the categorical terms of article XXII of the Constitution.

2 The Government possess no proof, nor does the note of the Imperial and Royal Government furnish them with any, that the *Narodna Odbrana* and other similar societies have committed up to the present any criminal act of this nature through the proceedings of any of their members. Nevertheless, the Royal Government will accept the demand of the Imperial and Royal Government and will dissolve the *Narodna Odbrana* Society and every other society which may be directing its efforts against Austria-Hungary.

3 The Royal Serbian Government undertake to remove without delay from their public educational establishments in Serbia all that serves or could serve to foment propaganda against Austria-Hungary, whenever the Imperial and Royal Government furnish them with facts and proofs of this propaganda.

4 The Royal Government also agree to remove from military service all such persons as the judicial enquiry may have proved to be guilty of acts directed against the integrity of the territory of the Austro-Hungarian Monarchy, and they expect the Imperial and Royal Government to communicate to them at a later date the names and the acts of these officers and officials for the purposes of the proceedings which are to be taken against them.

5 The Royal Government must confess that they do not clearly grasp the meaning or the scope of the demand made by the Imperial and Royal Government that Serbia shall undertake to accept the collaboration of the organs of the Imperial and Royal Government upon their territory, but they declare that they will admit such collaboration as agrees with the principle of international law, with criminal procedure, and with good neighbourly relations.

6 It goes without saying that the Royal Government consider it their duty to open an enquiry against all such persons as are, or eventually may be implicated in the plot of 28 June, and who happen to be within the territory of the kingdom. As regards the participation in this enquiry of Austro-Hungarian agents or authorities appointed for this purpose by the Imperial and Royal Government, the Royal Government cannot accept such an arrangement, as it would be a violation of the Constitution

and of the law of criminal procedure; nevertheless, in concrete cases communications as to the results of the investigation in question might be given to the Austro-Hungarian agents.

7 The Royal Government proceeded, on the very evening of the delivery of the Note, to arrest Commandant Voija Tankosić. As regards Milan Ciganović, who is a subject of the Austro-Hungarian Monarchy and who up to 28 June was employed (on probation) by the directorate of railways, it has not yet been possible to arrest him.

The Austro-Hungarian Government are requested to be so good as to supply as soon as possible, in the customary form, the presumptive evidence of guilt, as well as the eventual proofs of guilt which have been collected up to the present, at the enquiry at Sarajevo for the purposes of the later enquiry.

8 The Serbian Government will reinforce and extend the measures which have been taken for preventing the illicit traffic of arms and explosives across the frontier. It goes without saying that they will immediately order an enquiry and will severely punish the frontier officials on the Schabatz-Loznica line who have failed in their duty and allowed the authors of the crime of Sarajevo to pass.

9 The Royal Government will gladly give explanations of the remarks made by their officials whether in Serbia or abroad, in interviews after the crime which according to the statement of the Imperial and Royal Government were hostile towards the Monarchy, as soon as the Imperial and Royal Government have communicated to them the passages in question in these remarks, and as soon as they have shown that the remarks were actually made by the said officials, although the Royal Government will itself take steps to collect evidence and proofs.

10 The Royal Government will inform the Imperial and Royal Government of the execution of the measures comprised under the above heads, in so far as this has not already been done by the present note, as soon as each measure has been ordered and carried out.

If the Imperial and Royal Government are not satisfied with this reply, the Serbian Government, considering that it is not to the common interest to precipitate the solution of this question, are ready, as always, to accept a pacific understanding, either by referring this question to the decision of the International Tribunal of The Hague, or to the Great Powers which took part in the drawing up of the declaration made by the Serbian Government on 31 March 1909.

73 Lichnowsky to Jagow

Telegram 154
D.D. 180

London, 25 July 1914
D. 2.02 p.m.
R. 5.25 p.m.

Have just seen Sir E. Grey and talked as suggested in telegram 169.[1] The Minister accepted my explanations with a full comprehension of our point of view. Without any irritation or ill-feeling, he discussed with me again the general situation and seemed again to be a little more hopeful than yesterday, as Count Mensdorff had informed him on behalf of his Government that Austria did not intend to cross the Serbian border at once, if her demands should be refused, but only to mobilise.[2] Sir E. Grey is still without any information concerning the determination adopted at St Petersburg, but counts with certainty on the Austrian mobilisation being followed by that of Russia. Upon that, according to his opinion, the moment would have arrived at which to begin mediating between Austria and Russia in conjunction with us, France and Italy. Without our co-operation, he thought, all attempt at mediation would be futile, and he alone could not approach Russia and Austria. Whether France would participate with us, he did not yet know. He had talked with M. Cambon,[3] but had so far received no reply; he had told him at their talk that he had made the same proposal to me. He counted firmly on the agreement of France, although he did not know how far she was already committed to Russia.

The Minister draws a sharp line of distinction, as he told me again, between an Austro-Serbian and an Austro-Russian quarrel. Into the first he did not wish to mix, as it did not concern him. But an Austro-Russian strife meant, in the circumstances, a world war, such as we had jointly managed to avoid the year before by means of the ambassadorial conferences. Nor were European complications a matter of indifference to Great Britain, although she was *in no way committed by any sort of binding agreements*.

Therefore he wanted to join with us as before, and proceed hand in hand at the present time in the interest of European peace; and he hoped by our mutual mediation, with which he believed both France and Italy would probably associate themselves, to prevent an Austro-Russian war.

As far as concerned the Austrian note, he fully recognised the justice

[1] Zimmermann on 24 July to Paris, London, St Petersburg. In this he once again vigorously refuted the suspicion which had been expressed, that Germany was the driving force behind Austria's actions; *D.D.* 153.

[2] *Ö.D.* 10599.   [3] See *D.F.* XI, 23 and *B.D.* 98.

of the Austrian demand for satisfaction, as well as the desire for the punishment of all persons connected with the murder. He did not go into details of the note, but appeared to hope that by our mediation we might succeed in reaching an agreement on this matter also.

I deem it to be my duty to point out to Your Excellency that, according to my conviction, the British Government will strive to manifest toward us a friendly attitude, as unpartisan as possible, just so long as it believes in our honest desire for peace and in our efforts to cooperate with England, hand in hand, to avert the rising European thunderstorm. To refuse the proposition to mediate between Austria and Russia, however, or a recalcitrant attitude that would justify the supposition that we wished to bring about a war with Russia, would probably have the result of driving England unconditionally over to the side of France and Russia.[1]

74 Lichnowsky to Jagow

Telegram 155   London, 25 July 1914
D.D. 179   D. 2.00 p.m.
                                                                  R. 5.21 p.m.

I would like to call your attention again to the significance of Grey's proposal of a mediation *à quatre* between Austria and Russia.[2] I see in it the only possibility of avoiding a world war, in which for us there would be everything to lose and nothing to gain. If we refuse, Grey will not bestir himself again. As long as we are not mobilised, mediation will still be possible, and such a settlement of the quarrel as would be acceptable to Austria. Our refusal, however, would have a very disagreeable effect here, and I do not believe that, in case France should be drawn in, England would dare to remain disinterested. Once more, I urgently advise the acceptance of the English proposal and that it be announced to Vienna and St Petersburg.

[1] For Grey's version see 82.
[2] See 57.

75 Jagow to Lichnowsky

Telegram 176
D.D. 192

Berlin, 25 July 1914
D. 11.05 p.m.

Sir E. Grey's distinction between Austro-Serbian and Austro-Russian conflict entirely appropriate.[1] We wish to mix into the first no more than does England, and hold the view now as before that the matter must be localised by the non-interference of all Powers.[2] Therefore we earnestly hope that Russia, conscious of the seriousness of the situation and of her own responsibility, will refrain from any active intervention. Should an Austro-Russian strife arise, we shall, with the reservation of our known obligations as allies, be ready with the other Great Powers to inaugurate mediation between Austria and Russia.

76 Special Journal of the Russian Council of Ministers

Int. Bez. I, 5, 42

St Petersburg, 25 July 1914

Concerning the extension of the order for the period preparatory to war graciously approved on 2 March 1913.

On 25 July of this year Your Imperial Majesty graciously agreed to approve the Special Journal of the Council of Ministers of 24 July 1914 concerning the statement of the Foreign Minister about the latest moves of the Austro-Hungarian Government in relation to Serbia.[3] Through this Journal, amongst other things, the War and Navy Ministers have been entrusted in their respective capacities with requesting the gracious consent of Your Imperial Majesty to the mobilisation, as events require, of the four Military Districts of Kiev, Odessa, Moscow and Kazan, and of the Baltic and Black Sea Fleets, in addition to the speeding up of the completion of supplies of army equipment.

In response to the present turn of the diplomatic negotiations and in order that all departments may take the necessary measures for the preparation and smooth extension of the mobilisation of the Army, the Navy and the Fortresses, as well as the deployment of the Army on the frontiers opposite the threatened opponents, the Council of Ministers now considers it advisable from 26 July of this year to enforce throughout the entire Empire the order for the period preparatory to war laid down

[1] See 57.   [2] See 36 and 39.   [3] See 59.

in both schedules, whilst at the same time it empowers the War Minister to solicit the gracious consent of our Imperial Majesty to the implementation in the military department of other measures not provided for in the aforementioned schedules such as he may consider necessary in the circumstances and on the condition that he subsequently informs the Council of Ministers of the measures taken. In accordance with Article 2 of the above-mentioned order the beginning of the period preparatory to war is to be determined by ordinances of the Council of Ministers after they have been graciously approved by Your Majesty.

In the light of this the Council of Ministers resolves to put into operation the decree for the period preparatory to war in accordance with both schedules and in conformity with the particulars set out in this Journal.

The Council of Ministers regards it as its most humble and obedient duty to submit this decision for the gracious approval of Your Imperial Majesty.

77   Sazonov's draft of a report to Nicolas II

Int. Bez. I, 5, 47   St Petersburg, 25 July 1914

I take the liberty of submitting for the indulgence of Your Imperial Majesty the enclosed analysis of the pressing political questions on the chance that Your Imperial Majesty might deign to refer to them in your most exalted reply to the King of England.

Enclosure

. . .

At the present moment all matters relating to Persia recede into the background on account of the complications arising out of the exacerbation of Austro-Serbian relations.

The demands posited by Austria in Belgrade bear no relation either in form or in content to those omissions for which a measure of blame might possibly be imputed to the Serbian Government. Though it was admissible to request the latter for an enquiry to be instituted in Serbia on the basis of the facts brought to light in Austria-Hungary by the enquiry into the murder in Sarajevo, there can nevertheless be no justification for the posing of political demands which would be unacceptable to any state.[1]

[1] See 16 and 31.

The clear aim of this procedure—which is apparently supported by Germany—is the total annihilation of Serbia and disturbance of the political equilibrium in the Balkans.[1]

There can be no doubt that deceitful and provocative actions of this kind will meet with no sympathy in England from either the Government or public opinion.

If Austria persists any longer with this line of policy, Russia will not be able to remain indifferent and the possibility of grave international complications will have to be taken into account. It is to be hoped that in this event Russia and England will both find themselves on the side of right and justice and that the disinterested policies of Russia, whose sole aim it is to prevent the establishment of Austrian hegemony in the Balkans will find active support on the part of England.

It is absolutely essential to see beyond the limits of the present complications and to face the fact that it is now a question of the maintenance of the balance of power in Europe which is seriously threatened. It is to be hoped that England, whose policies for centuries have been directed at the maintenance of this balance, will likewise now remain faithful to the legacy of the past.

78 Chargé d'Affaires Bronevski to Sazonov

Telegram 124   Berlin, 25 July 1914
Int. Bez. I, 5, 63

Request urgent instructions. No. 1488[2] received.

I have expressed my opinion to Jagow in the manner indicated. He told me that the English Government had likewise requested him to recommend an extension of the time limit to the Vienna Government;[3] he had telegraphed Vienna about this,[4] and would also telegraph on the subject of our move but feared that his telegrams would be of no avail, on account of Berchtold's departure for Ischl and since insufficient time remained; besides, he is in doubt whether it would suit Austria to give way at the last moment and whether it might not increase Serbia's self-confidence.

I replied that a Great Power such as Austria could give way without damage to her prestige and cited all the relevant arguments in support of this but could obtain no more definite promises. The Foreign Minister

---

[1] See 35.   [2] See 61.   [3] See 57.
[4] But with no hint of support for the proposal; *D.D.* 171.

stated, *inter alia*, that we must be satisfied with the assurance given to Kudaschev yesterday that Austria was not seeking any territorial acquisitions;[1] perhaps Giesl's forthcoming departure after the expiry of the time limit indicated that the encounter would not follow immediately.[2] Austria had, however, requested the German Government to assume responsibility for the protection of the interests of Austrian subjects in Serbia in the event of a diplomatic rupture, and this it had consented to do.[3] In reply to vague hints that pressure would have to be exerted on Vienna for the avoidance of possible threatening consequences, the Foreign Minister each time answered evasively that he did not even want to think about such matters.

79 Crackanthorpe to Grey

Telegram 52   Belgrade, 25 July 1914
B.D. 114   D. 12.30 p.m.
                                                                R. 3.00 p.m.

Reply to Austrian note is now being drawn up at Council of Ministers. Under-Secretary of State for Foreign Affairs informs me that it will be drawn up in most conciliatory terms and will meet Austrian demands in as large measure as possible. He gave me in advance brief summary of projected reply.

Serbian Government consent to publication of declaration in *Official Gazette*. The ten points are accepted with reserves. Serbian Government declare themselves ready to agree to mixed commission of enquiry, provided that appointment of such commission can be proved to be in accordance with international usage. They consent to dismiss and prosecute those officers whose guilt can be clearly proved, and they have already arrested officer mentioned in Austrian note. They agree to suppress *Narodna Odbrana*.

Opinion of Serbian Government is that, unless Austrian Government desire war at any cost, they will accept full satisfaction offered in Serbian reply.

[1] See 48, 63 and 64.
[2] On the other hand, Jagow had only recently been urging Vienna to the exact opposite, i.e. a declaration of war at the earliest possible moment; see 71.
[3] See pp. 96 and 136.

80   Grey to Buchanan

Telegram 353   London, 25 July 1914
B.D. 112   D. 2.15 p.m.

Your telegram 166 of 24 July:[1] Austria and Serbia. You spoke quite
rightly in very difficult circumstances as to attitude of His Majesty's
Government. I entirely approve, and I cannot promise more on behalf
of His Majesty's Government. I do not consider that public opinion here
would or ought to sanction our going to war in the Serbian quarrel. But
if war does take place we may be drawn into it by development of other
issues, and I am therefore anxious to prevent war.

The brusque, sudden, and peremptory character of the Austrian
démarche makes it almost inevitable that in very short time Austria and
Russia will both have mobilised against each other. In this event, it seems
to me that the only chance of peace is for the other four Powers to join
in asking Austria and Russia not to cross frontier, and to give time for the
four Powers acting at Vienna and St Petersburg to endeavour to arrange
matters.

If Germany will adopt this view, I am strongly of opinion that France
and ourselves should act upon it. Italy no doubt would gladly cooperate.

But the cooperation of Germany would be essential.[2] No diplomatic
intervention or mediation would be tolerated by either Russia or Austria
unless it was clearly impartial and included friends or allies of both.

81   Rumbold to Grey

Telegram 90   Berlin, 25 July 1914
B.D. 122   D. 3.16 p.m.
                                                           R. 6.00 p.m.

Your telegram 196 of 24 July[3] acted on.

Secretary of State for Foreign Affairs says that on receipt of a telegram
at 10 this morning from German Ambassador at London, he immediately
instructed German Ambassador at Vienna to pass on to Austrian Minister
for Foreign Affairs your suggestion for an extension of time limit, and to
'speak to' his Excellency about it.[4] Unfortunately it appeared from press

---

[1] See 68.   [2] See 74.

[3] Grey's version of his discussion with Lichnowsky; see 57.

[4] But with no hint of his support (D.D. 164, 171); moreover the telegram was in fact only
despatched after the discussion with Rumbold.

that Count Berchtold is at Ischl, and Secretary of State thought that in these circumstances there would be delay and difficulty in getting time limit extended. Secretary of State said that he did not know what Austria-Hungary had ready on the spot, but he admitted quite freely that Austro-Hungarian Government wished to give the Serbians a lesson, and that they meant to take military action. He also admitted that Serbian Government could not swallow certain of the Austro-Hungarian demands.

Secretary of State said that a reassuring feature of situation was that Count Berchtold had sent for Russian representative at Vienna and had told him that Austria-Hungary had no intention of seizing Serbian territory.[1] This step should, in his opinion, exercise a calming influence at St Petersburg. I asked whether it was not to be feared that, in taking military action against Serbia, Austria would dangerously excite public opinion in Russia. He said he thought not. He remained of opinion that crisis could be localised. I said that telegrams from Russia in this morning's papers did not look very reassuring, but he maintained his optimistic view with regard to Russia. He said that he had given the Russian Government to understand that last thing Germany wanted was a general war, and he would do all in his power to prevent such a calamity. If the relations between Austria and Russia became threatening, he was quite ready to fall in with your suggestion as to the four Powers working in favour of moderation at Vienna and St Petersburg.

Confidential

Secretary of State again repeated very earnestly that he had had no previous knowledge of contents of Austro-Hungarian note, although he had been accused of knowing all about it. He confessed privately that as a diplomatic document note left much to be desired.

French Ambassador here learns from Vienna that Austrians are ready to act with eight army corps.

82 Grey to Rumbold

Telegram 197   London, 25 July 1914
B.D. 116   D. 3.00 p.m.

I have told German Ambassador that Austrian Ambassador has been authorised to inform me that rupture of diplomatic relations and military

_____
[1] See 48.

preparations but not operations on part of Austria would be the method of procedure on expiry of time limit.[1] I said this interposed a stage of mobilisation before actual crossing of frontier, which I had urged yesterday should be delayed.

We should now apparently be soon confronted by a moment at which both Austria and Russia would have mobilised. The only chance of peace would be for the four Powers, Germany, Italy, France and ourselves, to keep together if Russia and Austria did both mobilise, and to join in asking Austria and Russia not to cross frontier till there had been time for us to endeavour to arrange matters between them.[2]

German Ambassador read me a telegram from German Foreign Office saying that Germany had not known beforehand and had had no more than other Powers to do with the stiff terms of Austrian note to Serbia, but that having launched the note Austria could not draw back.[3] The Ambassador said, however, that what I contemplated was mediation between Russia and Austria; this was a different question, and he thought Austria might with dignity accept it and he expressed himself personally favourable to what I had suggested.

I endorsed his observation, saying that between Serbia and Austria I felt no title to intervene, but as soon as the question became one between Austria and Russia it was a question of the peace of Europe, in which we must all take a hand.

I impressed upon him that if Austria and Russia mobilised the participation of Germany would be essential to any diplomatic action for peace. We could do nothing alone. I had had no time to consult the French Government, who were travelling at the moment, and I could not be sure of their views; but if German Government were prepared to agree with my suggestion I was prepared to say to the French Government that I thought it the right thing to do.

83 Buchanan to Grey

Telegram 169   St Petersburg, 25 July 1914
Strictly confidential   D. 8.00 p.m.
B.D. 125   R. 10.30 p.m.

I communicated to Minister for Foreign Affairs this morning, in private letter, substance of your telegram 216 of 25 July to Paris,[4] and I this

[1] Berchtold to Mensdorff, 24 July; Ö.D. 10599.   [2] See 74.   [3] See 73, n. 1.
[4] B.D. 105. A reference to Berchtold's above-mentioned communication (82, 1st sentence).

afternoon discussed with him French Ambassador's suggested communication to Serbian Government recorded in your telegram 17 of 24 July
to Belgrade.[1]

As regards former, Minister for Foreign Affairs said that Austrian
Ambassador's explanations did not quite tally with information which
had reached him from German quarters. As regards latter, both his
Excellency and French Ambassador agreed that as delay accorded expires
this evening, it is too late to make such a communication. Minister for
Foreign Affairs said Serbia was quite ready to do as you suggested, and
to punish those proved to be guilty, but no independent State could be
expected to accept political demands put forward. From a conversation
he had with Serbian Minister yesterday, Minister for Foreign Affairs
thought that, in event of Austrian attack, Serbian Government would
abandon Belgrade and withdraw their forces to interior, while they would
at the same time appeal to Powers to help them. His Excellency was in
favour of such an appeal. Obligations taken by Serbia in 1909 to which
reference is made in Austrian ultimatum were given to Powers and not to
Austria, and he would like to see question placed on international footing.
Were Serbia to appeal to Powers, Russia would be quite ready to stand
aside and leave question in hands of England, France, Italy and Germany.
It was possible, he added, that Serbia might propose to submit question
to arbitration.

Minister for Foreign Affairs then told us that at Council of Ministers
held under his presidency this morning Emperor had sanctioned drafting
of Imperial Ukase, which is only to be published when Minister for
Foreign Affairs considers moment come for giving effect to it, ordering
mobilisation of 1,100,000 men. Necessary preliminary preparations for
mobilisation would, however, be begun at once.[2] On my expressing
earnest hope that Russia would not precipitate war by mobilising until you
had had time to use your influence in favour of peace, his Excellency
assured me that Russia had no aggressive intentions, and she would take
no action until it was forced on her.

French Ambassador then said he had received a number of telegrams
from Minister in charge of Ministry for Foreign Affairs,[3] that no one of
them displayed slightest sign of hesitation, and that he was in position
to give his Excellency formal assurance that France placed herself
unreservedly on Russia's side.

After thanking him, Minister for Foreign Affairs turned to me with
question 'And your Government?' I replied that you did not yet despair of
situation, and that great thing was to gain time. I repeated what I had said

[1] B.D., 102; see p. 168.　　　[2] See 76.　　　[3] D.F. XI, 8, 20.

to Emperor in audience—reported in my despatch 100, Secret, of 3 April[1] —that England could play rôle of mediator at Berlin and Vienna to better purpose as friend who, if her counsels of moderation were disregarded, might one day be converted into an ally, than if she were to declare herself Russia's ally at once. His Excellency said that unfortunately Germany was convinced that she could count upon our neutrality. With the exception of *The Times*, nearly the whole of English press was on the side of Austria, to whom Mr Gladstone had addressed warning of 'hands off'. The public had their spirit [group indecipherable]. They did not understand that Austria's action was in reality directed against Russia. She aimed at overthrowing present *status quo* in Balkans and establishing her own hegemony there. He did not believe that Germany really wanted war, but her attitude was decided by ours. If we took our stand firmly with France and Russia there would be no war. If we failed them now rivers of blood would flow and we would in the end be dragged into war.

French Ambassador remarked that French Government would want to know at once whether our fleet was prepared to play part assigned to it by Anglo-French Naval Convention.[2] He could not believe that England would not stand by her two friends, who were acting as one in this matter.

I said all I could to impress prudence on Minister for Foreign Affairs, and warned him, if Russia mobilised, Germany would not be content with mere mobilisation, or give Russia time to carry out hers, but would probably declare war at once. His Excellency assured me once more that he did not wish to precipitate a conflict, but unless Germany can restrain Austria I can regard situation as desperate. Russia cannot allow Austria to crush Serbia and become predominant Power in Balkans, and, secure of support of France, she will face all the risks of war. For ourselves position is a most perilous one, and we shall have to choose between giving Russia our active support or renouncing her friendship. If we fail her now we cannot hope to maintain that friendly cooperation with her in Asia that is of such vital importance to us. Attitude of Italy, according to Minister for Foreign Affairs, seems to be lukewarm, and she does not seem to have been consulted by Austria beforehand.

---

[1] Not included here.
[2] In raising this question the French Ambassador was acting without instructions from his Government. It was merely a private observation arising out of his own personal interpretation of the situation (see Introduction (to *B.D.*), p. xii—Note by the English editor).

84 Minutes of Clerk, Crowe, Nicolson and Grey on the German note
    of 21/24 July[1]

B.D. 100   London, 25 July 1914

Very strong support. G.R.C., 25 July 1914.

The answer is that owing to the extreme nature of the Austrian demands
and the time limit imposed, the localisation of the conflict has been made
exceedingly difficult.[2] Because the Austrian terms bear on their face the
character of a design to provoke a war. The statements made by Austria
and now reasserted by Germany concerning Serbia's misdeeds rest for
the present on no evidence that is available for the Powers whom the
Austrian Government has invited to accept those statements. Time ought
to be given to allow the Powers to satisfy themselves as to the facts which
they are asked to endorse. E.A.C., 25 July.

Telegrams are posted at the Clubs that the Conservative press at Berlin
have veered round, and are protesting against Germany being implicated
in a conflict which Austria-Hungary has conjured, and because Germany
was not consulted beforehand in regard to the ultimatum. I do not know
if this change of front has any significance. A.N.

If true it is a very surprising change of front. I have assumed in my
conversations with Prince Lichnowsky that a war between Austria and
Serbia cannot be localised. E.G.

85 Grey to Buchanan

Decree 295   London, 25 July 1914
Confidential
B.D. 132

I told Count Benckendorff today of what I had said to the German
Ambassador this morning as to the possibility of Germany, Italy, France
and ourselves working together in Vienna and St Petersburg to secure
peace after Austria and Russia had mobilised.[3]

Count Benckendorff was very apprehensive that what I said would give
Germany the impression that France and England were detached from
Russia.

I said that France and ourselves, according to my suggestion, would
be no more detached from Russia than Germany would be detached from

[1] See 39.   [2] See 31, 33 and 35.   [3] See 73 and 82.

her ally Austria. I had emphasised to Prince Lichnowsky that the participation of Germany in any such diplomatic mediation was an essential condition, and surely the situation was not made unsatisfactory for Russia if France and England held their hands, provided that Germany also held hers.

Count Benckendorff urged that I should give some indication to Germany to make her think that we would not stand aside if there was a war.

I said that I had given no indication that we would stand aside; on the contrary, I had said to the German Ambassador that, as long as there was only a dispute between Austria and Serbia alone, I did not feel entitled to intervene, but that, directly it was a matter between Austria and Russia, it became a question of the peace of Europe, which concerned us all. I had furthermore spoken on the assumption that Russia would mobilise, whereas the assumption of the German Government had hitherto been, officially, that Serbia would receive no support; and what I had said must influence the German Government to take the matter seriously. In effect, I was asking that, if Russia mobilised against Austria, the German Government, who had been supporting the Austrian demand on Serbia, should ask Austria to consider some modification of her demands, under the threat of Russian mobilisation. This was not an easy thing for Germany to do, even though we would join at the same time in asking Russia to suspend action. I was afraid, too, that Germany would reply that mobilisation with her was a question of hours, whereas with Russia it was a question of days; and that, as a matter of fact, I had asked that if Russia mobilised against Austria, Germany, instead of mobilising against Russia, should suspend mobilisation and join with us in intervention with Austria, thereby throwing away the advantage of time, for, if the diplomatic intervention failed, Russia would meanwhile have gained time for her mobilisation. It was true that I had not said anything directly as to whether we would take any part or not if there was a European conflict, and I could not say so; but there was absolutely nothing for Russia to complain of in the suggestion that I had made to the German Government, and I was only afraid that there might be difficulty in its acceptance by the German Government. I had made it on my own responsibility, and I had no doubt it was the best proposal to make in the interests of peace.

6 Mediation or Local War
26 – 28 July

After relations with Serbia had been broken off everything depended on whether Austria-Hungary would take the next step—declaration of war on Serbia. On the other hand, the Powers only really began their efforts at mediation now that the unexpectedly compliant Serbian reply had been made known. The following days saw a race between the Powers, in their moves to mediate, and Germany, in her endeavour to bring Austria-Hungary into the war at the earliest possible moment and so give still greater force to the *fait accompli* with which the world was to be confronted. For, as Jagow had intimated to Szögyény on 25 July: 'Here every delay in the beginning of war operations is regarded as signifying the danger that foreign powers might interfere' (71).

On 26 July, a Sunday, German pressure already began to tell on Vienna. There the original intention had been to declare war only after partial mobilisation and the deployment of troops had been completed, that is to say, on 12 August (42). But according to German logic, a plan for localisation would only hold good for a short time by very reason of the great 'danger that foreign powers might interfere'. Any delay caused by the Austrians would inevitably increase the chances of mediation and thus manoeuvre the German Government into 'the extremely difficult position of being exposed in the meantime to the mediation and conference proposals of the other Cabinets' (115).

When Jagow learned on 24 July of Austria's leisurely schedule as well as her intention of allowing a state of war 'to supervene only on the basis of an eventual declaration of war',[1] he evidently expressed his misgivings to Szögyény. At any rate, the Ambassador telegraphed Vienna the German view 'that if Serbia gives an unsatisfactory answer our declaration of war and war operations will follow immediately' (71). On the following day Berchtold, Tschirschky and Conrad consulted together over the pressure from Germany, whereupon the Ambassador 'warmly' supported the German point of view. The outcome of the German hint was that Berchtold who was usually so 'timid and irresolute' promptly followed the Germans' advice in complete contrast to the otherwise habitually bellicose Conrad. The Chief of General Staff was in no such hurry and would have much preferred to adhere to the old timetable. However, in the browbeating presence of Tschirschky the decision that the declaration of war on Serbia should be sooner was taken that day (86, 88), and on 27 July it was finally decided to declare war on 28 July.[2] Once again the Wilhelmstrasse was kept constantly up-to-date on the latest developments. On 27 July the Auswärtiges Amt learned from Tschirschky that it had been decided in Vienna 'to issue the official declaration of war tomorrow, or the day after tomorrow at the latest'. The reason given merely echoed German wishes and could thus cause no offence or surprise in Berlin: 'chiefly to frustrate any attempt at intervention'.[3] At 6.39 p.m. on the following day a telegram arrived from Tschirschky announcing that the declaration of war had been despatched to Belgrade at 11.00 a.m.[4]

But even now Berlin continued to press Vienna for a quickening of tempo. As though to dispel any doubts about the correctness of Szögyény's announcement of 25 July (71), on 27 July Jagow purposely renewed the German pressure for an immediate opening of hostilities, this time couched in an expression of regret 'that the term of the beginning' of Austrian 'military action should have to be postponed so far', namely until 12 August as Tschirschky had announced.[5]

Meanwhile the Powers continued with their efforts at mediation. After Vienna and Berlin had rejected an extension of the time-limit and mediation between Austria-Hungary and Serbia, there followed on 26 July what was certainly Grey's most important proposal: a four-power conference in London between those countries which were not directly involved, that is, England, France, Italy and Germany (93, 94). Once again the German Government immediately and brusquely declined, on the grounds that such a conference would be tantamount to an Areopagus before which Austria would be haled (96). Berlin even persisted in its

---

[1] Berchtold to Szögyény, 24, 7; *Ö.D.* 10580. See above, p. 200, n. 5.
[2] Conrad, *Dienstzeit*, IV, 132; *Ö.D.* 10855.
[3] *D.D.* 257.   [4] *D.D.* 311.   [5] *Ö.D.* 10792; *A.R.B.* II, 67.

refusal when Grey gave his assurance that this was not the intention and in any case was scarcely likely to occur.[1]

In St Petersburg an episode, little remarked by historians, demonstrated how easily the Austro-Hungarian crisis could have been resolved if there had been goodwill all round to avoid a *local* war. In a friendly discussion on 26 July Sazonov earnestly implored the German Ambassador to assist him in the preservation of peace with some kind of proposal for a formula for mediation. Off the cuff, Pourtalès outlined a compromise plan which could have opened a way out of the crisis: Vienna should modify some of the points in the ultimatum, whilst Belgrade would have to accept the revised conditions. As a wise precaution Pourtalès stressed that he was speaking without authority from his Government (90). Sazonov welcomed the suggestion with open arms and immediately translated the German Ambassador's idea into a proposal to Vienna that Szápáry should be authorised to hold a 'private exchange of views' so that together they could work out amendments to the conditions which offended the Russians.[2] The Russian advances met with no response in Vienna, and Berlin was equally reluctant to support Pourtalès' personal initiative.

Far from even considering this chance of avoiding a local war, the German Government was calculating more certainly than ever on a continental war. On 26 July there appeared in the *North German Gazette* a further semi-official notice, which frankly supported the Austrian ultimatum and, while indicating the desirability of localisation, it already spoke threateningly of the 'unavoidable settlement of the Austro-Serbian quarrel' if Serbia were to reject the demands (87).

On the same day the effect of the generals' trooping back to Berlin from their leave began to tell. Moltke presented the Auswärtiges Amt with the draft of a summons to the Belgian Government, by way of diplomatic preparation for the planned attack on France through Belgium. The summons was an attempt to justify the coming invasion by German troops with the help of fictitious reports of an imminent invasion of Belgium by French troops (91). The Auswärtiges Amt was by now so definitely banking on a continental war that on the same day a memorandum was drafted to the German Ambassadors in Paris, London and St Petersburg which laid down the official policy—adhered to in the days and decades that followed—of seeking to pin on to Russia the responsibility for a continental war.[3]

After the Serbian reply (72) became known in Europe, the moral position of Germany and Austria-Hungary rapidly deteriorated. On

---

[1] Grey to Goschen, 28 July; *B.D.* 218.   [2] *Int. Bez.* I, 5, 86.   [3] *D.D.* 234.

27 July Grey told Count Mensdorff, the Austro-Hungarian Ambassador in London, of his disappointment that Vienna 'treated the Serbian reply as if it had been a decided refusal to comply with [its] wishes, whereas it is really the greatest humiliation an independent state has ever been submitted to'.[1] The Auswärtiges Amt consequently switched to more flexible tactics, so as to check the growth of this bad impression in Europe. It now abandoned its purely negative attitude to efforts at mediation; instead, it adopted the aim of securing Britain's vital goodwill—in other words, her neutrality in the approaching continental war. Jagow, whilst actually regretting the delay in opening hostilities against Serbia[2]—in defiance of all the attempts at mediation by the other Powers—expounded the new tactics of flexibility to the Austrian Ambassador: in order to preserve Britain's goodwill, Berlin would pretend to adopt the role of mediator between London and Vienna without however identifying itself with the British proposals. As if to eliminate any misunderstanding Jagow made it clear that the German Government was for rejecting British proposals of mediation (95). This precautionary rider succeeded, as on the other two occasions when Berlin had likewise sought to forestall the possibility of a misunderstanding (26, 115).

That very day the Wilhelmstrasse found an opportunity to apply its new tactics when the Chancellor forwarded—late and without supporting it—another British proposal for mediation and explicitly justified this step in precisely the terms agreed between Jagow and Szögyény: 'By refusing every proposal for mediation, we should be held responsible for the conflagration by the whole world, and be set forth as the original instigators of the war. That would also make our position impossible in our own country, where we must appear as having been forced into the war. Our situation is all the more difficult, inasmuch as Serbia has apparently yielded to a very great degree. Therefore we cannot refuse the mediator's role, and must submit the English proposal to the consideration of the Vienna Cabinet, especially as London and Paris continue to make their influence felt in St Petersburg.'[3] In accordance with Jagow's tactics, the Chancellor expected in a subsequent briefing to Lichnowsky that Grey should appreciate this (wholly formal and fictitious!) show of meeting Grey's initiative (101) as indeed he had done on a previous occasion (81).

On 27 July, while Chancellor Bethmann Hollweg was informing the Kaiser of the situation[4] after the latter had returned early on his own

[1] *Ö.D.* 10813; *A.R.B.* II, 72.
[2] See above, p. 219.
[3] *D.D.* 277.   [4] *D.D.* 245.

initiative, Jagow was having to withstand a third wave of remonstrances from the diplomatic representatives of the Entente Powers. In all the discussions much was made of the connection between localisation of the Austro-Serbian dispute and prevention of an Austro-Russian conflict. Jagow, whilst working on Vienna for the speediest opening of hostilities, for tactical reasons maintained to Cambon that any attempt at mediation by the Great Powers could only be successful if things were not rushed. Jagow refused to intercede with Austria, but agreed in his conversation with Cambon to exert pressure on Austria surreptitiously. On the other hand, he withheld his support from the Russian proposal for mediation and tolerated rather than welcomed the bilateral discussions promoted by Pourtalès and Sazonov. He again employed the familiar arguments in rejecting the proposal for an Ambassadors' conference in London and turned a deaf ear to Cambon's urgent appeal to his conscience. In reply to Cambon's warning that he should harbour no illusions about Britain's attitude, the Secretary of State imperturbably declared 'You have your information, we have ours which is exactly the opposite. We are sure of English neutrality'.[1] Only Jagow's assurance that Germany would not counter Russian mobilisation with German mobilisation so long as the Russian mobilisation was only directed against Austria-Hungary (102, 103, 110) could provide some comfort. Even this small comfort proved illusory after a matter of days.

Although the Great Powers desperately tried to prevent the local war against Serbia as the best means of averting a major one (as Bienvenu-Martin, the acting French Foreign Minister, put it to Baron von Schoen, the German Ambassador in Paris), the German Government again on 28 July steadfastly rebutted all attempts at mediation.

Whilst Berlin was once more on 27 July urging the Austrians to make haste in starting the war against Serbia[2] and struggling withal to delay mediation, the German Government on 28 July quashed the sole initiative towards a settlement that emanated from Germany herself: Wilhelm II had only received the Serbian reply (72) early on 28 July after his premature return from his Scandinavian journey. He was quite taken aback and all his belligerence was suddenly gone. His comment was unequivocal: 'A brilliant performance for a time-limit of only 48 hours. This is more than one could have expected! A great moral victory for Vienna; but with it every reason for war drops away, and Giesl might have remained quietly in Belgrade. On the strength of this *I* should never have ordered mobilisa-

---

[1] L. Albertini, *Origins*, II, p. 250; Raymond Recouly, *Les heures tragiques d'Avant-Guerre* (Paris, 1922), p. 23.
[2] See above, p. 219.

tion!'¹ Accordingly he sent the Auswärtiges Amt written instructions to advise Vienna to be conciliatory; only the outstanding points needed to be negotiated. In addition the Kaiser proposed a limitation of military operations to the occupation of Belgrade to ensure that the Serbian promises were carried out (112).

Was this the great turning point? A ray of light on the horizon? There was certainly not a moment to be lost if peace were to be saved for although the Kaiser in Potsdam cannot have known it, the Austrian declaration of war on Serbia was dispatched only an hour later. Yet Chancellor Bethmann Hollweg took his time. He neither hastened to execute the imperial command which might even now have preserved the peace, nor did he adequately fulfil it but postponed his *démarche* at Vienna until he had received news of the declaration of war. He also falsified the imperial instructions in all essential points: he neither mentioned the Kaiser's central conclusion that every pretext for war was thereby removed, nor did he adhere to the remaining individual points. The Chancellor insisted on total subjection of Serbia, and the occupation of Belgrade was to serve as a means of enforcing this. Moreover, Tschirschky was required 'to avoid very carefully giving rise [in Vienna] to the impression that we wish to hold Austria back' (115). This aim, too, was in complete harmony with the arrangement between Jagow and Szögyény (95) and with the tactics to date. Instead of using his *démarche* as contribution to the avoidance of a local war, the Chancellor, when he should have been carrying out the Kaiser's peace mission on the evening of 28 July, was obsessed about incurring 'the odium of having been responsible for a world war, even, finally, among the German people themselves' (115). It is obvious that in such an atmosphere Vienna should have seen no occasion to break off the war against Serbia which had been so urgently desired by Berlin, after it was but a few hours old.

If the Austrians had known of the preparations for a great war which were advancing apace in Berlin at the same time, and if they had retained but a dim recollection of the recent deal between Jagow and Szögyény, they need scarcely have doubted that their interpretation of German intentions was substantially correct. As early as 26 July the completed drafts of innumerable laws and ordinances for the contingency of mobilisation lay ready in the Ministry of the Interior.² That Sunday Bethmann Hollweg handed the Kaiser a number of telegrams which had arrived, but for the time being withheld from his Monarch the Serbian reply and in its place presented him with a single document which merely required the signature and counter-signature of the Kaiser and his Chancellor for

¹ *D.D.* 271.   ² *DZA*, Potsdam, Reichsamt des Innern, no. 12144.

the entire batch to be passed on for the formality of ratification by the Federal Council.

Meanwhile, in Russia preparatory measures for mobilisation took their course. But on 26 July the Russian Minister of War, Sukhomlinov, had assured Major Eggeling, the German Military Attaché, that they were solely directed against Austria-Hungary; mobilisation itself was only to be proclaimed if Austrian troops should invade Serbia.[1] Russian military circles round Czar Nicolas hoped that Austria was merely bluffing and that, in the event, it would not come to the worst.[2] On 27 July Sazonov sought to use Austria's (albeit wholly unofficial) declaration of her territorial *désintéressement*, as a means—with Germany's assistance (100)—'to build a golden bridge' for Vienna by urging that the current dialogues with Vienna should be extended into authorised negotiations over a mitigation of the terms of the ultimatum (108).

Austria-Hungary's intransigence and especially her prompt declaration of war on Serbia on 28 July seem to have accentuated Russia's nervousness; Sazonov's reaction to the declaration of war was immediately to proclaim partial mobilisation and inform the German Government to this effect instead of actually waiting for an Austrian invasion of Serbia (118). He felt that he was covered by France, since Paléologue, the French Ambassador, had given him his (unauthorised!) assurance of French support.[3] At the same time Sazonov again sent an urgent plea to London that the British Government should make an unambiguous declaration of its solidarity with the Entente Allies, as he saw this to be the only chance of restraining Germany and avoiding general war (121).

French diplomacy was still partially paralysed by Poincaré's and Viviani's absence from Paris. Although they had cancelled their state visits to Christiania and Copenhagen on 27 July, they only arrived back in Paris in the afternoon of 29 July. The French Government was surprised at the rejection of the Serbian reply[4] and supported all proposals aimed at mediation between Vienna and Belgrade (103, 104, 105). On 26 and 27 July, Viviani informed the Russian Government that, in view of the crisis, France was ready to preserve peace by a show of solidarity.[5]

In Paris Schoen, the German Ambassador, visited the Quai d'Orsay several times in a bid to counteract the unfavourable impression on French public opinion created by German support of the ultimatum. He tried to lure the French Government into accepting the German policy of localisation by insisting on the 'solidarity' of both Powers in

[1] *D.D.* 242.   [2] *D.D.* 229; *Ö.D.* 10836.
[3] *Int. Bez.* I, 5, 172.   [4] *Ö.D.* 10739.
[5] *D.F.* XI, 138.

their endeavours for peace (89, 92, 106); his profuse protestations of peaceful intentions were bound to arouse strong suspicion in the French Foreign Ministry. In a lengthy discussion with Schoen on 28 July Bienvenu-Martin came out with what was certainly the most precise formulation of the whole problem, when he explained, according to Schoen's report, that 'the best means of avoiding a general war is by preventing a local one' (113). Nevertheless, France had been going ahead with her first cautious and secret military preparations since 25 July. The recall of the generals on 25 July and of officers and soldiers on leave for the harvest on 26 July was followed on 27 July by an order for the return to France of the majority of French troops in Morocco and instructions for preliminary safety measures on the railways. On 28 July the French Chief of General Staff—in anticipation of the political decision—informed Ignatiev, the Russian Military Attaché, of France's 'full and active readiness faithfully to execute her responsibilities as an ally'.[1]

The British Government would still give no firm undertakings. Although it addressed a number of indirect warnings to Berlin (97, 98, 99), they were not vigorous enough to convince the German Government. Even the order to the British Fleet not to disperse published on 27 July was plainly ignored by Berlin in its subsequent policy-making. Yet Crowe, like the Russians, pressed for a declaration of Britain's commitment, fearing that otherwise there was a threat that Britain would be isolated (107). On 28 July, in ignorance of Jagow's basic lack of enthusiasm for talks between Austria and Russia (102) and under the influence of misleading assurances from the Auswärtiges Amt that the dialogue between Vienna and St Petersburg was progressing favourably,[2] Grey postponed any further initiative in order to await the outcome of the advertised talks.[3] However, Grey did recommend to Lichnowsky that Vienna should be satisfied with the Serbian reply (97, 98, 99, 109). He explicitly informed Vienna and Berlin that he sought to avoid 'Austria's armed attack on Serbia' (98). That day Grey announced in the House of Commons: 'It must be obvious to any person who reflects upon the situation that from the moment the dispute ceases to be one between Austria-Hungary and Serbia and becomes one in which another Great Power is involved, it cannot but end in the greatest catastrophe that has ever befallen the Continent of Europe at one blow: no one can say what would be the limits of the issues that might be raised by such a conflict, the consequences of it, direct and indirect, would be incalculable'. On

---

[1] *Int. Bez.* I, 5, 180.
[2] Bethmann Hollweg to Lichnowsky, 27 July; *D.D.* 278.
[3] Grey to Goschen, 28 July; *B.D.* 223.

28 July he once more returned to his original (26 July) idea for a conference (93, 94), whilst adopting as his own and conveying to Berlin a
joint suggestion by Jules Cambon and Goschen, the British Ambassador,
that the German Government itself should propose the form of mediation
most acceptable to Austria and itself (119, 120).

The German answer to the attempts of the Powers to avoid a local
war between Serbia and Austria-Hungary by mediation and thus avoid
European War as its inevitable consequence, was to cling steadfastly to
its policy of localisation; in other words, primarily to a war against Serbia.
But from 26 July even its policy of localisation escalated a phase: now
that local war against Serbia was assured, the prime concern was to
manoeuvre the Reich into the most favourable position for embarking
on the continental war which had been made inevitable. Two things were
necessary for this, as was by now already apparent; the responsibility for
the war had to be shifted on to Russia, and British neutrality had to be
assured. Both aims stood a good chance of being achieved, if German
diplomacy succeeded in cornering Russia into such a position that she
became the first Great Power to proclaim general mobilisation.

86 Discussion between Conrad and Berchtold

Conrad IV, pp. 131f.   Vienna, 26 July 1914

At 12.30 in the afternoon of the same day (26 July) I went to see Count
Berchtold. There I met Herr von Tschirschky.[1] Later Baron Macchio and
Count Forgách joined us.

Herr von Tschirschky read out some notes. The Danish Minister had
reported that Russia was carrying out preparations for mobilisation in the
military districts facing the German and Austrian frontiers.

I objected that this certainly did not necessarily yet signify mobilisation but that one would have to watch Russia's actions and follow them
up pari passu. I asked to be kept fully informed of Russia's activities.

'Sweden', Herr von Tschirschky said, 'has told M. Poincaré that she
would stand unconditionally at the side of the Triple Alliance if it came
to a war with Russia.'[2] I expressed the view that it would be as well if
this could in some way be brought to Russia's notice, as this would
certainly have the effect of making her more cautious.

[1] For Tschirschky's version, see 88.
[2] See I. Geiss, *Julikrise und Kriegsausbruch 1914*, I, no. 342.

The German Ambassador said that in Italy the attitude of the news-papers was favourable. San Giuliano was extremely nervous, however, and had stated that Italy would not be compelled to fulfil the treaty obligations of the Triple Alliance if a large scale war resulted from Austria-Hungary's actions.

I interjected: 'I am afraid that this is undoubtedly Cadorna's influence;[1] he was described to me as a Francophile'.

Count Berchtold remarked that Italy probably wanted to do a deal with the aim of acquiring additional territory in the event of *our* winning any.

Herr von Tschirschky advised treating this in a dilatory manner, and telling Italy that compensation would be discussed at a suitable time. He then went on to talk about Germany's *démarche* in Paris[2] and Bratianu being upset, whilst adding that King Carol of Roumania was anxious to remain on the side of the Triple Alliance.

I then talked to Count Berchtold alone. He declared: 'We should like to deliver the declaration of war on Serbia as soon as possible so as to put an end to diverse influences. When do you want the declaration of war?'

I: 'Only when we have progressed far enough for operations to begin immediately—on approximately August 12.'

Count Berchtold: 'The diplomatic situation will not hold as long as that. Nor does anyone know whether there will be fighting on the frontier.'

I suggested that in this case matters would take their own course and proposed postponing a declaration of war for the time being, but sum-moning me if a postponement no longer seemed advisable from the diplo-matic point of view. We could certainly wait for a few days; it was not as urgent as all that. I recommended holding back Montenegro as long as possible and avoiding 'inciting' Bulgaria against Roumania, as we had to spare Roumania. Most important of all, however, was to gain a better understanding of Russia's attitude; it would be desirable to obtain such an understanding by 4 or 5 August[3] at the latest. Count Berchtold: 'That will not do!'

I resumed that as matters stood, if it was clear by this date that Russia was going to 'attack' us, we should proceed against Russia on our own initiative, but otherwise against Serbia; if Russia were subsequently to move against us, however, we would initially be weaker, in the northern theatre of operations.

---

[1] Cadorna was the new Italian Chief of Staff.   [2] See **39** and **55**.
[3] If it had only come to war against Serbia, the Second Army might possibly have crossed the Save-Danube after this date and thus engaged in action against Serbia—Note by Conrad.

87 Notice in the *North German Gazette*

Berlin, 26 July 1914

The demands brought against Serbia by Austria-Hungary on the grounds of the enquiry into the murder of the Heir Apparent in Sarajevo must appear justified if the arguments for these demands are treated with a gravity commensurate with the matter. It has been revealed that leading Serbian figures, including officials, were implicated in the long-range planning of the conspiracy against the life of the Archduke Franz Ferdinand and in intrigues against the unity of the Hapsburg Monarchy. The Austro-Hungarian Government has declared its willingness to allow the Powers to examine the material relating to the enquiry, a proof that it is convinced of the soundness of its investigations and the justness of its demands. If Serbia, contrary to expectations, were to reject these demands, it is to be hoped that, with a feeling for the seriousness of the situation, the Governments of the Great Powers will show a common concern for preventing the unavoidable settlement of the Austro-Serbian quarrel giving rise to far-reaching consequences.[1]

88 Tschirschky to Jagow

Telegram 105	Vienna, 26 July 1914
Confidential	D. 4.50 p.m.
D.D. 213	R. 6.20 p.m.

Count Berchtold read me a telegram from Count Szögyény in which the latter reports that the Berlin authorities consider the utmost rapidity in military operations and the immediate declaration of war to be necessary in order to avoid as far as possible the danger of the intervention of a third party.[2] The Minister had already requested Baron von Hötzendorf to come to him in order to discuss this point; he appeared while I was with the Minister.[3] I warmly supported our point of view—which was fully shared by Count Berchtold—to the Chief of the General Staff. Baron von Hötzendorf explained that commencing a campaign with insufficient forces was above all things to be avoided. The Hungarian corps on the northern Serbian border would be ready to march within a short time. The Austrian detachments along the western border of Serbia,

---

[1] See **36** and **39**.   [2] See **71**.   [3] For Conrad's version see **86**.

however, would take a longer time to prepare, owing to the lack of sufficient communication material; to wait that length of time was absolutely necessary. He was counting on being able to commence the general advance somewhere about 12 August.[1] For the rest, a formal declaration of war would probably prove superfluous, because, according to his certain information, hostile uprisings across the Bosnian border would be made by Serbia within the next few days.

89   Schoen to Jagow

Telegram 220   Paris, 26 July 1914
D.D. 235   D. 7.40 p.m.
                              R. 27 July, 0.07 a.m.

The Acting Minister for Foreign Affairs has assured me that our appeal for a united effort for the maintenance of peace had a very beneficial effect here and will receive befitting attention. Speaking for himself, he would gladly be willing to have pacifying influences set to work at St Petersburg, after it had been established in advance through Austrian assurances that no annexation was contemplated. Of course, he could not yet give me a formal explanation in the name of the French Government as to the method of influence, as he would first have to get in touch with the absent Premier.

The Minister interjected as an idea of his own, whether the exercise of pacifying influences at Vienna might not also be considered, since Serbia had apparently conceded most of the points and thereby opened up the opportunity for negotiation. I replied that any possible general representations of the Powers at Vienna would not appear to be conformable to our view that Austria-Hungary and Serbia ought to be let alone. The place where influence ought to be exercised was St Petersburg.

M. Bienvenu-Martin confidentially admitted, in the course of the conversation, that Sazonov's idea that only the Powers as a body were competent to pronounce judgment on Serbia's conduct, would be difficult to uphold legally. Minister expressed regret that my first *démarche*[2] here was so generally misinterpreted by the press, and assured me that the indiscretion did not originate at the Quai d'Orsay.

[1] On Jagow's reaction, see p. 219.
[2] On 24 July, see 55.

90 Pourtalès to Jagow

Telegram 163   St Petersburg, 26 July 1914
D.D. 238   D. 10.10 p.m.
                                                        R. 27 July, 10.45 a.m.

Count Szápáry had a lengthy conference with Sazonov this afternoon.[1]
Both participants, with whom I talked afterwards, emerged from it with
the same pleasant impression. The assurances of the Ambassador that
Austria-Hungary was contemplating no plan of conquest, and was simply
anxious to have the peace kept along its borders, visibly eased the
Minister's mind. The Austrian note was quietly discussed by Sazonov and
Count Szápáry. It developed from the discussion that Sazonov had no
objection to a number of the points. Concerning some of the other points,
the Minister told me, they might be able to come to an agreement as a
result of alterations in their form. Perhaps it was only a matter of words.
Austria, he said, made some demands which the Serbian Government
could not, as a matter of fact, carry out, without altering the Serbian
constitution, which at the present moment was impossible. But perhaps
a method for satisfying Austria might be found without literal compliance
with the demands. Sazonov also touched upon the idea of mediation in his
talk with my Austrian colleague, and suggested mediation by the Kings
of Italy and England. The Minister also asked me with urgency whether
I, too, might not be able to make some proposition. While insisting that I
was not empowered to make any proposition and could therefore only
suggest my own personal ideas, I replied that the following method might
perhaps be feasible. In case the Vienna Cabinet might be found willing
to modify to a certain extent the form of certain of the demands, which,
from the statements of Count Szápáry, did not seem to be entirely excluded as a possibility, it might be possible to get into immediate touch
with Austria-Hungary on this matter. Should an agreement be the result,
then Serbia [can] be advised by Russia to accept the demands on the
basis agreed upon between Austria and Russia, and to permit Austria to
be notified of this through the medium of some third Power.[2] Sazonov,
to whom I again emphatically insisted that I was not speaking in the
name of my Government, said that he would immediately telegraph to the
Russian Ambassador at Vienna along the lines of my proposal.[3]

---

[1] *Ö.D.* 10835; *Int. Bez.* I, 5, 86.
[2] This sentence was omitted from the versions telegraphed to the Kaiser, Lichnowsky
(Telegram 180, D. 12.10 p.m.) and Tschirschky (Telegram 161, D. 4.35 p.m.).
[3] An account by Sazonov is not available.

I have the impression that Sazonov, perhaps as the result of information from Paris and London, has lost some of his nerve and is now looking for a way out.[1] Minister earnestly requested of me that the German press be quieted down as much as possible. He promised to see to the same thing here.[2]

91 Jagow to Below

Decree 87[3]
D.D. 376

Berlin, 29 July 1914

The Imperial Government is in receipt of reliable information relating to the proposed advance of French armed forces along the Meuse, route Givet-Namur. They leave no doubt as to France's intention to advance against Germany through Belgian territory.[4]

The Imperial Government cannot help being concerned over the probability that Belgium, despite the best of intentions, will be unable to resist without assistance a French advance with a prospect of success so great that sufficient security against the menace to Germany may be found therein. It is for Germany a dictate of self-preservation that she anticipate the hostile attack. It would therefore fill the German Government with the deepest regret, should Belgium view as an act of hostility to herself the entrance of Germany upon Belgian soil, should she be forced by the measures of her opponents to do so in self-protection.

In order to avoid any misunderstanding, the Imperial Government makes the following statement:

1 Germany contemplates no hostile activities against Belgium. If Belgium should be willing to adopt an attitude of benevolent neutrality towards Germany in the prospective war, the German Government will bind itself to guarantee, at the conclusion of peace, [not only][5] the sovereign rights and independence of the Kingdom in their full extent, [but it will

---

[1] This sentence was omitted from the version transmitted to Tschirschky.

[2] Both the last sentences were omitted from the version transmitted to Lichnowsky.

[3] Chief of General Staff Moltke sent the draft to the *Auswärtiges Amt* on 26 July, together with a parallel note to the Netherlands promising respect for their neutrality; text in *D.D.* 426, n. 3. The note was dispatched to the German Minister at the Hague on 30 July (*D.D.* 426), and was delivered to the Netherlands Government on 3 August (*D.D.* 738, 797) in accordance with the instructions of 2 August (*D.D.* 674). The order was only sent to Below on 29 July (*D.D.* 375).

[4] From the very beginning these allegations were a complete fabrication.

[5] The passage placed in squared brackets was omitted in the version delivered to the Belgian Government on 2 August; *D.D.* 648.

even be prepared to favour with the best of good will any possible claims of the Kingdom for territorial compensation at the expense of France].[1]

2 Germany binds herself, under the above conditions, to evacuate the territory of the Kingdom as soon as peace shall have been concluded.

3 In case of the friendly attitude of Belgium, Germany will be willing, under an arrangement with the Royal Belgian authorities, to buy for cash all the necessities required by her troops, and to make good every damage that may possibly be occasioned by German troops.

Should Belgium oppose as an enemy the German troops, and in particular throw obstacles in their way by the resistance of the Meuse fortifications, or by the destruction of railroads, roads, tunnels or other artificial structures, Germany would be obliged, to her regret, to regard the Kingdom as an enemy. In such an event, Germany would be unable to undertake any obligations to the benefit of the Kingdom, but would have to leave the future regulation of the relations of the two nations to each other to the decision of arms.

The Imperial Government ventures to feel definitely hopeful that this eventuality may not occur, and that the Royal Belgian Government will be able to take appropriate measures to prevent any such occurrences as those hereinbefore mentioned. In such an event, the friendly ties that bind the two neighbouring nations would be subject to a further and a lasting consolidation.

Your Excellency will communicate this matter to the Royal Belgian Government in detail and in the strictest confidence, and will request the transmission of an unequivocal reply within twenty-four hours.[2] Your Excellency will make me a detailed telegraphic report concerning the reception with which your announcement is met there and of the definite reply of the Royal Belgian Government.

92 Note of Berthelot

D.F. XI, 109 (*F.Y.B.* 57)   Paris, 26 July 1914

After the visit which he paid to the Minister at 5 o'clock in the afternoon, Baron von Schoen went this evening at 7 o'clock to the Direction Politique, to ask that in order to avoid the appearance in the newspapers of com-

---

[1] The passage placed in squared brackets was omitted from the version delivered to the Belgian Government on 2 August; *D.D.* 648.

[2] On 2 August the time limit was reduced to 12 hours; *D.D.* 648.

ments intended to influence public opinion, such as that in the *Echo de Paris* of the evening before, and in order to define exactly the sense of the *démarches* of the German Government, a brief statement should be communicated to the press on the interview between the German Ambassador and the Minister for Foreign Affairs.

Herr von Schoen, in order to define what he had in his mind suggested the following terms, which the Acting Political Director took down at his dictation: 'During the afternoon the German Ambassador and the Minister for Foreign Affairs had a fresh interview, in the course of which, in the most amicable spirit, and acting in an identical spirit of peaceful co-operation (*sentiment de solidarité pacifique*), they examined the means which might be employed to maintain general peace.'[1]

The Acting Political Director replied at once, 'Then, in your opinion, everything is settled, and you bring us the assurance that Austria accepts the Serbian note or will enter into conversations with the Powers on this matter?' The Ambassador having appeared surprised and having vigorously denied the suggestion, it was explained to him that if there was no modification in Germany's negative attitude, the terms of the suggested 'note to the press' were exaggerated, and of a nature to give a false security to French opinion by creating illusion on the real situation, the dangers of which were only too evident.

To the assurances lavished by the German Ambassador as to the optimistic impressions which he had formed, the Acting Political Director replied by asking if he might speak to him in a manner quite personal and private, as man to man, quite freely and without regard to their respective functions. Baron von Schoen asked him to do so.

M. Berthelot then said that to any simple mind Germany's attitude was inexplicable if it did not aim at war; a purely objective analysis of the facts and the psychology of the Austro-German relations led logically to this conclusion. In the face of the repeated statement that Germany was ignorant of the contents of the Austrian note, it was no longer permissible to raise any doubt on that point; but was it probable that Germany would have arrayed herself on the side of Austria in such an adventure with her eyes closed? Did the psychology of all the past relations of Vienna and Berlin allow one to admit that Austria could have taken up a position without any possible retreat, before having weighed with her ally all the consequences of her uncompromising attitude? How surprising appeared the refusal by Germany to exercise mediating influence at Vienna now that she knew the extraordinary text of the Austrian note! What responsibility was the German Government assuming and what suspicions

[1] For the definitive text of the communiqué see **106**.

would rest upon them if they persisted in interposing between Austria and the Powers, after what might be called the absolute submission of Serbia, and when the slightest advice given by them to Vienna would put an end to the nightmare which weighed on Europe!

The breaking off of diplomatic relations by Austria, her threats of war, and the mobilisation which she was undertaking make peculiarly urgent pacific action on the part of Germany, for from the day when Austrian troops crossed the Serbian frontier, one would be faced by an act which without doubt would oblige the St Petersburg Cabinet to intervene, and would risk the unloosing of a war which Germany declares that she wishes to avoid.

Herr von Schoen, who listened smiling, once more affirmed that Germany had been ignorant of the text of the Austrian note, and had only approved it after its delivery; she thought, however, that Serbia had need of a lesson severe enough for her not to be able to forget it, and that Austria owed it to herself to put an end to a situation which was dangerous and intolerable for a great Power. He declared besides that he did not know the text of the Serbian reply, and showed his personal surprise that it had not satisfied Austria, if indeed it was such as the papers, which are often ill-informed, represented it to be.

He insisted again on Germany's peaceful intentions and gave his impressions as to the effect that might arise from good advice given, for instance, at Vienna, by England in a friendly tone. According to him Austria was not uncompromising; what she rejects is the idea of a formal mediation, the 'spectre' of a conference: a peaceful word coming from St Petersburg, good words said in a conciliatory tone by the Powers of the Triple Entente, would have a chance of being well received. He added, finally, that he did not say that Germany on her side would not give some advice at Vienna.

In these conditions the Political Director announced that he would ask the Minister if it appeared to him opportune to communicate to the press a short note in a moderate tone.

93 Grey to Missions in, Paris, Vienna, St Petersburg, Nisch, Berlin and Rome.

Telegrams 232, 159, 365, 18, 204, 198   London, 26 July 1914
B.D. 140
                                           D. 3.00 p.m.

Ask Minister for Foreign Affairs if he would be disposed to instruct Ambassador here to join with representatives of Italy, Germany, France, and myself in a conference to be held here at once in order to endeavour to find an issue to prevent complications. With this view representatives at Vienna, St Petersburg and Belgrade should be authorised in informing Governments to which they are accredited of above suggestion to request that pending results of conference all active military operations should be suspended.[1]

94 Nicolson to Grey

B.D. 144   London, 26 July 1914

I telegraphed to you an idea which occurred to me after reading Buchanan's telegram 169.[2] It seems to me the only chance of avoiding a conflict—it is I admit a very poor chance—but in any case we shall have done our utmost. Berlin is playing with us. Jagow did not really adopt your proposal to intervene at Vienna, and to be backed up by us and France, but simply 'passed on' your suggestion and told his Ambassador to speak about it.[3] This is not what was intended or desired. Mensdorff asked to see me this afternoon. It was only to announce officially that relations had been broken off with Serbia, and that Serbia was mobilising. He asked me what news we had from St Petersburg. I told him that the situation was most gravely viewed there, as was natural, but I gave him no details. I saw Benckendorff to whom I read Buchanan's 169.[2] He had no news, but impressed on me that Lichnowsky was convinced we could stand aside and remain neutral[4]—an unfortunate conviction—as were they to understand that our neutrality was by no means to be counted upon

---

[1] Only Goschen's reply has been selected for inclusion here; see 110. The remaining replies are to be found in *B.D.* 175, 183, 189, 198 and 202.

[2] See 83.

[3] See 81.

[4] Here either Nicolson or Buchanan was in error, unless Lichnowsky had deliberately sought to mislead his cousin, Benckendorff, for diplomatic reasons; see Lichnowsky's warning reports and telegrams 73 and 74.

and that we could not be expected to remain indifferent when all Europe was in flames, a restraining influence would be exercised on Berlin.

I have just heard you have approved my proposal[1]—I am glad, though I am not hopeful. Still no chance should be neglected.

I lunched with Stamfordham.[2] He told me Prince Henry[3] came over yesterday and breakfasted with the King this morning. Prince Henry said if Russia moved there would be an internal revolution and the dynasty be upset. This is nonsense—but it shows how anxious they are to make out to us that Russia will remain quiet and to spread about that we will be equally quiescent—a foolish procedure—(Prince Henry has gone back to Germany).

95 Szögyény to Berchtold

Telegram 307   Berlin, 27 July 1914
Strictly confidential   D. 9.15 p.m.
Ö.D. 10793   R. 28 July, 9.00 a.m.

Secretary of State in strictest privacy informed me that very shortly eventual English propositions of mediation would be communicated to Your Excellency through the German Government.

The German Government assures in the most *decided way that it does not identify itself* with these propositions, that on the contrary it advises to disregard them, but that it must pass them on, to satisfy the English Government.

The German Government holds the belief that it is just now of the very highest importance that England should not side with Russia and France. Therefore everything must be done to prevent the wire still working between Germany and England from being broken. If Germany candidly told Sir E. Grey that it refused to communicate England's wishes to Austria-Hungary, which it thinks will be more regarded, if they pass through Germany's hands, the above-mentioned eventuality might occur.

The German Government will, whenever England has such a request to make, tell Vienna explicitly that it[4] cannot support such proposals of intervention and only passes them on to please England.

[1] I.e. the proposal for an Ambassadors' conference; see **93**.
[2] Lord Stamfordham, Private Secretary to George V.
[3] Brother of Wilhelm II.
[4] The discussion between Jagow and Szögyény took place at approximately midday; see Heinz Günther Sasse 'Daten zum Kriegsaubruch, Deutschland' in *Berliner Monatshefte*, XII, 1934, pp. 707ff.

The British Government has through the German Ambassador in London yesterday, and through the British Ambassador, in Berlin, requested Herr von Jagow to support England's wishes with regard to a modification of the note to Serbia.[1] Jagow had answered that he would act according to Sir E. Grey's wish and would send his proposals on to you, but that he could not support them, because the conflict with Serbia was a question of *prestige* for the Austro-Hungarian Monarchy, which Germany shares to a certain extent.

He, the Secretary of State had therefore sent Sir Edward Grey's note on to Herr von Tschirschky, but without instructing him to present the note to Your Excellency;[2] it was thus possible to inform the English cabinet that far from refusing to comply with Sir E. Grey's wish, he had sent the note on to Vienna. Before concluding our conversation the Secretary of State repeated his view of the case, and begged me assure Your Excellency, that there might be no mistake, that though he had acted as middleman in this affair, he by no means wished to support the propositions for a mediation.

96 Bethmann Hollweg to Lichnowsky

Telegram 179   Berlin, 27 July 1914
D.D. 248   D. 1.00 p.m.

Had no knowledge here up to the present of Sir E. Grey's proposal to hold a conference *à quatre* there.[3] We could not take part in such a conference, as we would not be able to summon Austria before a European court of justice in her case with Serbia.[4] Sir Edward Grey makes a sharp distinction, as Your Excellency has expressly reported, between Austro-Serbian and Austro-Russian conflict, and is concerned about the former just as little as we ourselves.[5] Our mediation activities must be confined to a possible Austro-Russian clash.[6] In regard to the Austro-Serbian

[1] Evidently this is an allusion to Grey's intimation that Vienna should be content with the Serbian reply; *D.D.* 186, *B.D.* 149.   [2] *B.D.* 149.
[3] See 93. In fact the proposal only reached Berlin later.
[4] Szögyény reported Germany's refusal on 28 July; *Ö.D.* 10869.   [5] See 73.
[6] The draft contained the following sentence, subsequently deleted by Bethmann Hollweg: 'Your assumption that localisation is impossible had not yet been proved'. Before there was concrete evidence of the impossibility of localisation, however, or in other words before outbreak of world or continental war, the evidence could only be supplied by logical argument with reference to the existing state of affairs and it was this course that Lichnowsky undertook in vain to pursue. The proof could be supplied only by the failure of localisation, i.e. by the Great War; but once the infeasibility of localisation was proved, it was too late.

conflict, the method of a direct understanding between St Petersburg and Vienna as suggested by telegram (163) from St Petersburg[1] appears to me to be feasible. I therefore request you most urgently to advocate in London the necessity and the possibility of localisation.[2]

97 Lichnowsky to Jagow

Telegram 164   London, 27 July 1914
D.D. 258   D. 1.31 p.m.
                                                                R. 4.37 p.m.

Sir E. Grey had me call on him just now and requested me to inform Your Excellency as follows:

The Serbian Chargé d'Affaires had just transmitted to him the text of the Serbian reply to the Austrian note. It appeared from the reply that Serbia had agreed to the Austrian demands to an extent such as he would never have believed possible; except in one point, the participation of Austrian officials in the judicial investigation, Serbia had actually agreed to everything that had been demanded of her. It was plain that this compliance of Serbia's *was to be attributed solely to the pressure exerted from St Petersburg.*[3]

Should Austria fail to be satisfied with this reply, in other words, should this reply not be accepted at Vienna as a foundation for peaceful negotiations, or should Austria proceed even to the occupation of Belgrade, which lay quite defenceless before her, it would then be absolutely evident that Austria was only seeking an excuse for crushing Serbia. And thus that Russia and Russian influences in the Balkans were to be struck at through Serbia. It was plain that Russia could not regard such action with equanimity, and would have to accept it as a direct challenge. The result would be the most frightful war that Europe had ever seen, and no one could tell to what such a war might lead.[4]

We had repeatedly, and even yesterday, stated the Minister, turned to him with the request that he *make a plea for moderation at St Petersburg. He had always gladly complied with this request* and during the last crisis had subjected himself to reproaches from Russia to the effect that he was placing himself too much on our side and too little on theirs. Now he was turning to us with the request that we should make use of our influence

[1] See **90**.   [2] For Lichnowsky's reply see **98**.
[3] See **60**.   [4] See **57**.

at Vienna either to get them to accept the reply from Belgrade as satisfactory or as the basis for conferences. He was convinced that it lay in our hands to bring the matter to a settlement by means of the proper representations, and he would regard it as a good augury for the future *if we two should once again succeed in assuring the peace of Europe by means of our mutual influence on our allies.*

I found the Minister irritated for the first time. He spoke with great seriousness and seemed absolutely to expect that we should successfully make use of our influence to settle the matter. He is also going to make a statement in the House of Commons today in which he is to express his point of view. In any event, I am convinced that in case it should come to war after all, we should no longer be able to count on British sympathy or British support, as every evidence of ill-will would be seen in Austria's procedure. Also, everybody here is convinced, and I hear it in the mouths of all my colleagues, that the key to the situation is to be found in Berlin, and that, if peace is seriously desired there, Austria can be restrained from prosecuting, as Sir E. Grey expresses it, a foolhardy policy.[1]

98 Lichnowsky to Jagow

Telegram 165 London, 27 July 1914
D.D. 266 D. 6.17 p.m.
R. 8.40 p.m.

It is true that the Minister draws a sharp line of distinction between the Austro-Serbian and the Austro-Russian conflicts,[2] that is to say, he did not want to mix into the Austro-Serbian as long as it did not develop into an Austro-Russian conflict. As long as it remained an Austro-Serbian conflict he held himself in the background. But now he finds himself compelled to take a hand in it, as it threatens to develop into an Austro-Russian and thus into a European conflict. In this way the Austro-Russian conflict cannot be separated from the Austro-Serbian, as the former is based on the latter,[3] and the Minister has been talking to me from this point of view. An understanding between Austria and Russia depends on the settlement of the Austro-Serbian quarrel. Without such a settlement, every attempt at mediation appears entirely hopeless from the English point of view. How can I argue for localisation of the conflict, when nobody here has any doubt that by Austria's procedure important

[1] For Bethmann Hollweg's reply see 101.   [2] See 96.   [3] See 113.

Russian interests are in jeopardy, and that Russia will find herself compelled to intervene even against her own desire, in case no pressure on Vienna is exercised by us? I should be greeted by nothing but a cynical shrug of the shoulders.

If an understanding between Vienna and St Petersburg on the basis of the Austrian note as suggested in telegram 180[1] could be arrived at, together with the abstention from all military measures against Serbia, then everything that Sir E. Grey is striving for would be attained. What he wishes to avoid is Austria's armed attack on Serbia, because he fears the disturbance of the peace of Europe would be its result.[2]

He confirmed to me again today the fact that no calling in of the Russian reservists has taken place.

99 Lichnowsky to Jagow

Telegram 166   London, 27 July 1914
D.D. 265   D. 5.08 p.m.
                                                                     R. 8.40 p.m.

In addition to my telegram 164[3] of today, I would like to point out that our entire future relations with England depend on the success of this move of Sir Edward Grey. Should the Minister succeed at this significant moment, in which, despite all internal divisions, the entire British nation stands behind him, in preventing, with our cooperation, the situation from becoming more acute, I will guarantee that our relations with Great Britain will remain, for an incalculable time to come, of the same intimate and confidential character that has distinguished them for the last year and a half. The British Government, whether Liberal or Conservative, sees, in the maintenance of the peace of Europe on the basis of the balance of power by groups, its most vital interest,[4] and the conviction that it depends absolutely on us whether Austria shall endanger European peace by a stubborn prestige-policy, carries with it the assurance that any attitude of compliance on the part of Austria will be interpreted as proof of our honest desire to prevent, in conjunction with Great Britain, a Euro-

[1] A reference to Pourtalès' telegram of 26 July (see 90), which was forwarded to Tschirschky and Lichnowsky.

[2] See also 4.

[3] See 97.

[4] Zimmermann noted in the margin: 'What will happen to the balance of power, if Austria-Hungary gives in!'

pean war, to the benefit of our friendship with England and of our love of peace.

Should we, on the other hand, conceive our sympathies for Austria and the exact fulfilment of our alliance obligations to be of so much importance that every other point of view were overshadowed by them, and even the most important item of our foreign policy—our relations with England—subordinated to the special interests of our ally, I believe that it would never again be possible to restore those ties which have of late bound us together.

The impression is constantly gaining force here—and I noticed it plainly at my interview with Sir Edward Grey—that the whole Serbian question has devolved into a test of strength between the Triple Alliance and the Triple Entente. Therefore, should Austria's intention of using the present opportunity to overthrow Serbia ('to crush Serbia,' as Sir E. Grey expressed it) become more and more apparent, England, I am certain, would place herself unconditionally by the side of France and of Russia, in order to show that she is not willing to permit a moral, or perhaps a military, defeat of her group. If it comes to war under these circumstances, we shall have England against us. For the realisation that, in view of the far-reaching compliance of the Serbian Government, the war might have been avoided, will be of controlling significance in determining the attitude of the British Government.

100 Pourtalès to Jagow

Telegram 167
D.D. 282

St Petersburg, 27 July 1914
D. 8.40 p.m.
R. 28 July, 4.36 a.m.

Have just informed Sazonov of the contents of telegrams 126 and 128.[1] Minister requested me to thank Your Excellency for both communications, which made a very good impression on him, and to assure you in addition that the appeal to our long-preserved friendly relations was warmly echoed by him and stirred him deeply. Your Excellency might remain assured that Russia would not abuse the confidence in her love for peace. He was ready to go to the limit in accommodating Austria, and to exhaust all means to bring the crisis to a peaceful solution.

Since Austria had declared her territorial disinterestedness and had as

[1] *D.D.* 198, 219.

yet taken no hostile steps against Serbia, the moment had come, in his opinion, to seek the means by an exchange of views among the Powers 'to build a golden bridge' for Austria. What means should be proposed for the attainment of this end were immaterial to him. The desire to humiliate Austria lay far from his mind. But he urgently requested consideration of the fact that if those Austrian demands which infringed on the rights of Serbian sovereignty should be accepted, there would come into power a revolutionary régime which would be even worse than the present one. I replied that in any event, Serbia would have to swallow several bitter pills. Austria would probably not let herself be put off with lame excuses; whether some of the points might be formally modified, I was unable to judge. In any case, the Serbian provocations, which had now brought Europe to the verge of war for the third time within five years, must once and for all be put an end to, as present conditions had become simply intolerable for Europe. For this reason Europe ought not to try to stay Austria's arm in her present quarrel with Serbia. Sazonov did not wish to give up the hope that a moderation of some of the points of the demands put to Serbia might possibly be accomplished. He earnestly requested our cooperation along this line. There must be a way of giving Serbia her deserved lesson while sparing her sovereign rights. I said in reply, that guaranties must also be acquired for the future, in order that Serbia should not once again back out of the obligations she had assumed. If Serbia wished to be treated as a member of the European family of nations with equal rights, she would also have to behave herself as a civilised nation. The Minister's objections to this sort of criticism of Serbia were much more feeble than a day or two ago; his speech was just as conciliatory as it was yesterday.[1] In connection with the first part of telegram 128, Sazonov referred to yesterday's conversation of Major Eggeling with the Minister of War.[2]

[1] See 90.

[2] *D.D.* 242. Bethmann Hollweg added to the deciphered text the following significant observation: 'I am still in doubt as to whether we should communicate Sazonov's telegram in extenso to Lichnowsky. He informs Sir Edward of everything in a clumsy fashion and the latter might become still more compliant towards Russia, if he sees so plainly that the ties between Berlin and Petersburg have in no way been severed. At any rate, this could be the outcome. It will thus depend greatly upon the manner in which Lichnowsky is instructed and in which he speaks to Sir Edward.' See B.H., 287.

101   Bethmann Hollweg to Lichnowsky

Telegram 184   Berlin, 28 July 1914
D.D. 279   D. 2.00 a.m.

Sir Edward Grey has expressly and repeatedly stated that the Austro-*Serbian* conflict did not concern him, but that on the other hand he stood ready to mediate in case of an Austro-*Russian* conflict, and counted on our assistance in doing so.[1] We had declared ourselves to be in complete agreement with this point of view. Now, Sir Edward has deserted this ground and asks us to mediate to persuade Austria to accept the Serbian reply as satisfactory, or at least to look upon it as a basis for further conferences.[2]

The first petition cannot be acceded to. It is impossible for us to counsel Vienna to give a belated sanction to the Serbian reply, which they had immediately refused as unsatisfactory, even before it had come to our knowledge. We made great concessions to England when we undertook to inaugurate mediation in connection with the second petition. I feel sure that England will value this friendly advance of ours as it deserves. Whether the Serbian reply goes to the limit of what is possible, I am not yet able to judge, as it has just reached my hands.[3] The fact that Serbia mobilised before handing over her reply, however, is a suspicious circumstance. That permits one to suspect a bad conscience.[4] Sir Edward's assumption that Austria's object is the overthrow of Serbia seems to me to be all the less reasonable, inasmuch as she has expressly declared to Russia that she is looking for no territorial acquisition and that she would not infringe upon the right to existence of the Serbian Kingdom, a declaration that did not fail to make an impression on Russia.[5] Austria intends—and it is not only her right but her duty—to secure herself against the continuation of the undermining of her own existence through the Greater Serbia propaganda, which finally resulted in the crime of

[1] See **57** and **73**.

[2] See **97**.

[3] Two hours previously however, the Chancellor had given Tschirschky to understand that he must have been thoroughly acquainted with the Serbian reply, since Serbia had 'apparently made very considerable concessions'; *D.D.* 277.

[4] Or suspicion or fear that the Austro-Hungarian army would attack the Serbian capital, Belgrade, which lay on the common frontier between the two countries. This idea would not have been so far off the mark, since it had crossed the minds of influential figures in Vienna and Berlin from time to time (see **9**) and was only subsequently supplanted by Berchtold's and Tisza's more cautious method of approach. Moreover, the military preparations (see **32**) and the precipitate bombardment of Belgrade on 29 July show how justified the Serbian fears were in reality.

[5] See **100**.

Sarajevo. That has absolutely nothing at all to do with a policy of prestige or with playing off the Triple Alliance against the Triple Entente.

Deeply as we are engaged in all directions in attempting to maintain the peace of Europe, in full agreement with England, and, it is to be hoped, in continued cooperation with her, we cannot for that reason acknowledge the right of Russia or even of the Triple Entente to take the part of the Serbian intrigues against Austria.

I respectfully request that you regulate your arguments by these considerations.

102   Chargé d'Affaires Bronevski to Sazonov

Telegram 133   Berlin, 27 July 1914
Int. Bez. I, 5, 134

I have received your telegrams 1508 and 1509[1]. I spoke with the Foreign Secretary[2] in the sense indicated by you and asked him to support your proposal in Vienna that Szápáry should be authorised to draw up by means of a private exchange of views with you, a wording of the Austro-Hungarian demands which would be acceptable to both parties. Jagow answered that he was aware of this proposal and that he agreed with Pourtalès that, as Szápáry had begun the conversation, he might as well go on with it. He will telegraph in this sense to press Vienna with greater insistence.[3] I begged him to press Vienna with greater insistence to adopt this conciliatory line; Jagow answered that he could not advise Austria to give way, the mere passing on of Pourtalès' telegram to Vienna meant, however, that he would rather recommend such a way out of the situation.[4]

[1] *Int. Bez.* I, 5, 86.
[2] Jagow.
[3] No such telegram is included among the German Documents (*D.D.*). Only Pourtalès' Telegram 163 (see 90), with slight modifications, was sent to Tschirschky (in addition to Lichnowsky) on 27 July. See also 103 and 110.
  Likewise 81 and 101; in contrast, see 95.

103 Jules Cambon to Bienvenu-Martin

Telegram 199   Berlin, 27 July 1914
D.F. XI, 134 (*F.Y.B.* 67)   D. 12.55 p.m.
                                             R. 3.45 p.m.

Today I have had a conversation with the Secretary of State on the proposal by England that Germany should join the Cabinets of London, Paris and Rome to prevent hostilities between St Petersburg and Vienna.[1]

Herr von Jagow answered that he was disposed to join the Powers and do all he could to preserve peace.[2] He added that he was bound by obligations towards Austria, just as we towards Russia, however burdensome it might be to fulfil these obligations, for, he said, Germany —just as France—has no desire to enter a conflict which does not concern her directly. I answered that Sir Edward Grey's proposals opened the way to a peaceful issue. Herr von Jagow repeated once more that he was disposed to join in, but he remarked to me that, if Russia mobilised, Germany would be obliged to mobilise at once, that we should be forced to the same course also, and that then a conflict would be almost inevitable. I asked him if Germany would regard herself as bound to mobilise in the event of Russia mobilising only on the Austrian frontier; he told me 'No', and authorised me formally to communicate this limitation to you. He also attached the greatest importance to an intervention with Russia by the Powers which were friendly and allied to her in order to persuade her not to mobilise on the German frontier.

Finally, he remarked that if Russia attacked Austria, Germany would be obliged to attack at once on her side. The intervention proposed by England at St Petersburg and Vienna could, in his opinion, only come into operation if events were not precipitated. In that case, he does not despair that it might succeed. I expressed my regret that Austria, by her uncompromising attitude had led Europe to the difficult pass through which we were going, but I expressed the hope that intervention would have its effect.[3]

---

[1] See 93.

[2] Only a few hours previously Jagow had expressed his regret that, on the contrary, the military operations against Serbia were being too long drawn out and that events were not moving fast enough. See above, p. 219.

[3] An account of the discussions by Jagow is not available.

104 Bienvenu-Martin to Jules Cambon

Telegrams 339, 340   Paris, 27 July 1914
D.F. XI, 121 (*F.Y.B.* 61)   D. 12.45 p.m.

The three steps taken by the German Ambassador at Paris seem characteristic: on Friday[1] he reads a note in which the German Government
categorically place themselves between Austria and the Powers, approving
the Austrian ultimatum to Serbia, and adding that 'Germany warmly
desires that the dispute should remain localised, since any intervention of
another party must through the play of its alliances provoke incalculable
consequences';[2] the second day, Saturday, the effect having been produced, and the Powers having, on account of the surprise, the shortness
of the time-limit, and the risks of general war, advised Serbia to yield,
Herr von Schoen returns to minimise this step, pretending to be astonished
at the impression produced, and protests that intentions are attributed to
Germany which she does not harbour, 'since,' he says, 'there was neither
concert before nor threat afterwards';[3] the third day, Sunday, the result
having been obtained, since Serbia has yielded, as one might almost say,
to all the Austrian demands, the German Ambassador appears on two
occasions to insist on Germany's peaceful intentions and on her warm
desire to cooperate in the maintenance of peace, after having registered
the Austrian success which closes the first phase of the crisis.[4]

The situation at the moment of writing remains disturbing, on account
of the incomprehensible refusal of Austria to accept Serbia's submission,
of her operations of mobilisation, and of her threats to invade Serbia.
The attitude taken up from the beginning by the Austrian Government,
with German support, her refusal to accept any conversation with the
Powers, practically do not allow the latter to intervene effectively with
Austria without the mediation of Germany. However, time presses, for
if the Austrian army crosses the frontier it will be very difficult to circum-
scribe the crisis, Russia not appearing to be able to tolerate the occupation
of Serbia after the latter has in reality submitted to the Austrian note,
giving every satisfaction and guarantee. Germany, from the very fact of
the position taken up by her, is qualified to intervene effectively and be
listened to at Vienna; if she does not do this she justifies all suspicions
and assumes the responsibility for the war.

The Powers, particularly Russia, France, and England, have by their
urgent advice induced Belgrade to yield; they have thus fulfilled their

---

[1] I.e. of 24 July.   [2] See **39** and **55**.
[3] *D.D.* 166, 169, 170.   [4] See **92**.

part; now it is for Germany, who is alone able to obtain a rapid hearing at Vienna, to give advice to Austria, who has obtained satisfaction and cannot, for a detail easy to adjust, bring about a general war.

It is in these circumstances that the proposal made by the Cabinet of London is put forward; M. Sazonov having said to the British Ambassador that as a consequence of the appeal of Serbia to the Powers, Russia would agree to stand aside,[1] Sir Edward Grey has formulated the following suggestion to the Cabinets of Paris, Berlin and Rome: the French, German and Italian Ambassadors at London would be instructed to seek with Sir Edward Grey a means of resolving the present difficulties, it being understood that during this conversation Russia, Austria and Serbia would abstain from all active military operations.[2] Sir A. Nicolson has spoken of this suggestion to the German Ambassador, who showed himself favourable to it,[3] it will be equally well received in Paris, and also at Rome, according to all probability. Here again it is Germany's turn to speak, and she has an opportunity to show her goodwill by other means than words.

I would ask you to come to an understanding with your British colleague, and to support his proposal with the German Government in whatever form appears to you opportune.

105 Bienvenu-Martin to Fleuriau, French Chargé d'Affaires at London

Telegram 337
Urgent
D.F. XI, 123 (*F.Y.B.* 70)

Paris, 27 July 1914
D. 1.30 p.m.

I have received your telegram 143.[4]

The British Ambassador has communicated to me Sir E. Grey's proposal for common action by England, Germany, France and Italy at Vienna, Belgrade and St Petersburg, to stop active military operations while the German, Italian and French Ambassadors at London examine, with Sir Edward Grey, the means of finding a solution for the present complications.[5]

I have this morning directed M. Jules Cambon to talk this over with the British Ambassador at Berlin, and to support his *démarche* in whatever form he should judge suitable.[6]

[1] See 83.   [2] See 93.   [3] *B.D.* 139.
[4] D.F. XI, 115.   [5] See 93.   [6] See 104.

I authorise you to take part in the meeting proposed by Sir E. Grey. I am also ready to give to our representatives at Vienna, St Petersburg and Belgrade, instructions in the sense asked for by the British Government.

At the same time I think that the chances of success of Sir E. Grey's proposal depend essentially on the action that Berlin would be disposed to take at Vienna; a *démarche* from this side, promoted with a view to obtain a suspension of military operations, would appear to me doomed to failure if Germany's influence were not first exercised.

I have also noted, during Baron von Schoen's observations, that the Austro-Hungarian Government was particularly susceptible when the words 'mediation,' 'intervention,' 'conference' were used, and was more willing to admit 'friendly advice' and 'conversations'.[1]

106 Bienvenu-Martin to Ambassadors at Berlin, St Petersburg and London

Telegrams 341–2, 412–13, 338–9   Paris, 27 July 1914
D.F. XI, 133 (*F.Y.B.* 62)   D. 3.15 p.m., 3.45 p.m.

(Résumé on Schoen's second visit on 26 July, in the evening; *cf.* document 92.)

The note communicated was as follows: 'The German Ambassador and the Minister for Foreign Affairs have had a fresh interview, in the course of which they sought means of action by the Powers for the maintenance of peace.' This phrasing, deliberately colourless, avoided an appearance of solidarity with Germany which might have been misinterpreted.

This morning Herr von Schoen addressed a private letter to the Political Director under pretext of resuming his interview with the Minister, and has added: 'Note well the phrase in an identical spirit of peaceful co-operation. This is not an idle phrase, but the sincere expression of the truth.' The summary annexed to the letter was drawn up as follows: 'The Cabinet of Vienna has, formally and officially, caused it to be declared to that of St Petersburg, that it does not seek any territorial acquisition in Serbia, and that it has no intention of making any attempt against the integrity of the kingdom; its sole intention is that of assuring its own tranquillity. At this moment the decision whether a European war

[1] See 119 and 120.

must break out depends solely on Russia. The German Government have firm confidence that the French Government, with which they know that they are at one in the warm desire that European peace should be able to be maintained, will use their whole influence with the Cabinet of St Petersburg in a pacific spirit.'

I have let you know the reply which has been given (a French *démarche* at St Petersburg would be misunderstood, and must have as corollary a German *démarche* at Vienna, or, failing that, mediation by the four less interested Powers in both capitals).

Strictly confidential

Herr von Schoen's letter is capable of different interpretations. Perhaps it has for its object, like his *démarche* itself, to throw the responsibility for an eventual war on Russia and on France and to mask, by pacific assurances which have not been listened to, military action by Austria in Serbia intended to complete the success of Austria. A simpler explanation would be to assume that Herr von Schoen feared his government might see the note communicated to the press as his having badly executed his instructions, the main object of which were to ensure against eventual mobilisation of Russia on the German frontiers as such, a mobilisation which would be bound to provoke similar measures in Germany and to lead to war, as Herr von Jagow has indicated.[1]

I communicate the news to you by way of information and for any useful purpose you can put it to.

107 Buchanan to Grey

Telegram 173
B.D. 170

St Petersburg, 27 July 1914
D. 10.06 a.m.
R. 1.15 p.m.

Minister for Foreign Affairs had yesterday a long conversation with Austrian Ambassador, in which latter tried to explain away objectionable features of Austria's recent action. Minister for Foreign Affairs said that he perfectly understood Austria's motives, but ultimatum had been drafted in such a form as to render it impossible for Serbia to accept it as a whole. While some of demands were reasonable enough, others were not only incompatible with Serbia's dignity as an independent State, but could not possibly be put into immediate execution, as they entailed

[1] See 103.

revision of her existing laws. Russia, his Excellency added, was object of such suspicion in Austria that it would be useless for her to offer her good offices at Belgrade. He thought, however, England and Italy might be willing to collaborate with Austria with a view to putting an end to present tension. Ambassador promised to inform his Government of what his Excellency had said.[1]

In reply to question Minister for Foreign Affairs addressed to me, I said that I had in conversation, reported in my telegram 166 of 24 July,[2] correctly defined attitude of His Majesty's Government, and that you could not promise to do more. His Excellency was wrong in believing that we should promote cause of peace by telling Germany if she supported Austria by force of arms she would have us to deal with as well as France and Russia. Such a menace would but stiffen her attitude, and it was only by approaching her as a friend anxious to preserve peace that we could induce her to use her influence at Vienna to avert war. If, however, we were to succeed, his Excellency must do nothing to precipitate a conflict, and I therefore trusted that mobilisation ukase would be deferred as long as possible, and that when it was issued troops would not be allowed to cross frontier.

Minister for Foreign Affairs replied that he did not believe that we should succeed in winning over Germany to cause of peace unless we publicly proclaimed our solidarity with France and Russia. No effective steps towards mobilisation could be taken until Imperial ukase was issued, and if it was deferred too long Austria would profit by delay to make her military preparations complete, while Russia could do nothing. Order to mobilise might perhaps be accompanied by a statement that troops would be retained on this side of the frontier. He could not tell me when ukase would be issued, but spoke of day on which Austrian army entered Serbia as a likely date.

His Excellency strongly condemned arrest of Serbian General Putnik in Hungary as likely to aggravate present tension.[3]

Minute

Sir G. Buchanan spoke well.

I am afraid that the real difficulty to be overcome will be found in the question of mobilisation. Austria is already mobilising. This, if the war does come, is a serious menace to Russia who cannot be expected to delay her own mobilisation, which, as it is, can only become effective in something like double the time required by Austria and by Germany.

---

[1] Szápáry to Berchtold 27 July; *Ö.D.* 10835.
[2] See **68**.   [3] Putnik was released very soon afterwards.

If Russia mobilises, we have been warned Germany will do the same, and as German mobilisation is directed almost entirely against France, the latter cannot possibly delay her own mobilisation for even the fraction of a day.

From Sir M. de Bunsen's telegram 109[1] just come in, it seems certain that Austria is going to war because that was from the beginning her intention.

If that view proves correct, it would be neither possible nor just and wise to make any move to restrain Russia from mobilising.

This however means that within 24 hours His Majesty's Government will be faced with the question whether, in a quarrel so imposed by Austria on an unwilling France, Great Britain will stand idly aside, or take sides. The question is a momentous one, which it is not for a departmental minute to elaborate.

It is difficult not to remember the position of Prussia in 1805, when she insisted on keeping out of the war which she could not prevent from breaking out between the other Powers over questions not, on their face, of direct interest to Prussia.

The war was waged without Prussia in 1805. But in 1806 she fell a victim to the Power that had won in 1805, and no one was ready either to help her or to prevent her political ruin and partition.— E. A. C. July 27.

108 Buchanan to Grey

Telegram 174
B.D. 179

St Petersburg, 27 July 1914
D. 2.13 p.m.
R. 3.45 p.m.

French Ambassador informs me that since my conversation with Minister for Foreign Affairs, reported in my immediately preceding telegram of today[2] his Excellency has decided to propose direct conversation between Vienna and St Petersburg as to modifications to be introduced into Austrian demands.

Minute

This is confusing. In three consecutive days M. Sazonov has made one suggestion and two proposals all differing from each other.

1 The suggestions: If Serbia were to appeal to the Powers, Russia

[1] *B.D.* 175.   [2] See **107**.

would stand aside and leave question in hands of England, France, Italy and Germany (25 July).[1]

2 26 July: Proposal to Austrian Ambassador that England and Italy should collaborate with Austria with a view to putting an end to present tension.[2]

3 27 July: Proposal that Russia will converse directly with Vienna.[3]

One really does not know where one is with M. Sazonov and I told Count Benckendorff so this afternoon.—A. N.

109 Grey to Goschen

Telegram 208   London, 27 July 1914
B.D. 176   D. 3.00 p.m.

German Ambassador has informed me that German Government accept in principle mediation between Austria and Russia by the four Powers, reserving, of course, their right as an ally to help Austria if attacked. He has also been instructed to request me to use influence in St Petersburg to localise the war and to keep up the peace of Europe.

I have replied that the Serbian reply went further than could have been expected to meet the Austrian demands. German Minister for Foreign Affairs[4] has himself said that there were some things in the Austrian note that Serbia could hardly be expected to accept.[5] I assumed that Serbian reply could not have gone as far as it did unless Russia had exercised conciliatory influence at Belgrade, and it was really at Vienna that moderating influence was now required. If Austria put the Serbian reply aside as being worth nothing and marched into Serbia, it meant that she was determined to crush Serbia at all costs, being reckless of the consequences that might be involved. Serbian reply should at least be treated as a basis for discussion and pause. I said German Government should urge this at Vienna.

I recalled what German Government had said as to the gravity of the situation if the war could not be localised,[6] and observed that if Germany assisted Austria against Russia it would be because, without any reference to the merits of the dispute, Germany could not afford to see Austria

[1] See 83.   [2] See 107.
[3] *Int. Bez.* I, 5, 86.   [4] Jagow.
[5] Grey was clearly alluding to Jagow's declaration to Rumbold on 25 July; see 81.
[6] See 36, 39 and 87.

crushed. Just so other issues might be raised that would supersede the dispute between Austria and Serbia, and would bring other Powers in, and the war would be the biggest ever known; but as long as Germany would work to keep the peace I would keep closely in touch. I repeated that after the Serbian reply it was at Vienna that some moderation must be urged.[1]

110   Goschen to Grey

Telegram 96
B.D. 185

Berlin, 27 July 1914
D. 6.17 p.m.
R. 9.00 p.m.

Your telegram 232 of 26 July to Paris.[2]

Secretary of State for Foreign Affairs says that conference you suggest would practically amount to a court of arbitration and could not, in his opinion, be called together except at the request of Austria and Russia. He could not therefore, desirous though he was to cooperate for the maintenance of peace, fall in with your suggestion. I said I was sure that your idea had nothing to do with arbitration, but meant that representatives of the four nations not directly interested should discuss and suggest means for avoiding a dangerous situation. He maintained, however, that such a conference as you proposed was not practicable. He added that news he had just received from St Petersburg showed that there was an intention on the part of M. Sazonov to exchange views with Count Berchtold.[3] He thought that this method of procedure might lead to a satisfactory result, and that it would be best, before doing anything else, to await outcome of the exchange of views between the Austrian and Russian Governments.

In the course of a short conversation Secretary of State for Foreign Affairs said that as yet Austria was only partially mobilising, but that if Russia mobilised against Germany latter would have to follow suit. I asked him what he meant by 'mobilising against Germany.' He said that if Russia only mobilised in south Germany would not mobilise, but if she mobilised in north Germany would have to do so too, and Russian system of mobilisation was so complicated that it might be difficult exactly to locate her mobilisation. Germany would therefore have to be very careful not be taken by surprise.[4]

[1] For Lichnowsky's version, see **97**.   [2] See **93**.
[3] See **90**.   [4] Likewise Jagow—to Jules Cambon; see **103**.

Finally, Secretary of State said that news from St Petersburg had caused him to take more hopeful view of the general situation.[1]

Minute

So far as we know, the German Government has up to now said not a single word at Vienna in the direction of restraint or moderation. If a word had been said, we may be certain that the German Government would claim credit for having spoken at all. The inference is not reassuring as to Germany's goodwill.

At the same time the rapid succession of fresh proposals and suggestions coming from St Petersburg made it easier for Germany to find fresh excuses for her inactivity.[2]—E. A. C. 28 July.

111   Berchtold to Szögyény

Telegram 282   Vienna, 28 July 1914
Strictly confidential   D. 11.00 p.m.
Ö.D. 10863

Received Your Excellency's telegram 297 of 26 inst.[3] I have had analogous reports on the Russian armaments from the Imp. and Royal military attaché in St Petersburg.[4] I beg Your Excellency to go immediately to the Imperial Chancellor or the Secretary of State and inform him in my name of the following:

Concurrent news from St Petersburg, Kiev, Warsaw, Moscow and Odessa, show that Russia is making extensive military preparations. Herr Sazonov and the Russian War Minister both gave their word of honour that a mobilisation had not up to the present been ordered, but the latter told the German military attaché that the military districts, which come in question where Austria-Hungary is concerned, Kiev, Odessa, Moscow and Kazan, would be mobilised as soon as ever our troops crossed the Serbian frontier.

Under these circumstances, the Chief of the General Staff considers it *positively* necessary to obtain certainty, whether we can march against Serbia with strong forces, or whether we must reserve our chief army, to use it against Russia. From this question depends our entire plan of campaign against Serbia. If Russia is really mobilising the military

---

[1] An account by Jagow is not available. Grey's reply: *B.D.* 218.
[2] See **108** (minute).   [3] *Ö.D.* 10717.   [4] *Ö.D.* 10755.

districts in question, the time it is gaining, makes it absolutely imperative that Austria-Hungary, and under present circumstances Germany also, should immediately take comprehensive counter-measures.[1]

I consider this view of Baron Conrad most worthy of consideration and I request the Berlin cabinet to reflect, whether Russia should, in a friendly manner, be reminded that the mobilisation of the above-mentioned districts is equal to threatening Austria-Hungary and would have to be answered by counter-measures of a military character not alone by the monarchy, but by the allied German Empire also.

To facilitate a withdrawal on Russia's part, we think that such a step should be undertaken by Germany alone to begin with; but of course we are prepared to take our share in it. I think that plain language would at this moment be the most effective means for showing Russia the consequences of a threatening attitude adopted in the present situation. It might also be taken into consideration, whether the favourable dispositions reported from Bucharest to Berlin (Your Excellency's telegram 298 of yesterday)[2], should not be made use of, to influence Russia through Roumania.

With this aim in view, I think the German minister in Bucharest might without loss of time, be instructed to approach King Carol with the request to consider, that in the case of a European conflagration Roumania would stand on the side of the Triple Alliance. This could be done either by a solemn *démarche* in St Petersburg (eventually through a private telegram from King Carol to Emperor Nicolas) or simply through the publication of the fact that Roumania has joined the Triple Alliance. This explanation should, to be effective, be made at the latest on 1 August.

Your Excellency will conclude by saying that I trust the German factor in authority will, in view of the threatening attitude of Russia against both Empires, agree with my propositions.[3]

---

[1] See Conrad, *Dienstzeit*, IV, pp. 132ff., discussion with Berchtold on 27 July.
[2] Ö.D. 10718.
[3] Szögyény carried out the instructions in the afternoon of 29 July; D.D. 352.

112 Wilhelm II to Jagow

Handwritten   Neues Palais, 28 July 1914
D.D. 293   D. 10.00 a.m.

After reading over the Serbian reply,[1] which I received this morning, I am convinced that on the whole the wishes of the Danube Monarchy have been acceded to. The few reservations that Serbia makes in regard to individual points could, according to my opinion, be settled by negotiation. But it contains the announcement *orbi et urbi* of a capitulation of the most humiliating kind, and as a result, *every cause for war* falls to the ground.

Nevertheless, the piece of paper, like its contents, can be considered as of little value so long as it is not translated into *deeds*. The Serbs are Orientals, therefore liars, tricksters, and masters of evasion. In order that these beautiful promises may be turned to truth and facts, a *douce violence* must be exercised. This should be so arranged that Austria would receive a *hostage* (Belgrade), as a guaranty for the enforcement and carrying out of the promises, and should occupy it until the *petita* had *actually* been complied with. This is also necessary in order to give the army, now *unnecessarily* mobilised for the third time, the external *satisfaction d'honneur* of an ostensible success in the eyes of the world, and to make it possible for it to feel that it had at least stood on foreign soil. Unless this were done, the abandonment of the campaign might be the cause of a wave of bad feeling against the Monarchy, which would be dangerous in the highest degree. In case your Excellency shares my views, I propose that we say to Austria: Serbia has been forced to retreat in a very humiliating manner, and we offer our congratulations. Naturally, as a result, *every cause for war has vanished.*[2] But a *guaranty* that the promises *will be carried out* is unquestionably necessary. That could be secured by means of the *temporary* military occupation of a portion of Serbia, similar to the way we kept troops stationed in France in 1871 until the billions were paid. *On this basis*, I am ready to *mediate for peace* with Austria. Any proposals or protests to the contrary by other nations I should refuse regardless, especially as all of them have made more or less open appeals to me to assist in maintaining peace. This I will do in my own way, and as sparingly of Austria's *nationalistic feeling* and of the *honour of her arms* as possible. For the latter has already been appealed to on the part of the highest War Lord, and is about to respond to the appeal. Consequently it

[1] See 72.
[2] See the Kaiser's commentary to the Serbian reply on the morning of 28 July. In his approach to Vienna Bethmann Hollweg did not fall in with the first section of the Kaiser's instructions; see 115.

is absolutely necessary that it receives a visible *satisfaction d'honneur*; this is the *prerequisite* of my mediation. Therefore your Excellency will submit a proposal to me along the lines sketched out;[1] which shall be communicated to Vienna.[2] I have had Plessen write along the lines indicated above to the Chief of the General Staff, who is entirely in accord with my views.

113   Schoen to Bethmann Hollweg

Report 165   Paris, 28 July 1914
D.D. 350   R. 29 July, afternoon

In the course of a conversation with the acting Minister for Foreign Affairs, I casually made the remark that it was astonishing that the idea that we were urging Austria on and should therefore be responsible, if a general conflict grew out of the Austro-Serbian quarrel, not only found expression in the French press, but even seemed to haunt the minds of high-placed personages who ought to know better, and, coming from whose mouths, such insinuations might have an unfortunate effect. I did not want to be more definite, but I believe that M. Bienvenu-Martin understood me. He said that the press was not accusing us of driving Austria directly onward, but only of not restraining our ally. It was very hard to believe that Austria would have proceeded as she had, had she not been certain of our support; not that he wished to suggest, naturally, that our assurance that we had had no previous knowledge of the Austrian note was not entitled to absolute credence. But the fact was that we had said from the beginning that we approved of the procedure and the demands of Austria-Hungary, nor did we now seem inclined to hold back our ally from her course of action, which might lead to serious complications. But a moderate attitude on the part of Austria was the necessary preliminary to any successful mediation. The best means of avoiding a general war was by preventing a local one.[3] It was his opinion, therefore, that the latter should be the first aim of mediation, and that it should seek to satisfy Austria by the assurance of guaranties for Serbia's atonement and for her future good behaviour.

I replied to the Minister that after all that Serbia had done against the Dual Monarchy since her promise of the year 1909, without being restrained by that Power which was now upholding the principle of

[1] Evidently this was disregarded.   [2] See **115**.   [3] See **98**.

European supervision, we could not help but understand why Austria-Hungary should seek by force the rights and the peace that had not been granted her. We had not interfered in her quarrel with Serbia, had exercised no influence on her decisions, and could not do so now. All further dangerous consequences of the conflict would be avoided if all the Powers should decide to adopt a like attitude. We had stated from the beginning that the Powers should earnestly strive for the localisation of the conflict.[1] In accordance with that principle we should take part in all efforts to prevent a general conflagration, provided that their aim was not to prevent Austria-Hungary against her will from following up her only too justifiable demands.

114 Bethmann Hollweg to Wilhelm II

Immediate Report   Berlin, 28 July 1914
D.D. 308   D. ?
                                                     R. 10.15 p.m.

To Your Majesty:
I most humbly beg to report that I was compelled to make the *démarche*[2] command at Vienna by telegraph, as there is no longer any regular railroad connection with Vienna.

According to my most respectful opinion, it would be in suitable agreement with this move if Your Majesty would have the goodness to send a telegram to the Czar.[3] Such a telegram, should a war prove to be inevitable, would throw the clearest light on Russia's responsibility. I most humbly take the liberty of appending a draft of such a telegram.[4] Count Pourtalès has been instructed to tell Mr Sazonov that Your Majesty is endeavouring to persuade Vienna to hold a frank conference with St Petersburg for the purpose of explaining unambiguously and, it is to be hoped, in a manner satisfactory to Russia, the object and extent of Austria's procedure against Serbia. The declaration of war that has occurred in the meantime need make no difference.

---

[1] See 39.
[2] See 112, in other words the proposal for a pledge given by the occupation of Belgrade.
[3] On 27 July the Kaiser had already rejected as premature the idea of sending a telegram to the Czar; cf. the corresponding draft of a telegram from the night of 26–27 July; *D.D.* 233.
[4] See 117.

115 Bethmann Hollweg to Tschirschky

Telegram 174	Berlin, 28 July 1914
Urgent	D. 10.15 p.m.
D.D. 323	R. 29 July, 4.30 a.m.

The Austro-Hungarian Government has distinctly informed Russia that it is not considering any territorial acquisitions in Serbia. This agrees with Your Excellency's report to the effect that neither the Austrian nor the Hungarian statesmen consider the increase of the Slavic element in the Monarchy to be desirable. On the other hand, the Austro-Hungarian Government has left us in the dark concerning its intentions, despite repeated interrogations. The reply of the Serbian Government to the Austrian ultimatum, which has now been received, makes it clear that Serbia has agreed to the Austrian demands to so great an extent that, in case of a completely uncompromising attitude on the part of the Austro-Hungarian Government, it will become necessary to reckon upon the gradual defection from its cause of public opinion throughout all Europe.

According to the statements of the Austrian General Staff, an active military movement against Serbia will not be possible before 12 August.[1] As a result, the Imperial Government is placed in the extraordinarily difficult position of being exposed in the meantime to the mediation and conference proposals of the other Cabinets, and if it continues to maintain its previous aloofness[2] in the face of such proposals, it will incur the odium of having been responsible for a world war, even, finally, among the German people themselves. A successful war on three fronts cannot be commenced and carried on on any such basis. It is imperative that the responsibility for the eventual extension of the war among those nations not originally immediately concerned should, under all circumstances, fall on Russia. At Mr Sazonov's last conversation with Count Pourtalès the Minister already conceded that Serbia would have to receive her 'deserved lesson'.[3] At any rate the Minister was no longer so unconditionally opposed to the Austrian point of view as he had been earlier. From this fact it is not difficult to draw the conclusion that the Russian Government might even realise that, once the mobilisation of the Austro-Hungarian Army had begun, the very honour of its arms demanded an invasion of Serbia. But it will be all the better able to compromise with this idea if the Vienna Cabinet repeats at St Petersburg its distinct declaration that she is far from wishing to make any territorial acquisitions in Serbia, and that her military preparations are solely for the purpose of a temporary

---

[1] See **88**.   [2] See **95**.   [3] See **100**.

occupation of Belgrade and certain other localities on Serbian territory in order to force the Serbian Government to the complete fulfilment of her demands, and for the creation of guaranties of future good behaviour—to which Austria-Hungary has an unquestionable claim after the experiences she has had with Serbia. An occupation like the German occupation of French territory after the Peace of Frankfort, for the purpose of securing compliance with the demands for war indemnity, is suggested. As soon as the Austrian demands should be complied with, evacuation would follow.[1] Should the Russian Government fail to recognise the justice of this point of view, it would have against it the public opinion of all Europe, which is now in the process of turning away from Austria. As a further result, the general diplomatic, and probably the military, situation would undergo material alteration in favour of Austria-Hungary and her allies.

Your Excellency will kindly discuss the matter along these lines thoroughly and impressively with Count Berchtold, and instigate an appropriate move at St Petersburg. You will have to avoid very carefully giving rise to the impression that we wish to hold Austria back. The case is solely one of finding a way to realise Austria's desired aim, that of cutting the vital cord of the Greater Serbia propaganda, without at the same time bringing on a world war, and, if the latter cannot be avoided in the end, of improving the conditions under which we shall have to wage it, in so far as is possible.

Wire report.

116 Nicolas II to Wilhelm II

Telegram (unnumbered)   Peterhof Palace, 29 July 1914
D.D. 332   D. 1.00 a.m.
Int. Bez. I, 5, 170   R. 1.10 a.m.

Am glad you are back. In this most serious moment I appeal to you to help me. An *ignoble* war has been declared on a *weak* country. The *indignation* in Russia, *shared fully by me*, is *enormous*. I foresee that very soon I shall be *overwhelmed* by the *pressure* brought upon me, and be *forced* to take extreme measures which will *lead to war*. To try and avoid such a calamity as a European war, I beg you in the name of our old friendship to do what you can to *stop* your *allies* from *going too far*.[2]
In what does that consist?
Ally!

---

[1] See in contrast 112.   [2] Original in English. For Wilhelm's reply, see 131.

A confession of his own weakness, and an attempt to put the responsibility on my own shoulders. The telegram contains a concealed threat and an order-like summons to tie the hands of our ally. In case Your Excellency sent off my telegram[1] yesterday evening, it must have crossed this one. We shall see now, what effect mine has. The expression 'ignoble war' does not indicate any sense of Monarchial unity in the Czar, but rather a Pan Slavic conception; i.e., worry over a *capitis diminutio* in the Balkans in case of an Austrian victory. This might well first be waited for in its overall result. There will always be time later for negotiation and eventually for mobilisation, for which now Russia has no reason at all. Instead of summoning us to check our allies, His Majesty should turn to the Emperor Franz Joseph and deal with him in order to learn His Majesty's intentions. Should not copies of both the telegrams be sent to His Majesty the King at London for his information? The Socialists are making anti-military demonstrations in the streets; that must not be tolerated, in any event, not now; in case they are repeated I shall proclaim a state of martial law and have the leaders one and all *tutti quanti* locked up. Instruct Loebell[2] and Jagow[3] about this. We can tolerate no Socialist propaganda now!

117 Wilhelm II to Nicolas II

Telegram (unnumbered)
D.D. 335
Int. Bez. I, 5, 184

Berlin, 28 July 1914
D. 29 July, 1.45 a.m.

It is with the gravest concern that I hear of the impression which the action of Austria against Serbia is creating in your country. The unscrupulous agitation that has been going on in Serbia for years has resulted in the outrageous crime to which Archduke Franz Ferdinand fell a victim. The spirit that led Serbians to murder their own king and his wife still dominates the country. You will doubtless agree with me that we both, you and me, have a common interest, as well as all Sovereigns, to insist that all the persons morally responsible for the dastardly murder should receive their deserved punishment. In this politics play no part at all.

On the other hand I fully understand how difficult it is for you and your Government to face the drift of your public opinion. Therefore, with regard to the hearty and tender friendship which binds us both from long ago with firm ties, I am exerting my utmost influence to induce the Austrians to deal straightly to arrive to a satisfactory understanding with you. I confidently hope you will help me in my efforts to smooth over difficulties that may still arise.[4]

[1] See 117.
[2] Prussian Home Secretary.
[3] Berlin's Chief of Police.
[4] Original in English. For the Czar's reply, see 129.

118   Sazonov to Chargé d'Affaires Bronevski

Telegram 1539   St Petersburg, 28 July 1914
Int. Bez. I, 5, 168

Sent to Vienna, Paris, London and Rome
In consequence of Austria's declaration of war on Serbia, we shall declare
mobilisation in the military districts of Odessa, Kiev, Moscow and Kazan
tomorrow. Kindly bring this to the attention of the German Government
and emphasise the absence of any intentions of a Russian attack on
Germany. Our Ambassador in Vienna is not being recalled from his post
for the time being.

119   Goschen to Grey

Telegram 97   Berlin, 28 July 1914
B.D. 215   D. 2.03 p.m.
                                                               R. 2.45 p.m.

My telegram of yesterday.[1]

   Secretary of State for Foreign Affairs spoke yesterday[2] in same sense
to my French and Italian colleagues respecting your proposal. In talking
over his reply this morning my two colleagues and I found that to all of
us he had, while refusing proposed conference, said that nevertheless he
desired to work with us for maintenance of general peace. We therefore
deduced that if this wish on his part is sincere it is only to form of your
proposal that he objects. We therefore wondered whether it might be
possible for you to put proposal in another form omitting word 'conference', or perhaps even to propose to him that he himself should suggest
lines on which he would find it possible to work with us.[3]

Minutes

Sir E. Grey has telegraphed today to Berlin that he will suspend his
suggestion if there is any chance of direct exchange of views between
Vienna and St Petersburg.—G. R. C. 28 July 1914.
   Apart from that however there is much sound sense in the suggestion
that Germany should be asked, if as she says, she is so anxious to work for
peace, what *she* proposes the Powers should do.—E. A. C. 28 July.

   [1] See **110**.
   [2] I.e., of 27 July.
   [3] See also *D.F.* XI, 203.

I am a little tired of these protestations and should like to see some practical action. If direct conversations are to take place between Vienna and St Petersburg we had better not confuse the matter by making any fresh proposal.—A. N.

120 Grey to Goschen
Telegram 220   London, 28 July 1914
B.D. 223   D. 6.15 p.m.

Your telegram 97 of 28 July.[1]
German Government having accepted principle of mediation by the four Powers between Austria and Russia if necessary, I am ready to propose that German Minister for Foreign Affairs should suggest lines on which this principle may be applied, but I will keep the idea in reserve till we see how the conversations between Austria and Russia progress.

121 Buchanan to Grey

Telegram 177   St Petersburg, 28 July 1914
B.D. 247   D. 8.45 p.m.
                                                R. 29 July, 1.00 a.m.

I communicated to Minister for Foreign Affairs today substance of your telegram 208 of 27 July to Berlin,[2] and he begged me to thank you for language you had held to German Ambassador. He had received same disquieting news from Vienna as that reported in Sir M. de Bunsen's telegram [109?],[3] and accordingly took pessimistic view of the situation. I asked him whether he would be satisfied with assurances which I understood Austrian Ambassador had been instructed to give with regard to Serbia's independence and integrity. I was sure that His Majesty's Government would welcome any arrangement that would avert a European war, but it was important that we should know real intentions of Imperial Government. His Excellency replied at once that no engagement that Austria might take on these two points would satisfy Russia, and that on day that Austria crossed Serbian frontier order for mobilisation against Austria would be issued. I said that German Ambassador had in

<hr />

[1] See 119.   [2] See 109.   [3] B.D. 175.

conversation with myself contended that Russian Government could not pretend that their hands were being forced by public opinion as there was no excitement and no demonstrations. His Excellency replied that Ambassador was quite wrong and that it was only thanks to precautions taken by police that there had been no hostile demonstrations before Austrian and German Embassies. He had today received a telegram from Minister of the Interior, who was making a tour in the provinces, telling him that he need have no fear concerning internal disturbances, and that in event of war whole nation would be behind Government.

I asked whether it would not be possible in last resort for Emperor Nicolas to address personal appeal to Emperor of Austria to restrict Austria's action within limits which Russia could accept. His Excellency replied to my question by repeating that only way to avert war was for His Majesty's Government to let it be clearly known that they would join France and Russia.[1] Prince Henry of Prussia, he heard, was being sent on mission to England, and he trusted that His Royal Highness would not be left in doubt as to what England would do.[2]

As his Excellency had to report to Emperor this afternoon I was unable to ascertain result of conversation which he subsequently had with Austrian Ambassador, but from a hurried conversation which I had with latter I gathered that, while Austria is ready to discuss international question with Russia and to assure her that she has no ulterior aims directed either against Serbian independence and integrity or against Russia's interests in the Balkans, she considers her quarrel with Serbia is one that only concerns herself.

German Ambassador appealed to me to give moderating counsels to Minister for Foreign Affairs, and I told him that I had not ceased to do so from the beginning, and that it was now the turn of German Ambassador at Vienna to use his restraining influence. I warned his Excellency that Russia was thoroughly in earnest, and that nothing would avert general war if Austria attacked Serbia.[3] Ambassador had not received any instructions about suggestion of conference, and my French and Italian colleagues are still awaiting their final instructions before acting with me.

Minute

Russia has mobilised in Southern districts.—A. N.

[1] See **68** (minute).
[2] *D.D.* 374.
[3] Pourtalès did not report Buchanan's warning to Berlin. A more extensive account of the discussion with Pourtalès is to be found in Sir George Buchanan, *My Mission to Russia and Other Diplomatic Memories*, London, 1923.

7 British Neutrality and Russian General Mobilisation
29 – 31 July

On 28 July the German Government had succeeded in bringing about the *fait accompli* by its successful pressure in Vienna for an early declaration of war on Serbia. Now Vienna could no longer shrink back from the ultimate consequences, as had recently been the fear in Berlin.[1] The *fait accompli* was sealed by the shelling of Belgrade by the Austro-Hungarian batteries on the following day and this in fact opened the hostilities even before the deployment of troops against Serbia had been completed. The shelling of Belgrade can likewise have come as no surprise to the German Government, for by 20 July at the latest it was in possession of a report from the German Military Attaché in Vienna giving advance notice of the envisaged bombardment of the Serbian capital (32). Moreover the immediate opening of hostilities conformed with the German policy of creating a sudden *fait accompli* to baulk any attempts at mediation by the other Powers.

The precipitation of events by the antedating of the declaration of war and the start of hostilities even before the completion of Austrian mobilisation and of the deployment of troops against Serbia had a devastating effect, especially on Russia. There, the declaration of war on Serbia had already provoked the hasty decision for partial mobilisation (118), contrary to original intentions. The news of the bombardment of Belgrade now wrought a dramatic and fundamental change in the situation in St Petersburg, as the Russians saw this as the opening shot of an imminent invasion

[1] See above, p. 96.

of Serbia by Austrian troops. The rush of events precipitated by Berlin in Vienna was automatically attended by a similar stampede in St Petersburg. Under the impact of the news from Belgrade there was not only a deterioration in the hitherto friendly climate of the negotiations between Sazonov and Szápáry, but also Sazonov and the Czar now yielded to pressure from the Russian generals. The military held that war with Austria-Hungary was imminent and virtually inevitable with Germany. The well-known speed with which the Germans could mobilise, and the notorious slowness of the Russians, made the generals afraid of being caught off their balance if they hesitated for too long. In a hectic atmosphere on the afternoon of 29 July they won the day with an order for general mobilisation which was issued at 6.00 p.m. In the late evening, however, after receiving a telegram from Kaiser Wilhelm II, the Czar revoked the order and amended it to partial mobilisation instead.

Not only did the German Government cause a devastating and nigh irreparable precipitation of events in St Petersburg, with their all too successful disruption of the original Austrian timetable, but they proceeded to do likewise in Berlin. As late as 27 July Jagow had assured the Entente diplomats that Germany would not mobilise so long as Russian mobilisation was directed solely against Austria (102, 103, 110). On 29 July however the Wilhelmstrasse received a detailed memorandum 'on the political situation' from Moltke, the Chief of General Staff. In this, Moltke placed a diametrically opposed interpretation on Russian mobilisation by viewing it as sufficient justification for a general mobilisation in Germany (125). Moltke informed Conrad by telegraph to Vienna on the following day that 'in contrast to the already routine Russian mobilisations and demobilisations', this German mobilisation would 'unquestionably lead to war'.[1] Moreover, the German plan for mobilisation envisaged immediate occupation of Luxembourg and Liège, and thus the violation of the neutrality of two countries, as the curtain-raiser to a swift opening of the war against France, who had until now remained totally uncommitted.[2]

Once again German political leadership yielded to pressure from the military. From the 30 July onwards the German Government expressly demanded the revocation of the Russian mobilisation order, even against Austria. When on 30 July Jules Cambon drew Jagow's attention to the clash with his declaration of 27 July, the Secretary of State protested, with evident embarrassment, that the military had enforced a shift in position, adding that his declaration had anyway not been a 'definite

[1] Conrad, *Dienstzeit*, IV, p. 152.
[2] See G. Ritter, *Der Schlieffenplan. Kritik eines Mythos* (Munich, 1958).

commitment'.[1] But German general mobilisation in answer to Russian partial mobilisation made continental and world war virtually inevitable.

Bethmann Hollweg however still resisted immediate general mobilisation in Germany in the hope that Russia would make the first move, and confident in Germany's ability to mobilise with greater speed. Already on the 28 July Berchtold had urged in Berlin that Germany should threaten St Petersburg with mobilisation and so deter the Russians from ordering a partial mobilisation against Austria-Hungary (111). But Bethmann Hollweg had immediately refused,[2] nor was a repetition of the Austrian proposal of the 29 July (124) sufficient to dissuade him from his intention of baiting Russia into being the first Great Power to announce general mobilisation. The Chancellor also stood firm[3] when Falkenhayn on 29 July demanded a proclamation of the 'situation of the threatening danger of war' which meant the stage of military preparations immediately preceding mobilisation. Initially the generals showed their appreciation of the Chancellor's strategy of making Russia appear the aggressor so as 'at least to keep Britain out of the contest of nations'[4] or in other words to ensure Britain's neutrality in a continental war. But whether to placate the military or to further diplomatic preparations for the continental war which was drawing ever closer, Bethmann Hollweg subsequently threatened Paris and St Petersburg that only an immediate suspension of French and Russian preparations for war could prevent corresponding German counter measures, by which he was obviously referring to German mobilisation. To Paris the Germans made no mention whatsoever of mobilisation (it is interesting to note even in diplomatic niceties the German custom of discriminating between West and East, cultivated not only during but also after the two World Wars), whereas in St Petersburg they bluntly spoke of war (126, 127). The Chancellor probably calculated that if the Russians climbed down under the German threat, as they had done in 1909, localisation would have been achieved, general war at Serbia's and Russia's expense avoided and Russia would have forfeited her status as a World Power. If the Russians could not be forced to comply with German demands or were even panicked into general mobilisation, the Chancellor would have achieved one of his tactical goals in the July crisis, namely shifting on to Russia the odium for the outbreak of world war. It was for this reason that the Chancellor now initiated the famous exchange of telegrams between the Kaiser and the Czar, for on the evening of 28 July Bethmann Hollweg commended the first telegram to Nicolas with the explanation that 'such a telegram, should a war prove to be

[1] *D.F.* XI, 380.   [2] *D.D.* 299.

[3] Hans v. Zwehl, *Falkenhayn*, p. 57.   [4] Thus, G. Ritter, *Staatskunst*, II, p. 318.

inevitable, would throw the clearest light on Russia's responsibility' (114). The exchange of telegrams (116, 117, 129, 131, 142, 156, 157, 171, 175) was thus, from the German viewpoint, hardly more than part of the diplomatic manoeuvre to brand Russia as the aggressor and of the propagandist manoeuvre to smooth the way for German general mobilisation.

The extent to which the German Government calculated on a large-scale war is demonstrated by two incidents on 29 July. First, an ultimative demand to Belgium that she should offer no resistance to the transit of German troops (91) was sent to the German Minister in Brussels with the instructions that he was only to open the sealed envelope upon receipt of a specific order to do so.[1] Secondly, after an audience with the Kaiser in Potsdam, the so-called 'Potsdam Crown Council' of 29 July,[2] Bethmann Hollweg evidently with the agreement and approbation of the Kaiser tried to secure the coping stone of his political edifice—Britain's neutrality in the event of a continental war. Shortly before midnight he summoned the British Ambassador to the Wilhelmstrasse and officially asked him whether Britain would remain neutral if, in return, the Reich were to guarantee the territorial integrity of Belgium and France in Europe (though not in Africa). In addition, the Chancellor 'offered' an agreement of neutrality (but no naval agreement) for the post-war period (139). Germany had thus shown her hand and in exchange for vague assurances for the future, not only demanded British neutrality which held out the promise of victory, but also intimated that she had made up her mind to an infringement of Belgian neutrality, as the Foreign Office was not slow to recognise (139, minute).

Goschen merely gave the Chancellor a provisional reply, which left all the alternatives open, but which probably failed wholly to conceal the diplomat's surprise at the undiplomatic 'offer' (167). The British reply arrived almost immediately after Goschen's departure however; on the afternoon of 29 July Grey had disclosed to Lichnowsky, the German Ambassador, that England would not remain neutral in the event of a continental war (130). This information was doubly distressing to the Chancellor. He would not have spoken so openly if it had arrived earlier,

---

[1] Jagow to Below; 29 July; *D.D.* 375.

[2] No official documents on the discussion of 29 July exist; there are only private records by some of the participants. The most important of these is Alfred v. Tirpitz, *Politische Dokumente*, 2 vols. (Hamburg/Berlin, 1924–6), vol. II: *Deutsche Ohnmachtspolitik in Weltkriege*, pp. 2ff.; further references in Georg A. v. Müller, *Regierte der Kaiser? Kriegstagebücher, Aufzeichnungen und Briefe des Chefs des Marine-Kabinetts 1914–1918*, ed. by Walter Görlitz (Gottingen/Berlin/Frankfurt-am-Main, 1959), p. 36, and Hans v. Zwehl, *Erich von Falkenhayn General der Infanterie, Eine biographische Studie* (Berlin, 1926), p. 56.

as Jagow conceded with some embarrassment to Goschen the following day in the British Embassy (150, 167), but at least as important as this was the fact that British neutrality was not to be secured—the coping stone crashed to the ground and carried with it the entire edifice of the Chancellor's policy of localisation. The 'premises of his policy' had suddenly collapsed.[1]

After this heavy blow from London, Bethmann Hollweg spent the small hours of 30 July in an attempt to avert the catastrophe and salvage what remained of the pieces. To this end he sought to master the situation by exerting firm pressure on Vienna, only this time with an eye to moderation. Now, for a change, he wanted to gain time and so fell back on the Kaiser's proposal for a 'halt in Belgrade' (112). All of a sudden the Chancellor sought to restrain the Austrians and encourage them to meet the Russian suggestions (133, 134). However, the Germans were now repaid for their earlier policy of hustling Vienna into the war with Serbia, for Germany's pressure on her ally—this time in reverse direction—came too late, was too weak, and not sufficiently consistent to save the peace. The time Germany had caused others to lose with her policies could no longer be made good. Moreover, in seeking to exert a mediatory influence on Vienna, Bethmann Hollweg even now was motivated by certain tactical considerations: abroad he was anxious to allow the blame for the imminent continental war to fall on Russia, in the hope that Britain might still after all remain neutral, and at home he was mindful of preserving the unity of public opinion, with especial concern for the Social Democratic Party. It would have been sufficient for the Chancellor to declare: 'We have made a miscalculation, the war cannot be localised, Britain will not remain neutral, so we must call off the war; the Reich can no longer offer protection to the Danube Monarchy if she persists in the war against Serbia single-handed.' Yet at no point did he speak the decisive words. Nor did Bethmann Hollweg by any means take advantage of the remaining alternatives for preserving peace, even at a moment when he and his policies had been hurled into the most grave disarray; thus, in the early hours of 30 July, for example, he emphatically rejected the Russians' proposal for submitting the dispute to the Hague court of Arbitration.[2]

In the course of 30 July German mobilisation loomed ever larger. That morning on receipt of a telegram from the Czar to the effect that military preparations had already been concluded several days previously, the Kaiser noted with indignation: 'My work is at an end!' (132). Shortly before midday another telegram reached Berlin from St Petersburg in which Pourtalès reported extensive preparatory measures, still only

[1] F. Fischer, *Griff nach der Weltmacht*, p. 89 (3rd ed., p. 95).   [2] *D.D.* 391.

officially described in Russia as partial mobilisation.[1] One of these two incidents[2]—or both of them together—prompted the military to urge the Chancellor even more forcibly to proclaim a situation of imminent danger of war and Germany's consequent need for mobilisation. Moreover the military may have been apprised of the bad news from London (130), so that previous deference to British neutrality could now be abandoned. By some means hitherto unknown the news of Moltke's pressure for immediate German mobilisation seems to have reached the editorial staff of the quasi-official *Berliner Lokalanzeiger*, and, whether in genuine or ostensible error, was printed and distributed at 2.00 p.m. in Berlin in a special issue containing an announcement of German mobilisation. The Government immediately confiscated the special issue and sent a denial of the announcement to the Embassies of the Entente Powers.[3]

Bethmann Hollweg had no desire to be deprived by his generals of the tactical advantage of letting Russia be the first to order general mobilisation. For this reason, in a conversation with Moltke at 3.00 in the afternoon, he resisted pressure for mobilisation,[4] as he wanted first to await Austria's reply to his 'halt in Belgrade' proposal. Disillusioned, Moltke took the initiative into his own hands. At 2.00 p.m. he informed Lt. Col. Bienerth, the Austro-Hungarian Military Attaché in Berlin, that he desired Austria to mobilise immediately so that Germany as her ally could follow suit. Moltke also telegraphed Conrad direct: 'Stand firm against Russian mobilisation. Austria-Hungary must be preserved, mobilise at once against Russia. Germany will mobilise. Compel Italy to do her duty as an ally by compensation.'[5]

Just as Moltke was openly pressing the Chancellor to order immediate general mobilisation in Austria at a time when the latter still wanted to postpone this for political and tactical reasons, so it is quite possible that the General Staff, whether or not at Moltke's personal instigation, was covertly pursuing an identical aim by committing a calculated indiscretion in the *Berliner Lokalanzeiger*. Anyway, such an hypothesis would seem plausible. Since Moltke had submitted the Chancellor to external pressure (for general mobilisation in Austria), it is quite possible that he was also trying to exert internal pressure (by means of a calculated indiscretion through the *Berliner Lokalanzeiger*).

On the evening of 30 July the military achieved a decisive breakthrough: Moltke and Falkenhayn at last committed Bethmann Hollweg

---

[1] *D.D.* 410.

[2] L. Albertini (*Origins*, III, pp. 8ff.) decides in favour of the former explanation; G. Ritter (*Staatskunst*, II, p. 320) for the latter.

[3] *Int. Bez.* I, 5, 302, 303; *D.F.* XI, 330.   [4] A. v. Wegerer, *Ausbruch*, II, p. 112.

[5] Conrad, *Dienstzeit*, IV, p. 152.

and Jagow to giving an undertaking that the Government would make up its mind by midday on 31 July.[1] Both sides were satisfied with that time- and face-saving compromise: the generals because the outcome was hardly in doubt, now that events had gone so far; the Chancellor because he had won another respite, in the vague hope (all too justified by subsequent events) that Sazonov might after all lose his nerve and announce general mobilisation before the Germans.

At 11 a.m. on 31 July the military and political leaders reassembled to await news from St Petersburg. At 11.55, only five minutes before the self-imposed deadline, the eagerly awaited telegram from Pourtalès was delivered to the Chancellor: 'General mobilisation of the army and fleet ordered. First day of mobilisation, 31 July.'[2] The alibi for German mobilisation had finally been provided and Bethmann Hollweg could make the announcement, now that he had received news of the Russian general mobilisation. Falkenhayn immediately advised the Kaiser to make a proclamation of the situation of imminent danger of war, and Wilhelm II signed the relevant decree.[3] The same evening 'enquiries' in the nature of an ultimatum were sent to St Petersburg and Paris, consisting respectively of a demand for immediate cessation of Russian mobilisation and a query as to France's neutrality (158, 159). At the same time the Auswärtiges Amt was preparing the drafts of the declarations of war on Russia and France.[4] On the previous day, after learning of the intensity of the military preparations in Russia,[5] the Chancellor had abandoned his transitory efforts at exhorting the Austrians to moderation.

The tactical wavering in Berlin caused considerable confusion in Vienna and even a degree of temporary ill-feeling towards the German ally. The Chancellor's distortion of the Kaiser's 'halt in Belgrade' (112, 115) naturally had no braking effect on 29 July, especially as Tschirschky informed Berchtold[6] that he had been ordered for tactical reasons to avoid giving the impression that Berlin was seeking to restrain the Austrians. Now the Austrians were finally under way and they were unwilling to be deterred from their war against Serbia, even though the news of Russia's partial mobilisation had meanwhile been announced. In order to prevent what would, for Austria-Hungary, prove to be a deadly clash with Russia, Berchtold again tried, on 29 July, to induce Germany to mobilise against Russia, in the hope that Russia would once more, as in 1909, climb down

---

[1] Hans v. Zwehl, *Falkenhayn*, pp. 57f.
[2] *D.D.* 473.
[3] Falkenhayn to Bethmann Hollweg and Jagow, 31 July; *D.D.* 499.
[4] *D.D.* 608, 542.
[5] Bethmann Hollweg to Tschirschky, 30 July; *D.D.* 450, 451.
[6] Berchtold's minute of 29 July; *Ö.D.* 10939.

under the German threat (124). When Tschirschky, at the Chancellor's request, told Berchtold the following day that in order to create a favourable impression in Europe Vienna should accept British mediation in the Austro-Serbian conflict and content herself with the occupation of Belgrade (133), Berchtold merely gave a delaying reply (145); Vienna had no desire to be hampered in her military action against Serbia. All the same, Berchtold did instruct Szápáry to explain (though not to discuss) the contentious points with Sazonov, in conformance with the German desire for a resumption of the talks in St Petersburg (115).[1] On 31 July, under the added pressure of Moltke's urgent telegram,[2] Vienna decided on general mobilisation, even before learning the news of the Russian general mobilisation.[3] After the Council of Ministers (154) Berchtold gave what appeared to be a favourable answer to the British proposal of mediation (133) which had been forwarded by Berlin, but he qualified this with two conditions which were unacceptable from an objective point of view—continuation with the war against Serbia and an immediate end to Russian mobilisation (155).

By 30 July, such demands were already out of the question for Russia; instead, the final decisions were taken at St Petersburg on the same day. Two factors seem to have convinced Sazonov that war with Germany was now definitely inevitable and that Russian mobilisation was necessary in consequence: from Berlin Sverbejev, the Russian Ambassador, reported that Jagow's reaction to the announcement of partial Russian mobilisation (138) was in marked contrast to his comforting reassurance of 27 July,[4] and from Vienna there came a report of Tschirschky's remark to the effect that any form of conciliatory pressure on Austria would be useless.[5] When the military pressed the Czar over the telephone for a decree of general mobilisation, Sazonov joined their ranks and that afternoon finally obtained the Czar's permission to issue the order in question (137). Meanwhile at Pourtalès' insistence, Sazonov had drawn up a formula capable of satisfying Russia and inducing her to abandon mobilisation (141a, 146). But Sazonov himself did not really believe in the efficacy of such last-minute attempts at mediation, for he declared in a circular to his diplomatic mission that Russia would continue to rearm until Austria gave way.[6] After obtaining the Czar's assent to a general mobilisation Sazonov tried to conceal the fact for as long as possible but the secret could no longer be preserved when in the early morning of 31 July red placards with a call to arms hung from every wall. Neither the German

---

[1] Berchtold to Szápáry, 30 July; *Ö.D.* 11092.
[2] See above, p. 270.
[3] Conrad, *Dienstzeit*, IV, p. 153.
[4] See above, p. 222.
[5] *Int. Bez.* I, 5, 243.
[6] *Int. Bez.* I, 5, 279.

Ambassador's representations to Sazonov (160) nor his audience with the Czar were now sufficient to put an end to Russian general mobilisation.[1] At this Sazonov even declared to the German Ambassador that he could no longer guarantee that peace would be preserved (160).

The outline of a settlement appeared to emerge in the eleventh hour when Szápáry informed Sazonov that in his opinion the discrepancy between the Russian position (mitigation of the ultimatum) and the Austrian (elucidation of the ultimatum) could be bridged as it appeared to him 'that it came to the same thing' (168). Sazonov immediately seized on this conciliatory remark—so much so that Szápáry felt impelled expressly to remind him of the private nature of his utterance. Yet this would have provided a basis upon which Vienna (on whom the onus of preventing war with Russia clearly lay) could have started to build if sufficient time had remained.

Poincaré and Viviani arrived back in Paris shortly after midday on 29 July. Viviani, with Sazonov's backing, immediately appealed to Grey to reconsider his original (26 July) proposal for a conference (93).[2] The Council of Ministers determined on a middle course of seeking if possible to avoid general war whilst making military preparations for France's defence.[3] The reaction in Paris to the German 'enquiry' (126) was still one of reserve.[4] When Sazonov (by way of Izvolsky) referred to Paléologue's firm pledge that France would fulfil her treaty obligations (136), Viviani in St Petersburg even hinted that no such pledge had yet been given (148), as Viviani's instructions of 27 July, which Paléologue had interpreted thus, in reality only made mention of France's solidarity with Russia in the interests of preserving peace.[5] Since Viviani clearly recognised the significant propagandist and political role of the Russian general mobilisation he sought at the same time to add greater force to his counsel of restraint by urging on Sazonov that Russia should give Germany no pretext for general mobilisation[6] (148). It was for this reason that Jules Cambon also warned against premature general mobilisation in France (149). The news of the secret measures for the introduction of general mobilisation in Russia only reached Paris shortly before midnight.[7]

In the meantime with such measures as the 'protection of the frontier'

[1] Pourtalès to Jagow for Wilhelm II, 31 July; *D.D.* 535.
[2] Viviani to Paul Cambon, 29 July; *D.F.* XI, 260.
[3] Raymond Poincaré, *Au Service de la France. Neuf années de souvenirs*, 10 vols (Paris, 1926–33), vol. IV, *L'Union Sacrée*, pp. 371f.
[4] Schoen to Jagow, 29 July; *D.D.* 367.
[5] Viviani to Paléologue, 27 July; *D.F.* XI, 138.
[6] See also Izvolsky to Sazonov, 30 July; *Int. Bez.* I, 5, 291.
[7] Paléologue to Viviani, 30 July; *D.F.* XI, 359.

France took her military preparations a stage further to what virtually amounted to a partial mobilisation on 30 July. Notwithstanding this, the French Government ordered a withdrawal of French troops to a distance of approximately ten kilometres from the common frontier with Germany. At the same time Paris broached the question of the Anglo-French alliance; Viviani directed Paul Cambon to remind Grey of their correspondence in 1912 (148), and Poincaré attempted to make it clear to Bertie, the British Ambassador in Paris, that in the present circumstances only an unequivocal declaration of England's support for France could save the peace. On 31 July the French President renewed his pressure on England, this time on King George V himself.[1] Viviani supported the British version of the 'halt in Belgrade' proposal[2] and immediately forwarded it to St Petersburg with his recommendation;[3] he made it clear to Szécsen, however, that the Serbian question had by now faded into the background.[4] When Schoen delivered the ultimative German enquiry (159) at approximately 7.00 in the evening Viviani hedged at first with the aim of leaving France a free hand.[5] Yet there could no longer be any doubt of the determination of the French not to abandon their Russian ally to the Germans.

It was only in the last days of July that British policy broke away from its attitude of aloofness towards Germany. When Grey's announcement to Lichnowsky on 29 July (130) became known in Berlin it even began to open the Chancellor's eyes to the failure of his policy of localisation but it still did not succeed in inducing him to exert more than a transitory influence on Vienna for tactical reasons.[6] Despite this, Grey did not want to burn all his boats and he requested the Germans to make some proposal of their own for mediation.[7] However, the British diplomatists warned Vienna and Berlin against the illusion that 'the Triple Alliance would survive the ordeal of a world war' as Italy would not take part on the side of Germany and Austria;[8] an analogous warning was also sent to Vienna (122). As early as 29 July the British Cabinet discussed Britain's position in the event of a continental war and the possible violation of Belgian neutrality. Without yet committing themselves they sanctioned the preliminary measures for mobilisation of the Fleet which Churchill had ordered on his own initiative.[9]

[1] *D.F.* XI, 457.
[2] Grey to Buchanan, 30 July; *B.D.* 309.
[3] Viviani to Paléologue, 31 July; *D.F.* XI, 405.
[4] Szécsen to Berchtold, 31 July; *Ö.D.* 11164.
[5] Schoen to Jagow, 31 July; *D.D.* 528; Viviani to Paléologue, 31 July; *D.F.* XI, 438
[6] See above, p. 269.
[7] Grey to Goschen, 30 July; *B.D.* 263.
[8] Lichnowsky to Jagow, 29 July; *D.D.* 355.
[9] *Berliner Monatshefte*, XI, p. 69.

Germany's demands for neutrality on 29–30 July (139) only served to hasten a clarification of the situation in London. The reaction in the Foreign Office was strong and unequivocal, and Grey's outright refusal to Bethmann Hollweg (151) could only heighten the effect of his disclosure to Lichnowsky (130). Nevertheless Grey still declared himself willing to exert a mediatory influence on St Petersburg[1] and as before he avoided giving firm commitments to France and Russia. He wanted moreover to wait until he had received a definite undertaking from the German Government, and so he again recommended his version of a 'halt in Belgrade' to St Petersburg.[2]

The same procedure was gone over again on 31 July after Grey had greeted Lichnowsky's news of the resumption of the talks between Austria and Russia as a hopeful augury for the preservation of peace.[3] Grey in addition made another (his penultimate) proposal for mediation, whereby the four disinterested Powers were to obtain satisfaction for Austria from Serbia, whilst exacting from Vienna a guarantee of Serbia's sovereignty and integrity (163). Whereas Grey revealed to the German Ambassador that the British Navy was already on the verge of mobilisation,[4] he still refused to give Paul Cambon a pledge of solidarity with France, as only a German ultimatum to France would have enabled the British Government to propose to Parliament an intervention on the Continent (162).

England could no longer avoid intervening, however, as Crowe, in particular, pointed out in a memorandum (164). Consequently, London sent enquiries to Paris and Berlin to discover whether these Governments were prepared to respect Belgian neutrality, whilst Brussels received a call to stand firm.[5] The French Government sent a prompt reply in the affirmative which reached London just before midnight,[6] whereas Secretary of State Jagow merely evaded the issue (166).

[1] Lichnowsky to Jagow, 30 July; *D.D.* 435.
[2] *Int. Bez.* I, 5, 286, 288; *B.D.* 309.
[3] Lichnowsky to Jagow, 31 July; *D.D.* 489; Grey to Buchanan, 31 July; *B.D.* 340.
[4] Lichnowsky to Jagow, 31 July; *D.D.* 484.
[5] *B.D.* 348, 351.
[6] *B.D.* 380, 382.

122   Mensdorff to Berchtold

Telegram 119   London, 29 July 1914
Ö.D. 10973   D. 4.32 p.m.
                                                 R. 30 July, 9.00 a.m.

I have just spoken to Sir Edward Grey who declared that the situation
had grown far more serious and that he was very anxious today. Berlin
reports Russian mobilisation, from Vienna the refusal of the Imperial and
Royal Government to treat directly with Russia.[1] The danger of a great
European complication is hourly increasing.

He repeatedly said that we should probably have the support and the
sympathy of all the Powers if we were satisfied by Serbia's acceptance of
all our demands and that moreover all the Powers would guarantee to us
the keeping of these promises. I pointed out that after the declaration of
war and the beginning of hostilities this might be too late. 'Then it is
perhaps also too late for the prevention of the general war', he exclaimed.

I insisted that it was necessary to separate the Austro-Hungarian-
Serbian conflict from the question of a European war and that Russia
needed to be influenced not to provoke it by its intervention. Hereupon
Grey remarked: 'If the Powers are only to intervene in Russia in order
that it remains passive, this would be equal to giving you a free hand, a
thing that Russia will not accept. You must give us something, however
small, that we could make use of in St Petersburg.'

He refused to discuss the pros and cons of our point of view and said
that what concerned him were facts and the most important matter: how
can a European war be yet prevented? Also without any territorial
acquisitions we might bring Serbia into a state of vassalage[2] and thus
eliminate Russia completely from the Balkans.

I replied that according to our former arrangements with Russia (of
which we had spoken the day before yesterday) Serbia had advanced into
our sphere of influence. It would be absurd to think that Russian influence
could be eliminated from the Balkans if Belgrade ceased to be the pivot
of Russia's Balkan policy. It was we rather, who were in the position of
legitimate defence; the attempts to turn all our small neighbouring states
into enemies and the whole of the agitation directed against us, was
threatening our position as a Great Power and also the balance of Power
in Europe for which he had always stood, etc.

The Secretary of State was very pessimistic. 'Today St Petersburg is
still on speaking terms with Berlin, how will it be tomorrow?' He told

[1] *B.D.* 248, 249.   [2] See 35.

me he was in constant touch with the German Chancellor, who was also seeking means to mediate between Vienna and St Petersburg.

Afterwards I spoke to Tyrell, who confirmed that Sir Edward Grey was very anxious and continually endeavouring to find a way to prevent a conflagration.

Tyrell wholly confirms the view I hold gained of the attitude here, which I would sum up as follows: Great Britain seems to be trying by all means possible to keep out of a European complication; Russian interests leave England cool; but should it affect a vital interest of France's or what is more a question of the position of France as a Power, no English Government would be capable of preventing a participation of Great Britain on the side of France.

123 Szápáry to Berchtold

Telegrams 180, 181	St Petersburg, 29 July 1914
Secret	D. 11.00 p.m., 30 July, 1.00 a.m.
Ö.D. 11003, 11094	R. 30 July, 11.00 a.m., 3.15 p.m.

Having learnt from the German Ambassador, that Mr Sazonov seems very agitated in consequence of Your Excellency's refusal to continue exchange of views with Russia and of the supposed mobilisation of Austria-Hungary, which exceeds the necessary limits and seems therefore directed against Russia, I called on the Minister in order to clear up some apparent misunderstanding and at the same time to obtain closer insight into Russian plans.

The Minister started by claiming that Austria-Hungary had categorically refused a further exchange of views. On the strength of Your Excellency's telegram 191 of 28 inst.[1] I argued that Your Excellency had, it is true, after all that had happened altogether refused to discuss the texts of notes and the Austro-Hungarian-Serbian conflict, but that I could announce that I was in a position to propose a far broader basis for the exchange of views, by declaring that we did not wish to hurt Russian interests, that we had no intention of acquiring Serbian territory nor were we thinking of questioning Serbian sovereignty. I further felt convinced: I declared, that Your Excellency would always be ready to exchange views with St Petersburg concerning Austro-Hungarian and Russian interests.

[1] *Ö.D.* 10915.

Mr Sazonov thought that he would allow himself to be convinced with regard to the territorial question, but that he would insist on his view as regards the Sovereignty question seeing that the enforcing of our condition meant Serbian vassalage. The latter is calculated to upset the balance of power on the Balkan peninsula, while the former constitutes an interference with Russian interests. He then returned to a discussion of the Note, Sir E. Grey's action, etc., and assured me once more that our legitimate demands would be recognised and fully satisfied, but that this would need to be done in a form acceptable to Serbia. It was merely a case of quarrelling over words. I remarked that this was not a Russian, but a Serbian question, whereupon Sazonov claimed that in this case Russian interests were identical with the Serbian, so that I put an end to this futile discussion by changing the subject.

I mentioned having heard that Russia was alarmed at our having mobilised eight corps for the [conduct of war] against Serbia. Mr Sazonov asserted to me, that not he, who had known nothing of all this, but Emperor Nicolas, on the strength of information received from the Chief of the General Staff had expressed alarm. I tried to explain to the Minister that even a mere child in military matters could easily convince itself that our southern corps constituted no threat to Russia. I likewise drew attention to our experience in the Bosnian campaign.[1] At the same time I also mentioned the uncertain attitude of Montenegro, concerning which Mr Sazonov remarked that Herr von Giers had telegraphed, that the King had openly proclaimed his dislike of Serbia and his Austrophile sentiments. I replied that for all our confidence in Czar Nicolas and his utterances we could not discover any military guarantees in them. I hinted to the Minister that it were well if his Imperial Master were informed of the real situation, all the more so as it appeared urgently necessary, if peace were desired, promptly to end the military competition which threatened to establish itself on the strength of false information. Mr Sazonov said very enlighteningly that he could communicate this to the Chief of the General Staff who saw the Emperor every day. The Minister for his part, at a time like the present, went but to the usual Tuesday reception and was only informed by His Majesty himself what the military functionaries reported to him.

The Minister further told me that today an Ukase was being signed, ordering a mobilisation on a considerable scale. He could however assure me in the most official manner possible, that these troops were not destined to sweep down on us; they would only be kept in readiness in case Russia's interests in the Balkans were threatened. A 'note explicative'

[1] In 1878.

would establish this, for it was only a precautionary measure which Czar Nicolas considered justified, seeing that we not only possessed the advantage of easier mobilisation, but had also gained a great start on Russia.

I drew Mr Sazonov's attention most earnestly to the impression that a measure of this kind will make in Austria-Hungary. I could only [warn] that the note explicative might be calculated to moderate this impression, whereupon the Minister repeated his assurances concerning the harmlessness of these orders.

Whilst we were thus exchanging our views confidentially the Minister received a telephonic report of our having bombarded Belgrade.[1] He appeared as if transformed, tried to dish up all his former arguments again in a manner contrary to all logic and said that he now saw how right Czar Nicolas had been. 'You are only wanting to gain time by negotiations and are meanwhile advancing and bombarding an unprotected city. What else do you want to conquer when you are in possession of the capital?' and other childish utterances to this effect. The argument that an attitude of this kind towards Serbia constituted the reverse of a move against Russia did not weigh with the Minister. 'What is the good of our continuing our conversation if you act in this manner?' said he. I left him in a state of great agitation; and also my German colleague, who renewed his call had—at least for today—to renounce all hope of a calm interview.

Mounting indications of a diplomatic and military nature enabled us now to make a conjecture about Mr Sazonov's intended tactics. The Minister, like his Imperial Master, shuns war and without drawing immediate conclusions from our Serbian expedition seeks to dispute with us the fruits of the same, if possible without war, but if it should come to war, to enter the same better armed than at present. By mobilisation, accompanied by peaceful declarations apparently only directed against Austria-Hungary, but at the same time offering Roumania protection from the rear, it is intended to do everything possible to eliminate Germany and harass Austria-Hungary in her Serbian campaign and as soon as our operations have met with some success, to undertake the rescue of Serbia by Russia. If the remaining Balkan states were to stir and seek to profit by our actions, Roumania would be pushed forward in defence of the Peace of Bucharest. Should Austria-Hungary take a stand against this, it might come to a European war with Roumania on the side of Russia. If, however, Austria-Hungary and Germany should care even at this early stage to deduce the consequences of Russian mobilisation and forestall Russia gaining a military advantage, peaceful Russia would stand attacked and would have better prospects in this way of carrying along

[1] Strandtmann's brief telegram about the bombardment of Belgrade in *Int. Bez.* I, 5, 257.

with her France and perhaps even England, and our favourable moral and military situation in Europe would be damaged. Russia would be circumventing the straits in which she is placed by our just title to action against Serbia, and yet would still be in a position to protect her Balkan interests, perhaps even without war. By considerations such as these Czar Nicolas will have been won over to the idea of mobilisation, for which he certainly has little enthusiasm.

At all events, the possibility can by no means be discounted that military circles have been hard at work to reduce this complicated political calculation in whatever manner possible to a simpler formula and by creating a favourable climate of opinion and working on the Czar by way of false information, to precipitate events as far as possible once a certain preparedness for war has been achieved.

124 Berchtold to Szögyény

Telegram 291   Vienna, 29 July 1914
Ö.D. 10937   D. 30 July, 1.00 a.m.

Herr von Tschirschky has just told me that the Russian Ambassador informed him that he had received a notification from his Government that the military districts of Kiev, Odessa, Moscow and Kazan would be mobilised.[1] Russia had been slighted in her honour as a Great Power and has been compelled to have recourse to appropriate measures. The Russian mobilisation has been corroborated by our army corps commanders in Galicia, and today, according to a report from the Imp. and Royal Military Attaché, even Mr Sazonov made no further attempt to deny it in front of the German Ambassador. I request Your Excellency immediately to bring the foregoing to the attention of the German Government, and to emphasise that for military reasons our general mobilisation should be put in hand at once if the Russian measures for mobilisation are not immediately suspended. As a final attempt to avert a European war I should consider it desirable for our own and the German representatives in St Petersburg and possibly also in Paris to be given prompt instructions to explain in a friendly manner to the respective Governments that the continuance of Russian mobilisation would evoke counter-measures in Germany and Austria-Hungary and this would inevitably lead to grave consequences. Your Excellency may add that we shall naturally not allow ourselves to be dissuaded from our military action against Serbia. The Imp. and Royal Ambassadors in St Petersburg and Paris are receiving

[1] See 18.

instructions to deliver the aforementioned statement as soon as their German colleagues have received similar instructions. We are leaving it to the German Government to decide whether Italy should be informed of this step. In any case Herr von Mérey is to receive a transcript of this telegram charging him to inform the Italian Government as soon as German Ambassador receives instructions to this effect.

124a Pourtalès to Jagow

Telegram 183
Urgent
D.D. 343

St Petersburg, 29 July 1914
D. 1.38 p.m.
R. 2.52 p.m.

Argued subjects of telegrams 130 and 131[1] just now with Sazonov. They made a visibly good impression. Minister remarked, however, that up to the present there were unfortunately no existing evidences that Vienna was preparing to enter upon the road of direct conferences with St Petersburg[2]. Mr Schebeko, who had received instructions in regard to this matter, had so far made no report concerning any conversation with persons in authority, and Count Szápáry, too, stated that he had received no instructions. Consequently Austria's good faith was questionable.

Moreover, Austria had mobilized eight corps, and this measure must be regarded as in part directed against Russia. As a result Russia found herself compelled to mobilise the military districts on the Austrian frontier. The order for this was to be given today. When I made most earnest protest against these measures, Minister sought to convince me that in Russia mobilisation was far from meaning war, as it did among the western European nations; that the Russian army would doubtless be able to remain under arms for weeks to come without crossing the frontier. Russia wanted to avoid war, if it were in any way possible. I replied that these statements were not sufficient to satisfy me. The danger of every preparatory military measure lay in the counter-measures of the other side. It was obvious that the general staffs of the possible opponents of Russia would not be willing to sacrifice the advantage of getting a start over Russia in the matter of mobilisation, and would press for counter-measures. I earnestly begged him to consider this peril. Mr Sazonov assured me most solemnly once again that not the least thing was to happen to us. I replied with emphasis that, while the idea of a threat was far from my mind, he knew the obligations of our alliance with Austria.[3]

[1] Of 28 July; *D.D.* 300, 315.　　　　　　　　[2] See 123.
[3] For Sazonov's version see *Int. Bez.* I, 5, 218. For Bethmann Hollweg's answer of the same day, see *D.D.* 380.

125   Moltke to Bethmann Hollweg

D.D. 349
Berlin, 29 July 1914[1]
R. 29 July

Summary of the political situation

It goes without saying that no nation of Europe would regard the conflict between Austria and Serbia with any interest except that of humanity, if there did not lie within it the danger of general political complications that today already threaten to unchain a world war.[2] For more than five years Serbia has been the cause of a European tension which has been pressing with simply intolerable weight on the political and economic existence of nations. With a patience approaching weakness, Austria has up to the present borne the continuous provocations and the political machinations aimed at the disruption of her own national stability by a people which proceeded from regicide at home to the murder of princes in a neighbouring land. It was only after the last despicable crime that she took to extreme measures, in order to burn out with a glowing iron a cancer that has constantly threatened to poison the body of Europe. One would think that all Europe would be grateful to her. All Europe would have drawn a breath of relief if this mischief-maker could have been properly chastised and peace and order thereby have been restored to the Balkans; but Russia placed herself at the side of this criminal nation. It was only then that the Austro-Serbian affair became the thunder-cloud which may at any moment break over Europe.

Austria has declared to the European Cabinets that she intends neither to make any territorial acquisitions at Serbia's expense nor to infringe upon her status as a nation; that she only wants to force her unruly neighbour to accept the conditions that she considers necessary if they are to continue to exist side by side, and which Serbia, as experience has proved, would never live up to, despite solemn assurances, unless compelled by force.[3] The Austro-Serbian affair is a purely private quarrel in which, as has been said, nobody in Europe would have a profound interest and which would in no way threaten the peace of Europe but, on the contrary, would establish it more firmly, if Russia had not interfered with it.[4] This only was what gave the matter its menacing aspect.

Austria has only mobilised a portion of her armed forces, eight army corps, against Serbia—just enough with which to be able to put through her punitive expedition. As against this, Russia has made all preparations

---

[1] The draft dates from 28 July; see L. Albertini, *Origins*, II, p. 488.
[2] Berlin had also previously been aware of this, however; see 4.
[3] *Ö.D.* 10714.   [4] See 114 and 115.

to enable her to mobilise the army corps of the military districts of Kiev, Odessa and Moscow, twelve army corps in all, within the briefest period,[1] and is providing for similar preparatory measures in the north also, along the German border and the Baltic Sea. She announces that she intends to mobilise when Austria advances into Serbia, as she cannot permit the destruction of Serbia by Austria, though Austria has explained that she intends nothing of the sort.

What must and will the further consequences be? If Austria advances into Serbia she will have to face not only the Serbian army but also the vastly superior strength of Russia; thus she cannot enter upon a war with Serbia without securing herself against an attack by Russia. That means that she will be forced to mobilise the other half of her Army, for she cannot possibly surrender at discretion to a Russia all prepared for war. At the moment, however, in which Austria mobilises her whole Army, the collision between herself and Russia will become inevitable. But that, for Germany, is the *casus foederis*. If Germany is not to be false to her word and permit her ally to suffer annihilation at the hands of Russian superiority, she too, must mobilise. And that would bring about the mobilisation of the rest of Russia's military districts as a result. But then Russia will be able to say: I am being attacked by Germany. She will then assure herself of the support of France, which, according to the compact of alliance, is obliged to take part in the war, should her ally, Russia, be attacked. Thus the Franco-Russian alliance, so often held up to praise as a purely defensive compact, created only in order to meet the aggressive plans of Germany, will become active, and the mutual butchery of the civilised nations of Europe will begin.

It cannot be denied that the affair has been cunningly contrived by Russia. While giving continuous assurances that she was not yet 'mobilising', but only making preparations 'for an eventuality', that 'up to the present' she had called no reserves to the colours, she has been getting herself so ready for war that, when she actually issues her mobilisation orders, she will be prepared to move her armies forward in a very few days. Thus she puts Austria in a desperate position and shifts the responsibility to her, inasmuch as she is forcing Austria to secure herself against a surprise by Russia. She will say: You, Austria, are mobilising against us, so you want war with us. Russia assures Germany that she wishes to undertake nothing against her; but she knows perfectly well that Germany could not remain inactive in the event of a belligerent collision between her ally and Russia. So Germany, too, will be forced to mobilise, and again Russia will be enabled to say to the world: I did not want war,

[1] See 118.

but Germany brought it about. After this fashion things must and will develop, unless, one might say, a miracle happens to prevent at the last moment a war which will annihilate for decades the civilisation of almost all Europe.

Germany does not want to bring about this frightful war. But the German Government knows that it would be violating in ominous fashion the deep-rooted feelings of fidelity which are among the most beautiful traits of German character and would be setting itself against all the sentiments of the nation, if it did not come to the assistance of its ally at a moment which was to be decisive of the latter's existence.

According to the information at hand, France, also, appears to be taking measures preparatory to an eventual mobilisation. It is apparent that Russia and France are moving hand in hand as far as regards their preparations.

Thus, when the collision between Austria and Russia becomes inevitable, Germany, also, will mobilise, and will be prepared to take up the fight on two fronts.

With relation to the military preparations we have in view, should the case arise, it is of the greatest importance to ascertain as soon as possible whether Russia and France intend to let it come to a war with Germany. The further the preparations of our neighbours are carried, the quicker they will be able to complete their mobilisation. Thus the military situation is becoming from day to day more unfavourable for us, and can, if our prospective opponents prepare themselves further, unmolested, lead to fateful consequences for us.

126 Bethmann Hollweg to Schoen

Telegram 172   Berlin, 29 July 1914
Urgent   D. 12.50 p.m.
D.D. 341

Reports of French preparations for war are becoming more frequent. Kindly take up the matter with the French Government and call its attention to the fact that such activities would force us to take measures for self-protection. We should have to proclaim a state of 'risk of war', which, although it would not yet mean mobilisation or the calling in of any reserves to the colours, would nevertheless increase the tension. We continue to hope for the preservation of peace.[1]

[1] For Schoen's reply, see *D.D.* 367.

127 Bethmann Hollweg to Pourtalès

Telegram 134
D.D. 342

Berlin, 29 July 1914
D. 12.50 p.m.
R. 4.35 p.m.

Kindly call Mr Sazonov's serious attention to the fact that further continuation of Russian mobilisation measures would force us to mobilise, and in that case a European war could scarcely be prevented.[1]

128 Lichnowsky to Jagow

Telegram 174
D.D. 357

London, 29 July 1914
D. 2.08 p.m.
R. 5.07 p.m.

Have just had a talk with Sir Edward Grey, who considers the situation to be extremely serious. Yesterday's telegram from Sir Maurice de Bunsen, according to which Count Berchtold flatly declined Sazonov's proposal to empower Count Szápáry to confer with him about the Austro-Serbian quarrel, made a most unpleasant impression on him.[2] Even today Minister regards a direct exchange of opinions between Vienna and St Petersburg as the most feasible way, but asked me, however, what was to happen if, as the Vienna telegram seemed to indicate, the conferences were to collapse? Would we then be in a position to make any sort of a proposition? He had suggested a conference of the ambassadors here, which had not appeared to us to be feasible;[3] we had accepted the idea of a mediation *à quatre*, however, and he would be glad if we were in a position to make any kind of a proposal. I said that we regarded the Austro-Serbian quarrel as an affair in which we did not want to interfere, that we certainly could not expect Austria to submit to any humiliation. Austria was only doing what she had to do to create peace and order along her borders. This was also in the interest of the peace of Europe. Nor did Austria have any territorial acquisitions in view, but only the restoration of tolerable conditions.

He replied that he fully comprehended that Austria could not be humiliated, that there could be no talk of anything of that sort. He hoped that there might be found some way out which would permit Austria to

For Sazonov's reaction, see 137.   [2] *B.D.* 230.   [3] See 93 and 96.

receive full satisfaction, while not requiring Russia to stand inactively by until Austria had attained the final accomplishment of her warlike undertaking. That would be equal to the humiliation of Russia, which the latter could not possibly accept.

I replied that, as a matter of fact, Serbia did not concern Russia at all, and that Russia had all the less reason for interfering in this quarrel between neighbouring nations, since Austria had no intention of annexing Serbia.

He replied that even without annexation there was a way by which Serbia might be transformed into a vassal state of Austria. Russia could not and would not stand quietly by and see that accomplished. Russia's position among the orthodox Christians was at stake. He then made a suggestion as to whether it might not be possible to bring about an understanding as to the extension of Austria's military operations and as to the Monarchy's demands.[1]

I gathered again from the Minister's arguments today, that they are firmly convinced here, as I have repeatedly had the honour of reporting to Your Excellency, that unless Austria is willing to enter upon a discussion of the Serbian question, a world war is inevitable.

Sir E. Grey made here, half in joke, the remark that one never could tell whose house might remain unscorched in the midst of such a conflagration; that even little Holland was now arming herself.

The Minister was visibly pleased at my statement that Your Excellency had hitherto been endeavouring with some success to mediate between Vienna and St Petersburg,[2] and declared himself to be ready to participate in anything that promised the prospect of success.

I entreated the Minister again to warn St Petersburg against any precipitate decisions, and especially to prevent a general mobilisation there that would affect our frontiers also. The consequences would be beyond conception. The Minister promised me again to use his influence in this direction and to strive to keep them as cool-headed as possible.

The Minister informed me in conclusion that the Serbian Chargé d'Affaires at Rome had stated to the Marquis di San Giuliano that, with provision for certain interpretations as to the mode of participation by Austrian agents, Serbia would be inclined to swallow even Articles 5 and 6 of the Austrian note, thus accepting all demands. As it could not be assumed that Austria would be willing to enter upon direct negotiations with Serbia, the matter might be submitted to Serbia through the medium

---

[1] This idea of Grey's corresponded in principle to the Kaiser's proposal for a 'halt in Belgrade'; see 112.
[2] *D.D.* 314, 315.

of the Great Powers in the form of advice. Marquis di San Giuliano thought that on this basis an agreement might be arrived at. Above all, however, the Minister desired the immediate inauguration of the conferences. Sir E. Grey has had Marquis di San Giuliano referred to the Vienna and Berlin Cabinets, as, without their consent, he would not be in a position to take up the matter of a conference.

Finally, the Minister communicated to me a telegram from Sir George Buchanan, according to which the Russian Ministry for Foreign Affairs had informed the representatives of the foreign press that as the negotiations between Vienna and St Petersburg had come to an end without a result, Russia would feel herself obliged to regard the setting foot on Serbian soil by Austrian troops as a cause of war.[1]

129 Nicolas II to Wilhelm II

Telegram (unnumbered)   Peterhof Palace, 29 July 1914
D.D. 366   D. 8.20 p.m.
Int. Bez. I, 5, 214   R. 8.42 p.m.

Thanks for your conciliatory and friendly telegram.[2] Whereas official message[3] presented today by your Ambassador to my Minister was conveyed in a very different tone. Beg *you to explain this divergency*. It would be right to give over the Austro-Serbian problem to the *Hague conference*.[4] Trust in your wisdom and friendship.[5]

[1] See 121. In reality, only the question of Russian mobilisation against Austria was touched upon in the conversation with Buchanan.
[2] See 117.
[3] See 127.
[4] For the German reaction to this proposal see p. 269.
[5] For the Kaiser's reply see 142.

130 Lichnowsky to Jagow

Telegram 178   London, 29 July, 1914
D.D. 368   D. 6.39 p.m.
                                                    R. 9.12 p.m.

The worst and most scandalous piece of English pharisaism that I ever saw! I will never enter into a naval convention with such scoundrels.

That sets me out of the running.

Sir E. Grey just sent for me again. The Minister was entirely calm, but very grave, and received me with the words that the situation was continuing to grow more acute. Sazonov had stated that after the declaration of war he will no longer be in a position to negotiate with Austria direct, and *had requested them here to take up the mediation efforts again.* The Russian Government regards the cessation of hostilities for the present as a necessary preliminary to mediation.[1]

In spite of the Czar's appeal to me!

Good.

We have been trying to accomplish this for days, in vain!

Instead of mediation, a serious word to St Petersburg and Paris, to the effect that England would not help them would quiet the situation at once.

Sir E. Grey repeated his suggestion already reported, that we take part in a mediation *à quatre*, such as we had already accepted in principle.[2] It would seem to him to be a suitable basis for mediation, if Austria, after occupying Belgrade, for example, or other places, should announce her conditions.[3] Should Your Excellency, however, undertake mediation, a prospect I was able early this morning to put before him,[4] this would of course suit him equally well. But *mediation* seemed now to him to be urgently necessary, if *a European catastrophe were not to result.*

Sir E. Grey then said to me that he had a friendly and private communication to make to me, namely, that he did not want our warm personal relations and the in-

[1] *Int. Bez.* I, 5, 167.

[2] See **75**; moreover the relative clause is missing from the version of the telegram forwarded to the Kaiser.

[3] See **112** and **115**.

[4] The clause 'a prospect . . . before him' is missing from the copy of the telegram submitted to the Kaiser. This was plainly a reference to **128**.

timacy of our talks on all political matters to lead me astray, and he would like to *spare himself later the reproach (of) bad faith*. The British Government desired now as before to cultivate our previous friendship, and it could *stand aside as long as the conflict remained confined to Austria and Russia. But if we and France should be involved,* then the situation would immediately be altered, and the British Government would, *under the circumstances, find itself forced to make up its mind quickly.* In that event *it would not be practicable to stand aside and wait for any length of time.* 'If war breaks out, it will be *the greatest catastrophe* that the *world has ever seen.*' It was far from his desire to express any kind of a threat; he only wanted to protect me from disappointments and *himself* from the *reproach of bad faith*, and had therefore chosen the form of a private explanation.[1]

> *Aha! The common cheat!*
>
> *This means, we are to leave Austria in the lurch.*
> *Mean and Mephistophelian! Thoroughly English, however.*
>
> *Already made up.*
>
> *This means they will attack us.*
>
> *It remains.*

Sir E. Grey added also, that the *Government* of course had to *reckon with public opinion.* Up to the present it had in general been in favour of Austria, as the justice of a certain satisfaction due her was recognised; but now it was beginning *to turn completely to the other side,* as a result of Austrian stubbornness.

> *He has shown bad faith all these years just the same, down to his latest speech.*
> *We too!*
> *Newly created! If it wants to, it can turn and direct public opinion, as the press obeys it unconditionally.*
>
> *An absolute failure.*
>
> *With the aid of the jingo press.*

To my Italian colleague, who has just left me, Sir E. Grey said that he believed, if mediation were accepted, that he would be able to secure for Austria every possible satisfaction; there was no longer any question of a humiliating retreat for Austria, as the Serbs would in any case be punished and compelled, with the consent of Russia, to subordinate themselves to

[1] See the Kaiser's marginalia to 135.

Austria's wishes. Thus Austria could obtain guaranties for the future without a
war that would jeopardise the peace of
Europe.

England reveals herself in her true colours at a moment when she thinks that we are caught in the toils and, so to speak, disposed of! That mean crew of shopkeepers has tried to trick us with dinners and speeches. The boldest deception, the words of the King to Henry for me: 'We shall remain neutral and try to keep out of this as long as possible.'[1] Grey proves the King a liar, and his words to Lichnowsky are the outcome of a guilty conscience, because he feels that he has deceived us. At that, it is as a matter of fact a threat combined with a bluff, in order to separate us from Austria and to prevent us from mobilising, and to shift the responsibility for the war. He knows perfectly well that, if he were to say one single, serious, sharp and warning word at Paris and St Petersburg, and were to warn them to remain neutral, that both would become quiet at once. But he takes care not to speak the word, and threatens us instead! Common cur! England *alone* bears the responsibility for peace and war, not we any longer! That must also be made clear to the world.

131   Wilhelm II to Nicolas II

Telegram (unnumbered)   Berlin, 29 July 1914
D.D. 359   D. 29 July, evening
Int. Bez. I, 5, 238

I received your telegram[2] and share your wish that peace should be maintained. But as I told you in my first telegram,[3] I cannot consider Austria's action against Serbia an 'ignoble' war. Austria knows by experience that Serbian promises on paper are wholly unreliable. I understand its action must be judged as trending to get full guarantee that the Serbian promises shall become real facts. Thus my reasoning is borne out by the statement of the Austrian Cabinet that Austria does not want to make any territorial conquests at the expense of Serbia.[4] I therefore suggest that it would be quite possible for Russia to remain a spectator of the Austro-Serbian conflict without involving Europe in the most horrible war she ever witnessed. I think a direct understanding between your Government and Vienna possible and desirable and as I already telegraphed to you, my Government is continuing its exertions to promote it.[5] Of course military measures on the part of Russia which would be looked on by Austria as threatening would precipitate a calamity we both wish to avoid and

[1] *D.D.* 374.   [2] See 116.
[3] See 117.   [4] *Ö.D.* 10834.
[5] See 115.

jeopardise my position as mediator which I readily accepted on your appeal to my friendship and my help.[1]

132 Nicolas II to Wilhelm II

Telegram (unnumbered)	Peterhof Palace, 30 July 1914
D.D. 390	D. 1.20 a.m.
Int. Bez. I, 5, 275	R. 1.45 a.m.

Thank you heartily for your quick answer.[2] Am sending Tatistchev[3] this evening with instructions. The *military measures which have now come into force were decided five days ago* for reasons of *defence on account of Austria's preparations.* I hope from all my heart that these measures *won't in any way interfere* with your part as mediator which I greatly value. *We need your strong pressure on Austria* to come to an *understanding with us.*[4]

No! There is no thought of anything of that sort !!! Austria has only made a *partial* mobilisation against *Serbia* in the *south*. On the strength of that the Czar—as is openly admitted by him here—instituted 'mil. measures which have *now come into force*' against Austria and us and as a matter of fact five days ago. Thus it is almost a *week ahead* of us. And these measures are for *defence* against *Austria*, which is *in no way* attacking him !!! I cannot agree to any more mediation, since the Czar who requested it has at the same time secretly mobilised behind my back. It is only a manoeuvre, in order to hold us back and to increase the start they have already got. My work is at an end!

133 Bethmann Hollweg to Tschirschky

Telegram 192	Berlin, 30 July, 1914
Urgent	D. 2.55 a.m.
D.D. 395	R. 'midday'

The Imperial Ambassador at London telegraphs: 'Sir Edward Grey just sent for me . . . private explanation.'[5]

As a result we stand, in case Austria refuses all mediation, before a conflagration in which England will be against us; Italy and Roumania to all appearances will not go with us, and we two shall be opposed to four

[1] Original in English. For the Czar's reply see 132.
[2] See 131.
[3] Russian plenipotentiary officer in attendance on the German Kaiser.
[4] For Wilhelm II's reply see 157.
[5] Here Lichnowsky's latest telegram of 29 July (130) is cited.

Great Powers. On Germany, thanks to England's opposition, the principal burden of the fight would fall. Austria's political prestige, the honour of her arms, as well as her just claims against Serbia, could all be amply satisfied by the occupation of Belgrade or of other places.[1] She would be strengthening her status in the Balkans as well as in relation to Russia by the humiliation of Serbia. Under these circumstances we must urgently and impressively suggest to the consideration of the Vienna Cabinet the acceptance of mediation on the above-mentioned honourable conditions. The responsibility for the consequences that would otherwise follow would be an uncommonly heavy one both for Austria and for us.[2]

134 Bethmann Hollweg to Tschirschky

Telegram 193   Berlin, 30 July 1914
D.D. 396   D. 3.00 a.m.
                                                               R. 10.00 a.m.

Count Pourtalès telegraphs:[3] 'Sazonov, [who just had me sent for], informed me that the Vienna Cabinet had replied with a categorical refusal to the wish he had expressed here to enter upon direct conferences. As a result there was nothing left but to return to the proposal of Sir E. Grey for conversations *à quatre*. Minister stated that, in making this suggestion, the idea of expecting Austria to submit to a sort of European court of arbitration was far from his mind; that he was only looking for a way out of present difficulties, [and that in doing so he was grasping at every straw]. I replied again that I had no knowledge of the attitude of my Government towards Sir E. Grey's proposal, but that I could not help feeling that the order for Russian mobilisation, [in case it were really impending], was a great mistake, as long as they were insisting here that they really were serious in hoping to find a peaceable solution. Sazonov did not deny the imminence of mobilisation, but stated that Russia was compelled by Austria to take this step, but that mobilisation, however, was far from meaning war.'

This report does not agree with the impression that Your Excellency gave during the course of the conference of Count Berchtold with Mr

---

[1] See 115.

[2] Bethmann Hollweg had already indirectly raised the question of tactics when forwarding a telegram from London (*D.D.* 277) on the evening of 27 July; see also p. 221, and 134.

[3] The telegram reached Berlin at 9.45 p.m. on 29 July; the phrases in brackets were not transmitted to Vienna.

Schebeko.[1] Apparently there is some misunderstanding, which I beg to have cleared up. We can not expect Austria to deal with Serbia, with whom she is at war. The refusal to hold any exchange of opinions with St Petersburg, however, would be a serious error, as it would be direct provocation of Russia's armed interference, which Austria-Hungary is beyond all else interested to prevent.

We are, of course, ready to fulfil the obligations of our alliance, but must decline to be drawn wantonly into a world conflagration by Vienna, without having any regard paid to our counsel. Also, Vienna appears to disregard our advice in regard to the Italian question.

Please talk to Count Berchtold at once with all impressiveness and great seriousness.[2]

135 Pourtalès to Jagow

Telegram 189   St Petersburg, 30 July 1914
Urgent   D. 4.30 a.m.
D.D. 401   R. 7.10 a.m.

Just had one and a half hours' conference with Sazonov, who sent for me at midnight. Minister's purpose was to persuade me to advocate participation by my Government in a conference of four, in order to find a way to
Is Russian mobilisation a friendly means?!
move Austria by friendly means to drop those demands which infringe on the sovereignty of Serbia. I confined myself to promising to report the conversation, and took the stand that any exchange of opinions appeared to me to be a very difficult if not an impossible matter now that Russia had *decided to take the fateful step of*
Right.
mobilisation. Russia was demanding of us to do that to Austria which Austria was being reproached for doing
Very good.
to Serbia; to wit, *infringing upon her rights of sovereignty.* Since Austria had promised to *consider Russian interests* by her declaration of territorial disinterestedness, which,
Good.
on the part of a nation at war *meant a great deal*, the Austro-Hungarian Monarchy ought to be let alone while settling her affairs with Serbia. It would be time enough

[1] *D.D.* 356.
[2] For Tschirschky's reply, see *D.D.* 448.

Yes.

Nonsense! that sort
of policy conceals
within itself the
greatest dangers for
the Czar!

Aha! As I
suspected!

Nothing done as yet.

Right.

That was a partial
mobilisation of six
corps for a limited
purpose!

to return to the question of sparing Serbia's sovereign rights when *peace* was concluded. I added very earnestly that the whole Austro-Serbian matter took a *back seat* for the moment in the face of the *danger of a European conflagration*. I took great pains to impress the magnitude of this danger upon the Minister. Sazonov was not to be diverted from the idea that Russia could not leave Serbia in the lurch. No Government could follow such a policy here *without seriously endangering the Monarchy*.

During the course of the conversation *Sazonov wanted to argue* the inconsistency between the telegram of His Majesty the Emperor to the Czar[1] and Your Excellency's telegraphic instructions number 134.[2] I decidedly denied any, and pointed out that *even if we had already mobilised*, an appeal by my Most Gracious Master to the common interests of Monarchs *would not be inconsistent* with such a measure. I said that the communication I had made him this afternoon[3] according to the instructions of Your Excellency, had been no threat, but a friendly warning in the shape of a reference to the *automatic effect that the mobilisation here would have to have on us in consequence of the German-Austrian alliance*. Sazonov stated that the order for mobilisation *could no longer possibly be retracted*, and that the *Austrian mobilisation was to blame for it*.

From Sazonov's statements I received the impression that His Majesty's telegram did not fail of an effect on the Czar,[4] but that the Minister is busily striving to make sure that the Czar stands firm.

If mobilisation can no longer be retracted—*which is not true*—why, then, did the Czar appeal for my mediation three days afterward without mention of the issuance of the mobilisation order? That shows plainly that the mobilisation appeared to him to have been precipitate, and that after it he made this move *pro forma* in our direction for the sake of quieting his uneasy conscience, although he knew that it would no longer be of any use, as he did not feel himself to be strong enough to *stop* the mobilisation. Frivolity and weakness are to plunge the world into the most frightful war, which eventually aims at the destruction of Germany. For I have no doubt left about it: England, Russia and France have *agreed* among themselves—after laying the foundation of the *casus foederis* for us through Austria—to take the Austro-Serbian conflict for an *excuse* for waging a *war of extermination* against us. Hence Grey's cynical observation to

[1] See **131**.   [2] See **127**.   [3] I.e. 29 July.
[4] Under the influence of this telegram the Czar did in fact, once more, cancel the order for general mobilisation; see also **137**.

Lichnowsky 'as long as the war is *confined* to Russia and Austria, England would sit quiet, only when we and France *are mixed up in* it would he be compelled to make an active move against us';[1] i.e., either we are shamefully to betray our allies, *sacrifice* them to Russia—thereby breaking up the Triple Alliance, or we are to be attacked in common by the Triple Entente for our *fidelity to our allies* and punished, whereby they will satisfy their jealousy by joining in totally *ruining* us. That is the real naked situation *in nuce*, which, slowly and cleverly set going, certainly by Edward VII, has been carried on, and systematically built up by disowned conferences between England and Paris and St Petersburg; finally brought to a conclusion by George V and set to work. And thereby the stupidity and ineptitude of our ally is turned into a snare for us. So the famous '*encirclement*' of Germany has finally become a complete fact, despite every effort of our politicians and diplomats to prevent it. The net has been suddenly thrown over our head, and England sneeringly reaps the most brilliant success of her persistently prosecuted purely *anti-German world-policy*, against which we have proved ourselves helpless, while she twists the noose of our political and economic destruction out of our fidelity to Austria, as we squirm *isolated* in the net. A great achievement, which arouses the admiration even of him who is to be destroyed as its result! Edward VII is stronger after his death than am I who am still alive! And there have been people who believed that England could be won over or pacified, by this or that puny measure!!! Unremittingly, relentlessly she has pursued her object, with notes, holiday proposals, scares, Haldane, etc., until this point was reached. And we walked into the net and even went into the one-ship-programme in construction with the ardent hope of thus pacifying England!!! All my warnings, all my pleas were voiced for nothing. Now comes England's so-called gratitude for it! From the dilemma raised by our fidelity to the venerable old Emperor of Austria we are brought into a situation which offers England the desired pretext for annihilating us under the hypocritical cloak of justice, namely, of helping France on account of the reputed 'balance of power' in Europe, i.e., playing the card of all the European nations in England's favour against us! This whole business must now be ruthlessly uncovered and the mask of Christian peaceableness publicly and brusquely torn from its face in public, and the pharisaical hypocrisy exposed on the pillory!! And our consuls in Turkey and India, agents, etc., must fire the whole Mohammedan world to fierce rebellion against this hated, lying, conscienceless nation of shop-keepers; for if we are to be bled to death, England shall at least lose India.[2]

136   Sazonov to Isvolski

Telegram 1551   St Petersburg, 29 July 1914
Urgent
Int. Bez. I, 5, 221

The German Ambassador today informed me of the decision of his Government to mobilise, if Russia did not stop her military preparations.[3] Now, in point of fact, we only began these preparations in consequence of the mobilisation already undertaken by Austria, and owing to her evident unwillingness to accept any means of arriving at a peaceful settlement of her dispute with Serbia.

As we cannot comply with the wishes of Germany, we have no alternative but to hasten on our own military preparations and to assume

---

[1] See **130**.   [2] See also **179** (England and Turkey).   [3] See **127**.

that war is probably inevitable. Please inform the French Government of this, and add that we are sincerely grateful to them for the declaration which the French Ambassador made to me on their behalf, to the effect that we could count fully upon the assistance of our ally, France.[1] In the existing circumstances, that declaration is especially valuable to us.

It would be extremely desirable if England were also without delay to align herself with France and Russia, since only in this manner could she succeed in obviating a dangerous disturbance of the balance of power in Europe.[2]

137 Memorandum of the day of the Russian Ministry for Foreign Affairs
Int. Bez. I, 5, 224   St Petersburg, 29 July 1914

At 9.30 this morning the German Ambassador called up Baron Schilling on the telephone and said that he desired to see the Minister in order to make to him an 'agreeable communication.' Count Pourtalès, however, hastened to add, 'Toutefois pas trop d'optimisme'. Baron Schilling replied that latterly we had grown unaccustomed to 'pleasant' news from Berlin, and that therefore the Minister would certainly hear with pleasure what the Ambassador had to say.

S. D. Sazonov received Count Pourtalès at 11 a.m., who said that Germany was agreeable to continuing the attempts she had already made to induce the Vienna Cabinet to grant concessions. He requested, however, that strict secrecy should be maintained concerning this, as the announcement of such an intention on the part of the German Government might create the impression that the views of Austria and Germany were not fully in agreement in the present instance. In addition, the Ambassador insistently requested that the successful issue of the influence which Germany hoped to exercise in Vienna might not be hindered by a premature mobilisation on our part.[3]

After the Ambassador's departure the above-mentioned communication made by him was discussed by the Minister with A. A. Neratov, Baron Schilling and Prince Troubetzkoi. The question was raised whether Germany really intended to exert serious pressure in Vienna or whether the communication which Count Pourtalès was instructed to make was

---

[1] *Int. Bez.* I, 5, 172: Paléologue was acting without authority or was at any rate transgressing the limits set down in his instructions from Viviani of 27 July; see p. 224.

[2] See **107**.

[3] For Pourtalès' version of the above conversation, see *D.D.* 343.

only intended to lull us to sleep and so to postpone the Russian mobilisation and thus gain time wherein to make corresponding preparations. The general impression was that even if the sincerity of the German Government could be admitted, under the circumstances the possibility of arriving at any practical results in this direction must be doubted, because if Austria had gone thus far without the cooperation, or at least the tacit approval, of Germany, then it must be supposed that the influence of the latter in Vienna had greatly declined, and that therefore the German Government would not succeed in effecting much there at present.

At 3 p.m.[1] the German Ambassador came again to the Minister and read to him a telegram from the Imperial Chancellor, in which it was stated that if Russia continued her military preparations, even though she did not proceed to mobilise, Germany would find herself compelled to mobilise, in which case she would immediately proceed to take the offensive.[1] To this communication S. D. Sazonov sharply replied, 'Maintenant je n'ai plus de doute sur les vraies causes de l'intransigeance autrichienne.'[2] Count Pourtalès jumped up from his seat, and also sharply exclaimed, 'Je proteste de toutes mes forces, M. le Ministre, contre cette assertion blessante.'[3] The Minister drily replied that Germany still had an opportunity for proving the erroneousness of what he had said. The Minister and the Ambassador parted coolly.

Soon after the German Ambassador's departure, while A. A. Neratov and Baron Schilling were still in the Minister's cabinet, the telephone bell rang, and H.M. the Emperor personally informed S. D. Sazonov that he had just received a telegram from Kaiser Wilhelm, who urgently requested him not to allow events to develop into a war.[4] S. D. Sazonov utilised this opportunity to report to His Majesty concerning the announcement made to him a few minutes previously by Count Pourtalès, and pointed out how little the words of the Kaiser agreed with the instructions conveyed to his Ambassador. The Czar said that he was instantly telegraphing to Berlin to ask for an explanation of this apparent contradiction.[5] His Majesty gave permission to S. D. Sazonov to discuss the question of our mobilisation at once with the Minister for War and the Chief of the General Staff.

At this moment news was received of the commencement of the bombardment of Belgrade by the Austrians.[6]

[1] See 127; the telegram reached the German Embassy at 4.35 p.m.; according to Pourtalès the discussion only took place between 5.00 p.m. and 7.00 p.m.; see Pourtalès, *Am Scheidewege*, p. 45.

[2] 'Now I have no further doubts as to the true causes of Austria's intransigence.'

[3] 'Minister, I protest with all my might at this insulting assertion.'

[4] See 117.   [5] See 129.   [6] See 123.

The discussion between the three above-mentioned persons took place soon afterwards in the office of Lieut.-General Yanushkevich. In the adjoining room were Quartermaster-General Danilov, General Monke-vitz, and the Assistant to the Chief of the Chancellery of the Foreign Minister, N. A. Basili, in readiness immediately to carry out the arrange-ments necessitated by the decisions about to be come to. Those decisions were awaited with some trepidation, since all concerned knew how im-portant in respect of our military preparedness even a partial mobilisation would be if it were ordered, and still more a general mobilisation, as in the first case a partial mobilisation would render difficult a general mobilisation if such should prove subsequently necessary.

After examining the situation from all points, both the Ministers and the Chief of the General Staff decided that in view of the small probability of avoiding a war with Germany it was indispensable to prepare for it in every way in good time, and that therefore the risk could not be accepted of delaying a general mobilisation later by effecting a partial mobilisation now. The conclusion arrived at at this conference was at once reported by telephone to the Czar, who authorised the taking of steps accordingly. This information was received with enthusiasm by the small circle of those acquainted with what was in progress. Telegrams were at once dispatched to Paris and London to inform the respective Governments of the decision that had been come to.[1]

At the same time the Imperial Ambassador in Paris was instructed to thank the French Government for the declaration made by the French Ambassador yesterday. The Imperial Ambassador in London was directed to address to the English Government a request 'to range itself alongside of Russia and France without delay in order to prevent the European balance from being destroyed.'[2]

At about 11 p.m. the Minister for War informed the Foreign Minister by telephone that he had received orders from the Czar to stop the general mobilisation.

At about 1 a.m. the German Ambassador insistently requested the Minister to see him immediately, despite the lateness of the hour, on very pressing business.[3] S. D. Sazonov, who had already gone to bed, rose and received the Ambassador, who asked if we could not be satisfied with an assurance on the part of Austria not to violate the integrity of Serbia. The Minister replied that this would not suffice, and at the pressing

---

[1] See 136.   [2] See 136.

[3] According to Pourtalès (135) Sazonov demanded an interview with the German Ambassa-dor. This is scarcely probable, however, since Pourtalès had a commission to undertake with Sazonov and thus had a reason for coming to see the Minister.

request of the Ambassador drew up and handed to Count Pourtalès the text of a formula which set forth the conditions on which Russia would be willing to cease her armed preparations . . .[1]

138   Sverbejev to Sazonov

Telegram 140   Berlin, 29 July 1914
Int. Bez. I, 5, 241
Duplicate to Vienna

No. 1539[2] received.

In our friendly discussion the Minister[3] tried to convince me that the basis for our compromise with Austria might be the assurance given by the latter that she was not seeking any territorial gains but merely desired to teach Serbia a lesson for her inadmissible and provocative mode of behaviour. The conversation then turned to the rumour of our partial mobilisation, information of which the Foreign Minister claims only to have received today from the brief communication delivered to him in my presence. When Jagow learned from me that we had indeed been compelled to carry out the mobilisation of the four military districts mentioned in your telegram,[4] in connection with which I emphasised that these measures were in no way directed against Germany, he replied with considerable agitation that this unexpected news completely altered the situation and that he personally could now see no further possibility of averting a European war. 'If you mobilise against Austria and [take] measures against us' (I tried to talk him out of this) 'we shall be obliged to proclaim mobilisation against Russia,' then mobilisation against France would follow, and when all the Great Powers stood at arms war would seem to him inevitable.[5] At this, I pointed out to him that he had told the French Ambassador that our mobilisation on the Austrian frontier would still not be cause enough for the Germans to mobilise.[6] He could not deny that. But he added that all our measures on the [German] frontier were

---

[1] See **141**. According to Pourtalès, Sazonov had only drafted the formula on the morning of 30 July—not, then, the previous evening. L. Albertini, in *Origins*, II, p. 564, thus leaves the exact time open to question.
[2] See **118**.
[3] I.e., Secretary of State Jagow.
[4] See **118**.
[5] The effect of Moltke's memorandum (**125**) is here already clearly in evidence.
[6] See **103**.

precisely what caused Germany to think of her defence. On his enquiring whether Schebeko had been recalled, I replied in the negative. Towards the close of our discussion he read to me a telegram from Pourtalès which had been handed to him and which contained an account of your discussion with him on the subject of our partial mobilisation;[1] Jagow repeated to me that everything recounted here was, provisionally, his own personal view, but he would give me a definitive reply after immediate consultation with the Chancellor. A Council of Ministers is scheduled for tonight.

139 Goschen to Grey
Telegram 102   Berlin, 29 July 1914
Secret. Urgent   D. 30 July, 1.20 a.m.
B.D. 293   R. 30 July, 9.00 a.m.

Chancellor having just returned from Potsdam[2] sent for me again tonight and made the following strong bid for British neutrality in the event of war. He said he was continuing his efforts to maintain peace, but that in the event of a Russian attack on Austria, Germany's obligation as Austria's ally might, to his great regret, render a European conflagration inevitable, and in that case he hoped Great Britain would remain neutral. As far as he was able to judge key-note of British policy, it was evident that Great Britain would never allow France to be crushed. Such a result was not contemplated by Germany. The Imperial Government was ready to give every assurance to the British Government provided that Great Britain remained neutral that, in the event of a victorious war, Germany aimed at no territorial acquisitions at the expense of France.[3]

In answer to a question from me, His Excellency said that it would not be possible for him to give such an assurance as regards colonies.

Continuing, his Excellency said he was, further, ready to assure the British Government that Germany would respect neutrality and integrity of Holland as long as they were respected by Germany's adversaries.

As regards Belgium, His Excellency could not tell to what operations Germany might be forced by the action of France, but he could state that, provided that Belgium did not take sides against Germany, her integrity would be respected after the conclusion of the war.

[1] *D.D.* 343.
[2] From the so-called 'Potsdam Privy Council'.
[3] In contrast see **91**.

Finally, His Excellency said that he trusted that these assurances might form basis of a further understanding with England which, as you well know, had been the object of his policy ever since he had been Chancellor.

An assurance of British neutrality in conflict which present crisis might possibly produce would enable him to look forward to a general neutrality agreement between the two countries, the details of which it would, of course, be premature to discuss at the present moment.

His Excellency asked me how I thought you would view his request. I replied that I thought that you would like to retain full liberty of action, and that personally I did not consider it likely that you would care to bind yourself to any course of action at this stage of events.

After our conversation I communicated to His Excellency the contents of your telegram 227,[1] and he begged me to convey to you his best thanks.[2]

Minute

The only comment that need be made on these astounding proposals is that they reflect discredit on the statesman who makes them.

Incidentally it is of interest to note that Germany practically admits the intention to violate Belgian neutrality[3] but to endeavour to respect that of Holland (in order to safeguard German imports viâ the Rhine and Rotterdam).

It is clear that Germany is practically determined to go to war, and that the one restraining influence so far has been the fear of England joining in the defence of France and Belgium.—E. A. C. 30 July.

140 Berchtold to Szápáry

Telegram 198   Vienna, 30 July 1914
Ö.D. 11092   D. 1.20 p.m.

From Your Excellency's telegram 176 of 29 July[4] I gather that Mr Sazonov may possibly have misunderstood my answer concerning his proposal for the continuation of the conversation entered upon by Your Excellency.

I am of course, as always, ready to explain to Mr Sazonov the different points of our Note to Serbia, which however have since been forestalled

---

[1] *B.D.* 266.
[2] For Bethmann Hollweg's record of his declaration see *D.D.* 373. For further details of the discussion see 167. For Grey's reply see 151.
[3] See 91.   [4] *Ö.D.* 11001.

by events. At the same time I should also very much like to talk over amicably and confidentially questions directly concerning our relations with Russia according to the suggestion of the Russian Minister for Foreign Affairs,[1] which Mr Schebeko interpreted to me and which might clear up many matters which, I regret to say, are not quite clear and which might assure the so much desired peaceful development of neighbourly relations.

Will Your Excellency please ask Mr Sazonov, as though the question came from you, what subjects the Minister would like this conversation to embrace eventually; also, in a non-compromising manner, proceed to enter upon a discussion of matters in general, eliminating of course from the outset everything running counter to Russian interests, and express your readiness to report to me on the subject.

Please to act at once—perhaps in connection with the communications for Mr Sazonov forwarded to you in the instructions contained in telegram 199 of 30 inst.[2] in the above indicated sense, and report the result to me immediately.[3]

141   Szögyény to Berchtold

Telegram 328   Berlin, 30 July 1914
Strictly secret   D. 5.30 p.m.
Ö.D. 11030   R. 7.20 p.m.

Whilst hitherto I had been able to observe the greatest calm in all influential circles, concerning the eventuality of a European conflict, I must own, that I now have the feeling that in the last few days a state of nervousness has seized them which is not wholly only due to the greater imminence of the question of peace or war.

The reason for this change of feeling here is the fear I already reported in my telegrams, that Italy, in case of a general conflict, would not fulfil its duty as an ally of the Triple Alliance; but rather that its general attitude towards us might become downright doubtful.

If however the Triple Alliance, so runs the further argument of the German Government, cannot be considered as an integral whole, our chances in the great conflict must be considerably worse. Italy must therefore, absolutely, remain in the Triple Alliance and what is more, as an active factor.

[1] *Int. Bez.* I, 5, 188.   [2] *Ö.D.* 11020.   [3] For Szápáry's reply, see *Ö.D.* 11177.

Your Excellency is therefore most emphatically advised to interpret most liberally Article VII of the Treaty of the Triple Alliance and to meet Italy's wishes as concerns the question of compensation as much as possible and to declare as soon as possible that our readiness at once to enter upon negotiations regarding the interpretation of Article VII (with a view to the most far-reaching concessions) admitting at the same time our liability to grant compensation. (Whereby according to opinion prevalent here the Trentino is of course out of question.)

This wish of Germany's is not, according to my opinion due to a diminution of its fidelity as an ally towards Austria-Hungary, but solely based on the conviction that Austria-Hungary and Germany absolutely need Italy in order to enter the general conflict with safety.

The concessions to Italy communicated in Your Excellency's telegram 280 secret of 28 inst.[1] are according to report of the German Ambassador in Rome not considered sufficient by the Italian Cabinet.[2]

As the Imperial and Royal military attaché reports, the Chief of General Staff, Count Moltke, has spoken to him in the same sense concerning the absolute necessity of an immediate understanding with Italy.

I cannot help, in view of the gravity of the situation absolutely agreeing with the above reported conviction of the German Government.

141a Pourtalès to Jagow

Telegram 192
D.D. 421

St Petersburg, 30 July 1914
D. 1.01 p.m.
R. 3.52 p.m.

Have just talked with Sazonov according to instructions in telegram 139.[3] Minister repeated his declaration of last night[4] that assurance of territorial disinterestedness on the part of Austria-Hungary did not satisfy Russia. Any other policy he could not at the present time prosecute without endangering the life of the Czar. I requested Sazonov—stating in advance, however, that I believed any prospect of the fulfilment of his wishes by Austria to be hopeless—to formulate them once more for me, and in writing, and to bear in mind that, if there were in any case to be the least prospect of a peaceful solution, he would absolutely have to agree to some sort of a compromise. Minister thereupon set down the following:

---

[1] *Ö.D.* 10909.
[3] *D.D.* 380.
[2] Perhaps Szögyény means Flotow's Telegram 154, *D.D.* 419.
[4] See **135**.

'If Austria declares that in recognition of the fact that its conflict with Serbia has assumed the character of a question of European interest, it declares itself ready to eliminate from its ultimatum those points which infringe on Serbia's sovereign rights, then Russia agrees to suspend all military preparations.'

Even if these demands prove scarcely acceptable, it is still remarkable that Sazonov's document should not contain a word requiring the immediate suspension of Austria's punitive expedition. The Minister would not agree to my proposition that Russia might, perhaps, declare herself to be satisfied if Austria should give certain assurances along these lines upon the *Conclusion of Peace*.[1]

142 Wilhelm II to Nicolas II

Telegram (unnumbered)   Berlin, 30 July 1914
D.D. 420   D. 3.30 p.m.
Int. Bez. I, 5, 299

Best thanks for telegram.[2] It is quite out of the question that my Ambassador's language could have been in contradiction with the tenor of my telegram. Count Pourtalès was instructed to draw the attention of your Government to the danger and grave consequences involved by a mobilisation;[3] I said the same in my telegram to you. Austria has only mobilised against *Serbia* and only a *part* of her army. If, as it is now the case, according to the communication by you and your Government, Russia mobilises against Austria,[4] my role as mediator you kindly intrusted me with, and which I accepted at your express prayer, will be endangered if not ruined. The whole weight of the decision lies solely on your shoulders now, who have to bear the responsibility for peace or war.[5]

---

[1] See also Bethmann Hollweg's marginal note: 'What point of the Austrian ultimatum has Serbia really rejected? To my knowledge only the cooperation of Austrian officials in the judicial proceedings. Austria could forgo this cooperation on the condition that it occupies parts of Serbia with its troops until the completion of negotiations.' In conjunction with this see also Zimmermann's marginal note: 'Settled orally.' It is not known in which sense, but at all events the policy of the German Reich never reverted to the concession foreshadowed in the Chancellor's remark.

[2] See 129.

[3] See 127.

[4] See 118.

[5] For the Czar's reply, see 156.

143 Bethmann Hollweg to Tschirschky

Telegram 200
Urgent
D.D. 441

Berlin, 30 July 1914
D. 9.00 p.m.
R. 31 July, 3.00 a.m.

If Vienna declines to give in in any direction, especially along the lines of the last Grey proposal[1] (telegram 192), as may be assumed from the telephone conversation of Your Excellency with Mr von Stumm,[2] it will hardly be possible any longer to place the guilt of the outbreak of a European conflagration on Russia's shoulders.[3] His Majesty undertook intervention at Vienna at the request of the Czar since he could not refuse to do so without creating the incontrovertible suspicion that we wanted war. The success of this intervention is, of course, rendered difficult, inasmuch as Russia has mobilised against Austria. This we have announced to England today, adding that we had already suggested in a friendly tone, both at Paris and St Petersburg, the cessation of French and Russian war preparations,[4] so that we could take a new step in this direction only through an ultimatum, which would mean war. We suggested to Sir Edward Grey, nevertheless, that he work energetically along this line at Paris and St Petersburg,[5] and have just received through Lichnowsky his assurance to that effect.[6] If England's efforts succeed, while Vienna declines everything, Vienna will be giving documentary evidence that it absolutely wants a war, into which we shall be drawn, while Russia remains free of responsibility.[7] That would place us, in the eyes of our own people, in an untenable situation.[8] Thus we can only urgently advise that Austria accept the Grey proposal,[9] which preserves her status for her in every way.

Your Excellency will at once express yourself most emphatically on this matter to Count Berchtold, perhaps also to Count Tisza.

His Majesty this evening sent the following telegram to the Emperor Franz Joseph: 'I did not feel myself able to refuse the personal plea of the Czar that I undertake to attempt mediation for the prevention of a world conflagration and the maintenance of world peace,[10] and had proposals submitted to your Government yesterday and today through my Ambassador. Among other things, they provide that Austria should

[1] See 133. [2] See 145. [3] See 114, 115 and 125.
[4] See 126 and 127. [5] *D.D.* 409. [6] *D.D.* 435.
[7] See 114, 115 and 125.
[8] In other words, the coming war can only be justified in the eyes of the German people if they do not hold the Central Powers responsible. Thus, the onus must at all costs be shifted on to Russia.
[9] See 133. [10] See 116.

announce her conditions after occupying Belgrade or other places.[1] I should be honestly obliged to you, if you would favour me with your decision as soon as possible.[2]

144 Jagow to various Missions

Confidential   Berlin, 30 July 1914
D.D. 423

In view of the facts which the Austro-Hungarian Government made public in its note to the Serbian Government, the last doubt that the bloody deed to which the heir to the Austrian throne and his wife fell victims was at least planned with the connivance of members of the Serbian Government and army must vanish. It was the result of the Greater Serbia aspirations, which, for a number of years, have become a lasting disturbance both to the Austro-Hungarian Monarchy and to all Europe.

The Greater Serbian chauvinism stood out in particularly striking form during the Bosnian crisis. Only to the far-reaching self-control and moderation of the Austro-Hungarian Government, and to the energetic intervention of the Great Powers, can be credited the fact that the provocations to which Austria-Hungary was at that time subjected on the part of Serbia, did not lead to war. The assurance of future good behaviour which the Serbian Government gave at that period, it failed to live up to. With the connivance, or at least with the silent consent of official Serbia, the Greater Serbia propaganda has continued to increase both in extent and intensity. It would be consistent neither with its dignity nor with its right to self-protection, should the Austro-Hungarian Government any longer regard inactively the machinations on the other side of its border by which the security and the integrity of its territory are being constantly threatened. In this state of affairs, both the procedure as well as the demands of the Austro-Hungarian Government must be deemed to be justified.

The reply of the Serbian Government to the demands made on it by the Austro-Hungarian Government on 23 inst. through its representative at Belgrade, in the meantime, goes to prove that the ruling authorities in Serbia are not inclined to cease from their previous policy or from their subversive activities. Thus, there remains nothing for the Austro-Hungarian Government to do, unless it is willing to make the final sacrifice of its status as a Great Power, but to enforce its demands by the use of heavy pressure, or, if need be, by taking military measures.

[1] See 115.   [2] For Franz Joseph's reply see *Ö.D.* 11118, *D.D.* 482.

A number of Russian organs of public opinion consider it to be the self-evident right as well as the duty of Russia, actively to take the part of Serbia in the conflict between Austria-Hungary and Serbia. The *Nowoje Wremja* even believes itself authorised to dare to allege German responsibility for the European conflagration which would result from such a step by Russia, because Germany did not influence Austria-Hungary to yield. In this matter, the Russian press is distorting facts to suit itself. It was not Austria-Hungary which evoked the conflict with Serbia; but it was Serbia which, by unscrupulously favouring the Greater Serbia aspirations, even in portions of the Austro-Hungarian Monarchy, endangered the very existence of the latter and brought about conditions which ultimately found their expression in the criminal deed of Sarajevo. If Russia believes herself compelled to enter the conflict on behalf of Serbia, she certainly has a right to do so. But she must fully understand that by so doing she is adopting as her own the Serbian efforts to undermine the existence of the Austro-Hungarian Monarchy, and that she alone will be responsible if a European war results from the Austro-Serbian affair, which all the other Great Powers desire to localise.[1] This Russian responsibility is as clear as day, and weighs all the more heavily since Count Berchtold has officially announced to Russia that it (Austria-Hungary) desires neither to acquire any Serbian territory nor to encroach upon the status of the Kingdom of Serbia, but is merely anxious to put an end to the Serbian intrigues which are endangering its existence.[2]

The attitude of the Imperial Government in this matter is plainly fore-shadowed. The final object of the Panslavic agitations carried on against Austria-Hungary is, through the destruction of the Danube Monarchy, the breaking-up or the weakening of the Triple Alliance and, as a result, the complete isolation of the German Empire. Accordingly, our own self-interest summon us to the side of Austria-Hungary. The duty of preserving Europe from a general war, if that should be in any way possible, commands us at the same time to support those efforts which have the localisation of the conflict as their object, faithful to the principles of that policy which we have prosecuted for over forty-four years in the interest of the maintenance of European peace. However, should this conflagration centre be extended, contrary to our hopes, and owing to Russia's interference, then, true to the obligations of our alliance, we should have to support the neighbouring Monarchy with all the power of the Empire.

I request Your Excellency to utilise the foregoing communication for the regulation of your speech.

[1] See **114, 115, 125** and **143**.
[2] See Berchtold to Szápáry, 25 and 28 July; *Ö.D.* 10685, 10834.

145   Tschirschky to Jagow

Telegram 142   Vienna, 30 July 1914
D.D. 465   D. 31 July, 1.35 a.m.
                                                       R. 31 July, 4.35 a.m.

Telegram 192,[1] which arrived at noon, was brought to me immediately after being decoded at the Ministry of Foreign Affairs, while I was breakfasting with Count Berchtold. Immediately after getting up from table I carried out the instructions contained in it relative to Count Berchtold, in the presence of Count Forgách. The Minister, who listened, pale and silent, while it was read twice—Count Forgách taking notes— said at the conclusion that he would make a report to his Emperor at once about it.

I called the attention of the Minister particularly to the fact that the justifiable claims of Austria would seem to be fully protected by a castigation of Serbia together with the acquisition of guaranties for the latter's future good behaviour by the acceptance of the mediation proposal, and that the object declared from the beginning by the Monarchy to be that of the action against Serbia, would thus be attained without unchaining a world war. Under these circumstances, it seemed to me that a complete refusal of the mediation was out of the question. The honour of the Austrian arms would be satisfied by the occupation of Serbian territory by Austro-Hungarian troops. That this military occupation was to take place with the express consent of Russia unquestionably meant an important strengthening of Austrian influence with regard to Russia and in the Balkans. I begged both gentlemen to keep in mind the incalculable consequences of a refusal of the mediation.

When Count Berchtold left the room to change his dress for his audience with the Emperor, I appealed very seriously to Count Forgách's conscience; he too expressed it as his opinion that agreement to the mediation was requisite. Just the same, the restriction of the military operations now in progress appeared to him to be scarcely possible.

This afternoon, both before and after the telephone conversation with Mr. von Stumm,[2] I again took occasion to speak very seriously, from our points of view, with Count Forgách and Count Hoyos. Both of them assured me that restriction of the military operations was, in their opinion, out of the question, in view of the feeling in the Army and among the people. Count Tisza will appear in Vienna early tomorrow. His opinion must be obtained on this far-reaching decision.

[1] See 133.   [2] See 143.

Conrad von Hötzendorf was to submit to the Emperor this evening the order for general mobilisation as the reply to the measures already taken on the part of the Russians. They were not quite clear as to whether, in the present state of affairs, the mobilisation was called for.

146 Sazonov to Sverbejev

Telegram 1554   St Petersburg, 30 July 1914
Int. Bez. I, 5, 277
Very urgent
Communicated to Paris, London and Vienna

Request urgent dispositions.

The German Ambassador, who has just seen me, enquired whether we could not be content with Austria's promise not to violate the integrity of the kingdom of Serbia. I replied that this declaration was insufficient.[1]

Upon being urgently requested by the Ambassador to indicate on what conditions we would still agree to a suspension of our rearmament I dictated to him for urgent forwarding to Berlin the declaration contained under no. 2 in the telegram.[2]

Please telegraph urgently how the German Government reacts to this new proof of our readiness to do our utmost for a peaceful settlement of the question, because we cannot entertain the possibility of such negotiations merely being used by Austria and Germany to buy time in their favour.[3]

147 Memorandum of the day of the Russian Ministry for Foreign Affairs

Int. Bez. I, 5, 284   St Petersburg, 30 July 1914

Between 9 and 10 a.m. the Minister for Foreign Affairs spoke to the Minister for Agriculture by telephone. Both of them were greatly disturbed at the stoppage of the general mobilisation,[4] as they fully realized that this threatened to place Russia in an extremely difficult position in the event of relations with Germany becoming acute. S. D. Sazonov advised

[1] See 141.
[2] Sazonov's formula (*Int. Bez.* I, 5, 278) made up the second half of Telegram 1554; see 141.
[3] For Benckendorff's and Sverbejev's replies, see *Int. Bez.* I, 5, 286 and 305.
[4] See 137.

A. V. Krivoshein to beg an audience of the Czar in order to represent to His Majesty the dangers called forth by the change.

At 11 a.m. the Minister for Foreign Affairs again met the Minister for War and the Chief of the General Staff. Information received during the night still further strengthened the opinion which they all held that it was imperative to prepare for a serious war without loss of time. Accordingly the Ministers and the Chief of the Staff adhered to the view which they had expressed yesterday to the effect that it was indispensable to proceed to a general mobilisation. Adjutant-General Sukhomlinov and General Yanushkevich again endeavoured by telephone to persuade the Czar to revert to his decision of yesterday to permit a general mobilisation. His Majesty decidedly refused to do so, and finally shortly declared that the conversation was at an end. General Yanushkevich, who at this moment was holding the telephone receiver, only succeeded in reporting that the Minister for Foreign Affairs was there with him and asked to be allowed to say a few words to His Majesty. A somewhat lengthy silence ensued, after which the Czar expressed his willingness to hear the Minister. S. D. Sazonov requested His Majesty to receive him today, to enable him to present a report concerning the political situation which admitted of no delay. After a silence, the Czar asked: 'Is it all the same to you if I receive you at 3 o'clock, at the same time as Tatistchev, as otherwise I have not a free minute today?' The Minister thanked His Majesty and said that he would present himself at the hour named.

The Chief of the Staff warmly pleaded with S. D. Sazonov to persuade the Czar without fail to consent to a general mobilisation in view of the extreme danger that would result for us if we were not ready for war with Germany should circumstances demand the taking of decisive measures by us after the success of a general mobilisation had been compromised by recourse to a partial mobilisation. General Yanushkevich requested the Minister that in the event of his succeeding in persuading the Czar he would telephone to him to that effect from Peterhof, in order that he might immediately take the necessary steps, as it would be requisite first of all to stop as soon as possible the partial mobilisation which had already commenced and substitute fresh orders for those which had been issued. 'After that,' said Yanushkevich, 'I shall go away, smash my telephone and generally adopt measures which will prevent anyone from finding me for the purpose of giving contrary orders which would again stop our general mobilisation.'

On his return to the Foreign Office, S. D. Sazonov had an interview with the French Ambassador.[1]

[1] *D.F.* XI, 342.

Meanwhile A. V. Krivoshein informed S. D. Sazonov that in reply to his request that the Czar would receive him he was told that His Majesty was so extremely occupied today that he could not see him. Krivoshein then expressed a desire to see S. D. Sazonov before the latter went to Peterhof. It was decided that they should breakfast together at Donon's, and at 12.30 they and Baron Schilling met in a private room there. The general state of mind was tense and the conversation was almost exclusively concerned with the necessity for insisting upon a general mobilisation at the earliest possible moment, in view of the inevitability of war with Germany, which every moment became clearer. A. V. Krivoshein expressed the hope that S. D. Sazonov would succeed in persuading the Czar, as otherwise, to use his own words, we should be marching towards a certain catastrophe.

At 2 p.m. the Minister for Foreign Affairs left for Peterhof, together with Major-General Tatistchev, and both of them were received together there in the Alexander Palace by His Majesty. During the course of nearly an hour the Minister attempted to show that war was becoming inevitable, as it was clear to everybody that Germany had decided to bring about a collision, as otherwise she would not have rejected all the pacificatory proposals that had been made and could easily have brought her ally to reason. Under these circumstances it only remained to do everything that was necessary to meet war fully armed and under the most favourable conditions for ourselves. Therefore it was better to put away any fears that our warlike preparations would bring about a war, and to continue these preparations carefully rather than by reason of such fears to be taken unawares by war.[1]

The firm desire of the Czar to avoid war at all costs, the horrors of which filled him with repulsion, led His Majesty in his full realisation of the heavy responsibility which he took upon himself in this fateful hour to explore every possible means for averting the approaching danger. Consequently he refused during a long time to agree to the adoption of measures which, however indispensable from a military point of view, were calculated, as he clearly saw, to hasten a decision in an undesirable sense.

The tenseness of feeling experienced by the Czar at this time found expression, amongst other signs, in the irritability most unusual with him, with which His Majesty interrupted General Tatistchev. The latter, who throughout had taken no part in the conversation, said in a moment of silence: 'Yes, it is hard to decide.' His Majesty replied in a rough and

[1] This is in fact a precise description of the dilemma in which Russian policy was placed at this time.

displeased tone: 'I will decide'—in order by this means to prevent the General from intervening any further in the conversation.

Finally the Czar agreed that under the existing circumstances it would be very dangerous not to make timely preparations for what was apparently an inevitable war, and therefore gave his decision in favour of an immediate general mobilisation.

S. D. Sazonov requested the Imperial permission to inform the Chief of the General Staff of this immediately by telephone, and this being granted, he hastened to the telephone on the ground floor of the palace. Having transmitted the Imperial order to General Yanushkevich, who was waiting impatiently for it, the Minister, with reference to their conversation that morning, added: 'Now you can smash your telephone.'

Meanwhile His Majesty still cherished the hope of finding some means of preventing the general mobilisation from becoming an irrevocable *casus belli*. To this end the Czar, in a telegram dispatched to the Kaiser Wilhelm on this same day regarding the decision come to, gave his solemn word that despite the mobilisation referred to[1] . . .

148 Viviani to the French Ambassadors at St Petersburg and London

Telegrams 453, 373, 374   Paris, 30 July 1914
Confidential   D. 7.00, 7.10 a.m.
D.F. XI, 305 (*F.Y.B.* 101)

Mr Isvolsky came tonight to tell me that the German Ambassador has notified Mr Sazonov of the decision of his Government to mobilise the army if Russia does not cease her military preparations.[2]

The Minister for Foreign Affairs of the Czar points out that these preparations were only commenced after Austria had mobilised eight army corps and had refused to arrange peacefully her differences with Serbia. Mr Sazonov declares that in these circumstances Russia can only expedite her arming and consider war as imminent, that she counts on the help of France as an ally, and that she considers it desirable that England should join Russia and France without loss of time. For the rest the Government of the Republic is determined, as I have told you in my telegram of the 27 inst.,[3] not to neglect any effort towards a solution of the conflict in the interest of universal peace.

On the other hand, France is resolved to fulfil all the obligations of her

[1] The text ends abruptly here. For the Czar's telegram to Wilhelm II, see 156.
[2] See 127 and 136.   [3] See *D.F.* XI, 138; see also p. 224.

alliance. The conversation entered into between the Powers which are less directly interested still allows of the hope that peace may be preserved; I therefore think it would be well that, in taking any precautionary measures of defence which Russia thinks must go on, she should not immediately take any step which may offer to Germany a pretext for a total or partial mobilisation of her forces.

For London only

I would ask you to inform Sir Edward Grey, without delay, of these developments and remind him of the letters which you exchanged with him in 1912 on the subject of the investigations that the two Governments must undertake together in the event of tension in Europe.[1]

149 Jules Cambon to Viviani

Telegrams 225, 226	Berlin, 30 July 1914
Secret	D. 4.52, 5.15 p.m.
D.F. XI, 339 (*F.Y.B.* 105)	R. 6.10, 6.20 p.m.

Following my preceding telegram.[2]

One of the Ambassadors with whom I have very close relations saw Herr von Zimmermann at 2 o'clock. According to the Under-Secretary of State the military authorities are very anxious that mobilisation should be ordered, because every delay makes Germany lose some of her advantages. Nevertheless up to the present the haste of the General Staff, which sees war in mobilisation, had been successfully prevented.[3] In any case mobilisation may be decided upon at any moment. I do not know who has issued in the *Lokalanzeiger*, a paper which is usually semi-official, premature news calculated to cause excitement in France.

What matters is to make public mobilisation measures in France only after they have been definitely decided in Germany, so that British public opinion, which plays such an important role in what is happening, cannot attribute to us any initiative that led to war.

[1] See *D.F.* IV, no. 534, Appendix.
[2] *D.F.* XI, 330. In his telegram Cambon conveyed Jagow's denial of the German mobilisation announced in the *Lokalanzeiger*; see p. 270.
[3] See p. 270.

I have reasons to believe that all the measures for mobilisation which can be taken before the publication of the general order of mobilisation have already been taken here. It is apparently intended to make us publish our mobilisation first. It is up to us to undo that calculation and not to give way to impulses of impatience, which will certainly arise in the press and in public opinion in Paris.

150   Goschen to Grey

Telegram 103
B.D. 305

Berlin, 30 July 1914
D. 1.45 p.m.
R. 3.35 p.m.

Secretary of State for Foreign Affairs informs me that immediately on receipt of Prince Lichnowsky's telegram recording his last conversation with you[1] he asked Austro-Hungarian Government whether they would be willing to accept mediation on basis of occupation by Austrian troops of Belgrade or some other point and issue their conditions from there.[2] He has up till now received no reply, but he fears Russian mobilisation against Austria will have increased difficulties, as Austria-Hungary, who has as yet only mobilised against Serbia, will probably find it necessary also against Russia. Secretary of State for Foreign Affairs says if you can succeed in getting Russia to agree to above basis for an arrangement and in persuading her in the meantime to take no steps which might be regarded as an act of aggression against Austria, he still sees some chance that European peace may be preserved.

He begged me to impress on you difficulty of position of Germany in view of Russian mobilisation and military measures which he hears are being taken in France. Beyond recall of officers on leave—a measure which had been officially taken after, and not before, visit of French Ambassador yesterday—Imperial Government had done nothing special in way of military preparations. Something, however, would have soon to be done, for it might be too late, and if, and when, they mobilised, they would have to mobilise on three sides. He regretted this, as he knew France did not desire war, but it would be a military necessity.

His Excellency added that telegram received from Prince Lichnowsky last night[3] contains matter which he had heard with regret, but not exactly

---

[1] See 130.   [2] See 133.   [3] See 130.

with surprise, and at all events he thoroughly appreciated frankness and loyalty with which you had spoken.

He also told me that this telegram had only reached Berlin very late last night; had it been received earlier Chancellor would, of course, not have spoken to me in way he had done.[1]

151 Grey to Goschen

Telegram 231   London, 30 July 1914
B.D. 303   D. 3.30 p.m.
Your telegram 102.[2]

You must inform German Chancellor that his proposal that we should bind ourselves to neutrality on such terms cannot for a moment be entertained.

He asks us in effect to engage to stand by while French colonies are taken and France is beaten so long as Germany does not take French territory as distinct from the colonies.

From the material point of view such a proposal is unacceptable, for France could be so crushed as to lose her position as a Great Power, and become subordinate to German policy without further territory in Europe being taken from her.[3]

But apart from that, for us to make this bargain with Germany at the expense of France would be a disgrace from which the good name of this country would never recover.

The Chancellor also in effect asks us to bargain away whatever obligation or interest we have as regards the neutrality of Belgium. We could not entertain that bargain either.

Having said so much, it is unnecessary to examine whether prospect of a future general neutrality agreement between Germany and England would offer positive advantages sufficient to compensate us for tying our hands now. My answer must be that we must preserve our full freedom

[1] See **139** and **167**.
[2] See **139**.
[3] This very point was the essence of Bethmann Hollweg's subsequent policy towards France as formulated in his September Programme, if we make allowances here for the additional aim of annexing certain areas of French territory: see F. Fischer, *Griff nach der Weltmacht*, pp. 110f. English fears were thus thoroughly realistic and all too justified since a defeated France, integrated (even without direct annexation) into a German 'Central Europe' would have found herself in a state of permanent dependence upon a 'Greater Germany'.

to act as circumstances may seem to us to require in any development of the present crisis, so unfavourable and regrettable, as the Chancellor contemplates.

You should add most earnestly that the one way of maintaining the good relations between England and Germany is to continue to work together to preserve the peace of Europe; if we succeed in this object, the mutual relations of Germany and England will, I believe, be *ipso facto* improved and strengthened. For that object His Majesty's Government will work in that way with all sincerity and goodwill.

And if the peace of Europe can be preserved, and this crisis be safely passed, my own endeavour would be to promote some arrangement to which Germany could be a party, by which she could be assured that no hostile or aggressive policy would be pursued against her or her allies by France, Russia, and ourselves, jointly or separately. I have desired this and worked for it, as far as I could, through the last Balkan crisis, and, Germany having a corresponding object, our relations sensibly improved. The idea has hitherto been too Utopian to form the subject of definite proposals, but if this present crisis, so much more acute than any that Europe has had for generations, be safely passed, I am hopeful that the reaction and relief that will follow may make some definite rapprochement between the Powers more possible than before.[1]

152 Bertie to Grey

Telegram 95   Paris, 30 July 1914
B.D. 318   D. 8.15 p.m.
                                                                     R. 10.30 p.m.

I had audience of President of the Republic this evening in order to give him your message of congratulation on success of his visit to St Petersburg, for which he wishes me to thank you.

He told me that in middle of last night French Government received information that German Government had informed Russian Government that unless Russia stopped her mobilisation Germany would mobilise.[2] In middle of day a further report from St Petersburg stated that German communication had been modified and had become a request to be informed on what conditions Russia would consent to de-

---

[1] The text of Goschen's corresponding *démarche* of 31 July is to be found in *D.D.* 497. For Goschen's reply see *B.D.* 336.   [2] See **127** and **136**.

mobilisation, answer to which is that she will do so provided that Austria will give assurance that she will respect sovereignty of Serbia, and will submit certain of the demands of Austrian note not accepted by Serbia to an international discussion.[1]

President of Republic thinks that Austro-Hungarian Government will not accept these Russian conditions.[2] He is convinced that preservation of peace between Powers is in hands of England, for if His Majesty's Government announce that, in the event of conflict between Germany and France, resulting from present differences between Austria and Serbia, England would come to aid of France, there would be no war, for Germany would at once modify her attitude.[3]

I explained to him how difficult it would be for His Majesty's Government to make such an announcement. He, however, said that he must maintain that it would be in the interests of peace. France is pacific, she does not desire war, and she has not gone farther at present than to make preparations for mobilisation so as not to be taken unawares, and French Government will keep His Majesty's Government informed of everything that may be done in that way. French Government have reliable information that round Thionville and Metz German troops are concentrated ready for war.

President of Republic said that if there were a general war on the continent England would inevitably be involved in course of it, for protection of her vital interests, and a declaration by her now of her intention to support France, who desires to remain at peace, would almost certainly prevent Germany from embarking on a war.

Minutes

Sir E. Grey will no doubt approve Sir F. Bertie's language.

What must weigh with His Majesty's Government is the consideration that they should not by a declaration of unconditional solidarity with France and Russia *induce* and *determine* these two Powers to choose the path of war.

If and when, however, it is certain that France and Russia cannot avoid the war, and are going into it, my opinion, for what it is worth, is that British interests require us to take our place beside them as allies, and in that case our intervention should be immediate and decided.—E. A. C. 31 July.

I have answered this separately.[4]—E. G.

[1] See **141** and **146**.
[2] Jagow also shared this view; *Int. Bez.* I, 5, 305.
[3] See **68** (minute).
[4] For Grey's reply see *B.D.* 352.

153   Bunsen to Grey

Telegram 127   Vienna, 30 July 1914
B.D. 311   R. 9.00 p.m.

Russian Ambassador, on leaving Minister for Foreign Affairs this after-
noon came to French Embassy, where I happened to be, and gave French
Ambassador and myself account of his interview.[1] It was quite friendly.
Minister for Foreign Affairs said that of course as Russia had mobilised
Austria must do so also, but this was not to be considered as a threat, but
merely as adoption of military precautions similar to those taken across the
frontier. Also there was no objection to conversations between Russian
Minister for Foreign Affairs and Austrian Ambassador at St Petersburg
being continued, though Minister for Foreign Affairs did not say that they
could be resumed on basis of Serbian reply.

On the whole Russian Ambassador is not dissatisfied. He had begun to
pack up his things on the strength of rumour that Austria would declare
war in reply to mobilisation. Russian Ambassador now hopes that something may yet be done to prevent war with Austria, but he hears from
Berlin that German Secretary of State for Foreign Affairs was much
annoyed by mobilisation and threatened a German mobilisation both on
Russian and French frontiers, though Russian mobilisation was only
against Austria. Russian mobilisation is still kept dark in Vienna.

Minutes

This looks at last as if some German pressure were making itself felt at
Vienna. E. A. C. 31 July.

Surely it was Austria who mobilised before Russia did.[2] A. N.

154   Cabinet Council for Common Affairs

Protocol   Vienna, 31 July 1914
Ö.D. 11203   Morning[3]

Record of the Cabinet Council for Common Affairs held in Vienna on 31
July 1914 under the presidency of the Minister of the Imp. and Roy.
House and for Foreign Affairs Count Berchtold.

[1] *Ö.D.* 11093; *Int. Bez.* I, 5, 307; *D.F.* XI, 360.
[2] Partial mobilisation, yes, but not general mobilisation.
[3] The Council of Ministers took place in the morning.

Present: the Imp. and Roy. Prime Minister Count Stürgkh; the Hungarian Prime Minister Count Tisza; the Imp. and Roy. Joint Minister for Finances Ritter von Biliński; the Imp. and Roy. Minister of War Feldzeugmeister Ritter von Krobatin; the Royal Hungarian Minister a latere Baron Burián; the Deputy Chief of the Imp. and Roy. Naval Staff Rear-Admiral von Kailer.

Recorder: Councillor of Legation Count Hoyos.

Subject: Consultation regarding the English proposal of mediation[1] and compensations to be granted to Italy.

The president opens the session by reading a daily report of 30 inst. of the following tenor:[2]

Herr von Tschirschky has yesterday in the name of the State Chancellor transmitted a communication regarding an interview between Sir E. Grey and Prince Lichnowsky in which the English Secretary of State informed the German Ambassador of the following facts:

'Sazonov has informed the English Government that after Austria-Hungary's declaration of war on Serbia he was no longer in a position to negotiate directly with Austria-Hungary and therefore expressed the wish, that England again take up its mediation. The Russian Government pre-supposes the temporary ceasing of hostilities.'

Regarding this Russian statement Sir E. Grey remarked to Prince Lichnowsky, that England was thinking of a mediation *à quatre* and thought the same urgently necessary if a general war was not to ensue.

Privately Sir E. Grey had given the German Ambassador to understand that England might remain neutral if it were only a case of Russia's intervention, but that if Germany and France should also enter into action, it could not remain inactive but would be forced to make immediate decisions and act thereon. The English Cabinet must reckon with public opinion, which on account of the stubborn attitude of Austria was beginning to veer round.

To the Italian Ambassador, whom Sir E. Grey received shortly after Prince Lichnowsky, the English Secretary of State said he believed he could procure Austria-Hungary every possible sort of satisfaction. A humiliating withdrawal of Austria-Hungary was out of the question as the Serbians were at any rate to be punished and would—with the approval of Russia—be obliged to submit to the Austro-Hungarian demands. Austria-Hungary could therefore, also without starting a general war, obtain guarantees for the future.

Herr von Tschirschky was instructed to add to the above mentioned

[1] See 133.
[2] Not among the documents.

statements of Sir E. Grey the following considerations of the German State Chancellor:

If Austria-Hungary declined every sort of mediation, Austria-Hungary and Germany would find themselves opposed by a coalition of the whole of Europe, because neither Italy nor Roumania would go with them. Austria-Hungary's political prestige, the honour of its army and its justified claims on Serbia could be satisfied by the occupation of Belgrade and other points. Its relation to the Balkans—position in Russia—would by the humiliation of Serbia be a stronger one. Under these circumstances the German Cabinet must urgently and earnestly request the Imp. and Roy. Government to take into consideration the mediation of England under the said honourable conditions. It would be very difficult for Austria-Hungary and Germany to bear the responsibility of a negative attitude.

Continuing, Count Berchtold declares that he had, when the German Ambassador presented this English proposal to him, at once declared that a cessation of our hostilities against Serbia was impossible. He could not alone decide about the proposal of mediation but must await His Majesty's orders on the subject and discuss the affair in the Cabinet Council.

He had then reported to His Imp. and Roy. Majesty on the contents of the *démarche* of the German Ambassador. His Majesty had instantly declared that the cessation of hostilities against Serbia was impossible and had approved of the proposal to carefully avoid accepting the English offer on its merits, but agreed that we should in the form of our reply show, that we desired to meet England's wishes and thus also meet the wishes of the German State Chancellor by not offending the Government.

The reply to the German Government had not yet been elaborated, but he could already say now, that three fundamental principles had been observed in its wording viz:

1 The warlike operations against Serbia must continue.

2 We cannot negotiate concerning the English offer as long as the Russian mobilisation has not been stopped.

3 Our demands must be accepted integrally and we cannot negotiate about them in any way.[1]

As is known from experience, the Powers in such cases always try to make reductions when passing on the demands made by one power and it is very probable, that this would now also be tried, as the present constellation would make France, England and also Italy take Russia's part and we had a very doubtful support in the German representative in London. Anything might sooner be expected from Prince Lichnowsky

[1] See 155.

than that he would warmly represent our interests. If this whole action ended in nothing else than a gain of prestige, it would, according to his opinion, have been undertaken altogether in vain. A mere occupation of Belgrade would be of no good to us; even if Russia would allow it. All this was moonshine. Russia would pose as the saviour of Serbia and especially of the Serbian army; the latter would remain intact and in two or three years we could expect a renewed attack of Serbia under far more unfavourable conditions. He therefore had the intention of replying most courteously to the English offer making at the same time the afore-mentioned conditions and avoiding the discussion of facts.

The joint Minister for Finances points out that through our mobilisa-tion a completely new situation has been created. Proposals which might have been acceptable at an earlier date, are no longer acceptable now.

The Royal Hungarian Prime Minister declares that he is entirely of the opinion of the President and likewise thinks it would be dangerous to go into the facts of the English proposal. Our warlike operations in Serbia must certainly continue. He asked himself, however, whether it was already necessary to inform the Powers of our new demands on Serbia and would propose to reply to the English suggestion, by stating that we were ready to approach it in principle but only on the condition that our operations in Serbia be continued and the Russian mobilisation stopped.

The Imp. and Roy. Prime Minister explains that the idea of a con-ference is so odious to him that he would not even like to appear to accept it. He therefore finds Count Tisza's proposal the best. We must continue the war with Serbia and declare ourselves ready to continue negotiating with the Powers as soon as Russia stopped its mobilisation.

Chevalier von Biliński finds Count Tisza's suggestion extremely clever and by making the two conditions mentioned we would gain time. He too could not feel kindly towards the idea of a conference. The course of the London conference was so terrible a memory, that public opinion would revolt against the repetition of such a performance. He too was of opinion that the English offer must not be refused brusquely.

After Baron Burián had also expressed agreement, the proposal of Count Tisza was unanimously accepted and the fact established that the inclination was to accept the English proposal on the conditions formu-lated by Count Tisza.[1]

The President then lays stress upon the importance of Italy's remaining in the Triple Alliance. Now however Italy had taken the standpoint that we had provoked the conflict and that our proceedings against Serbia were

[1] See 155.

likewise aimed against Russia.[1] From everything the Marquis di San Giuliano had said it was clear, that the Italian attitude was inspired by a desire for compensation. Italy bases its wishes upon the wording of Article VII of the treaty of the Triple Alliance. Our interpretation is, that a right of compensation according to this article only then exists, if we occupy Turkish territories on the Balkans temporarily or for a longer time; as according to the spirit of the treaty there could only be a question of territories of the Ottoman Empire. Italy however insists that as in one part of the text the words *dans les Balkans* are mentioned, the whole Balkan peninsula is meant. Though the Italian conception might be refuted by a series of reasons, he must point out, that the German Government had also adopted the Italian point of view. In the course of the last week *démarches* had daily been made, in order to induce the Imp. and Roy, Government to join the two other allied countries in its acceptation of the question of compensation.[2]

The Imp. and Roy. Minister for War mentions that the Imp. and Roy. military attaché in Berlin had reported to him about interviews which he had had with the Kaiser Wilhelm and the Chief of the General Staff Count Moltke and in which both had most urgently pointed out how important an active intervention of Italy in the coming conflict was, and that it would therefore be most desirable that the Imp. and Roy. Government meet the wishes of Italy in the compensation question.[3]

The President declares that word had been sent to him from Rome that the coming war was against Italian interests, as its successful ending would strengthen our position in the Balkans. Under these circumstances Italy could only then intervene actively, if its claims were recognised. He had until now instructed the Imp. and Roy. Ambassador in Rome, to reply to the demands concerning the compensation by vague phrases and continue insisting on the fact that all idea of territorial aggrandisement was quite beyond our intentions. If however we should be forced against our will to undertake a non-temporary occupation, there would then still be time to approach the question of compensation. . . .

The Cabinet Council thereupon authorises the President on principle to promise Italy a compensation in the eventuality of a lasting occupation of Serbian territories on our part, and to speak of the relinquishment of Valona to Italy, if circumstances should demand it and Italy actually fulfil its duties as an ally; in which case Austria-Hungary would assure itself the decisive influence in North Albania.

The President then declares the discussion closed.

[1] Flotow to Jagow, 30 July; *D.D.* 419.   [2] See 134.
[3] Szögyény to Berchtold, 31 July; *Ö.D.* 11133/34.

155 Berchtold to Szögyény

Telegram 308
Ö.D. 11155

Vienna, 31 July 1914
D. 1 August, 3.45 a.m.

... [Text of the notes on Tschirschky's *démarche* on the basis of Bethmann Hollweg's instructions of July 30.[1]]

I ask Your Excellency to thank the Secretary of State for his communication by way of Herr von Tschirschky[1] and to explain to him that, despite the change which has occurred in the situation since Russia's mobilisation, we fully appreciate England's endeavours for the preservation of world peace and would be quite willing to enter more closely into Sir E. Grey's proposal to mediate between Serbia and ourselves. The prerequisites for our acceptance would, however, naturally be that our military action against the Kingdom should, for the time being, take its course, and that the British Cabinet should prevail upon the Russian Government to bring to a standstill the mobilisation of its troops against us, in which event we would naturally also put an immediate end to the defensive military counter-measures in Galicia to which we have been compelled by Russian mobilisation.[2]

156 Nicolas II to Wilhelm II

Telegram (unnumbered)
D.D. 487
Int. Bez. I, 5, 338

St Petersburg, Palace, 31 July 1914
D. 2.55 p.m.
R. 2.52 p.m.

I thank you heartily for your mediation which begins to give one hope that all may yet end peacefully. It is *technically* impossible to stop our military preparations which were obligatory owing to Austria's mobilisation. We are far from wishing war. So long as the negotiations with Austria on Serbia's account are taking place my troops shall not take any *provocative* action. I give you my solemn word for this. I put all my trust in God's mercy and hope in your successful mediation in Vienna for the welfare of our countries and for the peace of Europe.[3]

[1] See 133.
[2] See 154. The telegram was also despatched to London (telegram 194) and St Petersburg (telegram 208) at the same time.
[3] The telegram crossed with that from Wilhelm II; see 157.

157 Wilhelm II to Nicolas II

Telegram (unnumbered)   Berlin, 31 July 1914
D.D. 480   D. 2.04 p.m.
Int. Bez. I, 5, 357

On your appeal to my friendship and your call for assistance[1] I began to
mediate between your and the Austro-Hungarian Governments.[2] While
this action was proceeding your troops were mobilised against Austria-
Hungary, my ally. Thereby, as I have already pointed out to you,[3] my
mediation has been made almost illusory.

I have nevertheless continued my action. I now receive authentic news
of serious preparations for war on my eastern frontier. Responsibility for
the safety of my Empire forces preventive measures of defence upon me.
In my endeavours to maintain the peace of the world I have gone to the
utmost limit possible. The responsibility for the disaster which is now
threatening the whole civilised world will not be laid at my door. In this
moment it still lies in your power to avert it. Nobody is threatening the
honour or power of Russia who can well afford to await the result of my
mediation. My friendship for you and your Empire, transmitted to me
by my grandfather on his deathbed, has always been sacred to me and I
have honestly often backed up Russia when she was in serious trouble,
especially in her last war.

The peace of Europe may still be maintained by you, if Russia will agree
to stop the military measures which must threaten Germany and Austria-
Hungary.[4]

158 Bethmann Hollweg to Pourtalès

Telegram 153   Berlin, 31 July 1914
Urgent   D. 3.30 p.m.
D.D. 490   R. 11.10 p.m.

In spite of the still pending negotiations for mediation and although we
ourselves have up to the present hour taken no mobilisation measures of
any kind, Russia has mobilised her entire army and navy, thus against us
also.[5] For the security of the Empire, we have been compelled by these

[1] See 132.   [2] An allusion to 115.   [3] See 142.
[4] Original in English. The Kaiser made numerous alterations to the style and a number of
factual additions to the preliminary draft of the Auswärtiges Amt.
[5] *D.D.* 473. See pp. 265f., 271.

Russian measures, to declare a state of threatening danger of war, which does not yet mean mobilisation. Mobilisation must follow, however, in case Russia does not suspend every war measure against Austria-Hungary and ourselves within twelve hours and make us a distinct declaration to that effect.[1] Please inform Mr Sazonov of this at once, and wire the hour of your communication. I know that Sverbeev telegraphed to St Petersburg yesterday that we had mobilised,[2] which is untrue up to the present hour.[3]

159   Bethmann Hollweg to Schoen

Telegram 180
Urgent
D.D. 491

Berlin, 31 July 1914
D. 3.30 p.m.

In spite of the still pending negotiations for mediation and although we ourselves have taken no mobilisation measures of any kind, Russia has mobilised her entire army and fleet, thus against us also. As a result we have declared a state of threatening danger of war, which must be followed by mobilisation in case Russia does not suspend every war measure against Austria and ourselves within twelve hours. Mobilisation will inevitably mean war.[4] Please ask the French Government if it intends to remain neutral in a Russo-German war. Answer must be given within eighteen hours. Telegraph immediately hour at which the enquiry is made. Utmost haste necessary.[5]

Secret: If, as is not to be presumed, the French Government declares its intention to remain neutral, Your Excellency will inform the French Government that we shall have to demand the turning over of the fortresses of Toul and Verdun as a pledge of neutrality; these we would occupy and return after the completion of the war with Russia. Reply to last proposition must be here by four o'clock tomorrow afternoon.[6]

[1] On the same day (31 July) Jagow informed Jules Cambon of this measure and Cambon in turn passed on the news to Goschen. However Goschen's message only reached London early on 2 August; *B.D.* 455.

[2] See p. 270, n. 3.

[3] For Pourtalès' reply, see 160. For the text of the declaration of war on Russia, drafted the same evening, see *D.D.* 542.

[4] See 158.

[5] For Schoen's answer, see 173.

[6] Schoen did not mention this possible demand to Viviani. However, the French deciphering office subsequently succeeded in breaking the code not only of the entire telegram, but also of the secret final paragraph.

160 Pourtalès to Jagow

Telegram 209　　　　　　　　　　　St Petersburg, 1 August 1914
D.D. 536　　　　　　　　　　　　　　　　　D. 1.00 a.m.
　　　　　　　　　　　　　　　　　　　　　　R. 1 August

Have just carried out instructions,[1] at midnight. Mr Sazonov referred again to the technical impossibility of suspending the war measures, and attempted once more to convince me that we overestimated the significance of a Russian mobilisation, which was not comparable with that of our own. He urgently requested me to call Your Excellency's attention to the fact that the assurance of the Czar, on his word of honour, given in today's telegram from His Majesty the Czar Nicolas to His Majesty the Emperor and King,[2] should satisfy us as to Russia's intentions. I pointed out to him in return that the Czar by no means obligated himself under all circumstances to refrain from warlike action, but only so long as there still remained a prospect of composing the Austro-Russian quarrel on account of Serbia. I put to the Minister the direct question: could he give me a guaranty that Russia intended to keep the peace, even in the event that an agreement with Austria was not reached? The Minister was unable to give me an affirmative answer to this question. In that case, then, I replied, nobody can blame us for our unwillingness to allow Russia a longer start in mobilisation.

161 Memorandum of the day of the Russian Ministry for Foreign Affairs

Int. Bez. I, 5, 349　　　　　　　　　　St Petersburg, 31 July 1914

To avoid rendering more acute our relations with Germany the Minister for Foreign Affairs deemed it desirable to proceed to the general mobilisation as far as possible secretly and without making any public announcement concerning it. However, it appeared that this was impossible in a technical sense, and from the forenoon of 31 July announcements appeared in every street, printed on red paper, summoning men to the colours.

This could not but cause excitement among the foreign representatives, and one of the first of them who came to the Foreign Minister was the German Ambassador. S. D. Sazonov informed him that the decision taken

[1] See 158.　　　　[2] See 156.

by the Imperial Government merely constituted a precautionary measure necessitated by the unconciliatoriness manifested in Berlin and Vienna, and that Russia for her part would do nothing that was irrevocable, but that, despite her mobilisation, peace could be maintained if Germany would consent before it was too late to exercise a moderating influence upon her ally.

Count Pourtalès did not conceal his fears as to the reception that would be accorded to the measure in question by Berlin.[1]

162 Paul Cambon to Viviani

Despatch 357
D.F. XI, 459 (*F.Y.B.* 110)

London, 31 July 1914
R. 1 August

At the beginning of our conversation today, Sir E. Grey told me that Prince Lichnowsky had asked him this morning if Great Britain would observe neutrality in the conflict which is at hand. The Secretary of State for Foreign Affairs replied that, if the conflict became general, Great Britain would not be able to remain neutral, and especially that if France were involved Great Britain would be drawn in.

I then asked Sir E. Grey concerning the Cabinet Council which took place this morning. He replied that after having examined the situation, the Cabinet had thought that for the moment the British Government were unable to guarantee to us their intervention, that they intended to take steps to obtain from Germany and France an understanding to respect Belgian neutrality,[2] but that before considering intervention it was necessary to wait for the situation to develop.

Public opinion in Britain and the present mood of Parliament would not allow the Government to commit Britain formally at present. It is thought that the coming conflict will plunge the finances of Europe into trouble, that Britain was facing an economic and financial crisis without precedent and that British neutrality might be the only way of averting the complete collapse of European credit. Cabinet could not commit Parliament without consulting it beforehand; the question of Belgian neutrality could become an important factor and it is probably that point

[1] No first-hand account of this conversation from Pourtalès to his Government is available. According to the records of the German Embassy in St Petersburg Pourtalès did not speak to Sazonov that morning, but to his assistant Neratov; on this occasion Pourtalès also took the opportunity of delivering the memorandum on the German standpoint; see *D.D.* IV, p. 166.
[2] See p. 275.

which Parliament will raise first with the Cabinet. Finally, one wants to wait for further developments, since the disagreement between Russia, Austria and Germany is on a question in which Britain is not in the least interested.

I asked Sir E. Grey, if, before intervening, the British Government would await the invasion of French territory, and I remarked that intervention then would be too late. He answered by hinting at the possibility of an ultimatum to France or a comparable summary *démarche*. That would be such a fact as to enable the Government to propose intervention to the House of Commons.

I insisted on the fact that the measures already taken on our frontier by Germany showed an intention to attack in the near future and that, if Britain remained indifferent, she would repeat her mistake of 1870, when she did not see the dangers of the formation of a powerful Germany in the centre of Europe; I added that today the mistake would be the graver, since Britain, facing Germany, if that Power were to remain victorious, in isolation, would find herself in a state of dependence. I went on by pointing out that France counted on the assistance of Britain and that if we were let down those in favour of an alliance with Germany at the exclusion of Britain could feel justified. Finally, I requested Sir E. Grey to submit the matter once more to the Cabinet and to insist on pledges being given to us without delay.

Sir E. Grey replied that the opinion of the Cabinet had only been formed on the situation on the moment, that the situation might be modified, and that in that case a meeting of the Cabinet would be called together at once in order to consider it. Sir A. Nicolson, whom I saw on leaving the room of the Secretary of State, told me that the Cabinet would meet again tomorrow, and confidentially gave me to understand that the Secretary of State for Foreign Affairs would be certain to renew the discussion.

I have taken the necessary steps to secure that the letter of the President of the Republic should be given to the King this evening.[1] This step, which will certainly be communicated to the Prime Minister tomorrow morning, will, I am sure, have a favourable influence on the decisions of the British Cabinet.

[1] *D.F.* XI, 457.

163 Grey to Goschen

Telegram 241
B.D. 340

London, 31 July 1914
D. 2.45 p.m.

European crisis. My telegram 413 of 31 July to St Petersburg,[1] which has been repeated to you today.

I hope that the conversations which are now proceeding between Austria and Russia may lead to a satisfactory result. The stumbling-block hitherto has been Austrian mistrust of Serbian assurances, and Russian mistrust of Austrian intentions with regard to the independence and integrity of Serbia. It has occurred to me that in the event of this mistrust preventing a solution being found by Vienna and St Petersburg, Germany might sound Vienna, and I would undertake to sound St Petersburg, whether it would be possible for the four disinterested Powers to offer to Austria that they would undertake to see that she obtained full satisfaction of her demands on Serbia, provided that they did not impair Serbian sovereignty and the integrity of Serbian territory. As Your Excellency is aware, Austria has already declared her willingness to respect them.[2] Russia might be informed by the four Powers that they would undertake to prevent Austrian demands going the length of impairing Serbian sovereignty and integrity. All Powers would of course suspend further military operations or preparations.

You may sound the Secretary of State for Foreign Affairs about this proposal.[3]

I said to German Ambassador this morning that if Germany could get any reasonable proposal put forward which made it clear that Germany and Austria were striving to preserve European peace, and that Russia and France would be unreasonable if they rejected it, I would support it at St Petersburg and Paris and go the length of saying that if Russia and France would not accept it His Majesty's Government would have nothing more to do with the consequences; but, otherwise, I told German Ambassador that if France became involved we should be drawn in.

You can add this when sounding Chancellor or Minister for Foreign Affairs as to proposal above. If you think it desirable, you can also give Chancellor a memorandum of my telegram 231 of yesterday;[4] I presume you have told him of it verbally.[5]

[1] *B.D.* 335.
[2] This declaration, however, only applied to Serbia's territorial integrity.
[3] *D.D.* 496.
[4] See 151.
[5] For Goschen's reply see 165.

164   Crowe to Grey

Private   31 July 1914
B.D. 369

Will you pardon me if I venture to put before you in perhaps rather crude
words—they have of necessity been written rather rapidly—some simple
thoughts which the grave situation has suggested to my mind.

If you think them worthless please put them aside. Nothing is further
from my mind than to trouble you needlessly or add to your grave per-
plexities at this moment.

Enclosure in *B.D.* 369.

Memorandum by Sir E. Crowe, 31 July 1914

The theory that England cannot engage in a big war means her abdication
as an independent State. She can be brought to her knees and made to
obey the behests of any Power or group of Powers who *can* go to war, of
whom there are several.

The theory further involves not only that there is no need for any
British army or navy but also that there has been no such need for many
years. It cannot have been right to impose on the country the upkeep at
an enormous annual cost of an unnecessary because useless force.

If the theory were true, the general principle on which our whole
foreign policy has hitherto been declared to rest would stand proclaimed
as an empty futility. A balance of power cannot be maintained by a State
that is incapable of fighting and consequently carries no weight.

The fact that British influence has on several momentous occasions
turned the scale, is evidence that foreign States do not share the belief
that England cannot go to war.

At the opening of any war in all countries there is a commercial panic.

The systematic disturbance of an enemy's financial organisation and the
creation of panic is part of a well-laid preparation for war.

Commercial opinion is generally timid, and apt to follow pusillanimous
counsels. The panic in the city has been largely influenced by the deliberate acts of German financial houses, who are in at least as close touch with
the German as with the British Government, and who are notoriously in
daily communication with the German Embassy.

It has been the unremitting effort of Germany to induce England to
declare herself neutral in case Germany were at war with France and
Russia. The object has been so transparent that His Majesty's Government have persistently declined to follow this policy, as incompatible with

their duty to France and Russia and also to England herself. The proposal was again pressed upon us in a concrete form yesterday.[1] It was rejected in words which gave the impression that in the eye of His Majesty's Government the German proposal amounted to asking England to do a dishonourable act.[2]

If it be now held that we are entirely justified in remaining neutral and standing aside whilst Germany falls upon France, it was wrong yesterday to think that we were asked to enter into a dishonourable bargain, and it is a pity that we did not close with it. For at least terms were offered which were of some value for France and Belgium. We are apparently now willing to do what we scornfully declined to do yesterday, with the consequence that we lose the compensating advantages accompanying yesterday's offer.

The argument that there is no written bond binding us to France is strictly correct. There is no contractual obligation. But the Entente has been made, strengthened, put to the test and celebrated in a manner justifying the belief that a moral bond was being forged. The whole policy of the Entente can have no meaning if it does not signify that in a just quarrel England would stand by her friends. This honourable expectation has been raised. We cannot repudiate it without exposing our good name to grave criticism.

I venture to think that the contention that England cannot in any circumstances go to war, is not true, and that any endorsement of it would be an act of political suicide.

The question at issue is not whether we are capable of taking part in a war, but whether we should go into the present war. That is a question firstly of right or wrong, and secondly of political expediency.

If the question were argued on this basis, I feel confident that our duty and our interest will be seen to lie in standing by France in her hour of need. France has not sought the quarrel. It has been forced upon her.

[1] See **139**.
[2] See **151**.

165   Goschen to Grey

Telegram 113   Berlin, 31 July 1914
B.D. 385   D. 1 August 2.00 a.m.
                                         R. 1 August 3.45 a.m.

Your telegram 241.[1]

I spent an hour with Secretary of State for Foreign Affairs urging him most earnestly to accept your proposal[1] and make another effort to prevent terrible catastrophe of a European war.

He expressed himself very sympathetically towards your proposal,[1] and appreciated your continued efforts to maintain peace, but said it was impossible for the Imperial Government to consider any proposal until they had received an answer from Russia to their communication of today; this communication, which he admitted had the form of an ultimatum, being that, unless Russia could inform the Imperial Government within twelve hours that she would immediately countermand her mobilisation against Germany and Austria, Germany would be obliged on her side to mobilise at once.[2]

I asked his Excellency why they had made their demand even more difficult for Russia to accept by asking them to demobilise in south as well. He replied that it was in order to prevent Russia from saying all her mobilisation was only directed against Austria.

His Excellency said that if the answer from Russia was satisfactory he thought personally that your proposal merited favourable consideration, and in any case he would lay it before the Emperor and Chancellor, but he repeated that it was no use discussing it until the Russian Government had sent in their answer to the German demand.[3]

He again assured me that both the Emperor, at the request of the Czar, and the Imperial Foreign Office had even up till last night been urging Austria to show willingness to continue discussions[4]—and telegraphic and telephonic communications from Vienna had been of a promising nature[5] —but Russia's mobilisation had spoilt everything.[6]

Germany's demand to Russia[3] has been published tonight in the extra sheets, and large crowds are parading the streets singing patriotic songs.

Minute

M. de Etter[7] told me today that when he left St Petersburg on Wednesday[8]

[1] See 163.   [2] See 158.   [3] See 158.
[4] See 115, 133 and 134.
[5] Nothing to support this has been found among the German documents.
[6] An account by Jagow is not available.
[7] Councillor to Russian Legation in London.
[8] I.e. on 29 July.

no mobilisation of any degree was taking place there or in the 'Government' of St Petersburg. He came by the Nord Express through Germany. The German railways were filled in all directions with moving troops.—
E. A. C., 1 August,

166 Goschen to Grey

Telegram 114   Berlin, 31 July 1914
B.D. 383   D. 31 July 2.00 a.m.
                                    R. 1 August 3.30 a.m.

Your telegram 287 of 31 July to Paris:[1] Belgian neutrality.

Secretary of State for Foreign Affairs said that he could not possibly give me an answer before consulting the Emperor and the Chancellor. I said that I hoped that the answer would not be too long delayed. He then gave me to understand he rather doubted whether they could answer at all, as any reply they might give could not fail, in the event of war, to have the undesirable effect of disclosing to a certain extent part of their plan of campaign. After taking note of your request, he told me in confidence that Belgium had already committed certain acts which he could only qualify as hostile. On my asking him for details, he gave me as an instance that the Belgian Government had already embargoed a consignment of grain destined for Germany.[2]

In telling me that it was unlikely that the Imperial Government would be in a position to answer, he said that in any case it would be necessary for them to know what France replied to your enquiry.

I shall speak to him again on the subject tomorrow, but I am not very hopeful of obtaining a definite answer.[3]

[1] *B.D.* 348.
[2] There is no reference to this or any similar move in the German documents.
[3] The notes to this document are not reprinted here.

167   Goschen to Nicolson

Private	Berlin, 31[1] July 1914
B.D. 677	R. 5 September

You can imagine that I have been pretty busy since my return here on Monday[2] morning. I found Jagow ill and tired but nevertheless optimistic —his optimism being based, he told me, on the idea that Russia was not in a position to make war. I told him that that seemed to me to be rather a dangerous idea—particularly if it was shared by Austria! That this idea is prevalent among Austrians, at least some of them, was proved to me later in the day by Count Szögyény, who said to me later in the day that a *general* war was out of the question as Russia neither could, nor wanted to, go to war.

Jagow practically admitted to me that the Serbian reply went *very* far towards meeting the Austrian demands[3]—but he also admitted that Austria meant business and that nothing from Berlin or anywhere else would stop her from punishing Serbia, short of a complete acceptance of her demands. He also again assured me that the Austrian ultimatum was not submitted to Berlin before being sent in.[4] The general opinion here even among pro-Austrians is that Austria made her note brutal on purpose that it should not be accepted[5] . . .

Bethmann Hollweg's 'bid' for our neutrality[6] must have taken you by surprise; it certainly did me. His Excellency sent for me about 10.30 p.m.; told me that he had just come from a Council at Potsdam, at which the Emperor, Admiral von Tirpitz and the Minister of War had been present, that he had dined in ten minutes, and that, tired as he was, he had to have a long talk to Jagow after he had finished with me. He spoke to me from typewritten notes[7] which, however, he would not show me. I asked him as it was a matter of such importance whether I might draft my telegram there and then read to him what I had written. So I made a draft and read it to him. He suggested one or two slight alterations and then told me that it was exactly what he meant to say. He asked me what I thought of it. I told him frankly that it did not seem to me acceptable and that in any case I thought it was unlikely that His Majesty's Government would care to bind themselves to any particular course of action at the present stage. I would, however, send the telegram in exactly the same words as he had

---

[1] The letter was evidently begun on 30 July. Goschen wrote the last paragraph (not printed here) after his return from Germany after the outbreak of war.

[2] I.e. on 27 July.	[3] See in contrast **144**.

[4] See **41** and **43**.	[5] See **16** and **31**.

[6] See **139**.	[7] *D.D.* 373.

approved. On the following morning Jagow came round to see me early and spoke of a conversation between Sir Edward Grey and Lichnowsky— the report of which had been received late at night after I had left the Chancellor.[1] Had it been received earlier, Jagow said, the Chancellor would not have spoken to me in the way he had done. From what Jagow let drop in conversation I gather that Sir E. Grey had given Lichnowsky to understand that we might have to go with Russia and France—but strangely enough I have received no telegraphic account of this conversation as yet (30 July, 7 p.m.). Anyway Lichnowsky's report seemed to have depressed Jagow—though he praised the frankness and sincerity with which Sir E. Grey had spoken[2] . . .

[1] See 130.
[2] See 150.

8 From Continental War to World War

1 – 4 August

Since German mobilisation, 'in contrast to the already routine Russian mobilisations and demobilisations', would infallibly and 'inevitably lead to war', as Moltke himself telegraphed to Conrad,[1] war finally became certain after the German decision to mobilise on 31 July, a fact which is also confirmed by the immediate preparation of the German ultimatums and declarations of war on Russia and France.[2] There was no holding back now, and the course of events between the official beginnings of continental war on 1 August and of world war on 4 August may be likened in essence to a chain reaction which can no longer be halted. Hence also the analysis of diplomatic proceedings in the first four days of August can be contained in a considerably shorter space, although, in fact, the flood of diplomatic documents rose enormously in that brief span.

On 1 August the order for general mobilisation was issued almost simultaneously in Germany and France. A telegram from Lichnowsky, which seemed after all to hold out the prospect of British and French neutrality (170), caused a revealing confusion in Berlin. In reaction to the favourable news from London, Wilhelm II, only a short time after signing the mobilisation order, demanded a halt to the deployment in the west which was already in full swing and a redeployment of troops against Russia. Bubbling over with joy, the Kaiser even called for champagne for it seemed as if Russia alone remained in the field. Only Moltke turned sour and demurred: 'Now it only remains for Russia to bale out as well.'[3]

[1] See above, p. 266.   [2] See above p. 271.   [3] Müller, *Kriegstagebuch*, p. 39.

He vigorously opposed the Kaiser's request with the argument that the troops could not be suddenly redeployed without creating chaos in the army. This proves incidentally that, if the full deployment of the armies in the west[1] was already in full swing, while the decree for mobilisation was just being signed, actual German mobilisation cannot only have begun with the official command from Wilhelm II on 1 August. Initially the Kaiser had his way and ordered the 2nd Division in Trèves to call off their march into Luxembourg planned for 2 August, whilst Moltke shed tears in his study because his plan had been ruined before it could even be put into action.[2] Shortly before midnight, however, a further telegram from Lichnowsky, stating that there could be no question of the neutrality of the Western Powers,[3] clarified the situation and the final obstacle to the implementation of Moltke's and Ludendorff's modified Schlieffen Plan was removed.

At 7.00 in the evening in St Petersburg Ambassador Pourtalès delivered the German declaration of war, so that Russia was no longer able to 'bale out'. The declaration of war on France was still postponed in the vague hope that Paris would of its own accord declare war on Germany, or at least open hostilities.[4] As the prospects of such an obliging gesture on the part of the French seemed slight indeed, on 2 August the German Minister in Brussels received instructions to deliver the enclosed summons to the Belgian Government the same evening (91); it had been drafted as early as 26 July and sent to the German Minister on 29 July.[5] The delivery took place at 8.00 p.m. Central European Time and the Belgian Government promptly rejected the German demand on the following morning, 3 August,[6] after the time-limit for the reply to the German ultimatum had been reduced from 24 hours to 12 on Moltke's instructions on 2 August (179). Thus German troops began the invasion of neutral Belgium in the early hours of 4 August.

The *Reich* had, it is true, declared war on Russia on 1 August, but the German war plan was directed against France, which had only played an extremely indirect part in the July crisis. According to German logic the implementation of the Schlieffen Plan necessitated being on a war footing with France in addition to the invasion of neutral Belgium. Yet the violation of Belgian neutrality could only be lent a degree of plausibility in the

---

[1] K.-D. Erdmann, *Die Zeit der Weltkriege*, p. 20.
[2] Helmuth v. Moltke, *Erinnerungen, Briefe, Dokumente 1877 bis 1916* (Stuttgart, 1922), pp. 19ff.
[3] *D.D.* 603.
[4] Bethmann Hollweg to Wilhelm II, 2 August; *D.D.* 629. See p. 353, n. 2.
[5] *D.D.* 648.
[6] Below to Jagow, 3 August; *D.D.* 735.

eyes of the rest of the world if it could be shown that France offered a military threat to Germany and Belgium or at least if Germany and France were at war. In order to give some substance to the existence of an ostensible danger to Germany, the Berlin Government invented violations of the frontier by French troops.[1] Some of these fabrications were extraordinarily crude and their propaganda value turned out to be, on the whole, negative for their inventors: the most glaring examples were the claims that French planes had dropped bombs near Nuremberg and that 80 French officers in Prussian uniform had attempted to cross the German-Dutch frontier at Geldern (a good 250 kilometres from the French frontier).

Meanwhile the German Government cast round despairingly for allies. It was nominally on account of Austria-Hungary that the Reich was rushing headlong into the adventure of a world war, yet Vienna, whilst pursuing its local war against Serbia, as late as 1 August had still not achieved a state of war with Russia who, it was claimed, was threatening Austria-Hungary, and thus indirectly Germany too. On the contrary, despite mobilisation on both sides, the easing of tension which set in on 31 July[2] appeared on the 1 August to settle down to a basis for negotiation. Admittedly on 1 August Berchtold reiterated Franz Joseph's assent of the previous day to the redeployment of most of Austria's troops against Russia.[3] Nonetheless, it required several more admonitory warnings from Berlin before Austria-Hungary, on 6 August, finally declared war on Russia[4] who was supposed to constitute such a grave threat to her security. In doing this, Vienna finally put an end to 'the grotesque situation whereby Germany found herself in the war six days earlier than the ally for whose sake she took up the struggle in the first place'.[5]

In other respects, however, Germany's search for allies met with indifferent success: Italy declared her neutrality on 1 August on the grounds that this war was an Austrian war of aggression (172); Roumania was exposed to pressure from the Entente[6] and could see no reason for taking part—against her national interests—in a war against her friend and ally, Serbia, and, at that, on the side of Austria-Hungary, who stood in the way of the realisation of Roumanian national aspirations; Sweden, who at times had seemed to have strong sympathies for the German point of

---

[1] The most important German lies in *D.D.* 664, 693, 710, 734.
[2] See above, p. 273.
[3] *D.D.* 601.
[4] *D.D.* 627, 814, 870.
[5] G. Ritter, *Staatskunst*, II, 334.
[6] *Int. Bez.* I, 5, 341, 528.

view, similarly declared herself neutral.[1] Germany only succeeded in concluding a treaty with Turkey on 3 August, thus gaining an ally of doubtful value.[2] There also emerged the outline of an alliance with Bulgaria which led to the latter's entry into the war on the side of the Central Powers in 1915.

All links between St Petersburg and Vienna were abruptly severed by Germany's declaration of war on Russia. France meanwhile pursued her policy of preventing the isolation of Russia and herself in a war against Germany. In reply to Germany's ultimative 'enquiry' (159) Viviani fell back on the protection of French interests (173). At the same time the Council of Ministers endorsed the aim of fulfilling all obligations towards Russia (176). In France, too, practically the final decision had been taken, with the order for general mobilisation at 4.00 p.m. on 1 August. Now that continental war was imminent, the French Government strove harder than ever before to gain Britain's support. In a series of dramatic discussions Paul Cambon attempted to extract from Grey at least an assurance of England's commitment to her Entente allies, France and Russia, but Grey still hesitated to give an unequivocal pledge. However, his promise that the British Fleet would protect the French coast against a possible German naval attack was the first step in the direction desired by France.

Grey's freedom of action was crippled by a severe cabinet crisis, as a strong minority in the Cabinet firmly opposed British intervention on the Continent. The majority, however, endorsed the view that Britain could not simply acquiesce in a German violation of Belgian neutrality. On 3 August Grey still held back in a speech to the House of Commons (he did not, for instance, mention the German 'offer' of neutrality on 29–30 July (139)), but he intimated to Benckendorff, the Russian Ambassador, that by this time even he was definitely in favour of British participation in the war.[3] The violation of Belgian neutrality by German troops on 4 August (180, 181, 182) removed the final restraints (186). Last-minute appeals from Germany were no longer of any avail (182, 184, 185). In the early afternoon Grey despatched an ultimatum with a brief time-limit to the German Government, demanding the immediate withdrawal of German troops from Belgium, failing which Britain would enter

[1] For Sweden's attitude during the July crisis, see W. M. Carlgren, *Neutralität oder Allianz. Deutschlands Beziehungen zu Schweden in den Anfangsjahren des ersten Weltkriegs* (Stockholm, 1962), pp. 34ff.; a summary of his conclusions in *Julikrise und Kriegsausbruch 1914*, II, p. 14, note 4.

[2] The most important documents on German-Turkish relations during the July crisis in *Ö.D.* 10657, *D.D.* 399 (note), 411, 508, 662.

[3] Benckendorff to Sazonov, 4 August; *Int. Bez.* I, 5, 537.

into a state of war with Germany at midnight, Central European Time.[1] Secretary of State Jagow and Bethmann Hollweg rejected the British demand in a series of dramatic discussions (187, 188). It was on this occasion that the Chancellor made his famous remark about the 'scrap of paper'[2] over which England was now entering the war—even though it was a question of international agreements for the protection of Belgian neutrality. The remark was made in a situation of great tension and powerful emotions, since the Chancellor's policies had, in his own words, collapsed 'like a house of cards'. But the words were already implicit in embryonic literary form when Kurt Riezler, Bethmann Hollweg's closest collaborator and adviser, for whom the will to expansion and world domination was a fundamental principle of foreign policy, clear-sightedly predicted the situation of a great war:

'Arbitration treaties are created and international law is expanded, but events repeatedly prove the ease with which international papers are torn up. Ultimately it is no more than a consideration for the spectators at a time when the great nations still have room to develop side by side. . . . In a struggle in which everyone is involved and consideration for the spectators is ruled out, all agreements will be of no avail.'[3]

The First World War had begun after Germany had 'torn up the international papers' and in the Great War yet more 'agreements' were to follow for, as the Chancellor proclaimed in his speech to the Reichstag on 4 August: 'Necessity knows no law!'

168 Szápáry to Berchtold

Telegram 190 St Petersburg, 1 August 1914
Secret D. 10.45 a.m.
D.A. III, 97 R. 1.00 p.m.

Continuation of my telegram 189 of 31 ult.[4]

I therefore called upon Mr Sazonov who received me immediately. I explained to the Minister that I had received instructions in cipher[5] but that I had first of all to remark that the present situation in Vienna, created by the Russian general mobilisation, was wholly unknown to me, so that in

---

[1] Grey to Goschen, 4 August; *B.D.* 573.
[2] Goschen to Grey, 6 August; *B.D.* 671.
[3] K. Riezler, *Die Erforderlichkeit des Unmöglichen*, p. 230.
[4] *Ö.D.* 11179.
[5] See 140; also *Ö.D.* 11093.

interpreting my instruction, which had been sent me before the new situation had developed there, I should have to make allowances for the fact.

The Minister interrupted me excitedly, by saying, that the mobilisation had no significance; and that Emperor Nicolas had pledged his word to Kaiser Wilhelm, that the army would not budge, so long as a conversation tending towards an agreement was still going on with Vienna.[1] Moreover we had first mobilised, an assertion which I distinctly denied, so that the Minister said: 'let us leave this chronology aside'. There was no fear that the guns would go off by themselves and as concerned the Russian army, it was so well disciplined, that the Emperor with one word could make it retire from the frontier. I continued by saying that Your Excellency's[2] two instructions started from the misunderstanding that we had declined further negotiations with Russia. This was, as I had already informed him without instructions (my telegram 180 of 29 ult.[2]), a mistake. Your Excellency was not only ready to negotiate with Russia on a broad basis, but especially inclined to discuss the text of our note as far as its interpretation was concerned.

I knew, of course, that the Russian point of view was that the form of the note should be modified, whilst your Excellency was of opinion that its meaning could be explained.

This resulted in a discrepancy, which could not be overlooked, though on the whole it seemed to me that it came to the same thing.

Mr Sazonov said that this was good news, for he still hoped that in this way the matter might be directed into that channel which he had from the first imagined the best.

I insisted on the fact, that Your Excellency's instructions to me were a proof of good will, though I had again to remind him that the situation created since by the general mobilisation was unknown to me. I could only hope that the course of events had not gone too far already. In any case I had thought it my duty again to insist on the good will of the Imp. and Royal Government at the present most serious moment.

Mr Sazonov replied that he took note with satisfaction of this proof of good will; also, he would like to draw my attention to the fact that negotiations in St Petersburg would seem, for reasons easily understood, to promise less hope of success than those on the neutral ground of London. I answered, that Your Excellency, as I had already explained, started from the point of view of direct contact with St Petersburg, so that I was not in a position to give any opinion concerning his suggestion about London, but that I would report to Your Excellency on the subject.

Mr Sazonov seemed greatly relieved by my information and to

[1] See 171.   [2] See 123.

consider it of exaggerated importance[1] so that I always had to point out again the modified situation, the discrepancy of our initial views and so forth. Moreover, during the conversation two principal points were completely avoided. On my part the purely retrospective and theoretical character of a conversation—about the text of the note as I gathered it from Your Excellency's telegram, on his part, the question what should become of the military operations during the eventual negotiations?

With regard to the reservation which I made concerning the general Russian mobilisation, Your Excellency is absolutely free to declare my explanations as no longer having any bearing. On the other hand it seemed to me from the point of view of the distribution of parts, exceedingly important to have undertaken another step, which might well be described as extremely conciliatory. Should however Your Excellency today still think diplomatic negotiations practicable or opportune, a basis would seem to present itself here. For these reasons I hope that my proceedings will meet with Your Excellency's approval.

It would be most desirable that Britain as well would join France and Russia, without losing time, as only thus will she succeed in preventing a dangerous interference with the European balance of power.

169 Interview between Berchtold and Schebeko

Daily report 3737   Vienna, 1 August 1914
D.A. III, 99

The Imperial Russian Ambassador today called on me in the most friendly manner in order, as he said, to enquire for any news that might have come. He still hoped that it would be possible to settle the question at issue by direct negotiations. Considering the actual situation it would certainly be better to do this on neutral ground, London being especially suitable for the purpose. It was to be regretted that Germany evidently wanted to force on the war. Russia had already given the most binding assurances in Berlin that its military measures bore no hostile character towards the Monarchy or Germany.[2] Of course St Petersburg would have to insist as hitherto, that we did not solve the conflict with Serbia without consulting Russia, whose interests were engaged in this question.

I did not enter any further into these explanations of Mr Schebeko's, but began a friendly unofficial conversation in the course of which I drew

[1] *Int. Bez.* I, 5, 348.   [2] See **156**.

the attention of the Russian Ambassador to the manifold follies of the Russian Balkan policy. There was a far broader basis for discussions with Russia if she could only once make up her mind not always and entirely to make the fate of the Balkan States the touchstone of her attitude towards us.

Mr Schebeko replied likewise in a very friendly manner, discussed in a purely academical fashion the many obligations of Russia as an orthodox and Slav State, pointed out certain sentimental characteristics of the Russian people and took his leave with the remark that between us and Russia there was really only a great misunderstanding.

Immediately after this interview I received the visit of Monsieur Dumaine who spoke in just as peaceful a strain as his Russian colleague, lamented the warlike proceedings of Kaiser Wilhelm and expressed his conviction that a way must be found, to satisfy our just claims as well as Russia's interest in Serbia and open the way to peace.

170 Lichnowsky to Jagow

Telegram 205
D.D. 562

London, 1 August 1914
D. 11.14 a.m.
R. 4.23 p.m.

Sir E. Grey has just had me informed through Sir W. Tyrrell that he hopes, as the result of a Cabinet Meeting now in session, to be able to give me this afternoon some facts which may prove useful for the avoidance of the great catastrophe. Judging from Sir William's hints, this would appear to mean that in case we did not attack France, England would remain neutral and would guarantee France's neutrality. I shall learn more this afternoon.[1]

Sir E. Grey has just called me on the telephone and asked me if I thought I could assure him that in case France should remain neutral in a Russo-German war, we would not attack the French. I assured him that I could take the responsibility for such a guaranty, and he is to use this assurance at today's Cabinet session.[2]

[1] *D.D.* 570.
[2] For the reaction of officials in Berlin see pp. 336f.

171 Nicolas II to Wilhelm II

Telegram (unnumbered)   Peterhof Palace, 1 August 1914
D.D. 546
Int. Bez. I, 5, 384

I received your telegram.[1] Understand you are obliged to mobilise but wish to have the same guaranty from you as I gave you, that these measures *do not* mean war[2] and that we shall continue negotiating for the benefit of our countries and universal peace dear to all our hearts. Our long proved friendship *must* succeed, with God's help, in avoiding bloodshed. Anxiously, full of confidence await your answer.[3]

172 Flotow to Jagow

Telegram 168   Rome, 1 August 1914
Urgent   D. 1.14 p.m.
D.D. 568   R. 5.40 p.m.

Official communication in the *Tribuna* states: The Italian Government believes that neither by the letter nor the spirit of the Triple Alliance treaty is it obliged to take part in a war that does not bear the character of a war of defence; reserves the right, however, to determine subsequently in what way it can assume an attitude favouring the allies while preserving its own interests.

[1] See 157.
[2] The Kaiser could not give such an undertaking, since the German war plan envisaged the immediate occupation of Liège even before troops had been fully deployed; thus war was in effect linked with German general mobilisation.
[3] See 175.

173   Schoen to Jagow

Telegram 239
Urgent
D.D. 571

Paris, 1 August 1914
D. 1.05 p.m.
R. 6.10 p.m.

In connection with telegram 237.[1]

To the definite and repeated question, whether France would remain neutral in case of a Russo-German war, the Premier stated to me, *hesitatingly* that France would act in accordance with her interests. He based the uncertainty of this statement on the fact that he regarded the situation as changed since yester-

Do not know of any. I received none.

day. It is officially reported here that *Sir E. Grey's proposal of a general suspension of military preparations* has been accepted in principle by Russia,[2] and that

What does that mean?

Austria-Hungary has declared that she will not infringe on Serbia's territory or sovereignty.[3]

174   Lichnowsky to Jagow

Telegram 212
D.D. 596

London, 1 August 1914
D. 5.47 p.m.
R. 10.02 p.m.

Sir E. Grey has just read to me the following statement, which was unanimously drawn up by the Cabinet: 'The reply of the German Government with regard to the neutrality of Belgium[4] is a matter of very great regret, because the neutrality of Belgium does affect feeling in this country. If Germany could see her way to give the same positive reply as that which has been given by France,[5] it would materially contribute to relieve anxiety and tension here, while on the other hand, if there were a violation of the neutrality of Belgium

This drivel of Grey's shows that he absolutely doesn't know what he is to do. We will now await England's decision. I just learn that England has already cut the cable to Emden. A war measure, then! While she is still negotiating.

[1] *D.D.* 528.   [2] *Int. Bez.* I, 5, 343, 346, 348.   [3] *Ö.D.* 11121.
[4] See 166.   [5] *B.D.* 382.

by one combatant while the other respected it, it would be extremely difficult to restrain public feeling in this country.'

To my question, whether he could give me a *definite declaration on the neutrality of Great Britain* on the condition that we respected Belgian neutrality, the Minister replied that *that would not be possible for him*, though this question would play an important role in connection with public feeling here. Should we violate Belgian neutrality in a war with France, a reversal of public feeling would take place that would *make it difficult for the Government here to adopt an attitude of friendly neutrality*. For the present, *there was not the slightest intention of proceeding to hostilities against us.* But it would be difficult *to draw a line beyond which we might not go* without causing them on this side to step in. He kept returning to the question of Belgian neutrality and stated that in any case, this question would play an important role. He had also been wondering whether it would not be possible for *us and France* to remain facing each other *under arms, without attacking each other*, in the *event of a Russian war.* I asked him if he were in a position to say whether France would agree to a pact of that sort. Since we intended neither to ruin France nor to conquer any territory, I could imagine that we might enter upon that sort of an agreement, if it assured us of Great Britain's neutrality.

The Minister said that he *would inform himself*, but he did not fail to realise the difficulty of retaining the soldiers of both sides in a state of inactivity.

My impression as a whole is, that if it is possible in any way, they want here, to

Marginal notes (left):

Then he's a false rascal!

He lies! He told Lichnowsky so himself four days ago!

So he already has my offer of yesterday afternoon, that is very plain! And then the King talks of a misunderstanding! Rot!

Marginal notes (right):

Humbug! it has not adopted it so far.

Unless an English equivalent is named!

The rascal is crazy or an idiot! Besides that, the French have begun the war and the violation of international law with their bomb-hurling planes.

keep out of the war, but that the reply of
the Secretary of State to Sir Edward
Goschen concerning Belgian neutrality has
caused an unfavourable impression.

My impression is that Mr Grey is a false dog who is afraid of his own meanness and false
policy, but who will not come out into the open against us, preferring to let himself be forced
by us to do it.

175   Wilhelm II to Nicolas II

Telegram (unnumbered)
D.D. 600
Int. Bez. I, 5, 416

Berlin, 1 August 1914
D. 10.30 p.m.

Thanks for your telegram.[1] I yesterday pointed out to your Government
the way by which, alone, war may be avoided.[2] Although I requested an
answer for noon today, no telegram from my Ambassador conveying an
answer from your Government has reached me as yet. I therefore have
been obliged to mobilise my Army.[3]

Immediate, affirmative, clear and unmistakable answer from your
Government is the only way to avoid endless misery. Until I have received
this answer, alas, I am unable to discuss the subject of your telegram.
As a matter of fact I must request you to immediately order your
troops on no account to commit the slightest act of trespassing over our
frontiers.[4]

176   Izvolsky to Sazonov

Telegram 222
Int. Bez. I, 5, 409
Duplicate to London

Paris, 1 August 1914

I received at 11.00 a.m. your telegram concerning Germany's declaration
of war on Russia.[5] I at once communicated it[6] personally to the President
of the Republic, who immediately called a Council of Ministers. Poincaré

[1] See 171.   [2] See 157.   [3] See pp. 270, 336.
[4] Marginal note by Nicolas II: 'Received after declaration of war.'
[5] *Int. Bez.* I, 5, 393 and 394.
[6] At approximately 11.30 p.m.; see R. Poincaré, *L'Union Sacrée*, pp. 495f.

told me quite categorically that the entire Council of Ministers, like himself, was firmly resolved to carry out to the letter the obligations devolving on France as a result of the treaty of alliance. However, there arises from this a series of highly complicated questions of a political as well as a strategic nature. According to the constitution, the Government requires a resolution in Parliament before any declaration of war, and two days are needed to recall Parliament. Although Poincaré has no doubt that this resolution will be passed, he would prefer to avoid public debate on the implementation of the treaty of alliance; therefore, and for reasons which have primarily to do with Britain, it would be preferable if the declaration of war should emanate not from France, but from Germany. Further, it must be borne in mind that today is only the first day of French mobilisation and that it would be more advantageous to both allies if France were only to begin military operations when mobilisation has reached a more advanced stage. Moreover, Poincaré pointed out that Germany would not wait for France to declare war on her, but would make a surprise attack without allowing her to complete mobilisation. Immediately after the conclusion of the debate of these questions by the Council of Ministers, Poincaré will send for me to inform me of the outcome.

177   Grey to Bertie

Telegram 299   London, 1 August 1914
B.D. 426   D. 8.20 p.m.

After the Cabinet Meeting today, I told M. Cambon that the present position differed entirely from that created by the Morocco incidents. In the latter, Germany made upon France demands that France could not grant, and in connection with which we had undertaken special obligations towards France. In these, public opinion would have justified the British Government in supporting France to the utmost of their ability. Now, the position was that Germany would agree not to attack France if France remained neutral in the event of war between Russia and Germany. If France could not take advantage of this position, it was because she was bound by an alliance to which we were not parties, and of which we did not know the terms. This did not mean that under no circumstances would we assist France, but it did mean that France must take her own decision at this moment without reckoning on an assistance that we were not now in a position to promise.

M. Cambon said that he could not transmit this reply to his Government and he asked me to authorise him to say that the British Cabinet had not yet taken any decision.[1]

I said that we had come to a decision: that we could not propose to Parliament at this moment to send an expeditionary military force to the continent. Such a step had always been regarded here as very dangerous and doubtful. It was one that we could not propose, and Parliament would not authorise unless our interests and obligations were deeply and desperately involved.

M. Cambon said that the French coasts were undefended. The German fleet might come through the Straits any day and attack them.

I said that that might alter public feeling here, and so might a violation of the neutrality of Belgium. He could tell his Government that we were already considering the Belgian point, and that I would ask the Cabinet to consider the point about the French coasts. He could say that the Cabinet had not yet taken any decision on these points.

Minute

I have spoken to the P.M., and attach great importance to the point being settled tomorrow.—*E. G.*, 1.8.14.

178 Nicolson to Grey

Notice
B.D. 424
                          London, 1 August 1914

M. Cambon pointed out to me this afternoon that it was at our request that France had moved her fleets to the Mediterranean, on the understanding that we undertook the protection of her northern and western coasts. As I understand you told him that you would submit to the Cabinet the question of a possible German naval attack on French northern and western ports[2] it would be well to remind the Cabinet of the above fact.

[1] Cambon was thrown into complete confusion by this disclosure; see Harold Nicolson, *Sir Arthur Nicolson, Bart., First Lord Carnock. A study in the old diplomacy*, London, 1930, pp. 418–19.
[2] See 177.

179 Moltke to Jagow

Secret   Berlin, 2 August 1914
D.D. 662   R. 2 August, afternoon
A.A. vol. 12

I have the honour of presenting herewith to the Foreign Office some suggestions of a military-political nature, to which I attribute some value from a military point of view.   *v. Moltke*

Switzerland[1]

Switzerland has mobilised. Following reports which have arrived here, she is already afraid of French violation of her neutrality,[2] as evidenced by the accumulation of French troops on her western border. It will be of advantage to assure Switzerland that Germany is prepared to secure her neutrality with military aid. For this eventuality a treaty of alliance with Switzerland has been prepared by me, one copy of which is in my hands and the other in the hands of the Chief of Swiss General Staff. This treaty, putting all Swiss armed forces under the control of the German High Command, needs only to be ratified and exchanged. This agreement has to be kept absolutely secret until a diplomatic discussion along these lines has taken place, lest premature publication should discredit the Chief of the Swiss General Staff in the eyes of his Government or expose him to the reproach of unilateral political action.

Turkey

The treaty of alliance with Turkey should be made public immediately. Turkey ought to declare war on Russia as soon as possible.[3]

England

Attempts must be made to instigate an uprising in India, if England takes a stand as our opponent.[4]

The same thing should be attempted in Egypt;[4] also in the Dominion of South Africa.[4]

Should England make her neutrality in the German-Austro-Russo-French war dependent upon Germany's assurance 'that she would act

[1] The section on Switzerland was not published in *D.D.* 662; it was evidently excised in 1919 out of deference to Switzerland as a neutral country; see *Julikrise und Kriegsausbruch 1914*, vol. I, p. 32; more details on the significance of the document, and Switzerland's attitude to Germany at the beginning of the world war are also to be found here; vol. II, p. 622.

[2] This never happened.

[3] Rosenberg's marginal note of 4 August: 'The matter has been settled as desired.'

[4] That was also what happened: see F. Fischer, *Griff nach der Weltmacht*, pp. 146ff.

with moderation in case of a victory over France' (Foreign Office, no. 218, of 2 August 1914),[1] then this assurance could be given her unconditionally and in the most binding form. It is not of consequence to us to ruin France—it is only of consequence to us to vanquish her. England's neutrality is of such importance to us that this concession could be made unconditionally.[2]

Sweden

We should strive to get Sweden to mobilise her entire armed forces immediately and to proceed as soon as possible with her 6th Division against the Finnish border.[3] Sweden's undertakings should be so guided that her measures would inspire and maintain in Russia the fear of an attack by her on Finland, as well as the possible landing of Swedish troops on the Russian coast. We must promise unconditionally to fulfil all of Sweden's desires, whether they relate to regaining Finland or are desires in other directions, so long as they are compatible with German interests.

Should Sweden declare herself willing to enter upon a joint war with Germany, then notice of this fact should at once be given at Copenhagen, with the request that the example of Sweden be followed.

Similar demands should be made of Norway, with allusion to Russia's aspiration—well recognised in Norway—to possess an ice-free harbour on the Norwegian coast, a wish that Russia would unquestionably turn at once into fact, were she to emerge a victor from the present war. The Russian aspirations can be effectually blocked, if the Scandinavian nations will join with Germany to oppose Russia's unappeasable hunger for territory.

Germany has absolutely no intention of infringing upon the political status of the Norwegian kingdom, and would gladly oppose all Russia's schemes to this end, both at present and in the future.

Denmark

No further measures are necessary. Let our already announced declaration agreeing to respect her neutrality remain, so long as our opponents' measures do not force us to new counter-measures.

The Balkans

It is necessary to bring about as soon as possible a clarification of the situation in the Balkans. Austria must state frankly whether, under the present conditions of war, she will allow the agreements, which she has made with

---

[1] Lichnowsky to Jagow; *D.D.* 641.   [2] See 139.
[3] General Staff to Jagow, 1 August; *Julikrise und Kriegsausbruch 1914*, II, No. 1015a.

Bulgaria, to be realised. The attitude of Greece, and that of Roumania, must be also clarified.

All the information that can be obtained by us concerning the Balkan states must be passed on to Austria and to Turkey immediately.

Should Italy join in the war, she, too, should be kept fully and permanently instructed as to the situation in the Balkans. The information which, to my knowledge, has been received here, to the effect that Roumania was forced to remain neutral in a Russo-Austrian conflict, but had faithfully promised that under no circumstances would she go over to Russia's side, is of the greatest importance to Austria and must be communicated to her at once.

Belgium

So far as I know, the reply to Germany's summary demand[1] is supposed to arrive, at the latest, tomorrow, Monday, 3 August, at 2 p.m. I propose that a respite of twelve hours be granted for making the reply.[2] If this should not be possible, in the opinion of the Foreign Office, the time set for presenting the demand should be altered accordingly. But I consider a twelve-hour respite to be the better plan.

Presentation of the note to Holland,[3] simultaneously with the copy of the note to Belgium.

The same thing simultaneously in England, with the additional announcement that Germany, even in the event of a hostile clash with Belgium, will not threaten her status as a nation, but, on the other hand, will, after the conclusion of peace, guarantee that Belgium's integrity is preserved. England should be asked in this case to regard Germany's procedure merely as an act of compulsory self-protection against a French menace to German territory.[4]

Italy

It is absolutely necessary that Italy be brought to declare immediately whether or not she is willing to take an active part in the approaching war, in accordance with the obligations of her alliance. To me it is of no importance that Italy should carry out to its full extent her agreement to despatch bodies of troops to Germany; if she should send only one division of cavalry, that would appear sufficient to me. It is not of consequence that Italy should support us actively with a strong force, but it is of conse-

---

[1] See **91**.
[2] This took place immediately; *D.D.* 648.
[3] See p. 231, note 3.
[4] Jagow's corresponding order to Lichnowsky was despatched to London at 5.30 p.m. the same afternoon; *D.D.* 667.

quence that the Triple Alliance as such should enter upon the war united. That would be shown by the smallest conceivable contribution of troops. I call attention to that document No. 2 of General Pollio given to the Foreign Office, 'le Gouvernement me charge de dire à Votre Excellence . . . .'[1]

Should Italy decide to take part in the war, it is necessary for us to receive early information as to the military measures planned by Italy, as well as the announcement of the date of the first day of mobilisation in Italy, which could be accomplished by direct communication between the two General Staffs.

Russia

A declaration of war against Russia, or, respectively, of Russia against us, has become of no consequence, owing to the Russian invasion across our eastern boundary. If no declaration of war from Russia has reached us, or should be presented only after the first Russian operations, then Russia has acted contrary to the Hague agreements.

France

Our possible declaration of war is entirely independent of the move made in Belgium. One does not necessarily follow the other. I do not consider it necessary yet to deliver the declaration of war to France;[2] on the other hand, I am counting on the likelihood that, if it is held back for the present, France, on her part, will be forced by public opinion to organise warlike measures against Germany, even if a formal declaration of war has not been presented. Presumably France will move into Belgium in the rôle of the protector of Belgian neutrality, just as soon as the step taken by Germany in Belgium[3] becomes known in Paris.

On our side arrangements have been made so that the crossing of the French frontier will be avoided until activities on the part of France render it necessary.

Japan

Japan should be urged to use this favourable opportunity for satisfying her various aspirations in the Far East now, preferably by means of inaugurating hostilities against a Russia tied up by a European war.

---

[1] Not in *D.D.* or among the documents of the Auswärtiges Amt.

[2] See also *D.D.* 629: Bethmann Hollweg to Wilhelm II, on the morning of 2 August: 'In accordance with understanding with Ministry of War and General Staff, presentation of declaration of war to France not necessary today for any *military* reasons. Consequently it will not be done, in the hope that the French will attack us.'

[3] See **91**.

Such desires as Japan believes she could accomplish by means of German cooperation must be promised her. We can promise Japan anything that she wishes from us in this direction.

Persia

Persia should be urged to use the favourable opportunity for shaking off the Russian yoke, and, if possible, to go hand in hand with Turkey.[1]

180 Moltke to Jagow

Secret   Berlin, 3 August 1914
D.D. 788   R. 10.00 p.m.

The Belgian Government must be informed on Tuesday, 4 August, at 6 a.m., that, to our regret, we shall be forced by the Royal Belgian Government's attitude of refusal towards our well-meant proposals,[2] to put into execution the measures of self-protection against the French menace which we have already described as unavoidably necessary, even if we do have to do it by force of arms.

This communication is a necessity, inasmuch as our troops will already be entering upon Belgian territory early tomorrow morning. I think this declaration will suffice, as Belgium has stated to us that she will oppose with force of arms any invasion.[3] I consider a declaration of war undesirable, as I am still counting on the possibility of being able to come to an understanding when the Belgian Government realises the seriousness of the situation.[4]

181 Bethmann Hollweg to Lichnowsky

Telegram 223   Berlin, 3 August 1914
D.D. 790   D. 10.25 p.m.

Please state to Sir Edward Grey that if we should take the step of violating Belgian neutrality, we would do so compelled by the duty of self-

---

[1] Mirbach's note by the words 'together with Turkey': 'Presumably that would only lead to an endless and fruitless exchange of views between the two dilatory and over cautious Moslem Governments.' More recently, see also Ullrich Gehrke, *Die deutsche Politik in Persien im ersten Weltkrieg* (Ph.D. dissertation), Hamburg, 1959.
[2] See 91.   [3] See p. 337.   [4] See 182.

preservation. We found ourselves in a position of military constraint. While France had also before that time made strong military preparations and while we had up until then confined ourselves in a military way to only the most urgent measures of military preparation for self-defence, the unfortunate Russian mobilisation had suddenly exposed us to the danger of being swallowed up by the floods from east and west. The preliminaries of the French mobilisation had demonstrated that mobilisation is fated to bring war in its train. Then, wedged in between east and west, we had to make use of every means to save ourselves. It is not by any means a case of intentional violation of international law, but the act of a man fighting for his life. I had devoted all my efforts as Imperial Chancellor towards gradually bringing about, in partnership with England, a state of affairs which would make the madness of self-destruction on the part of Europe's civilised nations impossible. Russia, by treacherously playing with fire, has brought these intentions to naught.[1] Say that I firmly hope that England, by her attitude in this world crisis, will lay a foundation on which, after it has come to an end, we may bring to realisation all that Russia's policy has for the present destroyed.

182   Jagow to Below

Telegram 48   Berlin, 3 August 1914
Urgent   R. 10.35 p.m.
D.D. 791

Your Excellency will inform the Belgian Government tomorrow, Tuesday, 4 August, at six a.m., that, to our regret, we shall be forced by its attitude of refusal towards our well-meant proposals, to put into execution the measures of self-protection against the French menace which we have already described as unavoidably necessary, even if we have to do it by force of arms.[2]

[1] See **114**, **115**, **125** and **142–4**.
[2] See **180**.

183 Paul Cambon to Viviani

Telegram 186   London, 3 August 1914
D.F. XI, 661 (*F.Y.B.* 143)   D. 11.52 a.m.
                                                R. 2.30 p.m.

Your Telegram 451.[1]

Sir E. Grey, to whom I communicated your telegram while suggesting how absolutely necessary it was for Your Excellency to give today some indication of British intentions, told me that at present he was not in a position to give me precise information on what he was going to say, as this was to be laid down in a Cabinet meeting this morning and might be modified according to the mood of the House of Commons. But he authorised me to inform you that you could state that he was making explanations to the Commons as to the present attitude of the British Government and that the chief of these declarations would be as follows:

'In case the German fleet came into the Channel or entered the North Sea in order to go round the British Isles with the object of attacking the French coasts or the French navy and of harassing French merchant shipping, the British fleet would intervene in order to give to French shipping its complete protection, in such a way that from that moment Great Britain and Germany would be in a state of war.'

Sir Edward Grey explained to me that the mention of an operation by way of the North Sea implied protection against a demonstration in the Atlantic Ocean.

On my return to the Embassy I received your telephonic communication relating to the German ultimatum addressed to Belgium.[2] I immediately communicated it to Sir Edward Grey.

184 Moltke to Jagow

Secret   Berlin, 4 August 1914
D.D. 804

1 For the purpose of carrying through the war that has broken out, it is of the very greatest importance—an importance that cannot be over-emphasized—that the importation of foodstuffs into Germany through Italy remain unimpeded. Since Italy has not been willing to observe the obligations of her alliance, but has promised to observe a benevolent

---

[1] *D.F.* XI, 621.   [2] See **91**.

neutrality, the least she can do to prove this benevolence is to put no difficulties in our way in this connection.

I request that activities towards this end be undertaken at Rome at once. It is a question of life or death for us.[1]

2 I request that the following be transmitted at once to London:

Germany wishes again to emphasise the fact that in her procedure in Belgium she was not guided by the intention of taking possession of Belgian territory on some frivolous pretext, even in the event of a hostile clash with Belgium. Germany's declaration to the Netherlands that she would not set foot on Dutch territory during this war, but, on the other hand, was determined to observe the strictest neutrality with regard to the Netherlands,[2] is the best substantiation of the assurance just given. The English Government is able to see for itself that if Germany were cherishing any intention of acquiring Belgian territory, such an acquisition could only be of value if the same intention were being cherished towards Holland. It is here emphasised once again, that Germany's procedure in Belgium was compelled, and could not help but be compelled, by the knowledge, acquired from reliable sources, of France's intended military operations. Germany could not afford to expose herself to the danger of attack by strong French forces in the direction of the Lower Rhine.[3] Germany was forced to act on the principle that the offensive is the best defensive, which England, always ready to take the most energetic steps in time of war, should certainly understand better than anybody else. In this war it is a question for Germany, not only of her whole national existence and of the continuation of the German Empire, created through so many bloody sacrifices, but also of the preservation and maintenance of German civilisation and principles as against uncivilised Slavdom.

Germany is unable to believe that England will be willing to assist, by becoming an enemy of Germany, in destroying this civilisation—a civilisation in which English spiritual culture has for ages had so large a share. The decision as to this lies in England's hands.

Note

I would ask that this despatch be sent to London *uncoded*, and that the Ambassador be advised to read it to Sir Edward Grey.[4] It will not do us

---

[1] Accordingly a telegram was immediately despatched to Flotow; *D.D.* 806.

[2] For the text of the parallel note to the Netherlands Government see *D.D.* 426, note 3.

[3] The aims imputed to the French were no less of a fabrication on 4 August than they had been on 26 July, when Moltke had drafted the summons to Belgium and the note to the Netherlands.

[4] See **185**.

any harm if this note, by reason of its uncoded form, should also become known elsewhere.

3 Note to the Foreign Office: It is necessary continually to maintain towards the Belgian Government, even after the German invasion has taken place, the stand that Germany is ready at any moment to hold out to Belgium the hand of a brother, and is ever willing to enter upon negotiations concerning an acceptable *modus vivendi*, subject to the prosecution of the war forced upon us by France's procedure.[1]

The indispensable basis of these negotiations, however, would have to remain the opening of Liège to the passage of German troops, and Belgium's assurance that she would not undertake the destruction of any railroads, bridges or artificial structures. Other demands than these would not be required from a military point of view.

185   Jagow to Lichnowsky

Telegram 226   Berlin, 4 August 1914
D.D. 810   D. 10.20 a.m.

Please dispel any mistrust that may subsist on the part of British Government with regard to our intentions, by repeating most positively formal assurance that, even in the case of armed conflict with Belgium, Germany will, under no pretence whatever, annex Belgian territory.[2] Sincerity of this declaration is borne out by fact that we solemnly pledged our word to Holland strictly to respect her neutrality.[3] It is obvious that we could not profitably annex Belgian territory without making at the same time territorial acquisitions at expense of Holland. Please impress upon Sir E. Grey that German army could not be exposed to French attack across Belgium, which was planned according to absolutely unimpeachable information.[4] Germany had consequently to disregard Belgian neutrality, it being for her a question of life or death to prevent French advance.

[1] See p. 357, note 3.
[2] See in contrast 91, where the preservation of Belgium's territorial integrity was made conditional upon the German army being granted a free transit.
[3] See p. 357, note 2.
[4] This idea (on 4 August) that the French were intending to attack Germany through Belgium was again a complete fabrication.

186 Lichnowsky to Jagow

Telegram 245
D.D. 820

London, 4 August 1914
D. 10.02 a.m.
R. 1.37 p.m.

Yesterday I was not yet acquainted with the complete text of Sir E. Grey's speech, of which only a short parliamentary report was available. Since today's publication of its content in full, however, I must correct my impressions of yesterday[1] by saying that I do not believe that we shall be able to count much longer on England's neutrality.

As I have repeatedly reported to Your Excellency, the question of the violation of Belgian neutrality constituted one of the most important factors in England's self-restraint.[2] Mr Asquith as well as Sir E. Grey had called this to my attention, and, as reported, I was able to convince myself before the session, that Sir E. Grey was in a state of intense excitement as the result of the violation of Belgian territory by our army.[3]

What form British intervention will take, and whether it will take place at once, I am not able to judge. But I do not anticipate that, as I thought yesterday, from my knowledge gained only from extracts of the speech, the British Government will keep out, unless we are in a position to evacuate Belgian territory in the very shortest possible time. Hence we shall probably have to reckon on England's early hostility. The reception which met Sir E. Grey's speech in the House can be interpreted to mean that, outside of the left wing of its own party, the Government will have behind it the overwhelming majority of Parliament in any active policy the purpose of which is the protection of France and Belgium.

The news that reached here yesterday concerning the invasion of Belgium[4] by German troops brought about a complete reversal of public opinion, to our disadvantage. The appeal of the King of the Belgians,[5] made in moving language, has materially strengthened this impression.

---

[1] *D.D.* 801.
[2] See 174; also *D.D.* 641, 676, 799 and 801.
[3] *D.D.* 764.
[4] It is not clear what the basis for these reports was; they were in anticipation of events by one day, since the German invasion only began on the morning of 4 August.
[5] Text in the first Belgian Grey Book, no. 25.

187   Goschen to Grey

Telegram 136   Berlin, 4 August 1914
B.D. 666   R. 13 August

Your telegram 266 of 4 August.[1]

Secretary of State for Foreign Affairs regrets that he cannot give assurance demanded as German troops passed Belgian frontier this morning.

He begs me to assure you that this was military necessity and matter of life and death for Empire; every other line of attack would have taken too long and enabled Russia to concentrate. They had been ready to give, and had in fact given, assurances to Belgium that every compensation would be given to her after the war, and that her neutrality in every other way except as regards passage of troops would be respected.[2] Belgium, he admitted, had acted quite naturally and very loyally in this matter.

188   Goschen to Grey

Telegram 137   Berlin, 4 August 1914
B.D. 667   R. 13 August

Your telegram 270 of 4 August.[3]

Both Chancellor and Secretary of State for Foreign Affairs regretted that they could give no other answer than that which they gave me this afternoon.[4] I told them that in that case I had been instructed to ask for my passports.

My interview with the Chancellor was very painful. He said that he could not but consider it an intolerable thing that because they were taking the only course open to them to save the Empire from disaster, England should fall upon them just for the sake of the neutrality of Belgium. He looked upon England as entirely responsible for what might now happen.

I asked him whether he could not understand that we were bound in honour to do our best to preserve a neutrality which we had guaranteed. He said: 'But at what price!'

[1] *B.D.* 573.
[2] See also **91**.
[3] *B.D.* 594.
[4] See **187**.

Conclusion

The outbreak of the First World War was not the result of blind, un-fathomable fate, nor need its causes defy rational analysis by the historian. There is no reason to refer the matter to some inscrutable higher force nor to give up in despair, in a fit of what has been called 'historical nihilism'.[1] It is equally inadmissible to stifle the discussion by charging that the new results (new only for Germany) were a renewal of the accusations levelled against Germany at Versailles or by claiming that everything was already settled so that no more research was necessary. A new look at July 1914 in the 1960s has nothing to do with the so-called verdict of Versailles in 1919. The traditional German view was, as we now know, largely mani-pulated by the German Auswärtiges Amt of the Weimar period and was challenged by scholarly historians like Renouvin, Schmitt and Albertini.[2] Even the agreement between German and French historians of 1951–2[3] cannot end the matter. They merely give recommendations for rewriting textbooks in France and Germany, and no amount of genuine consensus can dispense with the need for free research, discussion and criticism.

[1] 'Gathering Storm, 1914' in *Times Literary Supplement* (5 August, 1965), p. 1.

[2] See above, p. 10, n. 2. After the recent, more conventional, study by Laurence Lafore, *The Long Fuse: an interpretation of the origins of World War I* (London, 1966), the issue of the *J.C.H.*, vol. I, 3, which is devoted to '1914', shows that Fritz Fischer and his group are more in basic agreement with contemporary historians on the First World War outside Germany than are his German critics, as reflected by Wolfgang J. Mommsen's essay on the Fischer controversy in the same issue. See Mommsen, 'The Debate on German War Aims' in *J.C.H.*, vol. I, 3, pp. 47–72.

[3] See above, p. 10, n. 5.

A final analysis should not in any way be an accusation or a verdict, but simply a summary of events and arguments. What matters above all else is to assess the responsibility for causing the First World War as objectively as possible, not in moral but, as it were, in scientific terms. This can only be achieved by a critical approach to all traditional creeds and dogmas, by leaving out politics (as rarely happened in the past on the German side) and by a 'patient and careful evaluation of the original sources'.[1]

A detailed discussion of the causes of the war can speedily discard two standard arguments, because they are commonplaces which do not substantially explain anything. It is, of course, true that the war was a result of the tensions in the age of imperialism. But this is no more helpful than to say that the Wars of the Roses were a result of the tensions in the age of feudalism, or that a motor accident was caused by the bad state of roads or by the density of traffic. An enquiry into the immediate causes will have to consider the circumstances which led to the accident in the given place and time. By the same token, it is not enough to be satisfied with the statement that in 1914 no one really wanted the world war. Hardly anyone in his senses wanted (or wants) a world war, and apart from the years of the war itself, no one has ever seriously maintained that Germany wanted the First World War. The correct, but commonplace, statement also implies that the Entente Powers did not want the war, and this should help to overcome lingering German resentments and prejudices. The desire of any Power to bring about the First World War, therefore, is no longer a point of dispute.

Yet world war did break out, and the real causes have to be analysed. To avoid emotional judgments it seems advisable to make a two-fold distinction: first between the three stages or phases of war, second between *desiring* and merely *causing* any of the three. In July and August 1914 three kinds of war appear to have been telescoped within one week; local war (Austria-Hungary against Serbia), continental war (Austria-Hungary and Germany against Russia and France), and world war (Britain joining the continental war). The discussion has to concentrate on finding out which Power desired or merely sparked off one particular kind of war. Thus by desiring the local war it might be possible to cause the continental or even the world war.

Clearly, the Power or Powers who encouraged the local war against Serbia had the greatest share in causing the World War, as all concerned knew perfectly well that war against Serbia would provoke Russia's intervention and might lead to a world war. Why was it not possible to find a peaceful solution in July 1914? This time war *was* envisaged from the first

[1] G. Ritter, *Staatskunst*, vol. I, p. 24.

moment of the crisis—war there would be, even if only against tiny Serbia. This is why the diplomatic crisis could not follow, as it were, its natural course, but was speedily pushed aside, resulting in an actual state of war on 28 July.

Among the Powers involved, we can easily eliminate those who certainly did not want the local war or continental war: Britain, Russia and France. They all tried desperately to stave off the war against Serbia, because they knew it could not be localised. Their very argument against it was that 'the best method of avoiding a general war is to prevent a local one' (113).[1] Serbia did not want such a war either, at least not in July 1914, because her leaders knew that she would be crushed by Austria-Hungary. Serbia's almost complete acceptance of the Austrian ultimatum is in itself proof enough of her anxiety to ward off the threatening war.[2] Furthermore, neither the Triple Entente nor Serbia took the initiatives that made for war, but only reacted to the actions of the other side.

The decisive factor is to be found in German policy in July 1914. Austria did, it is true, envisage war against Serbia, did prepare for it by the ultimatum of 23 July, by breaking off diplomatic relations and by partial mobilisation on 25 July, and did actually open hostilities by the declaration of war on Serbia on 28 July and the artillery bombardment of Belgrade on 29 July. But war against Serbia would have been out of the question without the approval of the dominating Power in the Triple Alliance—the German Reich. Immediately after the murder at Sarajevo, spirits in Vienna were running high, and there was strong pressure for immediate war against Serbia, in particular from most of the German-speaking press in Austria, from the military and from high officials in the Austrian-Hungarian Foreign Ministry. Yet all those in power, including Conrad, were prepared to let their final decision depend on the attitude of the German Government. It was only after Berlin had given the Austrians the green light and promised to cover their rear against Russian intervention, it was only after the Germans had urged their allies to make war against Serbia as soon as possible, that the Austrians finally made up their minds, and even then not without hesitation and misgiving. The Austrians may have been prompted into action by the veiled threat made by the Germans that Austria now had her last chance to prove herself as a great power and as worthy to be a German ally.[3]

On the other hand, the Germans suspected that their ally would not be tough enough and might be satisfied with less than a military subjection of Serbia. They feared that Austria could, by delaying action too long,

---

[1] See above, pp. 161, 219.   [2] See above, p. 169.
[3] See above, p. 99.

provide the Serbians with the chance of giving in peacefully, so that the Austrians would have lost their last opportunity of strengthening their position by a short successful war and by a military victory over Serbia (15, 28, 33).

It has been argued again and again that the German Government was not informed of Austrian intentions to go to war and disapproved of them, at least internally, once they became known in Berlin.[1] This line, however, was nothing but a diplomatic lie manufactured by Berlin in the July crisis for consumption abroad, and historians today should no longer accept it uncritically as the truth. The documents prove beyond doubt that Berlin not only knew of the possibility of war against Serbia, but actually pressed for it. By 11 July, the Auswärtiges Amt knew of the intentions and general tenor of the ultimatum when it was prepared (16), and only feared that it would not come early enough or would not be harsh enough. By 14 July Berlin was informed of the Austrian intention to break off diplomatic relations with Belgrade, as part of the 'action' against Serbia. The Auswärtiges Amt not only approved of such a move but also forecast a similar measure to be taken by Germany.[2] By 19 or 20 July Berlin must have known of Austrian preparations for a possible bombardment of Belgrade (32). Thus, if the German Government had really wished, there would have been ample time to make representations in Vienna or to show concern about too aggressive a policy against Serbia. If the German Government did not take such steps, it was because they wanted the 'punitive expedition' against Serbia actually to take place.

By giving Austria a free hand and urging her to make war against Serbia as soon as possible, the German Government in fact created the crisis of July 1914. Berlin was well aware that Russia would be forced to intervene, making world war inevitable. It is most unlikely that the German statesmen had forgotten their experience of the two preceding years,[3] and in early July 1914 the Auswärtiges Amt did repeat that realistic warning (4). Some fragments of the Riezler diary confirm what could be gathered from diplomatic documents generally known for decades, that Bethmann Hollweg had seen the risk of world war, and had consciously accepted it when inaugurating his policy.[4] The second question asked above also inevitably leads to the paramount German share in causing the First World War. It has been shown that it was Germany who in the last analysis had made war against Serbia possible and thereby introduced the decisive element which made a peaceful solution virtually impossible. Germany was also responsible for precipitating developments and severing

[1] G. Ritter, *Staatskunst*, II, p. 321.
[2] See above, p. 96.   [3] See above, pp. 42–44.   [4] See above, p. 74.

all diplomatic links. Even if the Austrians had declared war against Serbia without German pressure, they originally intended to do so only after their mobilisation against Serbia was complete, on about 12 August. It was only after German representations, made first by Jagow on 25 July and vigorously supported by Tschirschky the following day in Vienna, that the Austrian Government decided to declare war on Serbia before the completion of their mobilisation (42, 71, 86, 88).

The reasons for the German hurry emerge clearly from the documents: if Vienna delayed the 'punitive expedition' too long, Germany and Austria would be exposed to the mediatory pressure of the other Powers, and it would become increasingly difficult to maintain the intransigent position of 'localising', which meant waging, the war against Serbia (155). Only quick action could cut the ground from beneath all attempts at mediation between Vienna and Belgrade, and this was achieved by precipitating the declaration of war on Serbia. There was a second 'advantage' in creating the *fait accompli*: the declaration of war and the immediate opening of hostilities—again, urged by Berlin (71)—made it impossible for Austria to go back to a peaceful solution. The Austrians could no longer bale out (*abschnappen*) as Moltke feared of the Russians as late as 1 August.[1]

There are hardly any more doubts possible about the overall share of Germany in causing the First World War. Yet the more liberal version of the traditional German view, that all the Powers were equally guilty, has been recently reaffirmed by Karl Dietrich Erdmann, and this in spite of new materials and arguments, and the fact that Erdmann himself admitted that 'by the Riezler diary . . . some things are really corrected'.[2] Erdmann offered a slightly modified formula: according to him all the Powers could have prevented the war, if only they had seriously desired peace. This modern version of the old Lloyd George dictum does not hold water when inspected more closely: the Triple Entente did try to prevent the one kind of war which was bound to spark off the fatal chain reaction—local war—because they wanted to prevent continental war (113); they had always warned Germany of the illusion of 'localisation'. Once all efforts at mediation had failed because of German and Austrian intransigence, once the critical threshold had been crossed on 28 July by the war against Serbia, there was no way of holding back the course of events. In the actual situation, and according to the standards of the age of imperialism, Russia and France could not remain passive and yield to the combined German-Austrian blackmail. They behaved, it should be noted, exactly in the way Bethmann Hollweg had originally expected.[3]

[1] See above, p. 336.   [2] *Der Spiegel* (21 October, 1964), p. 49.   [3] See above, p. 61.

Even more questionable is Erdmann's attempt to explain how the Powers could have prevented the First World War:

> Austria, if she had accepted the Serbian answer to the ultimatum; Russia, if she had dropped Serbian nationalism; France, if she had not promised Russia to be faithful to her commitments in this crisis; England, if she had made her position clear in the case of an European conflict; and Germany, if she had held back Austria.[1]

The statements on Austria and Germany cannot be objected to, except, perhaps, that the Austrians possibly did not dare to accept the Serbian answer because they feared German displeasure at committing an act of inexcusable weakness. The statement on Britain is doubtful, to say the least. If England had declared herself neutral, world war would have been prevented, but not continental war, because then one of the conditions of certain German victory would have been fulfilled. If Britain had declared herself openly and at an early stage for Russia and France (a move which Grey dared not make for reasons of domestic policy, but which Crowe in the Foreign Office and Sazonov in St Petersburg strongly urged), Germany might perhaps have backed down, as Crowe and Sazonov hoped. But this is far from certain. After all, the German Government could still have beaten a retreat on 29 July, when British intervention became certain. The argument implied by Erdmann sounds even stranger if one remembers that so far, Crowe's and Sazonov's demands that Britain should support her partners early and energetically enough had always been seen by German historians as proof of Russian and British war-mongering, of the war guilt of the Entente Powers.

Russia could not drop Serbia and her traditional interests in the Balkans under the combined Austrian-German threat of a great war, unless she was prepared to abdicate as a Great Power. France could not but act according to the obligations of a treaty of alliance, which was almost a quarter of a century old, and which envisaged the situation that actually arose in July 1914: a provocation arising from Germany and/or Austria, which was bound to upset the balance of power in Europe. If France had dropped Russia in July 1914, German victory over Russia would have been certain, and an isolated France would have had to face an overwhelmingly powerful Germany, the hegemonial Power on the Continent.

Erdmann's formula, therefore, is hardly more than a theoretical construction, which contributes little to our understanding of the situation in July and August 1914. It amounts to the not very helpful statement that

---

[1] K-D. Erdmann, 'Zur Beurteilung Bethmann Hollwegs' in *G.W.U.* 9 (1964), p. 535. This is a slightly modified version of a formula presented by Erdmann a few years earlier; see K-D. Erdmann, *Die Zeit der Weltkriege*, p. 23.

the First World War could have been prevented if the aggressors had not attacked and their victims had not defended themselves. Today it can no longer be doubted that Germany was the aggressor, for the German policy of deliberately provoking Russia with the help of a local *blitzkrieg* against Serbia to be executed by Austria drove Russia, France and Britain to the wall and into a position where they could not but react against massive German ambitions.

After establishing Germany's overwhelming share in causing the First World War we may turn to secondary questions: what were German motives? What was the connection between *Weltpolitik*, German policy in July 1914 and subsequent German war aims? Was the aggression premeditated? Was it meant to achieve all or some of those war aims which were formulated in Germany immediately after the outbreak of the war? Such questions bristle with difficulties, as documentary evidence is almost completely lacking. Still, a tentative answer can be given. The material referred to in the Chapter, 'Origins of the First World War', seems to show that the ruling circles of Wilhelmine Germany were well aware that *Weltpolitik* involved a risk of world war. Here is the element of premeditation. The Kaiser and Spahn in 1912 and the Chancellor in 1913 made uncannily accurate forecasts of the constellation which led to war in July 1914.[1]

It is harder to decide whether German leaders envisaged conquests before August 1914. As will be shown below, certain war aims began to emerge in the last days of July 1914. The war appears to have breached a dam in German society and let loose a fantastic flood of annexationist schemes. Such ideas could hardly have originated in the excitement of the war; the desire to make Germany a fully-fledged World Power had always entailed the idea of spreading German influence. The war hysteria seems to have crystallised these diffuse and vague sentiments.

To strike at the root of the problem, a more penetrating psychological study of German pre-war society and its unhealthy collective state of mind is needed. Here the recent concept of the 'Copenhagen complex' may prove useful. As Jonathan Steinberg has rightly pointed out:

> There is something incongruous about Schlieffen's and Moltke's apprehension. Odd as the idea of Ludendorff in his bath was to John Maynard Keynes, the image of the aged Count Schlieffen sitting in his study obsessed by spectral hordes pouring over the frontiers of the Reich is surely odder? Here was Germany, the greatest power the continent of Europe had ever known, a land full of the noise and smells of industrial expansion, guarded by the world's most terrible army, augmented by the world's

[1] See above, pp. 41f., 44.

second most powerful high seas fleet, a society literally bursting with every conceivable expression of strength, and here were her leaders, nervously expecting Sir John Fisher at any moment or the hordes of invading Slavs.[1]

The 'Copenhagen complex' was followed by what could be called the 'encirclement complex', and there were more complexes in Wilhelmine society to disturb the public mind, such as British envy of Germany, French revanchism, Russian Pan-Slavism. The realities behind them were microscopic, their emotional impact in Germany tremendous. Yet they suggest a way of understanding pre-war Germany a little better: if the 'Copenhagen complex' was a negative psychological reflex of German intentions to challenge Britain by *Weltpolitik* and a German Battle Fleet,[2] the 'encirclement complex' may have been a subconscious compensation of the German desire for further expansion. The German obsession with Russian military recovery by 1916 or 1917, which was given as the main justification for launching a preventive war in 1914, seems to betray a basic German trauma: the Entente Powers would become too powerful for Germany and her ramshackle ally. Since it is highly improbable that the Entente would have attacked the Central Powers in 1917 or later, one can only conclude that German leaders must have felt that they would have lost any chance by 1917 to impose *their* will on Europe, short of going to war; and they would have lost a war of aggression started in 1917 or after.

By the same token, the 'British envy' complex reflects Germany's curious love-hate of Britain, best personified in the Kaiser and the Führer. German obsession with 'French revanchism' probably reflects a guilt complex over the annexation of Alsace-Lorraine and indicates what Germany would have done in a similar situation—the Second World War after all did bring the temporary re-annexation of Alsace-Lorraine. The 'Russian Pan-Slavism' complex reflects Pan-German ideas in reverse: the powerful influence ascribed to Russian Pan-Slavism by German propaganda tallies with the enormous powers of Pan-Germanism in German society.

Together, these complexes amounted to a feeling that the rest of the world was hostile to Germany, and this in turn resulted in Germany's political agoramania. This can be seen as a psychological reflection of the desire to expand Germany's power, necessarily at the expense of her neighbours, and to be different from the rest of mankind. There was even a masochistic glorying in the fact that she had to face a 'world of enemies',

---

[1] See above, p. 36.
[2] J. Steinberg, *The Copenhagen Complex*, p. 41.

who were unwilling to accept the blessings of German standards, reputed to heal the world one day.[1] Such wicked unwillingness appeared only as another proof of hostility against Germany.

A further complex should be mentioned—the Bismarck complex. Shortly after Bismarck's fall a veritable Bismarck cult arose in Germany, leading to a constant search for precedences in Bismarck's policies. Wilhelmine Germany was, as it were, constantly looking over her shoulders in search of guidance from Germany's greatest statesman. The obsession with Bismarck could be carried to absurd lengths: in the middle of the First World War Bethmann Hollweg had in all earnest to answer the ever-present question, 'What would Bismarck have done?', put to him by Bismarck's biographer, Erich Marcks, during the agitation, which pressed for an open discussion about German war aims.[2]

The solemn debates about what Bismarck would have done, the elaborate exegesis of the Bismarck codices were, however, doubly irrelevant to the German situation then (and after). The towering figure of the Iron Chancellor could, with its complexities, with Bismarck's well-known tactical flexibility (vulgarly named opportunism), mean anything to anybody. Bismarck defied any attempt at straightforward ideological annexation by one of the main wings of German Patriotism. Furthermore, 'Bismarck's heirs', or self-appointed disciples, chose to misinterpret their hero on two important points: they ignored or forgot his warning that an attempt at converting Germany's latent hegemony into an open one would spell disaster for the Reich itself, an insight which betrayed Bismarck's appreciation of the subtle dialectics of power politics and Germany's geographical situation in Central Europe. Secondly, they perverted his whole approach to politics. For him it was 'the art of the possible', whereas for Riezler, perhaps the most sophisticated of German thinkers and politicians in the age of *Weltpolitik*, it apparently had something to do with demanding the impossible.[3]

All these complexes produced a dangerous emotional instability. Taken together with Prussian militarism, Conservative-Liberal bureaucracy and the industrial energies of the Ruhr, the Saar and Upper Silesia, the result was a strange mixture of huge economic and military power on the one hand, and of hopeless political and social bankruptcy on the other. Superficially modernised German political institutions and ideas fitted, as Michael Balfour suggested with slight exaggeration, more into the Stone

---

[1] See above, p. 34.

[2] F. Fischer, *Griff nach der Weltmacht*, p. 112.

[3] See the revealing title of Riezler's magnum opus, *Die Erforderlichkeit des Unmöglichen. Prolegomena zur einer Theorie der Politik*, etc.

Age than into the twentieth century.[1] Behind that awe-inspiring structure
of power and weakness, each strengthening the other, was that explosive
bundle of ambitions, romantic nostalgia, resentments, fears and complexes that made up the German political neurosis in ever-new forms. On
top of it were vain (Bülow) or mediocre (Bethmann Hollweg) political
leaders and a near-neurotic Kaiser (followed after the interval of the
Weimar Republic by the still more neurotic Führer). With his virtues and
shortcomings, the Kaiser most perfectly embodied the German nation in
hot pursuit of their elusive and self-destructive *fata morgana*, called
'equality' in terms of power. The Kaiser and his Chancellors proved
unable to direct the enormous potential of the German nation into peaceful channels, to find constructive solutions for the sharp internal conflicts
within German society. Their failure made a rational German foreign
policy even less probable, and made the great collision even more unavoidable by conjuring up a host of largely self-fulfilling prophesies,
which all ended in the final ruin of the Reich in 1945.

German jitters before 1914 and expansive policies during the war also
indicate an ideological motivation, but this is bound up with *Weltpolitik*.
Half a century after the event German motives come into focus. The
murder at Sarajevo seemed to offer the golden chance for the Reich to become a fully-fledged World Power by establishing herself firmly on the
Continent, either by war or by the threat of war. At the same time, it
seemed possible to strengthen Germany's position as the bulwark of con-
servatism in the world by crushing the national revolutionary movement
in the Balkans and humiliating or conquering those Powers which, directly
or indirectly, were upholding the democratic principle at home or abroad.

This is what Jagow seems to have had in mind when he insisted that
'the maintenance of Austria, and in fact of the most powerful Austria possible, is a necessity for us both for *internal*[my italics] and external reasons'
(30). The reasoning of the German *White Book* of 2 August 1914 points
to the same underlying factor. The *White Book*, largely conceived by
Kurt Riezler, already used the racist vocabulary of a more sinister future,
but it suggests the same when it maintains that, by Austria's gradual
collapse and by the 'subjection of all the Slavs under one Russian sceptre',
the 'position of the Teutonic race in Central Europe' would become
'untenable'.[2]

---

[1] Michael Balfour, *The Kaiser and His Times* (London, 1964), p. 369. The best German treatment of Wilhelm II is still Emil Ludwig's brilliant psychological study, *Wilhelm II* (Berlin,
1928). Recently it was republished, with a postscript by this author, where some of the points
raised above are discussed in detail.

[2] For an English version of the *German White Book* see C.D.D., pp. 405–34; the quotation
on p. 406.

Everyone will admit that Germany from 1914 to 1918 was not driven to act as she did by 'a mere lust of conquest for the sake of conquest'. Crowe's shrewd analysis of 1907[1] was echoed and confirmed, first by the Kaiser on 4 August 1914 in defending German action, and then later by Gerhard Ritter in castigating Fritz Fischer.[2] But conquest, as envisaged in German war aims, had a definite political function, and was subordinated to one supreme aim—the strengthening of the Reich and the defeat of the sinister forces of national revolution and democracy that were threatening the military, conservative and aristocratic empires in Central Europe. This is why German diplomacy in July 1914 again and again stressed to Czarist Russia the necessity of maintaining the monarchic principle by the solidarity of the conservative Powers, as an argument for Russia to drop revolutionary Serbia (see documents **28, 33, 58, 62, 100**). Perhaps nothing infuriated the Kaiser more than the refusal of the Russians to play that game, and the Czar's ideological 'betrayal' by lining up with national revolutionaries, republicans and liberals against the stronghold of the monarchic and conservative principles. The desire to achieve the final breakthrough as a world power and the panic of an anachronistic but powerful conservative system incapable of coping in a peaceful and constructive way with newly emergent social and political forces, probably drove the German statesmen to their ideological, pre-emptive strike.

Such a wider perspective also helps to solve the paradox between the subjectively defensive mood of German patriotism from 1914 onwards and its offensive expansion in the war: German policy aimed at defending the conservative Reich against the new forces in the world, the most radical ones on the level of states then being organised in Serbia and her national revolutionary or national democratic movement. In a rapidly changing world the Germans wanted to conserve their social and political order, but the way they chose to go about it was to take the offensive, the calculated risk of war and enforce a showdown at the least disadvantageous moment.[3]

After Klaus Epstein recently dismantled so brilliantly on one page one of the standard arguments of traditional German historiography,[4] the nagging insistence on the 'defensive' character of German policies and actions during the First World War becomes even more irrelevant, for in the wider historical context it degenerates into a mere quibble over words,

[1] See above, pp. 29f.
[2] G. Ritter, *H.Z.*, 194/3, p. 135 (Ullstein no. 616, p. 137).
[3] See above, pp. 47, 123.
[4] Klaus Epstein, 'Gerhard Ritter and the First World War' in *J.C.H.*, vol. I, 3, p. 198. The article is a critical review of the third volume of G. Ritter's *Staatskunst und Kriegshandwerk*.

such as 'defensive' and 'offensive'. Looking back from the mid-1960's we can understand the German mood of 1914, that strange mixture of ideological despair, political bankruptcy and overwhelming economic and military power. From this sprang that blind, proud and explosive stubbornness that persuaded the Reich to plunge into the abyss rather than work out a political solution with the new revolutionary forces in the world. German desperation chose 'suicide for fear of death' (Bismarck) by engineering the first example of unsuccessful brinkmanship in our century, in a situation which, in July 1914, rapidly escalated into world war. We can understand German motives even better, since Hitler and the Third Reich staged a repetition on an even grander and more destructive scale, only 25 years later; since Britain and France acted, on a more limited scale, in a similar mood of despair and political bankruptcy over Suez and Nasser in 1956, and since the United States have recently worked itself into a similar mood of desperate helplessness towards newly emerging revolutionary forces, which they tried to crush in 1961 in Cuba, and are still trying to wipe out in Vietnam.

That there has been no world war since 1945 is because the fear of the absolute weapon has checked the 'normal' process of escalation, which was touched off in 1914 comparatively easily in a world without atomic weapons. Compared with the informality with which wars have broken out since 1939 and compared with the massive and sustained provocations some countries have had to suffer since 1945, Austrian statesmen look ridiculously fussy with their insistence that a formal declaration of war be delivered to Serbia, while the Germans look much more modern with their insistence on a *blitzkrieg* against Serbia, if possible without any time-wasting niceties such as ultimata or declarations of war. On the other hand, both the Serbians and Russians appear extremely touchy over their insistence on Serbian sovereignty and over the few artillery shells lobbed across the Danube into Belgrade on 29 July 1914, by contrast with the military intervention of the United States in South Vietnam since 1960, and with the permanent air bombardment of North Vietnam since February 1965.

But this way of looking at the events of 1914 is not really permissible, because it means substituting the prevailing rules of 1914 by experiences and judgments of our own time. However, the historical comparison illustrates the debasement of international and political morals which began when the German Government opened Pandora's box in an act of sheer political and ideological despair.

In such a world-wide perspective of the direct consequence of *Weltpolitik* and policy in July 1914, Germany's aims in the First World War seem even more anachronistic and bizarre. The attempt to set up the Reich as the hegemonial power on the continent—by the combination of old-fashioned annexations in East and West, of buffer or vassal states under German political control and of the fairly modern concept of a *Mitteleuropa*, reaching from the North Cape to the Persian Gulf—did not seem too absurd for the German mind. What evidence is there of German expansionist plans existing by July 1914? If the German Government during the diplomatic crisis of that month was apparently successful in avoiding the use of certain compromising documents which one would normally have expected in regular diplomatic transactions,[1] it is even less to be expected that they would lay down plans of conquest before the war or to let them be seen after the war.[2] Nevertheless, two points ought to be borne in mind: first, the experience of 1870, when Prussia entered the war against France as a 'defensive' move, when Bismarck very soon manipulated German public opinion into demanding the annexation of Alsace-Lorraine,[3] and when those Socialists who dared to dissent were speedily imprisoned. So far, it has not yet been proved whether the Chancellor or the Auswärtiges Amt manipulated the German press similarly from 1914 onwards; from what we know it seems unlikely that they did, although the idea should not be excluded. However, it can be shown that German war aims already made their appearance in the last days of July 1914: the German ultimatum to Belgium, conceived by Moltke as early as 26 July, included the 'offer' to Belgium to respect Belgian territorial integrity, if she were to allow German troops to pass unhindered (91). By the same token the Chancellor generously 'promised' to abstain from annexations in Belgium and France, if Britain were to remain neutral, but he refused to extend the same promise to Belgian and French colonies in Africa (139). As neither condition underlying the German 'offers' materialised—Belgian passivity and British neutrality—Germany could claim a free hand in pressing for annexations after a victorious war. At least indirectly, annexations of Belgian and French territory were foreshadowed in the two German moves, and, directly, annexations in Africa, as part of the drive for what became known as *Mittelafrika*, the colonial counterpart to *Mitteleuropa*.

In any case, the result for the world would have been the same, if Germany had deliberately provoked a war which rapidly escalated into world war, in order to achieve all the direct and indirect conquests

[1] For the lacunae in the German documents on July 1914 see I. Geiss, *Julikrise*, vol. I, pp. 32–4.
[2] See above, p. 30.
[3] See above, p. 18, note 2.

indicated in her war aims, instead of taking the course of action that she did, pretending afterwards to have been attacked and therefore forced in self-defence to secure all those safeguards for future German security (*Sicherungen*). The main effect was simply to convince German socialists of the righteousness of the German cause when defending the Fatherland and to confuse generations of German historians, until the secret documents could be inspected by a fresh generation of historians. For the latter, German innocence in the First World War is no longer a point of national honour; it is more important to them to establish the facts, no matter how painful this may be today for political feeling in Germany.

The analysis of German war aims in the First World War has opened up new historical perspectives, at least for Germans. It emerged that Germany's bid for the status of a world power under the Kaiser was re-peated under strikingly similar circumstances only 25 years later by Hitler and the Third Reich. Although the German aim to give the world a new order along German, let alone Nazi, lines, was absurd, a comparison with German ideas and actions under the Kaiser shows that the Führer's aims made sense—by German standards at least and as long as Hitler seemed to be a success. The striking similarity between German war aims in the two World Wars (in spite of some significant differences) gave rise to the concept of what has been called the 'continuity' of German history.[1] Con-tinuity has nothing to do with postulating an identity between the most important political phases and dominant forces in recent German history. But it is a first German attempt at finding the common denominator be-tween all the seemingly nonsensical changes in the German political scene during the last half century. The hidden unity between the 'liberal' and conservative wings of German patriotism on the one hand, and the chauvinist (Pan-German and later Fascist) wing of German patriotism on the other, can be seen in the rejection of the modern world, that is, of the social and political implications of the industrial revolution.[2]

The crystallisation of the German ideological resentment against the modern world has been the concept of the 'Reich' with its implied bid for

[1] There is no detailed discussion yet by a German historian of continuity in recent German history. A survey of the problem will be given by an anthology, edited and introduced by J. C. G. Röhl, *From Bismarck to Hitler: The Problem of Continuity in German History*, due for publication in autumn 1968.

[2] The rejection of the modern world by the German mind is admirably summed up by Gerhard Ritter's classical dictum, which he made, nearly half a century ago, in the context of Luther's historical stature: 'Recently it has often been argued whether Martin Luther belongs to the Middle Ages or to the "modern world". Much more important seems to us the question, whether we [the Germans] do want to belong to the "modern world", if it is understood to be represen-ted mainly by the ideas of Anglo-Saxon and Latin (*romanische*) culture.' G. Ritter, *Luther: Gestalt und Symbol* (Munich, 1925), p. 154.

German hegemony at least on the continent. The establishment of such a hegemonial position would have been the consequence of both German *Weltpolitik* and German war aims from 1914 to 1918, whether or not German statesmen recognised or consciously aimed at it. German policy in July 1914 provided the necessary historical link between those two sets of expansionist ideas, because the war seemed to make room for a new political order. The fact that German ambitions remained as many dreams, that they resulted in defeat and the opposite of what was to be achieved, does not mean that those ambitions and dreams were not real,[1] as millions of soldiers and non-combatants were to feel from 1914 to 1918.

A rational analysis of the events of July 1914 and of their historical consequences by Germans themselves could go far towards destroying many illusions that continue to be fostered in present-day Germany, and to overcoming some of the deep-rooted political prejudices and resentments in German society. It should be obvious by now that all evils in recent German history were of German making, and that we cannot blame others for it. Dramatic insights like these, new by German standards, might contribute to the development of less nationalistic views in German society, might result in finding a rational solution for the perennial German question. This means the acceptance of a more realistic and modest place for Germany in a modern world that is changing even more rapidly and turbulently than in July 1914.

[1] This seems to be implied by the term *Weltmachtträumer* used by Ritter and Erdmann, which belittles the tremendous importance of the Pan-Germans before and during the First World War.

Documents and Sources

Bibliography

Only titles referred to in the text or documents are quoted below. A working bibliography is to be found in L. Albertini, *The Origins of the War of 1914*. Also useful, although out of date now, is A. v. Wegerer, *Bibliographie zur Vorgeschichte des Weltkrieges* (Berlin, 1934).

DOCUMENTARY MATERIAL

Abbreviations used in text are indicated at end of each entry.

Diplomatische Aktenstücke zur Vorgeschichte des Krieges 1914. Ergänzungen und Nachträge zum Österreichisch–Ungarischen Rotbuch (28. Juni bis 27. August 1914), 3 vols (Wien, 1919). *D.A.* English edition: *Austrian Red Book*. Official Files pertaining to Pre-War History, 3 parts (London, 1920)

Österreich–Ungarns Aussenpolitik von der Bosnischen Krise 1908 bis zum Kriegsausbruch 1914. Diplomatische Aktenstücke des Österreichisch–Ungarischen Ministeriums des Äussern, ed. Ludwig Bittner, Alfred Pribram, Heinrich Srbik and Hans Uebersberger, 8 vols (Wien, 1930), *Ö.D.*

Die Deutschen Dokumente zum Kriegsausbruch. Vollständige Sammlung der von Karl Kautsky zusammengestellten amtlichen Aktenstücke mit einigen Ergänzungen, ed. Walter Schücking and Max Montgelas, 3 vols (Berlin, 1919, 3rd edition 1927). *D.D.*

Bayerische Dokumente zum Kriegsausbruch und zum Versailler Schuldspruch, ed. Pius Dirr (München, 1922, 3rd edition 1925). *Bayr. Dok.*

Deutsche Gesandtschaftsberichte zum Kriegsausbruch. Berichte und Telegramme der badischen, sächsischen und württembergischen Gesandtschaften in Berlin aus dem Juli und August 1924. Commissioned by the Auswärtiges Amtes, ed. August Bach (Berlin, 1937). *Bach.*

Die Grosse Politik der Europäischen Kabinette 1871–1914. Sammlung der diplomatischen Akten des Auswärtigen Amtes, ed. Joh. Lepsius, A. Mendelssohn-Bartholdy, Fr. Thimme, 39 vols (Berlin, 1922/27). *G.P.*

Julikrise und Kriegsausbruch 1914. Eine Dokumentensammlung, ed. Imanuel Geiss, 2 vols (Hannover, 1963–4)

Die Internationalen Beziehungen im Zeitalter des Imperialismus. Dokumente aus den Archiven der Zarischen und der Provisorischen Regierung. German edition ed. Otto Hoetzsch, ser. I, vols 4 and 5 (Berlin, 1931/34). *Int. Bez.* 4 or 5

Livre Jaune Français. Documents diplomatiques 1914. La guerre européenne. Pièces relatives aux négotiations qui ont précédé les déclarations de guerre de l'Allemagne à la Russie (1 août 1914) et à la France (3 août 1914) (Paris, 1914). English translation from the *French Yellow Book* in *Collected Diplomatic Documents. F.Y.B.*

Documents Diplomatiques Français (1871–1914). Ministère des Affaires Etrangères. Commission de Publication des Documents Relatifs aux Origins de la Guerre de 1914, 3rd series, vols X, XI (Paris, 1936). *D.F.* X or XI

British Documents on the Origins of the War 1898–1914, ed. by G. P. Gooch and Harold Temperley, 11 vols (London, 1926–38). *B.D.*

Collected Diplomatic Documents relating to the Outbreak of the European War (London, 1915). *C.D.D.*

PUBLISHED WORKS—GENERAL, PRE-WAR IMPERIALISM, JULY 1914

Books

Albertini, Luigi, *Le origini della guerra del 1914,* 3 vols (Milano, 1942–3); English edition: *The Origins of the War of 1914* (London, New York, Toronto, 1952–7; 2nd impression 1966)

Anrich, Ernst, *Die englische Politik im Juli 1914.* Eine Gesamtdarstellung der Julikrise (Stuttgart, 1934)

Barnett, Correlli, *The Sword Bearers.* Studies in Supreme Command in the World War (London, 1963)

Barnes, Harry E., *The Genesis of the World War.* An introduction to the problem of War Guilt (New York, London, 1929)

Bernhardi, Friedrich v., *Deutschland und der nächste Krieg* (6th edition, Stuttgart, Berlin, 1913)

Bethmann Hollweg, Theobald von, *Betrachtungen zum Weltkriege,* 2 vols (Berlin, 1919–20)

Buchanan, Sir George, *My Mission to Russia and other Diplomatic Memories*, 2 vols (London, 1923)

Böhme, Helmut, *Deutschlands Weg zur Grossmach*. Studien zum Verhältnis von Wirtschaft und Staat während der Reichsgründungszeit 1848–1881 (Köln, 1966)

Bülow, Fürst von, *Denkwürdigkeiten*, 3 vols (Berlin, 1931–32); English edition, *Memoirs 1903–1910* (London, 1931)

Carlgren, W. M., *Neutralität oder Allianz*. Deutschlands Beziehungen zu Schweden in den ersten Anfangsjahren des ersten Weltkriegs (Stockholm, 1962)

Conrad von Hötzendorf, Franz Freiherr, *Aus meiner Dienstzeit 1906–1918*, 5 vols (Wien, Leipzig, München, 1922)

Dedijer, Vladimir, *The Road to Sarajevo* (New York, London, 1966)

Dehio, Ludwig, *Deutschland und die Weltpolitik im 20 Jahrhundert* (München, 1955)

Delbrück, Clemens von, *Die wirtschaftliche Mobilmachung in Deutschland* (München, 1924)

Einem, von, *Erinnerungen eines Soldaten 1853–1933* (2nd impression, Leipzig, 1933)

Erdmann, Karl Dietrich, *Die Zeit der Weltkriege, in : Handbuch der deutschen Geschichte*, hgb. von Herbert Grundmann, vol. IV, 2nd impression (Stuttgart, 1961)

Eulenburg, Philipp, *The Kaiser's Friend*, ed. Johannes Haller (London, n. d.)

Fay, Sydney, B., *The Origins of the World War*, 2 vols (New York, 1928)

Fellner, Fritz, *Der Dreibund*. Europäische Diplomatie vor dem Ersten Weltkrieg (München, 1960)

Fischer, Fritz, *Griff nach der Weltmacht*. Die Kriegszielpolitik des kaiserlichen Deutschland 1914/18 (Düsseldorf, 1961, 3rd impression 1964); English edition: *Bid for Power* (London, 1967)

Gehrke, Ullrich, *Die deutsche Politik in Persien im ersten Weltkrieg*. Diss. (Hamburg, 1959)

Groener, Wilhelm, *Lebenserinnerungen : Jugend, Generalstab und Weltkrieg*, ed. Friedrich Frhr. von Gaertringen (Göttingen, 1957)

Hallgarten, George W. F., *Imperialismus vor 1914*. Die soziologischen Grundlagen der Aussenpolitik europäischer Grossmächte vor dem Ersten Weltkrieg, 2 vols (2nd edition, München, 1963)

Hantsch, Hugo, *Leopold Graf Berchtold*. Grandseigneur und Staatsmann, 2 vols (Köln/ Graz/ Wien, 1963)

Haselmayer, Friedrich, *Diplomatische Geschichte des Zweiten Reichs von 1871–1918*, 6 vols (München, 1955–64)

Hauser, Oswald, *Deutschland und der englisch-russische Gegensatz 1900–1914* (Göttingen, Berlin, Frankfurt/M., 1958)

Herzfeld, Hans, *Die deutsche Rüstungspolitik vor dem Weltkriege* (Bonn, Leipzig, 1923)
Die moderne Welt 1789–1945, 2 vols (3rd edition, Braunschweig, 1960)

Hinsley, C. F., *Power and the Pursuit of Peace* (Cambridge, 1963)

Hoyos, Graf Alexander von, *Der deutsch-englische Gegensatz und sein Einfluss auf die Balkanpolitik Österreich-Ungarns* (Berlin, 1922)

Hubatsch, Walther, *Deutschland im Weltkrieg 1914–1918* (Frankfurt/M., Berlin, 1966)
Germany and the Central Powers in the World War 1914–1918 (Lawrence, Kansas, 1963)

Jagow, Gottlieb von, *Ursachen und Ausbruch des Weltkrieges* (Berlin, 1919)

Jerussalimski, A. S., *Die Aussenpolitik und die Diplomatie des deutschen Imperialismus am Ende des 19. Jahrhunderts* (Berlin, 1954)

Kann, Robert A., *The Multinational Empire*: Nationalism and National Reform in the Habsburg Monarchy, 1848–1914 (New York, 1950)

Kantorowicz, Hermann, *Der Geist der englischen Politik und das Gespenst der Einkreisung Deutschlands* (Berlin, 1929)

Kehr, Eckart, *Schlachtflottenbau und Parteipolitik 1894–1901*. Versuch eines Querschnitts durch die innenpolitischen, sozialen und ideologischen Voraussetzungen des deutschen Imperialismus. Historische Studien vol 197 (Berlin, 1930, 2nd impression 1966)
Der Primat der Innenpolitik. Gesammelte Aufsätze zur preussisch-deutschen Sozialgeschichte im 19. und 20. Jahrhundert, ed. Hans-Ulrich Wehler, preface Hans Herzfeld (Berlin, 1965)

Kiderlen Wächter, *der Staatsmann und Mensch*. Briefwechsel und Nachlass, ed. Ernst Jäckh, 2 vols (Stuttgart, Berlin, Leipzig, 1925)

Kloster, Walter, *Der deutsche Generalstab und der Präventivkriegsgedanke* (Stuttgart, 1932)

Kruck, Alfred, *Geschichte des Alldeutschen Verbands 1890–1939* (Wiesbaden, 1954)

Langer, William L., *European Alliances and Alignments 1871–1890* (New York, 1931, 2nd impression 1951)
The Diplomacy of Imperialism 1890–1902, 2 vol. (New York, 1935, 2nd impression 1950)

Luckau, Alma, *The German Delegation at the Paris Peace Conference* (New York, 1941)

Lutz, Hermann, *Lord Grey and the World War* (London, 1928)

Margutti, Albert von, *Vom alten Kaiser*. Persönliche Erinnerungen an Franz Joseph I (Leipzig, Wien, 1921)

Meinecke, Friedrich, *Die deutsche Katastrophe* (Wiesbaden, 1947); English edition, *The German Catastrophe*, translated by Sydney B. Fay (Cambridge, Mass., 1950, 2nd edition 1963)

Moltke, Helmuth von, *Erinnerungen, Briefe, Dokumente 1877–1916* (Stuttgart, 1922)

Mommsen, Wolfgang J., *Max Weber und die deutsche Politik 1890–1920* (Tübingen, 1959)

Monger, George W., *The End of Isolation: British Foreign Policy 1900–1907* (London, Edinburgh, 1963)

Müller, George A. von, *Regierte der Kaiser?* Kriegstagebücher, Aufzeichnungen und Briefe des Chefs des Marinekabinetts 1914–1918, ed. Walter Görlitz (Göttingen, Berlin, Frankfurt/M., 1959)
Der Kaiser: Aus den Tagebüchern des Chefs des Marinekabinetts Admiral George Alexander von Müller, ed. Walter Görlitz (Göttingen, Berlin, Frankfurt, 1965)

Naumann, Victor, *Dokumente und Argumente* (Berlin, 1928)

Nicolson, Harold G., *Sir Arthur Nicolson, Bart., First Lord Carnock*. A study in the old diplomacy (London, 1930)

Plehn, Hans, *Deutsche Weltpolitik und kein Krieg* (Berlin, 1913)

Pogge-v. Strandmann, Hartmut/I. Geiss, *Die Erforderlichkeit des Unmöglichen.* Deutschland am Abend des ersten Weltkrieges (Frankfurt, 1965)

Poincaré, Raymond, *Au Service de la France.* Neuf années de souvenirs, 10 vols (Paris, 1926/33)

Recouly, Raymond, *Les heures tragiques d'avant-guerre* (Paris, 1922)

Redlich, Josef, *Schichsalsjahre Österreichs 1908–1918.* Das politische Tagebuch Josef Redlichs, ed. Fritz Fellner, 2 vols (Graz, Köln, 1953)

Remak, Joachim, *Sarajevo*, London, 1959

Renouvin, Pierre, *Les Origines Immédiates de la Guerre* (Paris, 1925)

Riezler, Kurt, *Die Erforderlichkeit des Unmöglichen.* Prolegomena zu einer Theorie der Politik und zu anderen Theorien (München, 1912)

Ritter, Gerhard, *Europa und die deutsche Frage.* Betrachtungen über die geschichtliche Eigenart des deutschen Staatsdenkens (München 1948), 2nd edition as: *Das deutsche Problem.* Grundfragen deutschen Staatslebens gestern und heute (München, 1962, 2nd impression 1966)
The Schlieffen Plan: Critique of a Myth (London, 1958)
Lebendige Vergangenheit. Beiträge zur historisch-politischen Selbstbesinnung (München, 1958)
Staatskunst und Kriegshandwerk. Das Problem des 'Militarismus' in Deutschland, 3 vols (München, 1954–64)

Röhl, John C., *Germany without Bismarck 1890–1900* (London, 1967)

Ruedorffer, J. J. (= Kurt Riezler), *Grundzüge der Weltpolitik* (Stuttgart, Berlin, 1914)

Sasse, Heinz Günther, *England/Deutschlands Widerpart*. Die deutsch-englischen Beziehungen von 1815–1940 (Berlin, 1941)

Schlieffen, Graf Alfred von, *Gesammelte Werke*, 2 vols (Berlin, 1913)

Schlieffen, Generalfeldmarschall Graf Alfred von, *Briefe*, ed. and introduced by Eberhard Kessel (Göttingen, 1958)

Schmitt, Bernadotte E., *The Coming of the War 1914*, 2 vols (New York, London, 1930)

Schüssler, Wilhelm, *Deutschland zwischen Russland und England*. Studien zur Aussenpolitik des Bismarckschen Reiches 1879–1914 (Leipzig, 1940, 4th impression 1941)

Singer, Ladislaus, *Eine Welt bricht zusammen*. Die letzen Tage vor dem Weltkrieg (Graz/Wien/Köln, 1961)

Steglich, Wolfgang, *Die Friedenspolitik der Mittelmächte 1917/18*, vol. I (Wiesbaden, 1964)

Steinberg, Jonathan, *Yesterday's Deterrent, Tirpitz and the Birth of the German Battle Fleet* (London, 1965)

Taylor, A. J. P., *The Hapsburg Monarchy 1809–1918*. A History of the Austrian Empire and Austria–Hungary (London, 1948, Penguin Books, 1964)

Thimme, Annelise, *Hans Delbrück als Kritiker der Wilhelminischen Epoche* (Düsseldorf, 1955)

Tirpitz, Alfred von, *Politische Dokumente*, 2 vols (Hamburg, Berlin, 1924–6)

Uebersberger, Hans, *Österreich zwischen Russland und Serbien*. Zur südslawischen Frage und der Entstehung des 1. Weltkrieges (Köln, 1958)

Wegerer, Alfred von, *Der Ausbruch des Weltkrieges*, 2 vols (Hamburg, 1939)

Wendel, Hermann, *Die Habsburger und die Südslawenfrage*. Das Werk des Untersuchungsaussches, 1st series, vol. 10 (Berlin, 1930)

Winckler, Martin, *Bismarcks Bündnispolitik und das europäische Gleichgewicht* (Stuttgart, 1964)

Wirsing, Giselher, *Der masslose Kontinent*. Roosevelts Kampf um die Weltherrschaft (Jena, 1942)
Das Zeitalter des Ikaros (Jena, 1944)

Zeman, Z. A. B., *The Break-up of the Hapsburg Empire, 1914–18*. A Study in National and Social Revolution (London, New York, Toronto, 1961)

Zwehl, Hans von, *Erich von Falkenhayn, General der Infanterie*. Eine biographische Studie (Berlin, 1926)

Articles

Abbreviations of Journals
F.A.Z.—Frankfurter Allgemeine Zeitung
G.W.U.—Geschichte in Wissenschaft und Unterricht
H.J.—Historical Journal (Cambridge)
H.Z.—Historische Zeitschrift
J.C.H.—Journal of Contemporary History
Vh.Z.G.—Vierteljahrshefte für Zeitgeschichte

Andrew, Christopher, 'German World Policy and the Reshaping of the Dual Alliance', in *J.C.H.*, I, no. 3 (July 1966), pp. 137–51

Bestuzhev, I. V., 'Russian foreign policy February–June 1914', in *J.C.H.*, I, no. 3, pp. 93–112

Dedijer, Vladimir, 'Sarajevo: Fifty Years After', in *Foreign Affairs*, July 1964, pp. 569ff.

Dieckmann, Fritz, 'Die Kriegsschuldfrage auf der Friedenskonferenz von Paris 1919', in *H.Z.*, 197/1 (August 1963), pp. 1–101

Fisher, Charles A., 'The Changing Dimensions of Europe', in *J.C.H.*, vol. I, no. 3, pp. 3–20

Geiss, Imanuel, 'The Outbreak of the First World War and German War Aims', in *J.C.H.*, vol. I, no. 3, pp. 75–91.

Hagen, Maximilian von, 'Deutsche Weltpolitik und kein Krieg', in *H.Z.*, 179/2 (April 1955), pp. 297–307

Hillgruber, Andreas, 'Riezlers Theorie des kalkulierten Risikos und Bethmann Hollwegs politische Konzeption in der Julikrise 1914', in *H.Z.*, 202/2 (April 1966), pp. 333–51.

Hubatsch, Walther, 'Ursachen und Anlass des Weltkrieges, in *1914–1939–1944. Schicksalsjahre deutscher Geschichte*, ed. Klaus-Jürgen Müller (Boppard, 1964); 'So kam es zum Ersten Weltkrieg', in *Deutsche Korrespondenz* (4 July 1964)

Holborn, Hajo, 'Diplomats and Diplomacy in the Early Weimar Republic', in *The Diplomats 1919–1939*, ed. Gordon Craig and Felix Gilbert (Princeton, 1953)

Lipgens, Walter, 'Bismarck, die öffentliche Meinung und die Annexion von Elsass und Lothringen 1870', in *H.Z.*, 199/1 (August 1964), pp. 31–112

Röhl, John C. G., 'A Document of 1892 on Germany, Prussia and Poland', in *H.J.*, vol. VII (1964), no. 1, pp. 143–9
'The Disintegration of the Kartell and the Politics of Bismarck's Fall from Power, 1887–1890', in *H.J.*, vol. IX (1966), no. 1, pp. 60–89

Steinberg, Jonathan, 'A German Plan for the Invasion of Holland and Belgium, 1897', in *H.J.*, vol. VI (1963), no. 1, pp. 107–19
'The Copenhagen Complex', in *J.C.H.*, vol. I, no. 3, pp. 23–46

Wehler, Hans-Ulrich, 'Der Fall Zabern'. Rückblick auf eine Verfassungskrise des wilhelminischen Kaiserreichs', in *Die Welt als Geschichte*, vol. 23 (1963)

Zechlin, Egmont, 'Die türkischen Meerengen—ein Brennpunkt der Weltgeschichte', in *G.W.U.*, 17/1 (January 1966), pp. 1–31

THE FISCHER CONTROVERSY

Again, this is not intended to be an exhaustive bibliography. Titles with an asterisk are re-printed in Lynar's anthology, which contains a bibliography for until early 1964.

Augstein, Rudolf, 'Bethmann—einen Kopf kürzer?' in *Die Zeit* (25 September 1964)

Dehio, Ludwig, 'Deutschlands Griff nach der Weltmacht?' Zu Fritz Fischers Buch über den Ersten Weltkrieg', in *Der Monat*, no. 161 (February 1962), pp. 65–9

Erdmann, Karl Dietrich, 'Zur Beurteilung Bethmann Hollwegs', in *G.W.U.*, 15/9 (September 1964), pp. 525–40
'Bethmann Hollweg, Augstein und die Historiker-Zunft', in *Die Zeit* (2 October 1964)

Fischer, Fritz, 'Deutsche Kriegsziele: Revolutionierung und Separatfrieden im Osten 1914–1918', in *H.Z.*, 188/2, pp. 249–310 *
'Weltpolitik, Weltmachtstreben und deutsche Kriegsziele', in *H.Z.*, 199/2 (October 1964), pp. 265–364

Freund, Michael, 'Bethmann Hollweg, der Hitler des Jahres 1914?, Zu einer Spätfrucht des Jahres 1914 in der Geschichtsschreibung,' in *F.A.Z.*, 28/29 March 1964 *

Gerstenmaier, Eugen, 'Die Last des Vorwurfs. Zweimal deutsche Kriegsschuld?' in *Christ und Welt* (2 September 1964); also in *Bulletin der Bundesregierung* (4 September 1964) and E. Gerstenmaier, *Neuer Nationalismus?* (Stuttgart, 1965)

Herzfeld, Hans, 'Literaturbericht', in *G.W.U.*, 13/4 (April 1962), pp. 246–54
'Die deutsche Kriegspolitik im Ersten Weltkrieg, in *Vh.Z.G.*, 11/3 (July 1963), pp. 224–45

Hölzle, Erwin, 'Griff nach der Weltmacht?' in *Das Historisch-Politische Buch*, X, 3 (March 1962), pp. 65–9

Lynar, Ernst W. Graf, ed.: *Deutsche Kriegsziele 1914–1918* (Ullstein–Bücher no. 616) (Berlin, 1964)

Mann, Golo, 'Der Griff nach der Weltmacht', in Neue Zürcher Zeitung (28 April 1962) *

Ritter, Gerhard, 'Griff nach der Weltmacht?' in *Lübecker Nachrichten* (20 May 1962)
 'Eine neue Kriegsschuldthese? Zu Fritz Fischers Buch Griff nach der Weltmacht', in *H.Z.*, 194/4 (June 1962), pp. 646–68 *
 '*Der Erste Weltkrieg*'. Studien zum deutschen Geschichtsbild. Schriftenreihe der Bundeszentrale für Politische Bildung, no. 64 (Bonn, 1964)
 'Zur Fischer-Kontroverse', in *H.Z.*, 200/3 (June 1965), pp. 783–7
 'Die politische Rolle Bethmann Hollwegs während des Ersten Weltkrieges', in *Congrès International des Sciences Historiques* (Vienne, 29 Août–5 Septembre 1965) vol. IV, pp. 271–8

Wirsing, Giselher, '. . . auch am Ersten Weltkrieg schuld?' in *Christ und Welt* (8 May 1964)
 'Der Bauchredner', in *Christ und Welt* (10 July 1964)

Zechlin, Egmont, 'Deutschland zwischen Kabinettskrieg und Wirtschaftskrieg. Politik und Kriegführung in den ersten Monaten des Weltkrieges 1914', in *H.Z.*, 199/2 (October 1964), pp. 247–458
 'Bethmann Hollweg, Kriegsrisiko und SPD 1914', in *Der Monat*, no. 208 (January 1966), pp. 17–32
 'Motive und Taktik der Reichsleitung 1914. Ein Nachtrag', in *Der Monat*, no. 209 (February 1966), pp. 91–5

Index

393